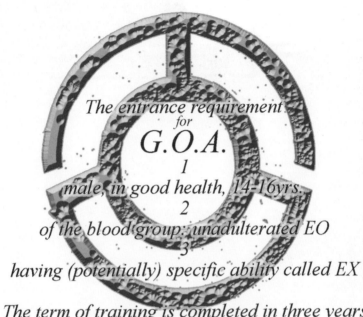

The entrance requirement
for
G.O.A.
1
male, in good health, 14-16yrs.
2
of the blood group: unadulterated EO
3
having (potentially) specific ability called EX

The term of training is completed in three years

the Candidate for Goddess™

Translators - Alethea & Athena Nibley
English Adaptation - Marv Wolfman
Copy Editor - Aaron Sparrow
Retouch and Lettering - Yoohae Yang
Cover Design - Harlan Harris

Editor - Rob Tokar
Digital Imaging Manager - Chris Buford
Pre-Press Manager - Antonio DePietro
Production Managers - Jennifer Miller, Mutsumi Miyazaki
Art Director - Matt Alford
Managing Editor - Jill Freshney
VP of Production - Ron Klamert
President & C.O.O. - John Parker
Publisher & C.E.O. - Stuart Levy

E-mail: info@TOKYOPOP.com
Come visit us online at www.TOKYOPOP.com

A  Manga

TOKYOPOP Inc.
5900 Wilshire Blvd. Suite 2000
Los Angeles, CA 90036

The Candidate For Goddess Vol. 1

THE CANDIDATE FOR GODDESS TM & © 1997 Yukiru Sugisaki.
All Rights Reserved. First published in 1997 by Wani Books.
English publication rights arranged through Wani Books.

English text copyright ©2004 TOKYOPOP Inc.

ISBN: 1-59182-747-7

First TOKYOPOP printing: April 2004

10 9 8 7 6 5 4 3 2 1

Printed in the USA

the Candidate for Goddess™

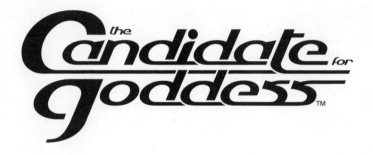

VOL. 1

BY
YUKIRU SUGISAKI

TOKYOPOP®
LOS ANGELES • TOKYO • LONDON

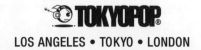

The Candidate for Goddess
Characters

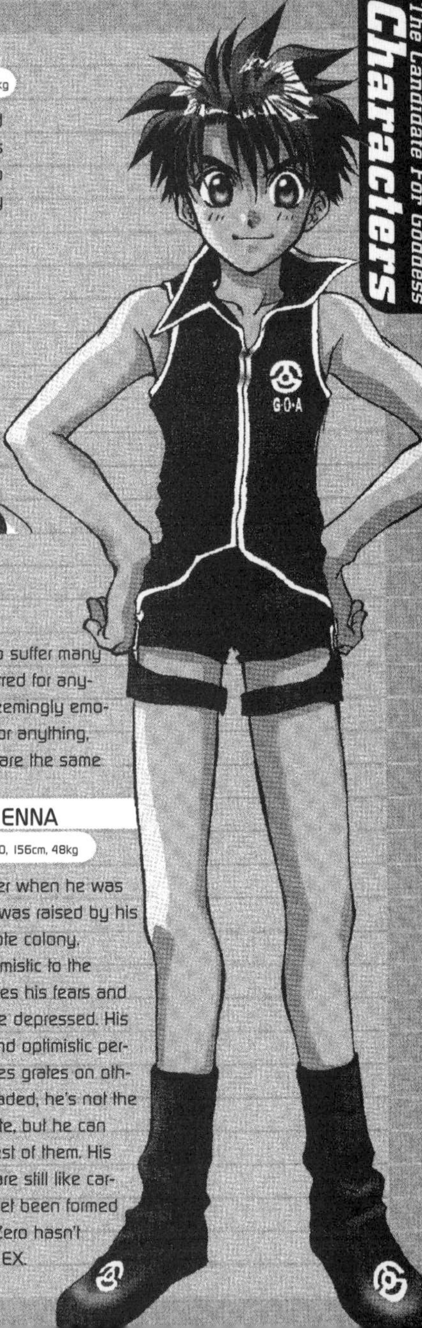

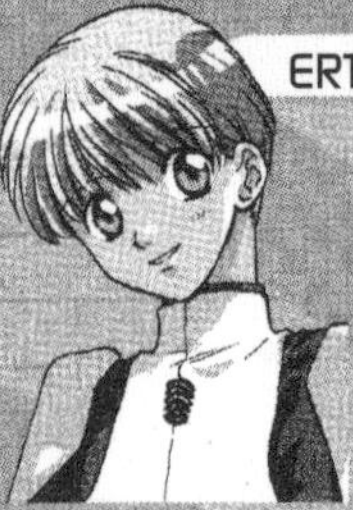

ERTS VIRNY COCTEAU

Age 14, Blood type E0, 156cm, 47kg

Orphaned very young and forced to enter the G.O.A., Erts is gentle and doesn't like to fight. His grades are very good. Erts is Zero's friend.

CLAY CLIFF FORTRAN

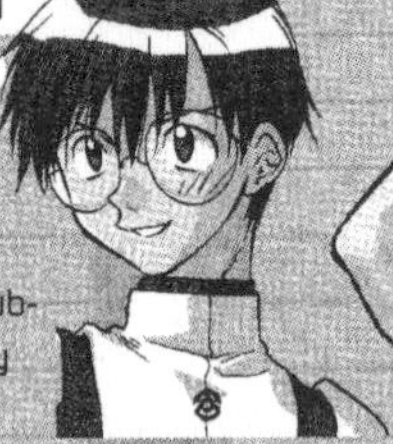

Age 15, Blood type E0, 159cm, 53kg

The class brain, Clay came to the G.O.A. not to be a pilot, but to study and theorize. Interested in many different subjects. His catch phrase is "Very interesting."

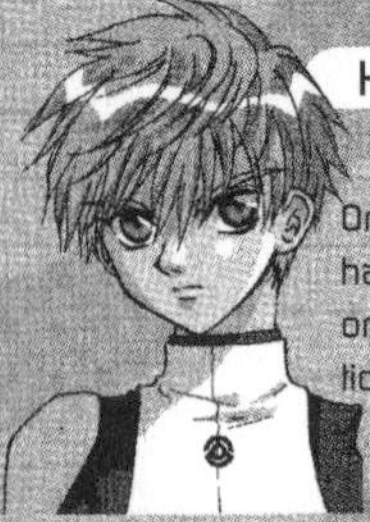

HIEAD GNER

Age 15, Blood type E0, 160cm, 52kg

Orphaned in the war and forced to suffer many hardships, Hiead has a strong hatred for anyone raised in comfort. Cold and seemingly emotionless, he doesn't trust anyone or anything, especially Zero. These rivals share the same EX abilities.

ZERO ENNA

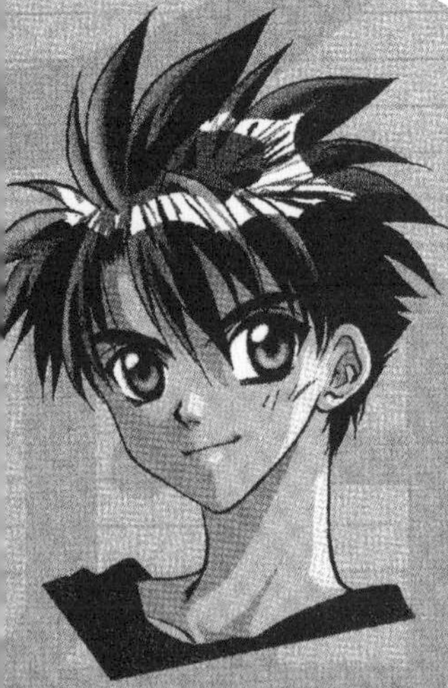

Age 15, Blood type E0, 156cm, 48kg

Zero lost his father when he was very young and was raised by his mother on a remote colony. Cheerful and optimistic to the extreme, Zero hides his fears and refuses to ever be depressed. His straightforward and optimistic personality sometimes grates on others. A bit thickheaded, he's not the smartest candidate, but he can move with the best of them. His piloting abilities are still like carbon that hasn't yet been formed into a diamond. Zero hasn't yet mastered his EX.

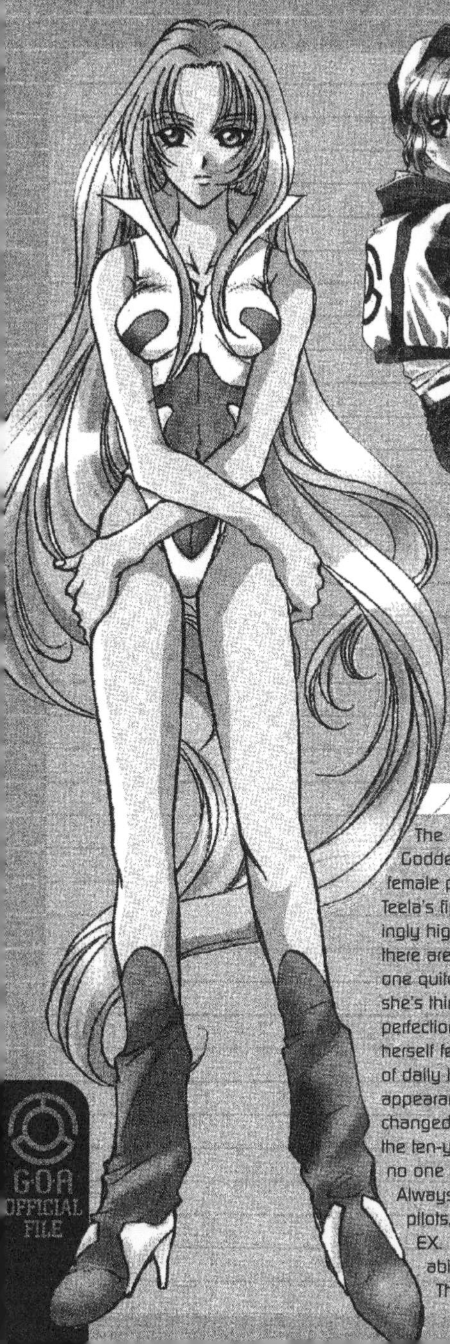

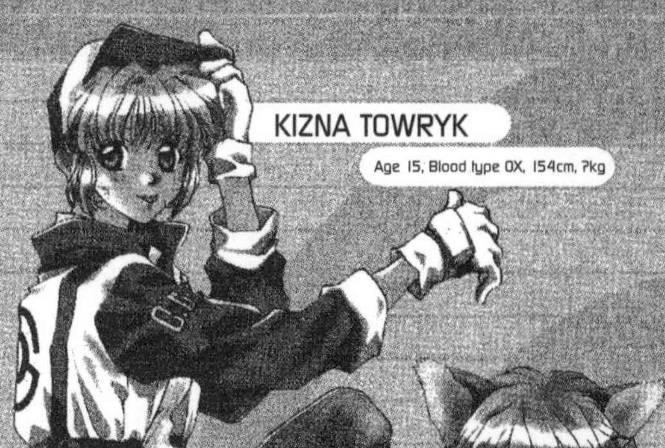

KIZNA TOWRYK

Age 15, Blood type OX, 154cm, 7kg

The personal repairer for the practice Ingrid Zero pilots. Kizna wants to be Zero's equal, and not inferior to him. Sometimes, Kizna talks like a man, but because of her rational personality, the other mechanic girls in her class look up to her. She has dexterous fingers and makes an excellent mechanic. She really likes sweet things.

TEELA ZAIN ELMES

Age 15, Blood type EO, 156cm, 42kg

The best of the five Goddesses and the only female pilot. Faithful to her task, Teela's fighting ability is frighteningly high. Nearly flawless, there are times when no one quite knows what she's thinking. Seeking perfection, she won't let herself feel the emotions of daily life. Her outward appearance has hardly changed since she saved the ten-year-old Zero, but no one knows why. Always the top of the pilots, Teela has two EX. One is the same ability as Zero's. The other...

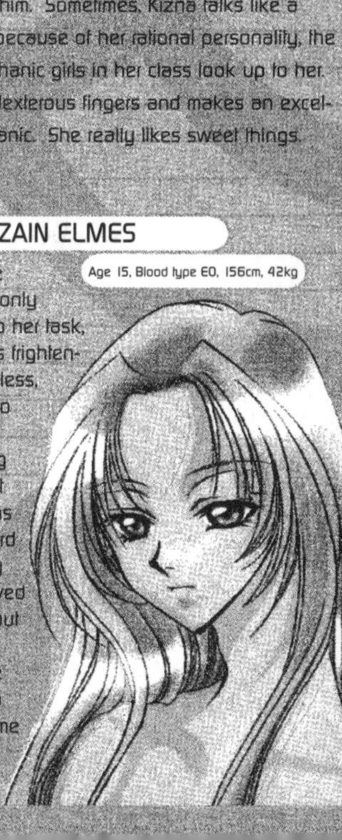

G·O·A OFFICIAL FILE

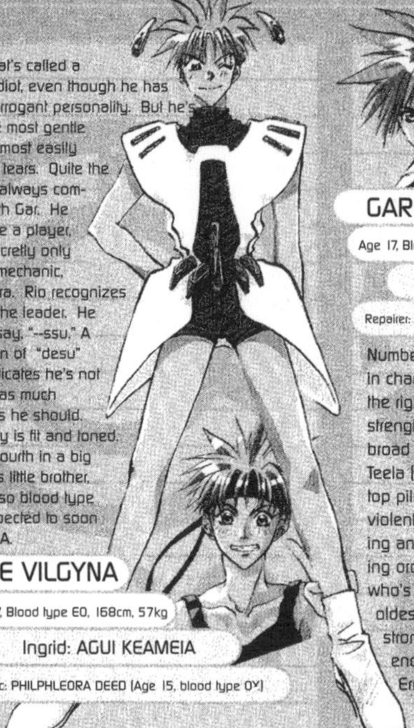

Rio is what's called a cheerful idiot, even though he has a rather arrogant personality. But he's easily the most gentle pilot and most easily moved to tears. Quite the flirt, he is always competing with Gar. He seems like a player, but he secretly only likes his mechanic, Philphleora. Rio recognizes Teela as the leader. He tends to say, "--ssu," A contraction of "desu" which indicates he's not showing as much respect as he should. Rio's body is fit and toned. He's the fourth in a big family. His little brother, who is also blood type EO, is expected to soon enter G.O.A.

RIOROUTE VILGYNA

Age 17, Blood type EO, 168cm, 57kg

Ingrid: AGUI KEAMEIA

Mechanic: PHILPHLEORA DEED (Age 15, blood type OX)

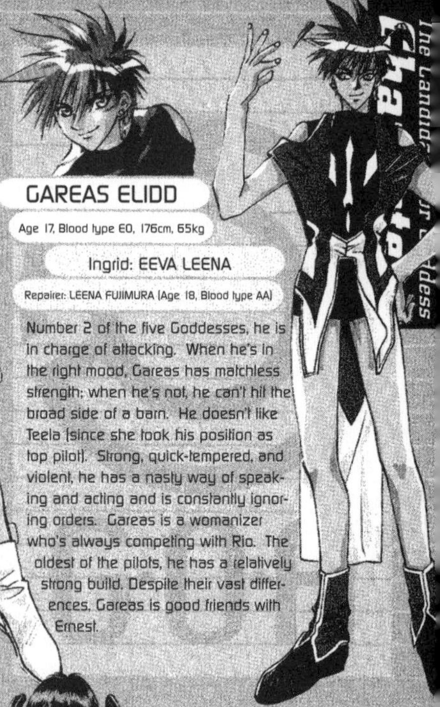

GAREAS ELIDD

Age 17, Blood type EO, 176cm, 65kg

Ingrid: EEVA LEENA

Repairer: LEENA FUJIMURA (Age 18, Blood type AA)

Number 2 of the five Goddesses, he is in charge of attacking. When he's in the right mood, Gareas has matchless strength; when he's not, he can't hit the broad side of a barn. He doesn't like Teela (since she took his position as top pilot). Strong, quick-tempered, and violent, he has a nasty way of speaking and acting and is constantly ignoring orders. Gareas is a womanizer who's always competing with Rio. The oldest of the pilots, he has a relatively strong build. Despite their vast differences, Gareas is good friends with Ernest.

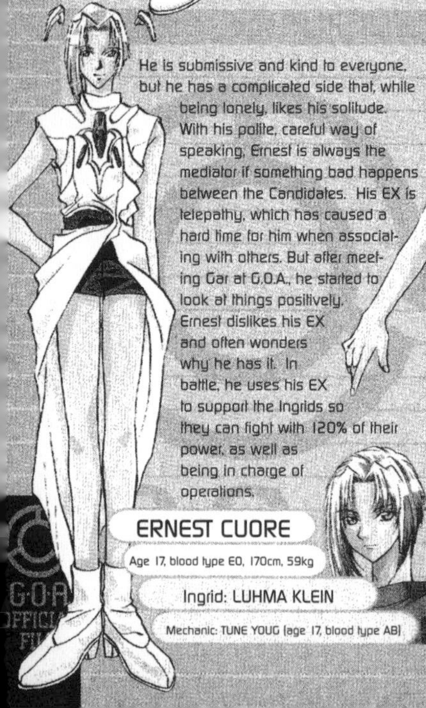

He is submissive and kind to everyone, but he has a complicated side that, while being lonely, likes his solitude. With his polite, careful way of speaking, Ernest is always the mediator if something bad happens between the Candidates. His EX is telepathy, which has caused a hard time for him when associating with others. But after meeting Gar at G.O.A., he started to look at things positively. Ernest dislikes his EX and often wonders why he has it. In battle, he uses his EX to support the Ingrids so they can fight with 120% of their power, as well as being in charge of operations.

ERNEST CUORE

Age 17, blood type EO, 170cm, 59kg

Ingrid: LUHMA KLEIN

Mechanic: TUNE YOUG (age 17, blood type AB)

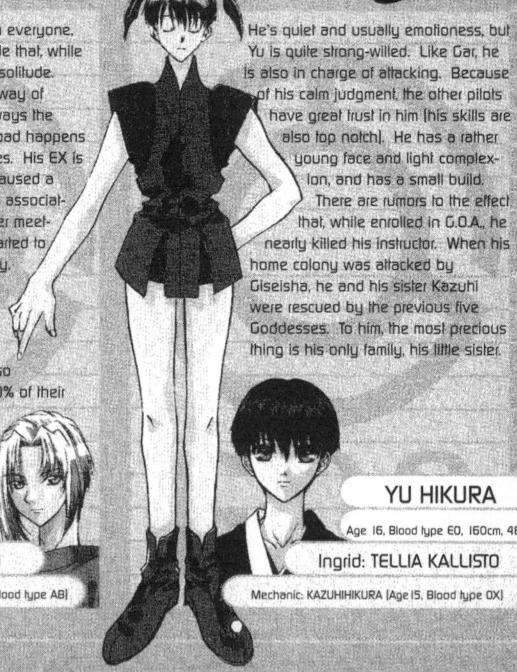

He's quiet and usually emotionless, but Yu is quite strong-willed. Like Gar, he is also in charge of attacking. Because of his calm judgment, the other pilots have great trust in him (his skills are also top notch). He has a rather young face and light complexion, and has a small build. There are rumors to the effect that, while enrolled in G.O.A., he nearly killed his instructor. When his home colony was attacked by Giseisha, he and his sister Kazuhi were rescued by the previous five Goddesses. To him, the most precious thing is his only family, his little sister.

YU HIKURA

Age 16, Blood type EO, 160cm, 48kg

Ingrid: TELLIA KALLISTO

Mechanic: KAZUHIHIKURA (Age 15, Blood type OX)

女神候補生

THE CANDIDATE FOR GODDESS

杉崎ゆきる

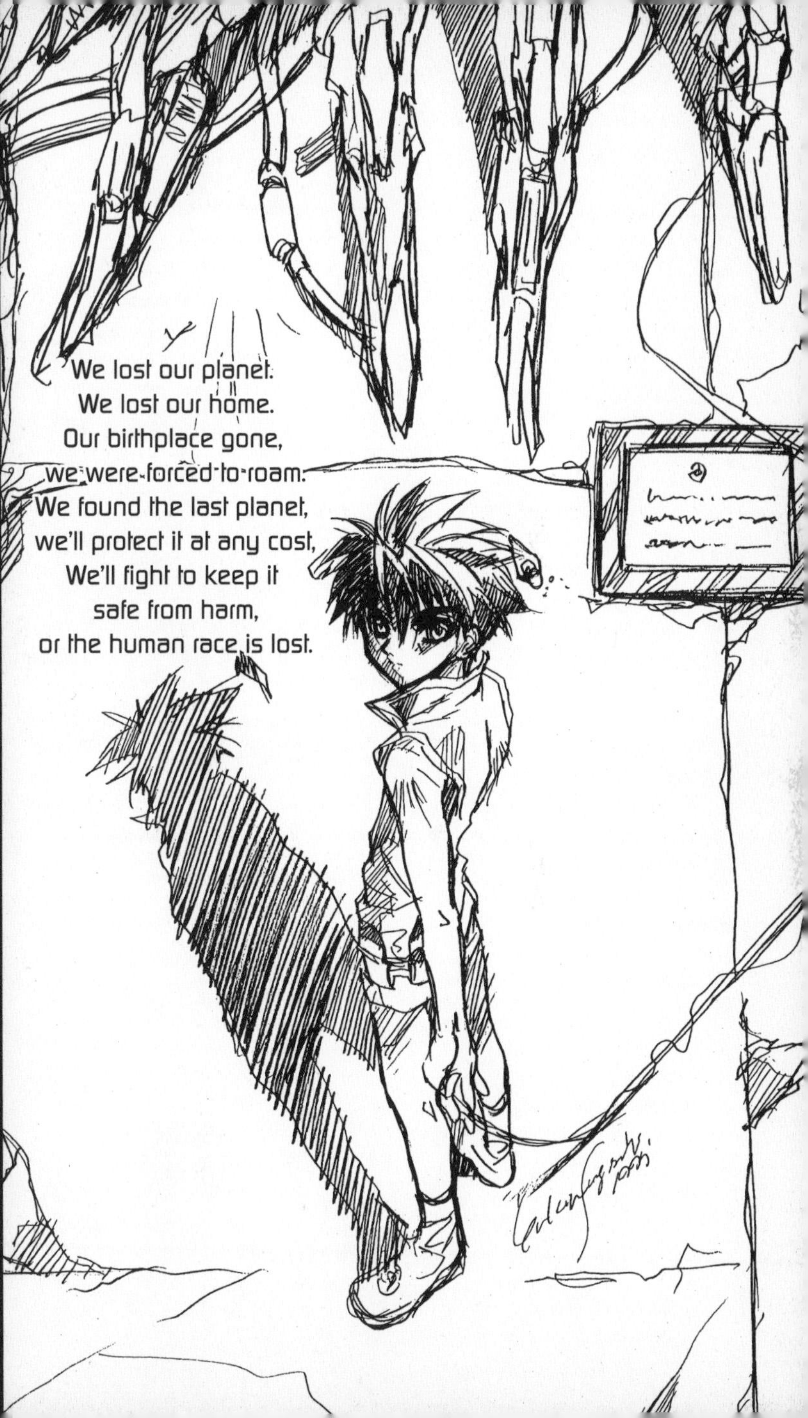
We lost our planet.
We lost our home.
Our birthplace gone,
we were forced to roam.
We found the last planet,
we'll protect it at any cost,
We'll fight to keep it
safe from harm,
or the human race is lost.

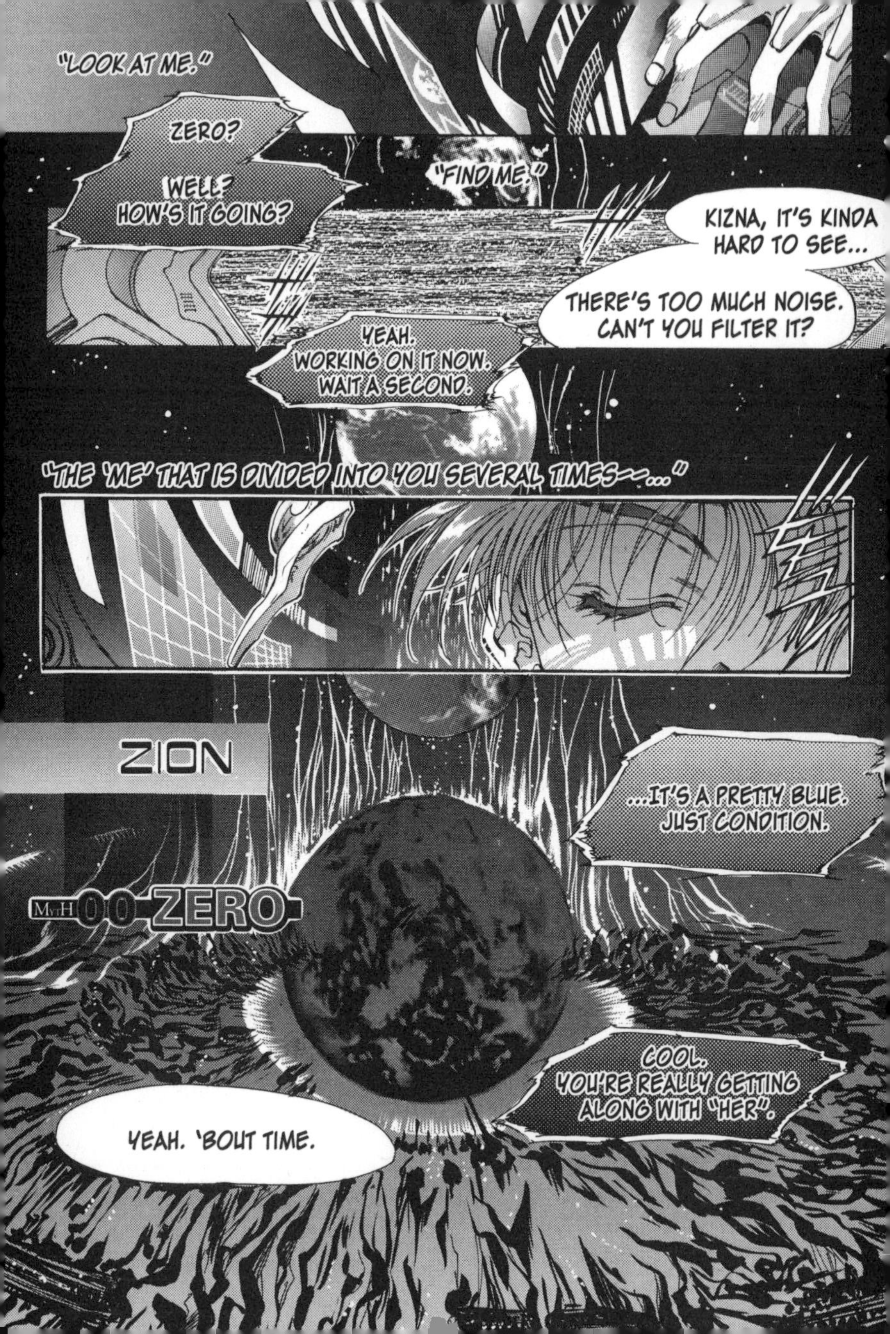
"LOOK AT ME."
ZERO?
WELL? HOW'S IT GOING?
"FIND ME."
KIZNA, IT'S KINDA HARD TO SEE...
THERE'S TOO MUCH NOISE. CAN'T YOU FILTER IT?
YEAH. WORKING ON IT NOW. WAIT A SECOND.
"THE 'ME' THAT IS DIVIDED INTO YOU SEVERAL TIMES--..."
ZION
...IT'S A PRETTY BLUE. JUST CONDITION.
MYTH 00 ZERO
COOL. YOU'RE REALLY GETTING ALONG WITH "HER".
YEAH. 'BOUT TIME.

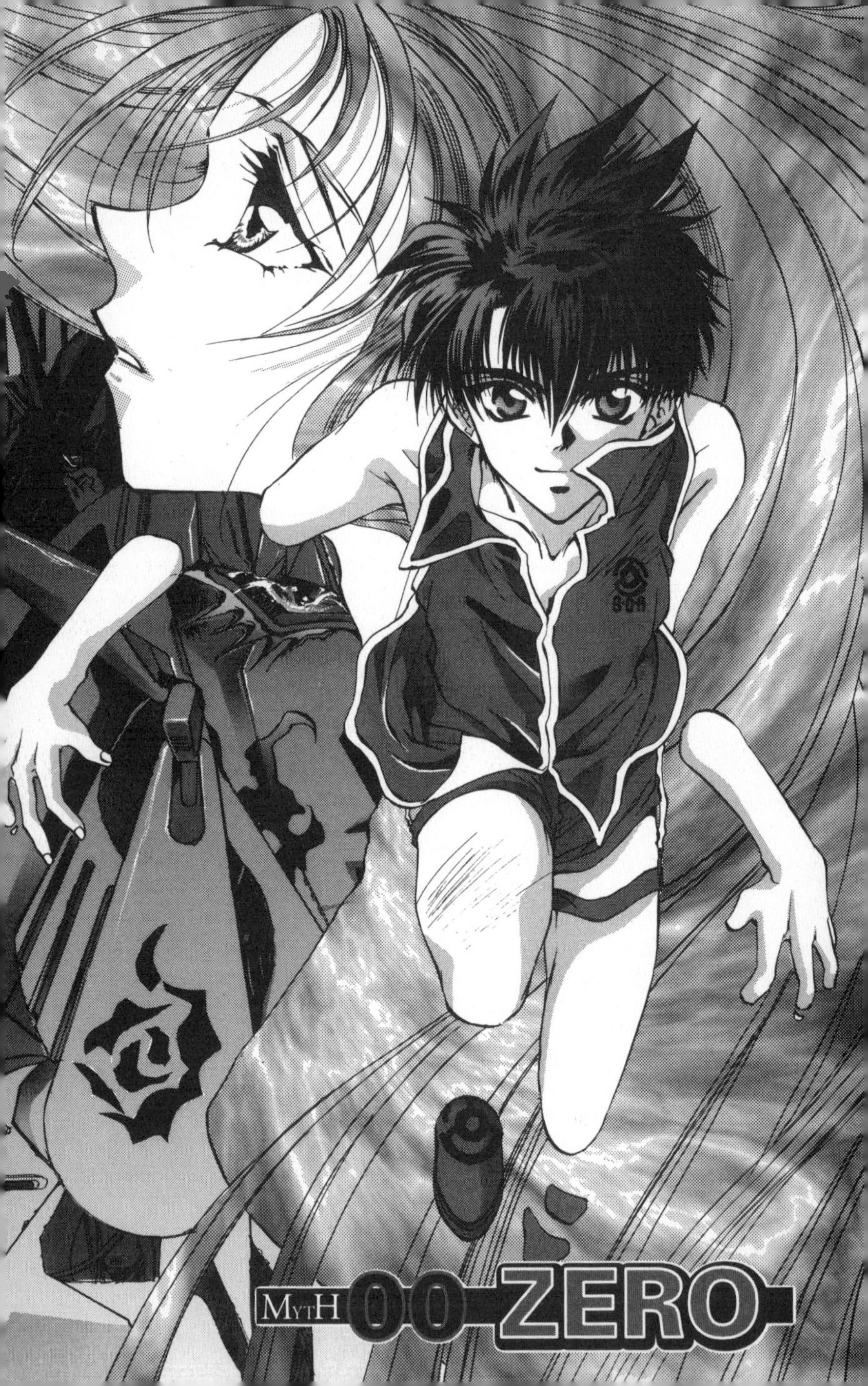
MyTH 00 ZERO

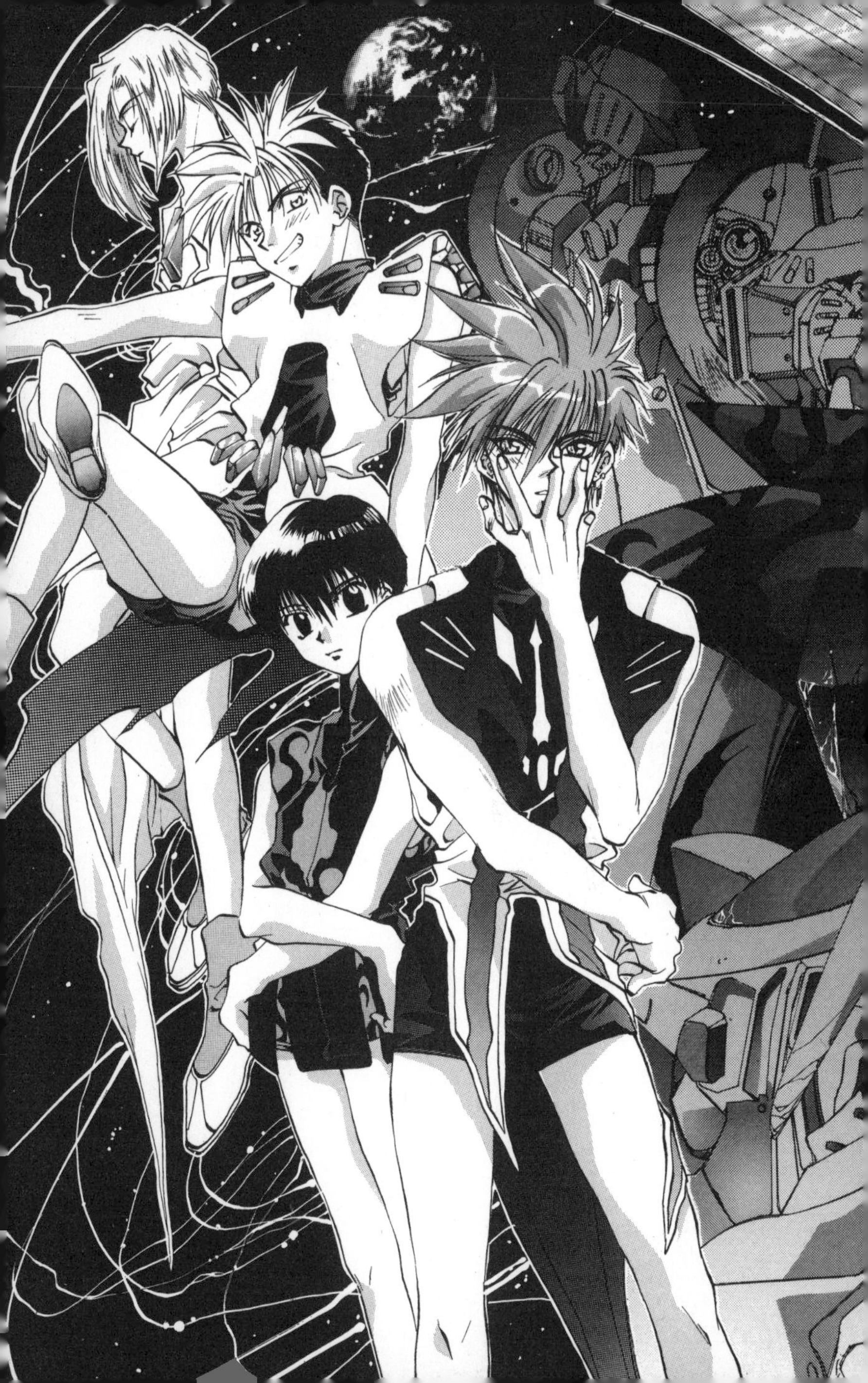

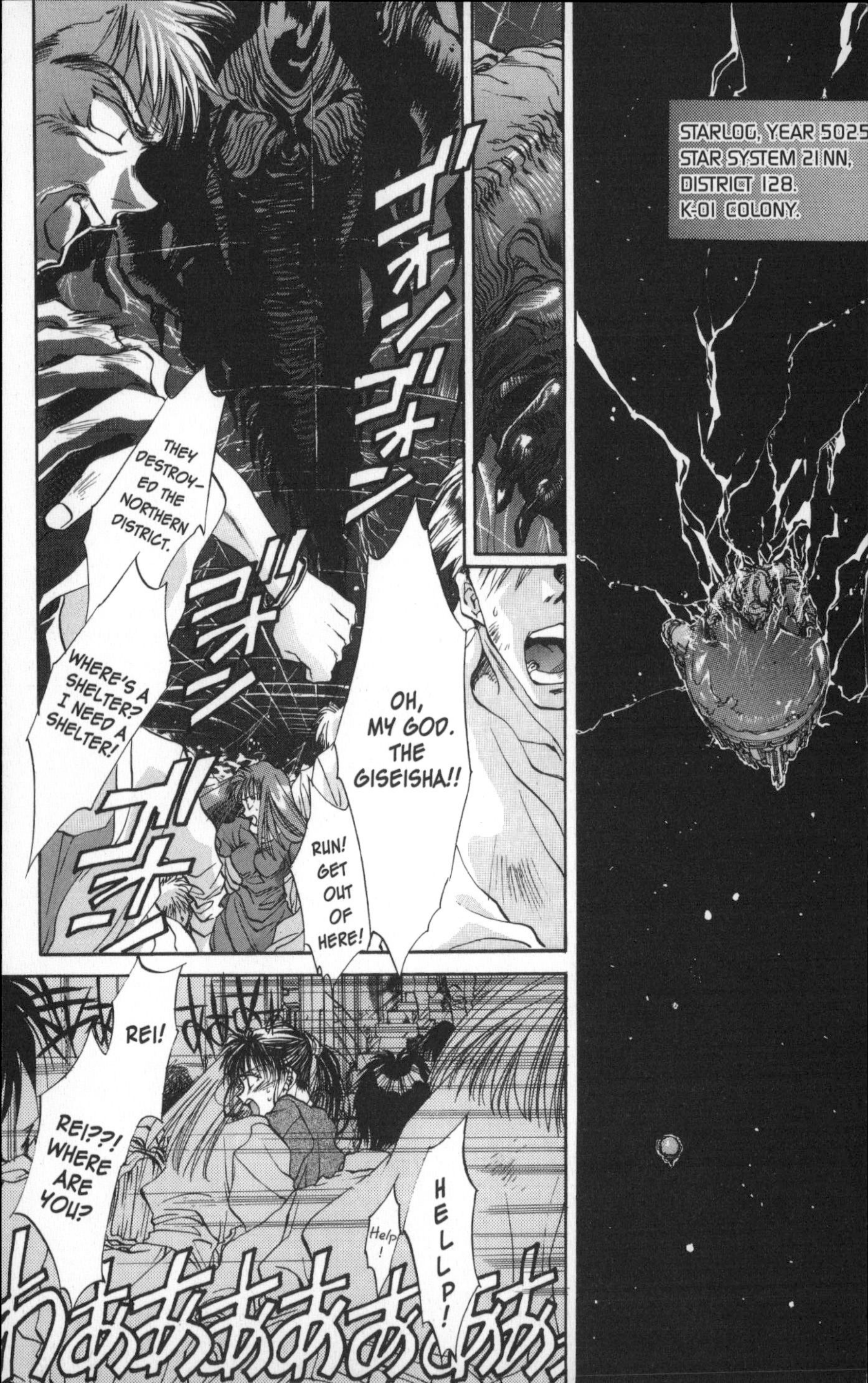
STARLOG, YEAR 5025
STAR SYSTEM 21NN,
DISTRICT 128.
K-01 COLONY.
OH, MY GOD. THE GISEISHA!!
THEY DESTROY-ED THE NORTHERN DISTRICT.
RUN! GET OUT OF HERE!
WHERE'S A SHELTER? I NEED A SHELTER!
HELLP!
Help!
REI!
REI!??! WHERE ARE YOU?

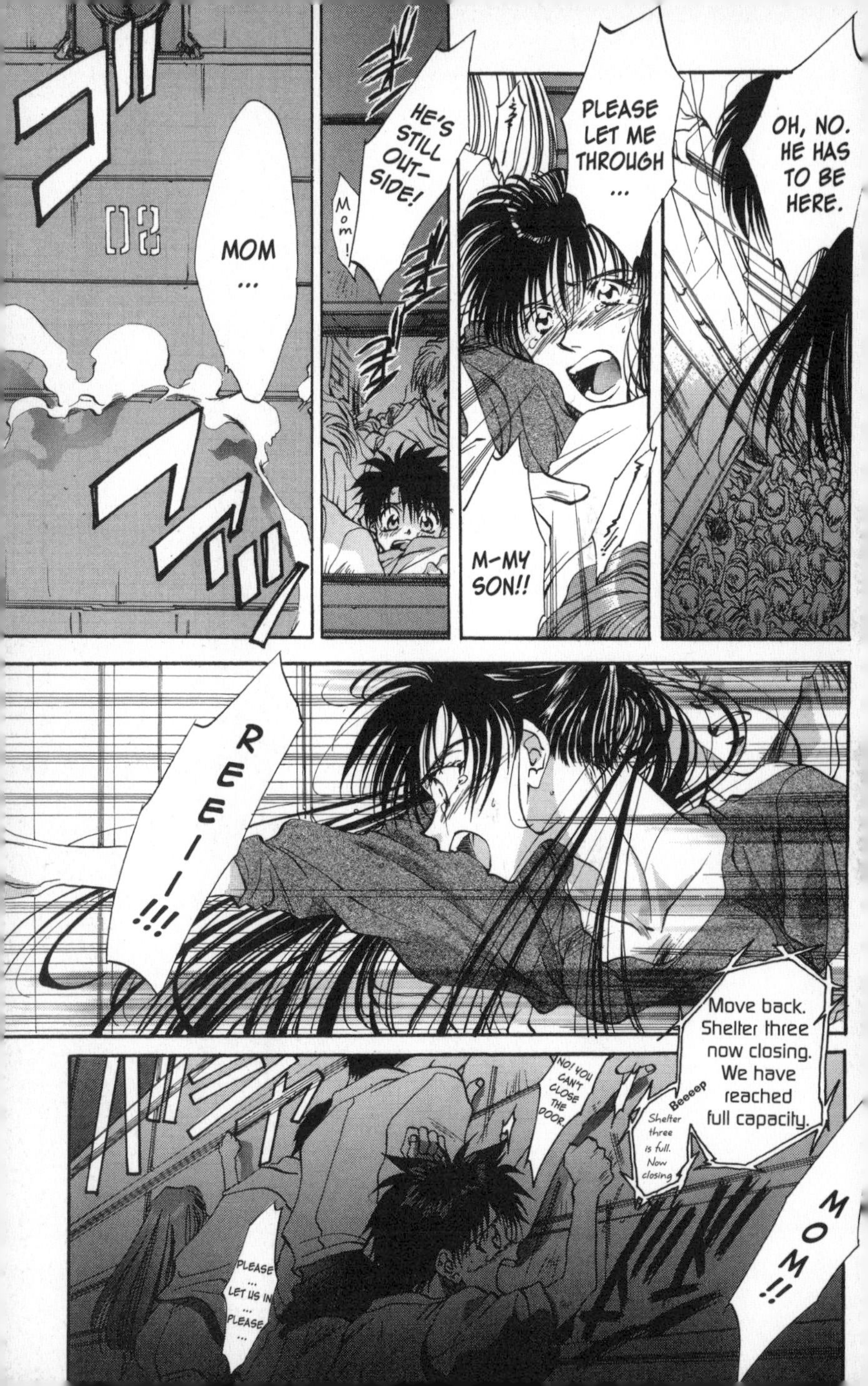
OH, NO. HE HAS TO BE HERE.
PLEASE LET ME THROUGH ...
M-MY SON!!
HE'S STILL OUT-SIDE!
Mom!
MOM ...
REEIII!!!
MOM!!
Move back. Shelter three now closing. We have reached full capacity.
Beeeep
Shelter three is full. Now closing
NO! YOU CAN'T CLOSE THE DOOR
PLEASE ... LET US IN ... PLEASE ...

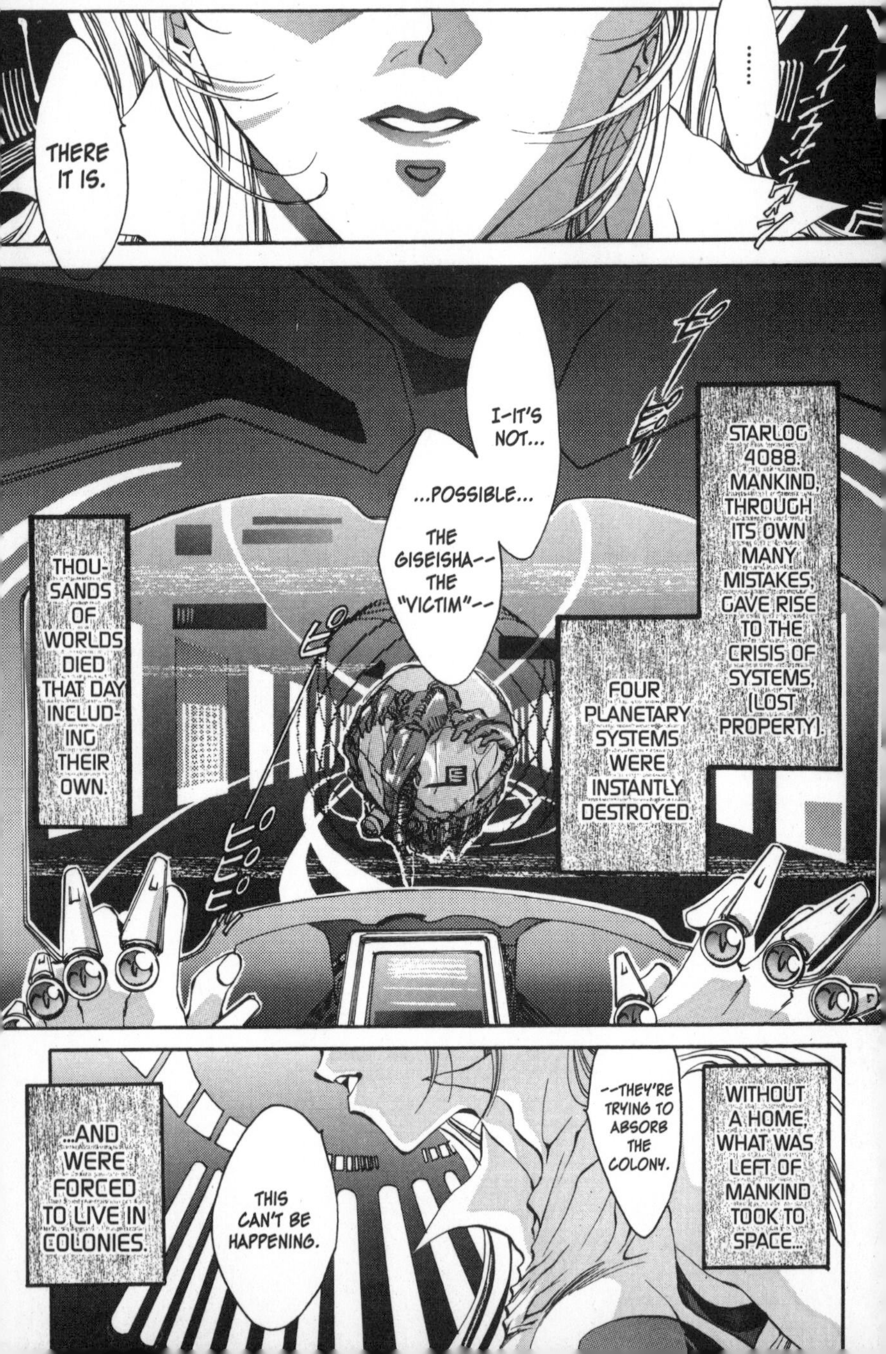
......
THERE IT IS.
STARLOG 4088. MANKIND, THROUGH ITS OWN MANY MISTAKES, GAVE RISE TO THE CRISIS OF SYSTEMS, (LOST PROPERTY).
I-IT'S NOT...
...POSSIBLE...
THE GISEISHA--THE "VICTIM"--
FOUR PLANETARY SYSTEMS WERE INSTANTLY DESTROYED.
THOUSANDS OF WORLDS DIED THAT DAY INCLUDING THEIR OWN.
WITHOUT A HOME, WHAT WAS LEFT OF MANKIND TOOK TO SPACE...
--THEY'RE TRYING TO ABSORB THE COLONY.
THIS CAN'T BE HAPPENING.
...AND WERE FORCED TO LIVE IN COLONIES.

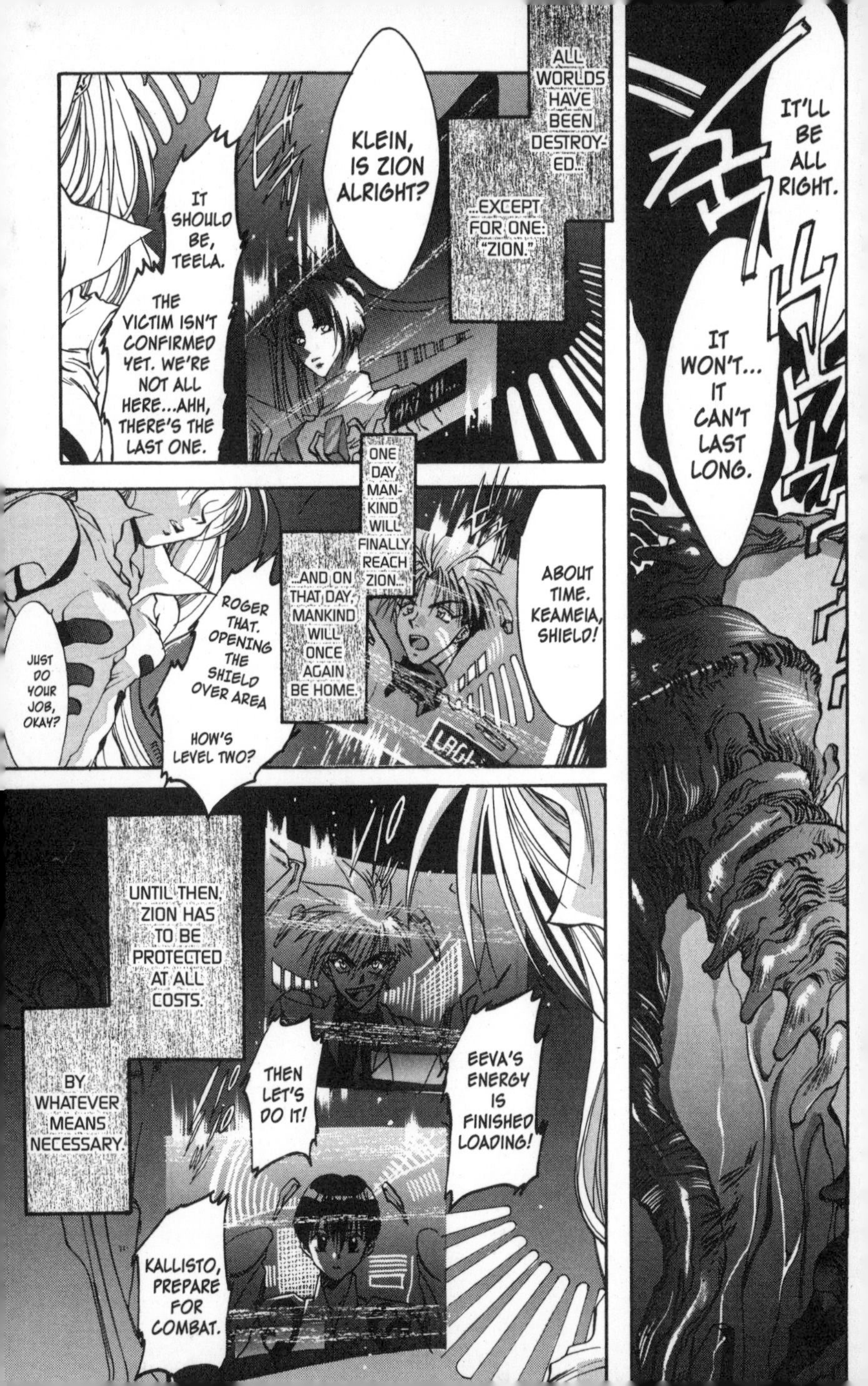
IT'LL BE ALL RIGHT.
IT WON'T... IT CAN'T LAST LONG.
ALL WORLDS HAVE BEEN DESTROY-ED...
...EXCEPT FOR ONE: "ZION."
KLEIN, IS ZION ALRIGHT?
IT SHOULD BE, TEELA.
THE VICTIM ISN'T CONFIRMED YET. WE'RE NOT ALL HERE...AHH, THERE'S THE LAST ONE.
ONE DAY MAN-KIND WILL FINALLY REACH ZION...
ABOUT TIME. KEAMEIA, SHIELD!
...AND ON THAT DAY, MANKIND WILL ONCE AGAIN BE HOME.
ROGER THAT. OPENING THE SHIELD OVER AREA
JUST DO YOUR JOB, OKAY?
HOW'S LEVEL TWO?
UNTIL THEN, ZION HAS TO BE PROTECTED AT ALL COSTS.
EEVA'S ENERGY IS FINISHED LOADING!
THEN LET'S DO IT!
BY WHATEVER MEANS NECESSARY.
KALLISTO, PREPARE FOR COMBAT.

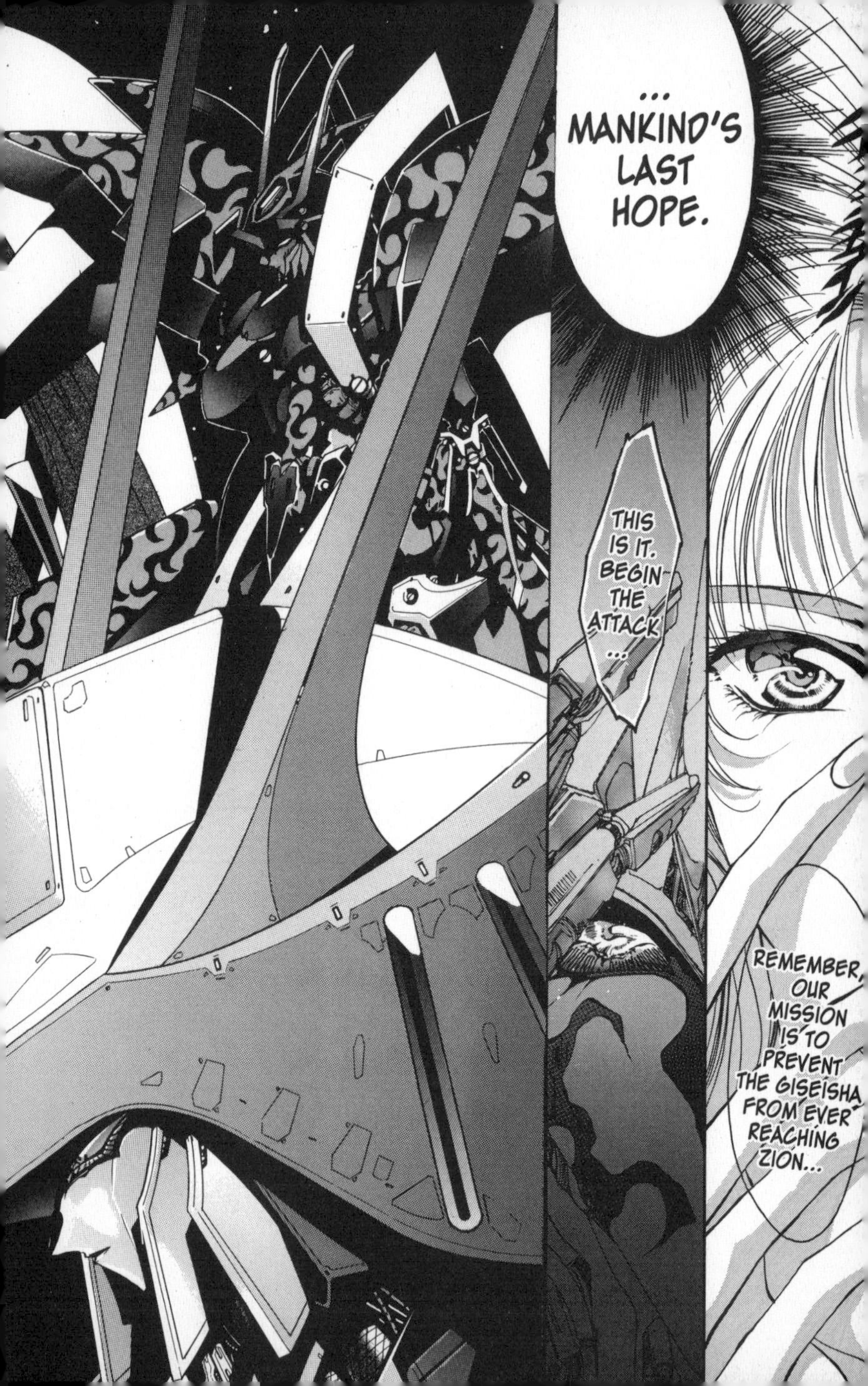
... MANKIND'S LAST HOPE.
REMEMBER, OUR MISSION IS TO PREVENT THE GISEISHA FROM EVER REACHING ZION...
THIS IS IT. BEGIN THE ATTACK ...

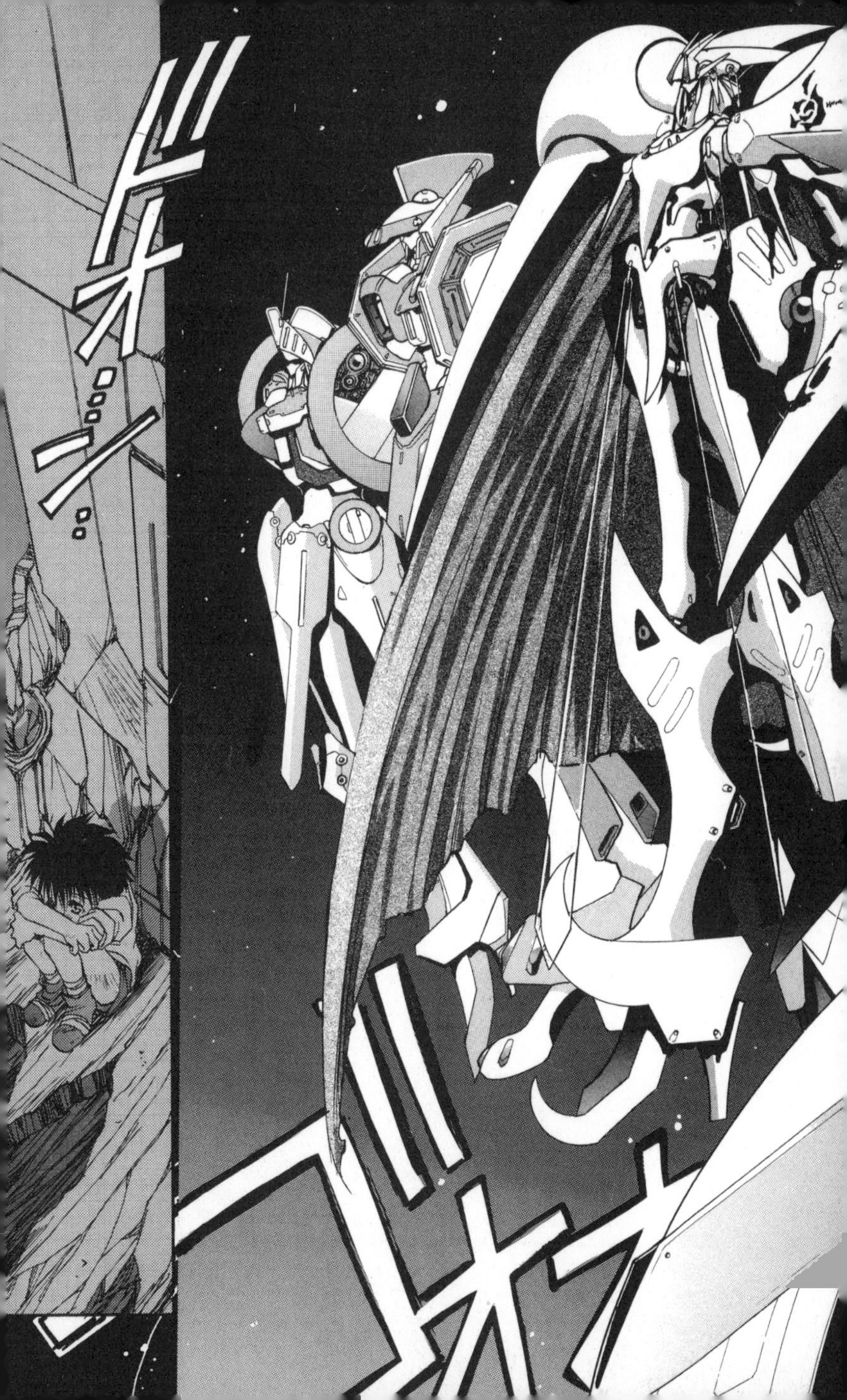
ドオ・・・ン

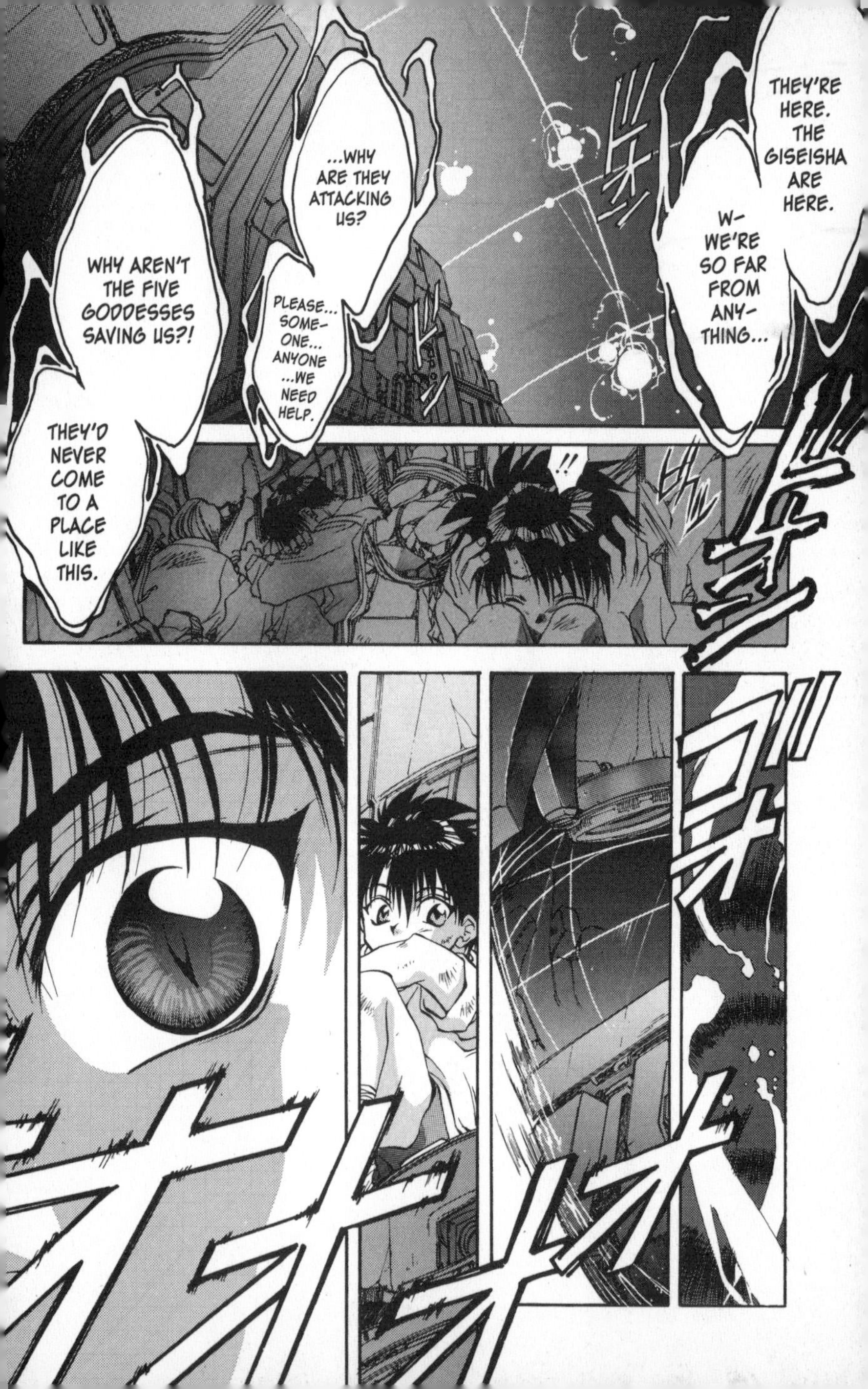
THEY'RE HERE. THE GISEISHA ARE HERE.
W-WE'RE SO FAR FROM ANYTHING...
...WHY ARE THEY ATTACKING US?
PLEASE... SOMEONE... ANYONE ...WE NEED HELP.
WHY AREN'T THE FIVE GODDESSES SAVING US?!
THEY'D NEVER COME TO A PLACE LIKE THIS.
!!

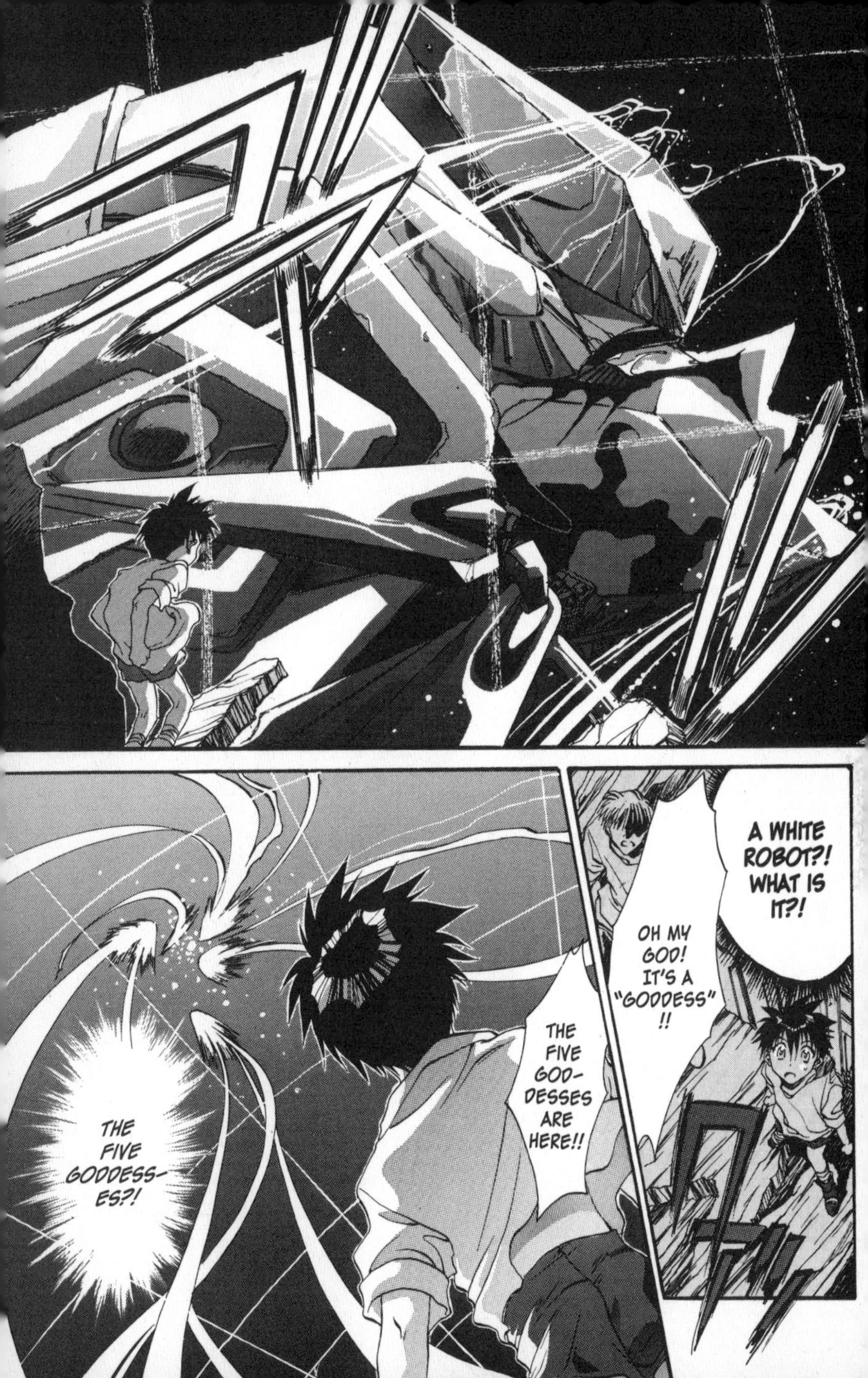
A WHITE ROBOT?! WHAT IS IT?!
OH MY GOD! IT'S A "GODDESS" !!
THE FIVE GOD-DESSES ARE HERE!!
THE FIVE GODDESS-ES?!

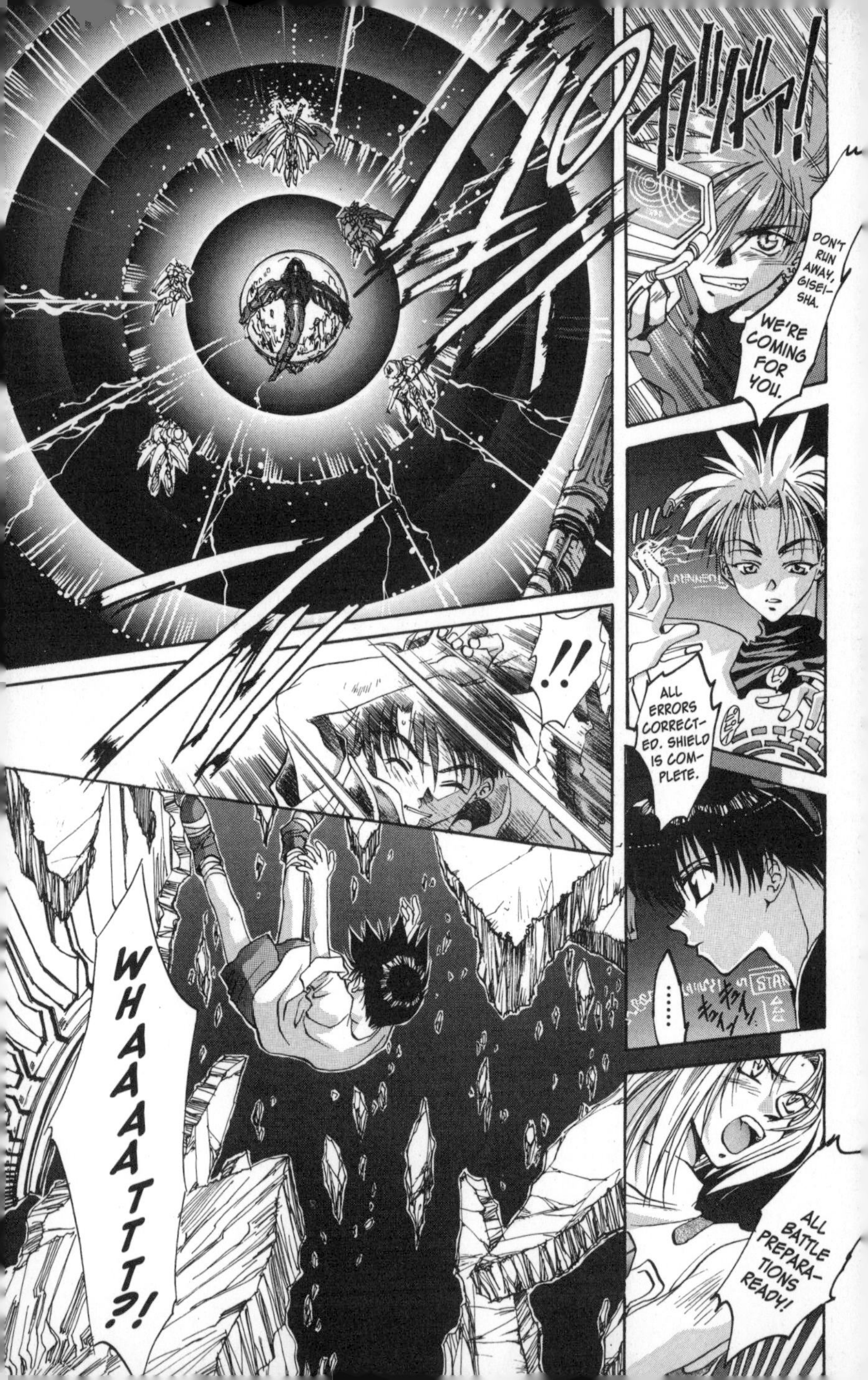
DON'T RUN AWAY, GISEI-SHA.
WE'RE COMING FOR YOU.
ALL ERRORS CORRECT-ED. SHIELD IS COM-PLETE.
......
ALL BATTLE PREPARA-TIONS READY!
!!
WHAAAATTTT?!

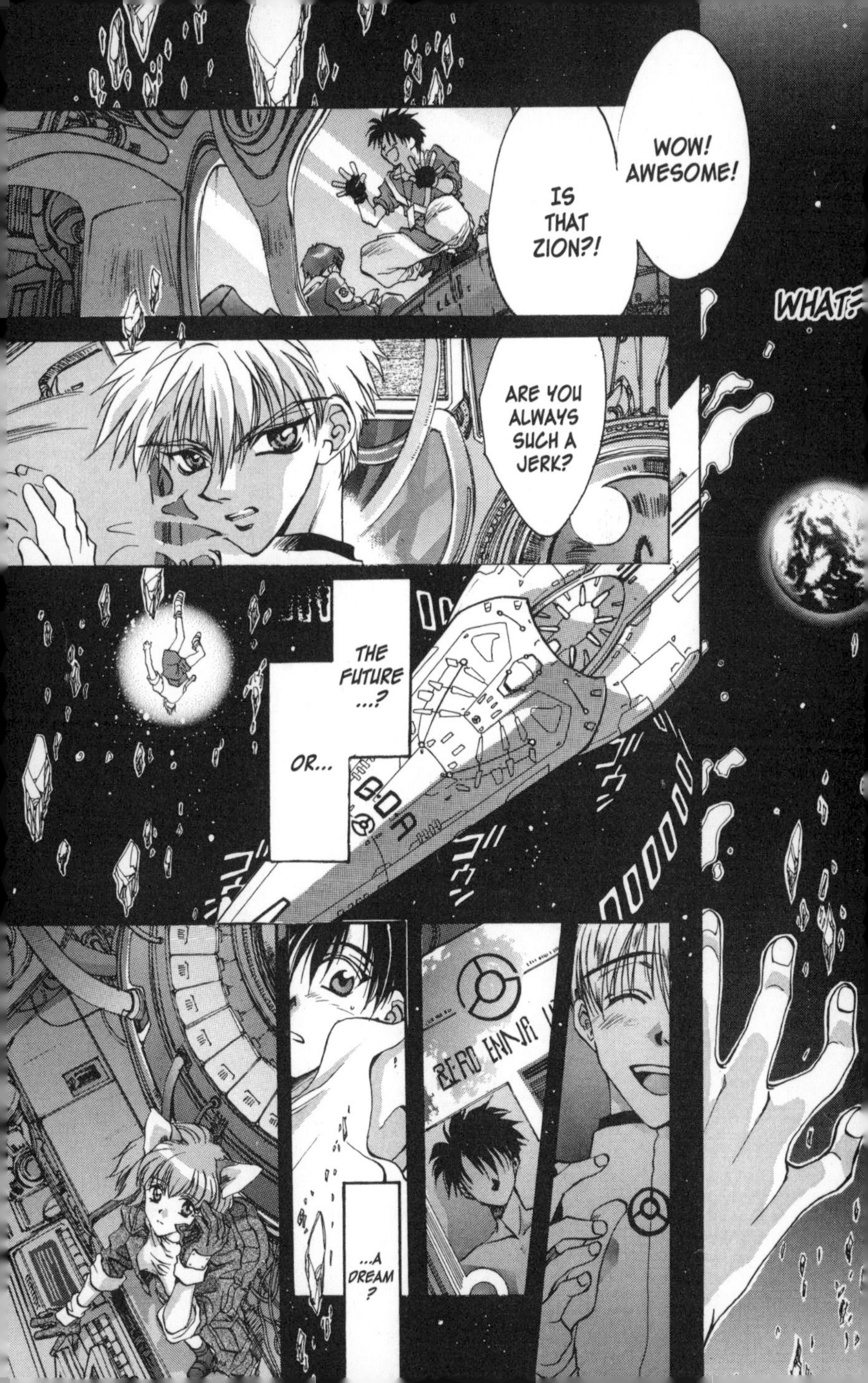
WOW! AWESOME!
IS THAT ZION?!
WHAT!?
ARE YOU ALWAYS SUCH A JERK?
THE FUTURE ...?
OR...
...A DREAM?

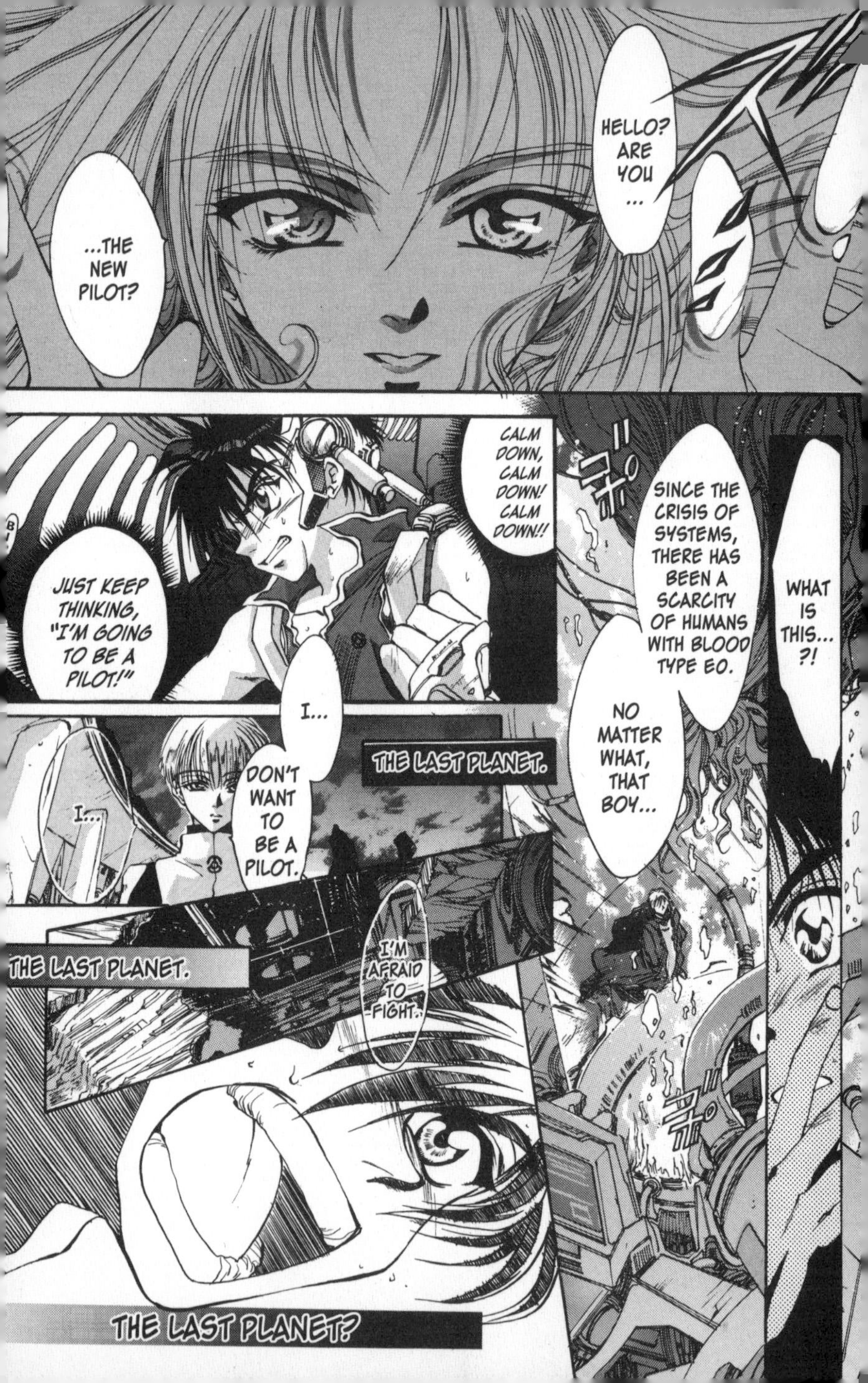
HELLO? ARE YOU ...
...THE NEW PILOT?
WHAT IS THIS...?!
SINCE THE CRISIS OF SYSTEMS, THERE HAS BEEN A SCARCITY OF HUMANS WITH BLOOD TYPE EO.
NO MATTER WHAT, THAT BOY...
CALM DOWN, CALM DOWN! CALM DOWN!!
JUST KEEP THINKING, "I'M GOING TO BE A PILOT!"
I...
DON'T WANT TO BE A PILOT.
THE LAST PLANET.
I...
THE LAST PLANET.
I'M AFRAID TO FIGHT.
THE LAST PLANET?

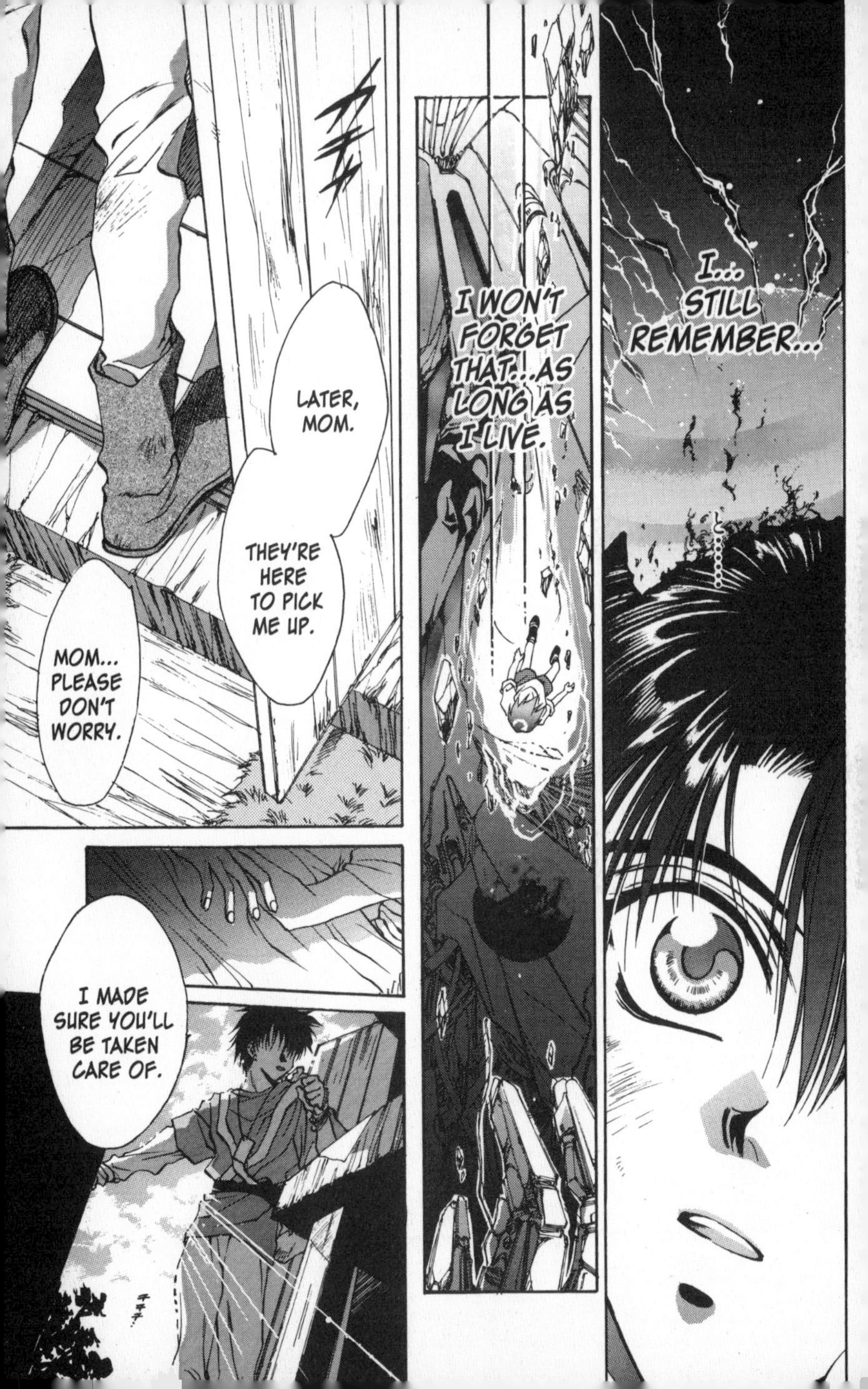
I... STILL REMEMBER...
I WON'T FORGET THAT...AS LONG AS I LIVE.
LATER, MOM.
THEY'RE HERE TO PICK ME UP.
MOM... PLEASE DON'T WORRY.
I MADE SURE YOU'LL BE TAKEN CARE OF.

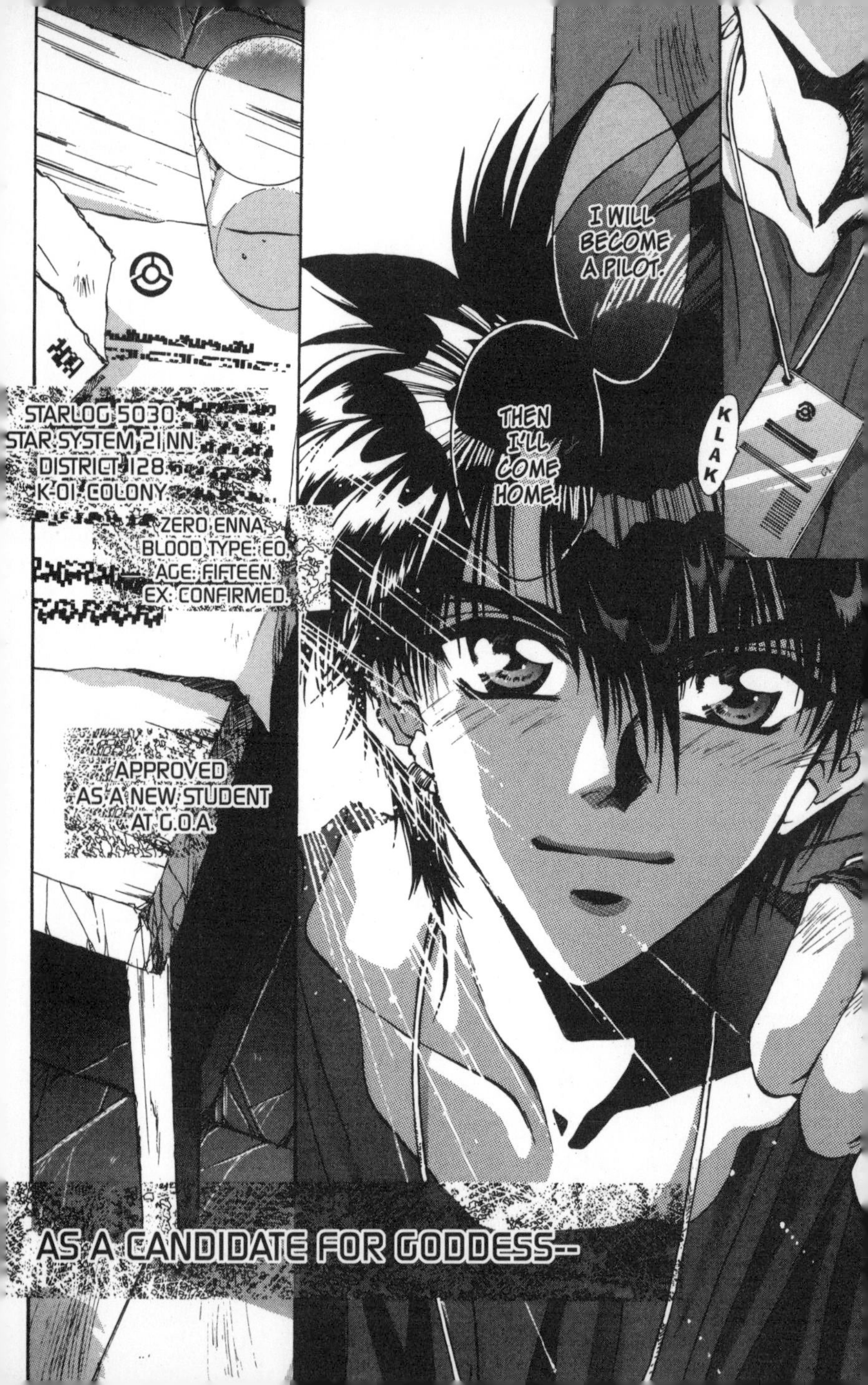
I WILL BECOME A PILOT.
KLAK
THEN I'LL COME HOME.
STARLOG 5030. STAR SYSTEM 21 NN. DISTRICT 128. K-01 COLONY
ZERO ENNA. BLOOD TYPE: EO. AGE: FIFTEEN. EX: CONFIRMED.
APPROVED AS A NEW STUDENT AT G.O.A.
AS A CANDIDATE FOR GODDESS--

Teela Zain Elmes

age:15	type:EO	156cm	42kg

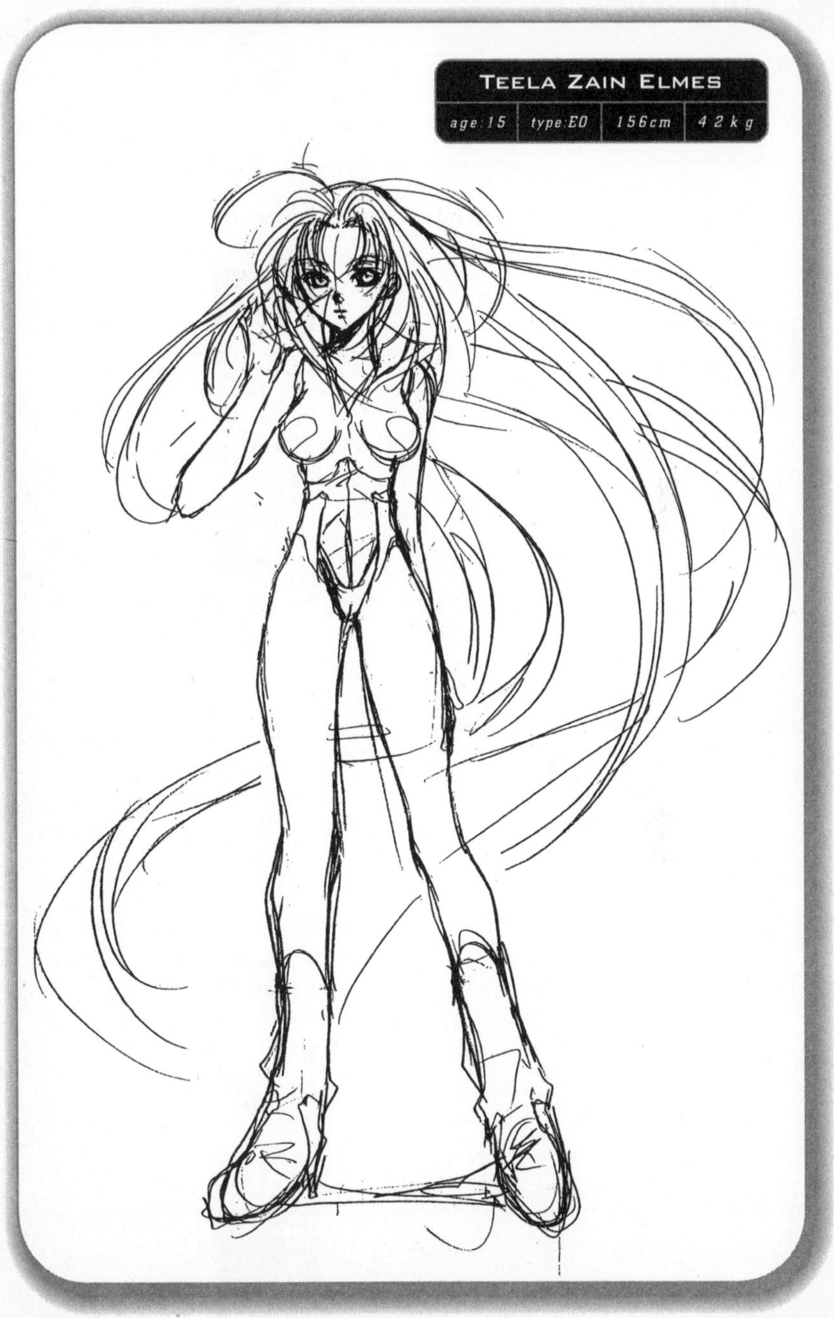

I hear a voice.
Inside hope and hesitation,
Your voice, calling me.

I hear a sound.
Inside hope and emptiness,
Far away, nearby, from the end of the world.

The flow of the wind over the earth
Quietly goes around the turning planet.

Static that is about to be cut off by consciousness,
Instead of all memories,
The light shines on the last memory,
As if to reach you, whom I have yet to see.

Look at me. Find me.
The me that is divided into you several times.

Today and tomorrow and even the future,
Even if I close my eyes,
I will look for you.

The flow of the wind over the earth
Quietly goes around the turning planet.

Find me, sleeping in the darkness.
Me, inside of you, to keep living.

Today and tomorrow and forever,
Even if everything is destroyed
I will look for you.

Today and tomorrow and even the future,
Even if I close my eyes,
I will look for you.

I will look for you.

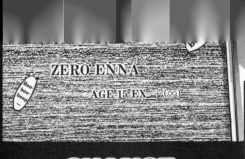

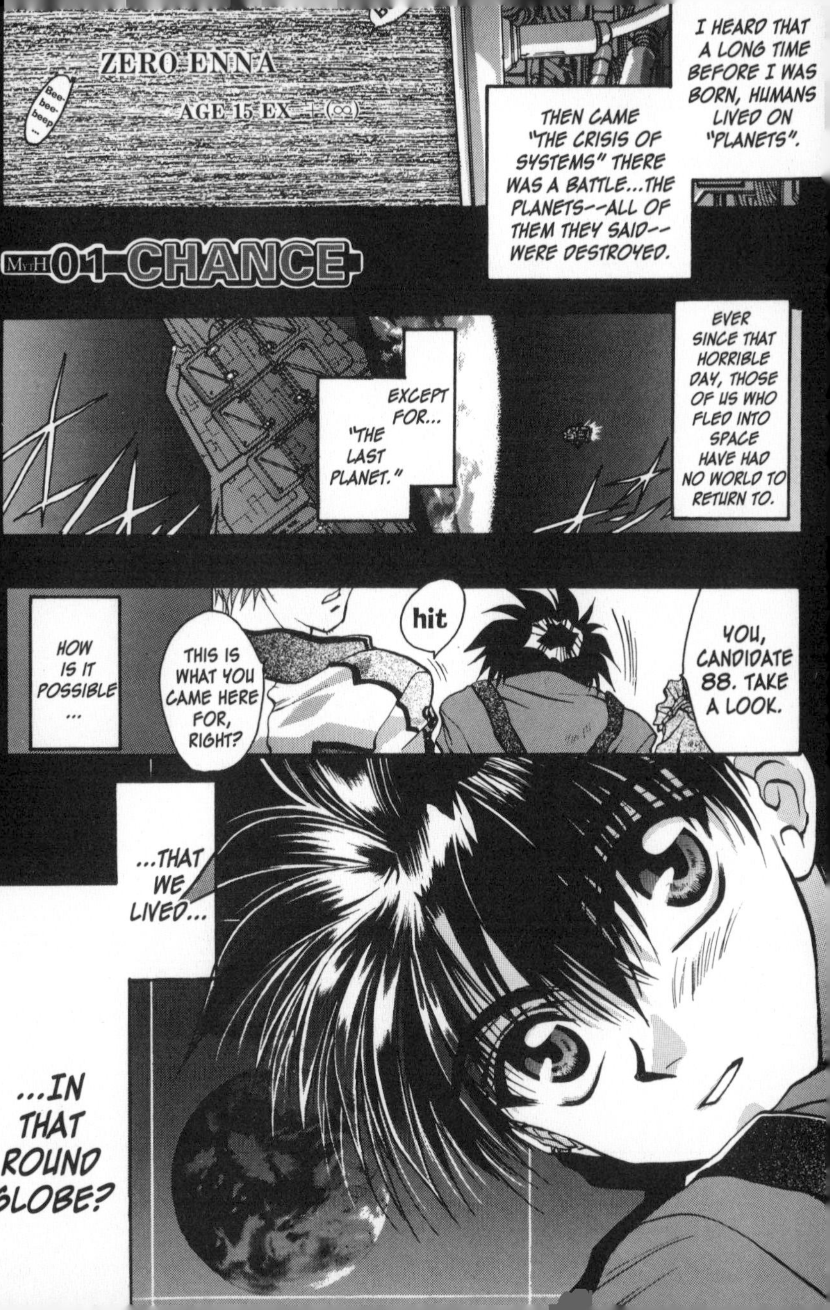
I HEARD THAT A LONG TIME BEFORE I WAS BORN, HUMANS LIVED ON "PLANETS".
THEN CAME "THE CRISIS OF SYSTEMS" THERE WAS A BATTLE...THE PLANETS--ALL OF THEM THEY SAID--WERE DESTROYED.
ZERO ENNA
AGE 15 EX + (∞)
Bee-bee-beep...
MYTH 01 CHANCE
EVER SINCE THAT HORRIBLE DAY, THOSE OF US WHO FLED INTO SPACE HAVE HAD NO WORLD TO RETURN TO.
EXCEPT FOR... "THE LAST PLANET."
YOU, CANDIDATE 88. TAKE A LOOK.
hit
THIS IS WHAT YOU CAME HERE FOR, RIGHT?
HOW IS IT POSSIBLE ...
...THAT WE LIVED...
...IN THAT ROUND GLOBE?

MyTH 01 CHANCE

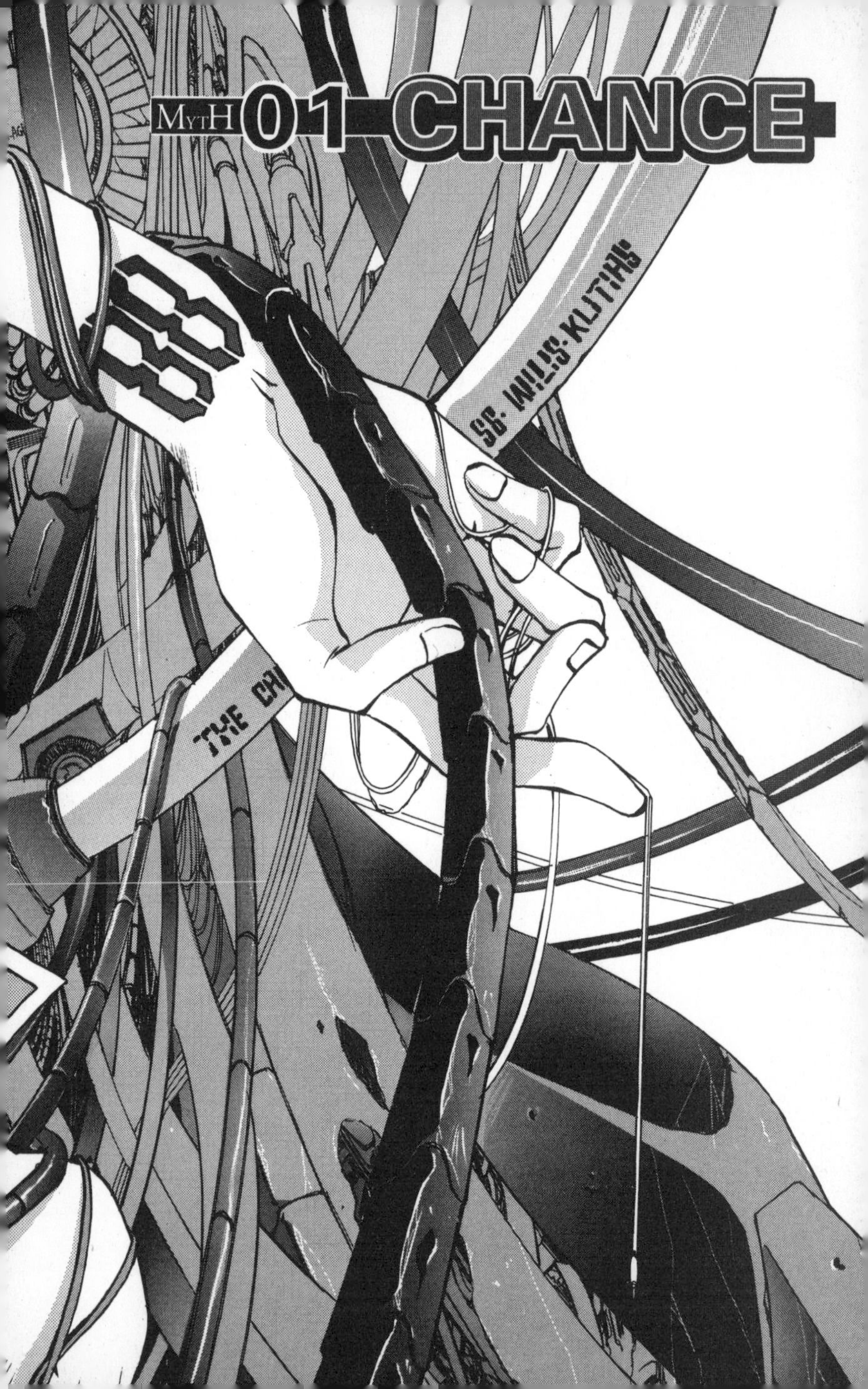

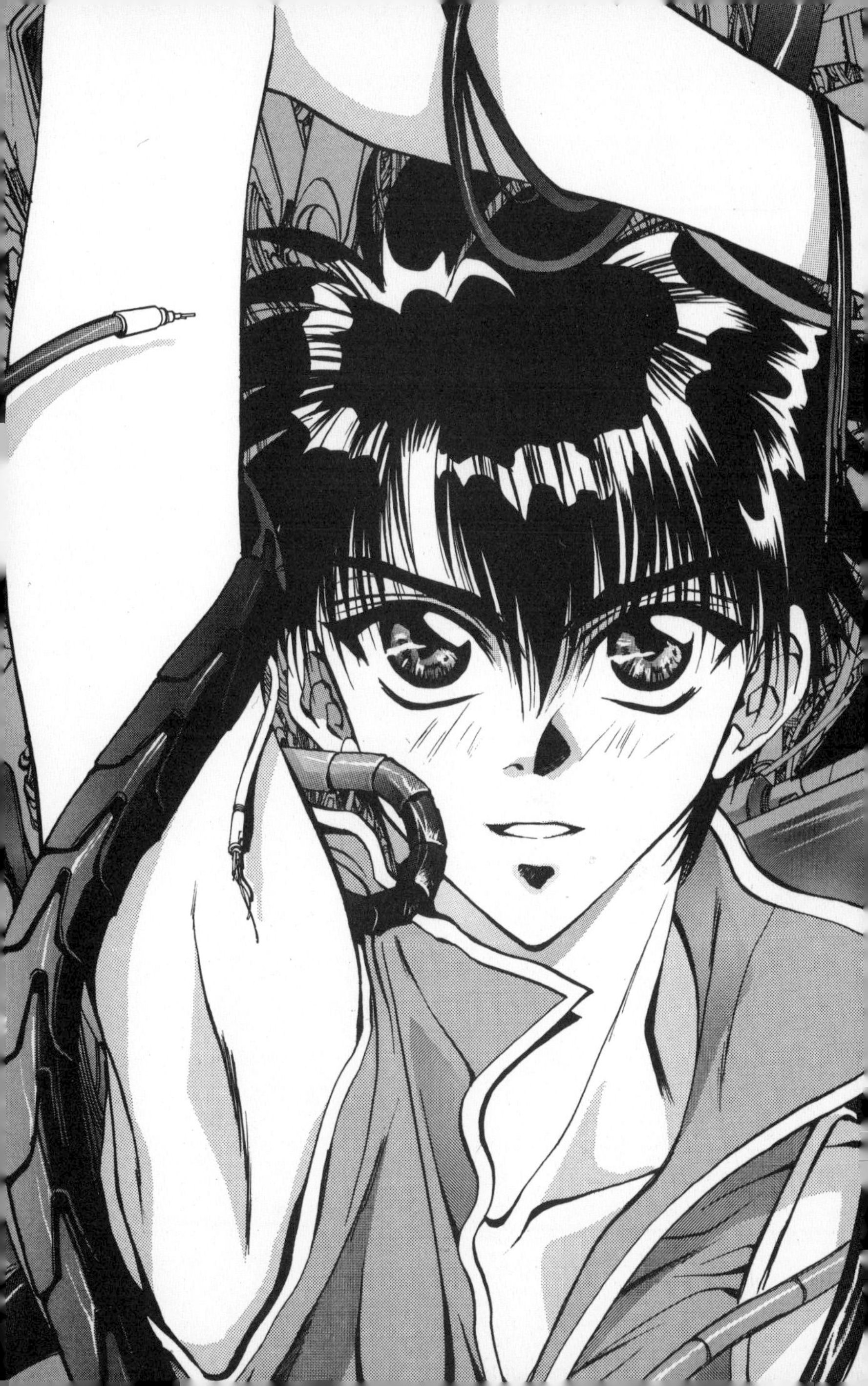

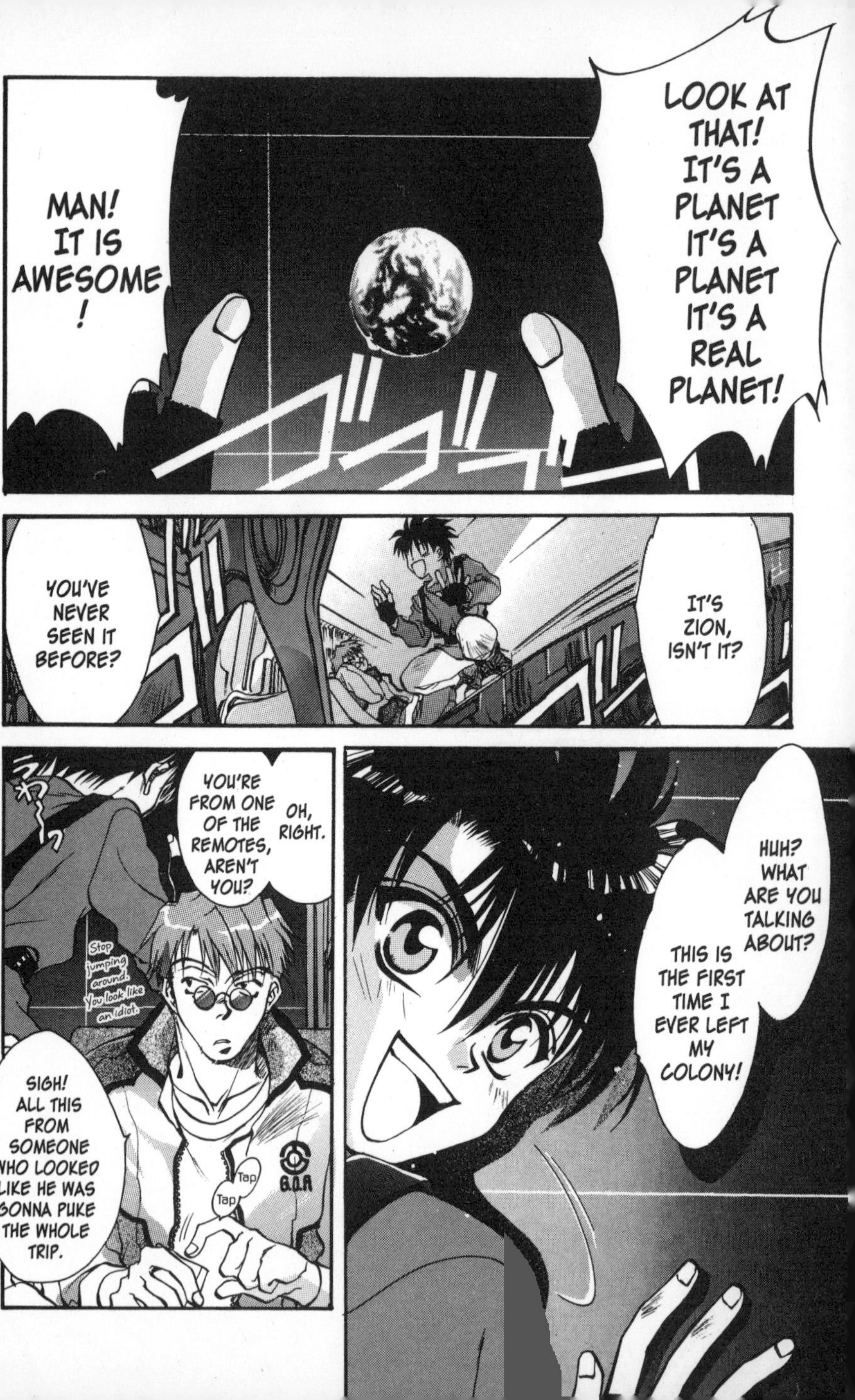
LOOK AT THAT! IT'S A PLANET IT'S A PLANET IT'S A REAL PLANET!
MAN! IT IS AWESOME!
IT'S ZION, ISN'T IT?
YOU'VE NEVER SEEN IT BEFORE?
HUH? WHAT ARE YOU TALKING ABOUT?
THIS IS THE FIRST TIME I EVER LEFT MY COLONY!
OH, RIGHT.
YOU'RE FROM ONE OF THE REMOTES, AREN'T YOU?
Stop jumping around. You look like an idiot.
SIGH! ALL THIS FROM SOMEONE WHO LOOKED LIKE HE WAS GONNA PUKE THE WHOLE TRIP.
Tap
Tap
G.O.A

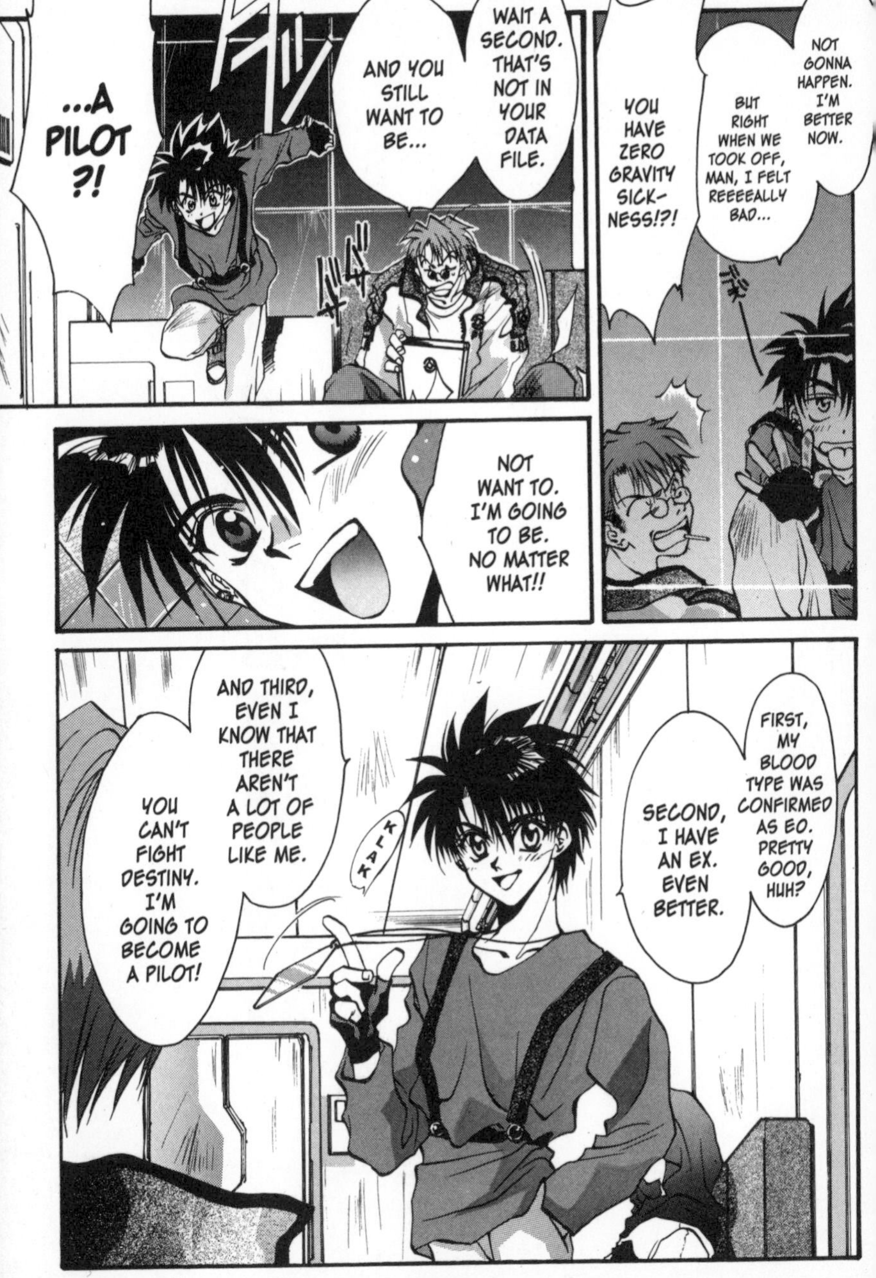
NOT GONNA HAPPEN. I'M BETTER NOW.
BUT RIGHT WHEN WE TOOK OFF, MAN, I FELT REEEEALLY BAD...
YOU HAVE ZERO GRAVITY SICKNESS!?!
WAIT A SECOND. THAT'S NOT IN YOUR DATA FILE.
AND YOU STILL WANT TO BE...
...A PILOT ?!
NOT WANT TO. I'M GOING TO BE. NO MATTER WHAT!!
FIRST, MY BLOOD TYPE WAS CONFIRMED AS EO. PRETTY GOOD, HUH?
SECOND, I HAVE AN EX. EVEN BETTER.
AND THIRD, EVEN I KNOW THAT THERE AREN'T A LOT OF PEOPLE LIKE ME.
KLAK
YOU CAN'T FIGHT DESTINY. I'M GOING TO BECOME A PILOT!

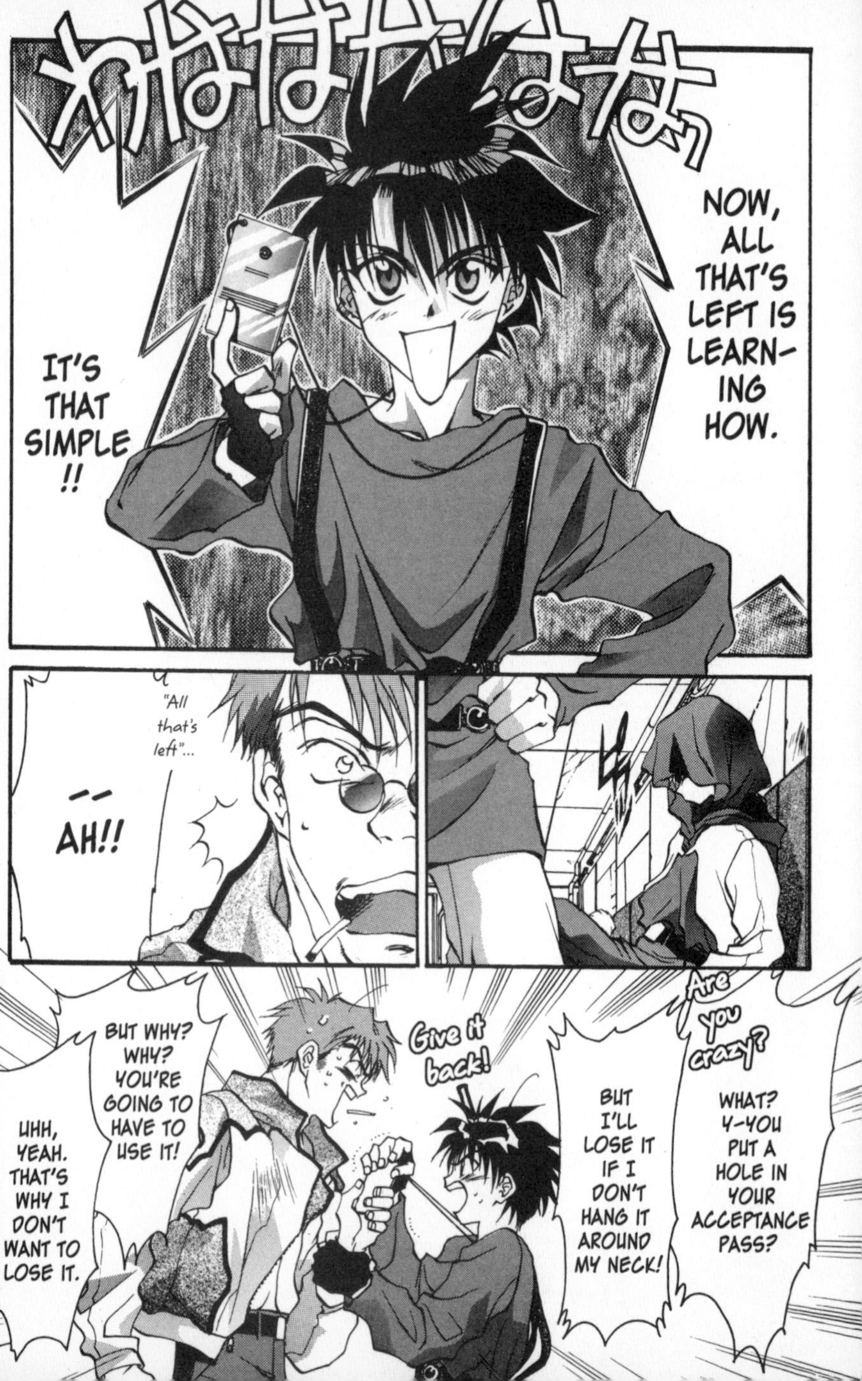
NOW, ALL THAT'S LEFT IS LEARNING HOW.
IT'S THAT SIMPLE !!
"All that's left"...
-- AH!!
Are you crazy?
WHAT? Y-YOU PUT A HOLE IN YOUR ACCEPTANCE PASS?
BUT I'LL LOSE IT IF I DON'T HANG IT AROUND MY NECK!
Give it back!
BUT WHY? WHY? YOU'RE GOING TO HAVE TO USE IT!
UHH, YEAH. THAT'S WHY I DON'T WANT TO LOSE IT.

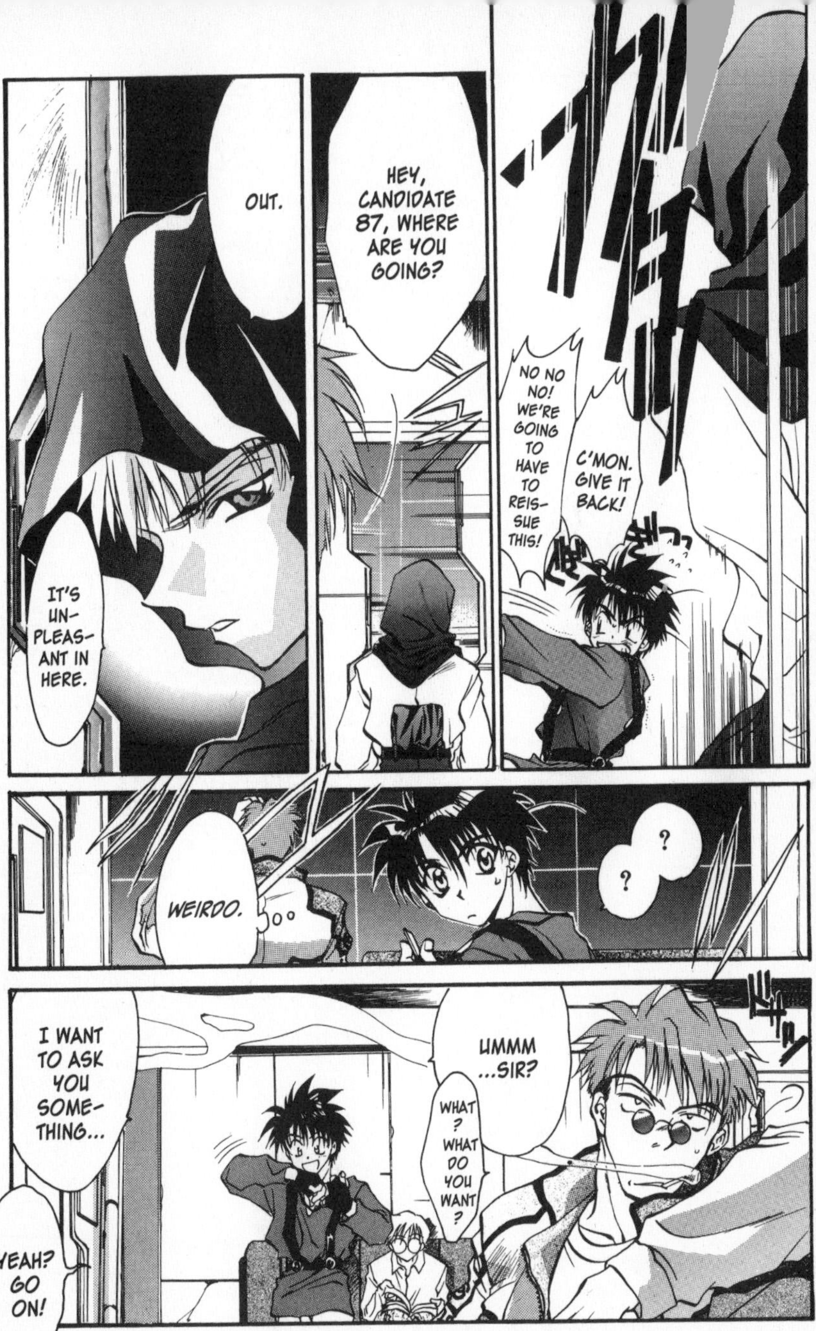
C'MON. GIVE IT BACK!
NO NO NO! WE'RE GOING TO HAVE TO REIS-SUE THIS!
HEY, CANDIDATE 87, WHERE ARE YOU GOING?
OUT.
IT'S UN-PLEAS-ANT IN HERE.
?
?
WEIRDO.
UMMM ...SIR?
WHAT? WHAT DO YOU WANT?
I WANT TO ASK YOU SOME-THING...
YEAH? GO ON!

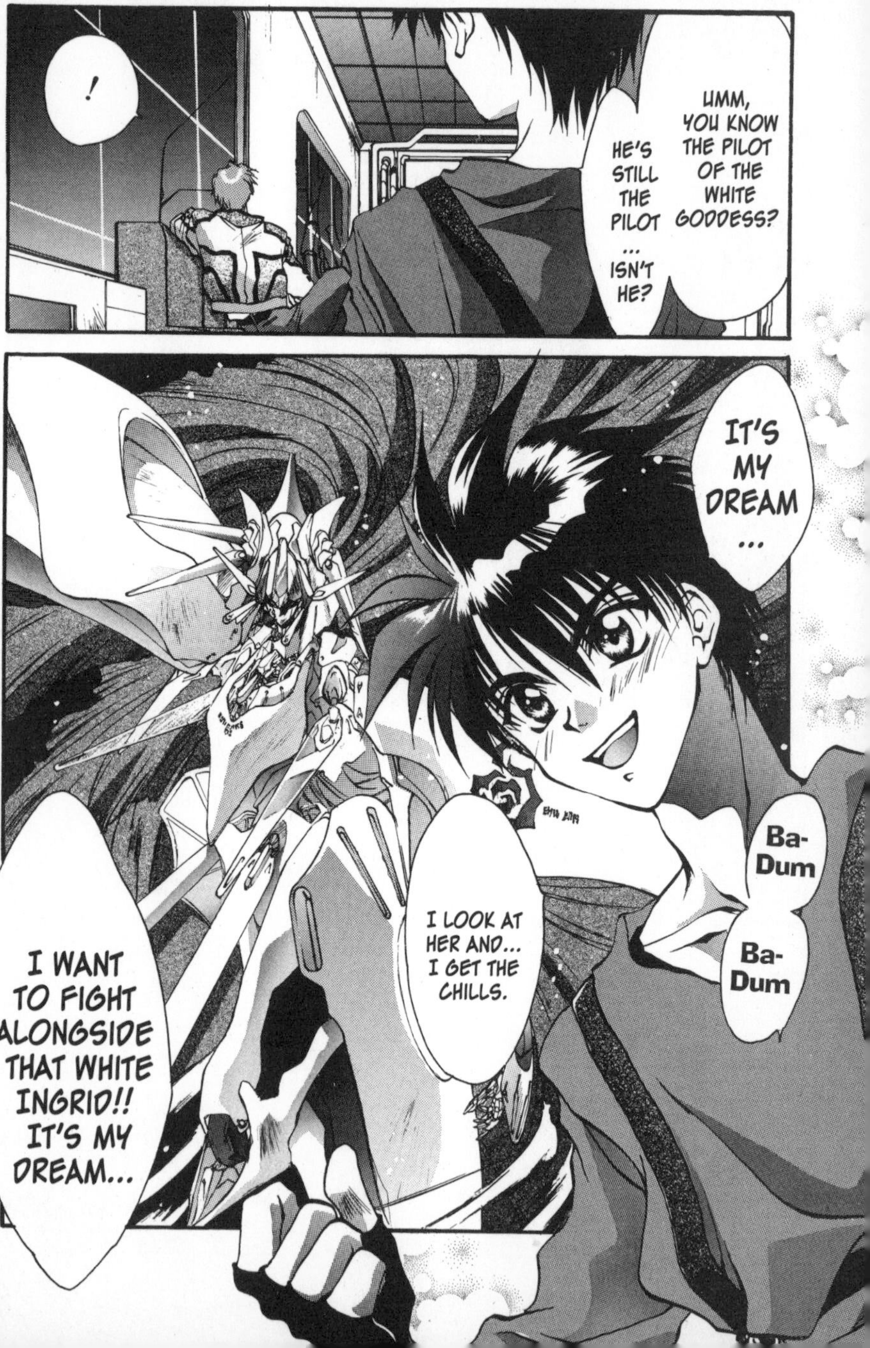
UMM, YOU KNOW THE PILOT OF THE WHITE GODDESS?
HE'S STILL THE PILOT ... ISN'T HE?
!
IT'S MY DREAM ...
Ba-Dum
Ba-Dum
I LOOK AT HER AND... I GET THE CHILLS.
I WANT TO FIGHT ALONGSIDE THAT WHITE INGRID!! IT'S MY DREAM...

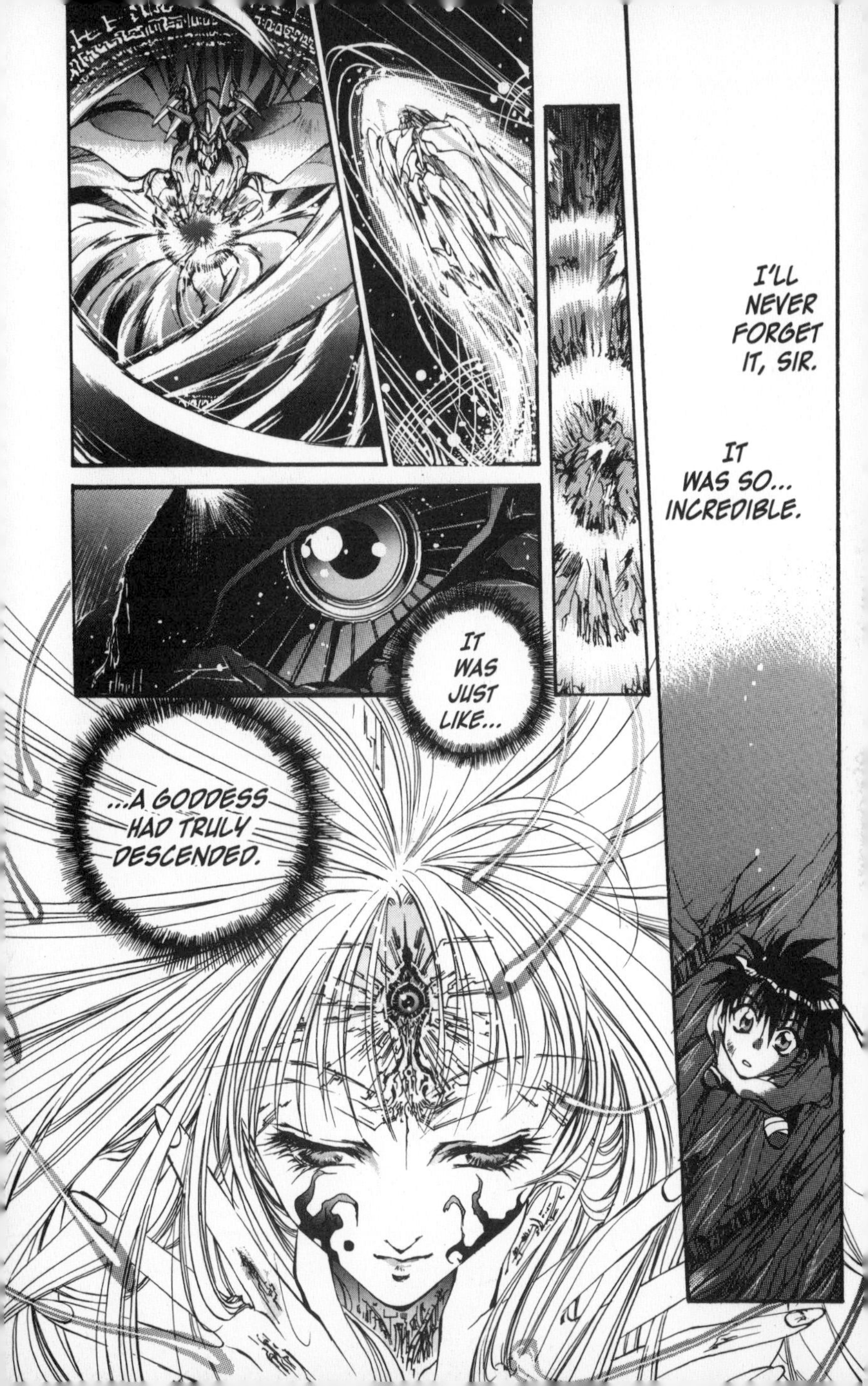
I'LL NEVER FORGET IT, SIR.
IT WAS SO... INCREDIBLE.
IT WAS JUST LIKE...
...A GODDESS HAD TRULY DESCENDED.

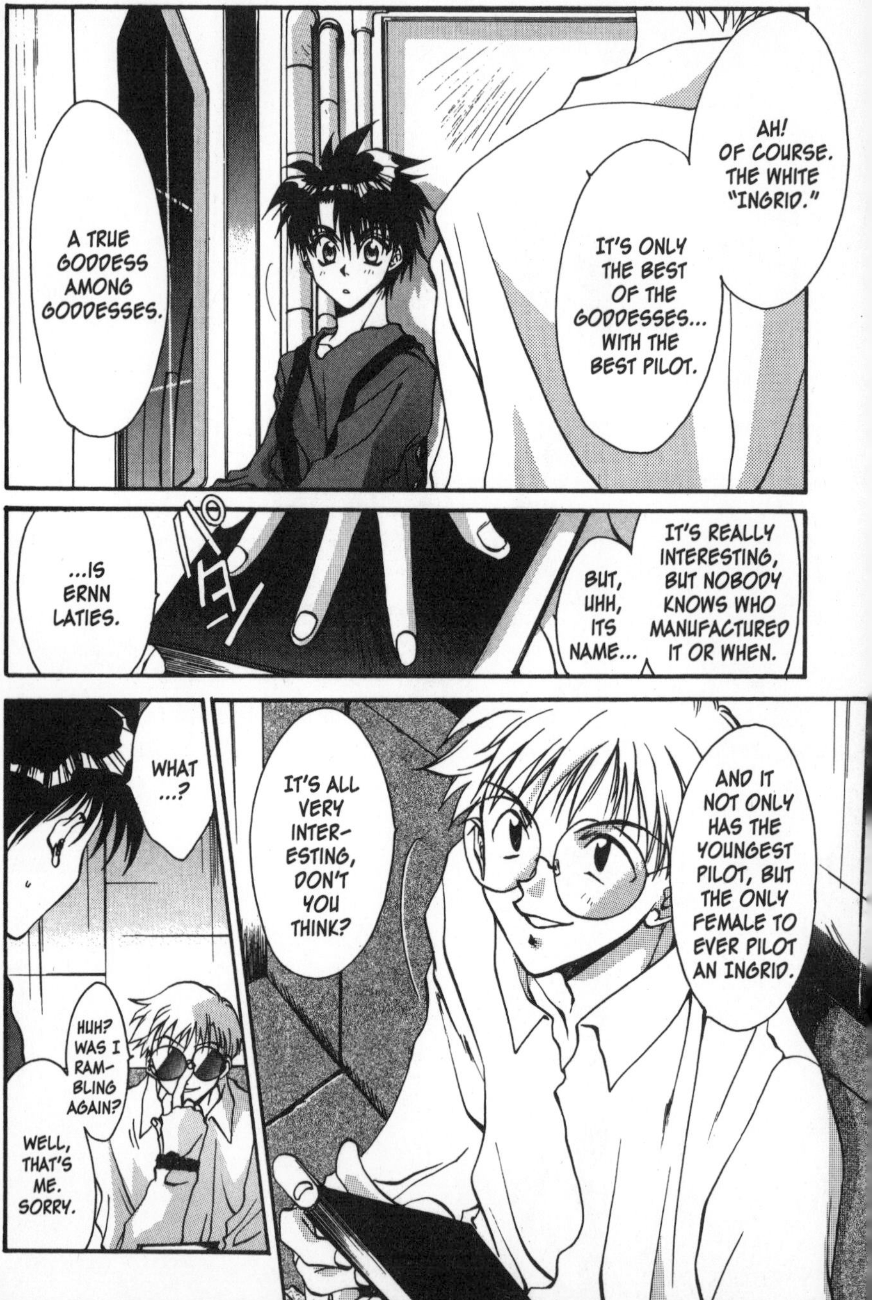
AH! OF COURSE. THE WHITE "INGRID."
IT'S ONLY THE BEST OF THE GODDESSES... WITH THE BEST PILOT.
A TRUE GODDESS AMONG GODDESSES.
IT'S REALLY INTERESTING, BUT NOBODY KNOWS WHO MANUFACTURED IT OR WHEN.
BUT, UHH, ITS NAME...
...IS ERNN LATIES.
AND IT NOT ONLY HAS THE YOUNGEST PILOT, BUT THE ONLY FEMALE TO EVER PILOT AN INGRID.
IT'S ALL VERY INTER-ESTING, DON'T YOU THINK?
WHAT ...?
HUH? WAS I RAM-BLING AGAIN?
WELL, THAT'S ME. SORRY.

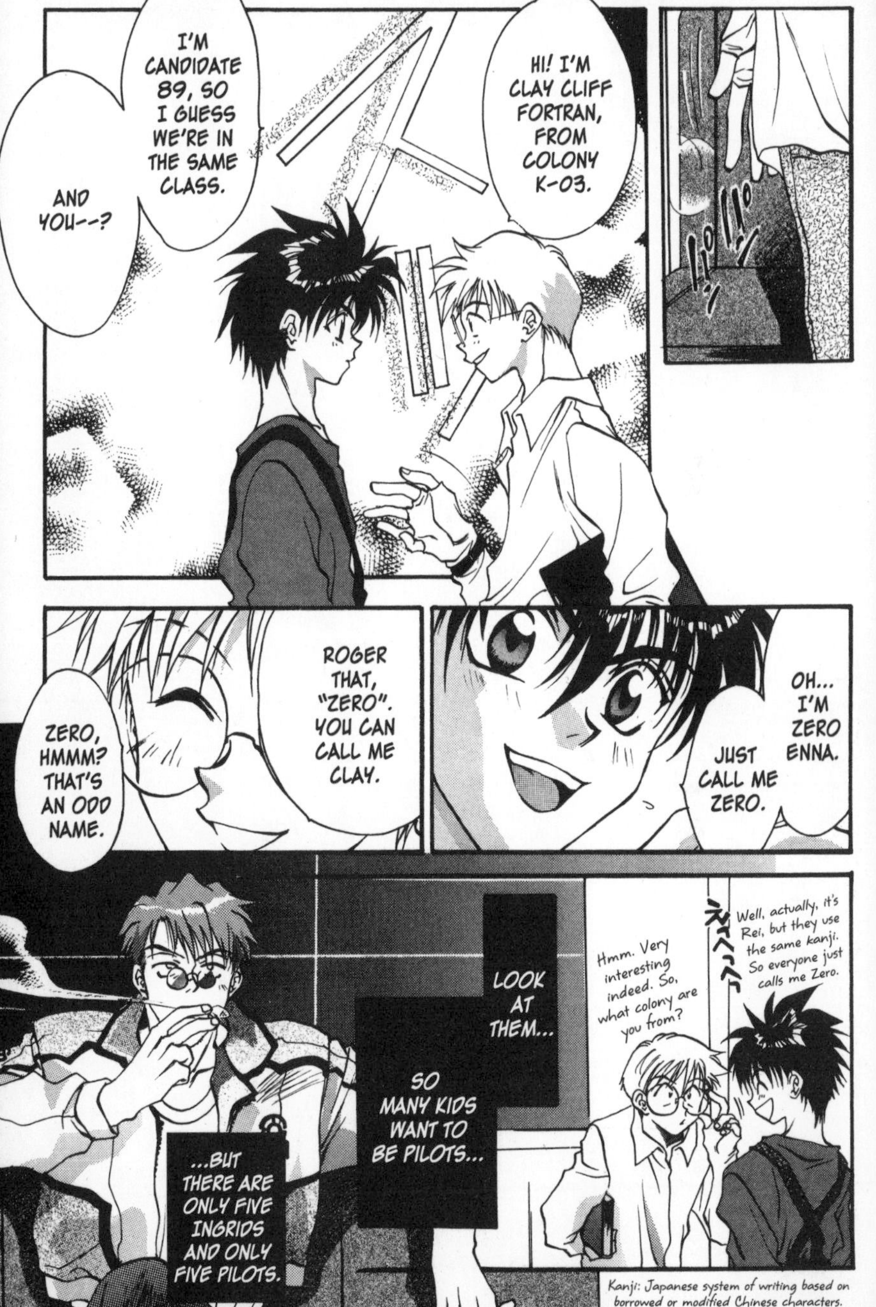
HI! I'M CLAY CLIFF FORTRAN, FROM COLONY K-03.
I'M CANDIDATE 89, SO I GUESS WE'RE IN THE SAME CLASS.
AND YOU--?
OH... I'M ZERO ENNA.
JUST CALL ME ZERO.
ROGER THAT, "ZERO". YOU CAN CALL ME CLAY.
ZERO, HMMM? THAT'S AN ODD NAME.
Well, actually, it's Rei, but they use the same kanji. So everyone just calls me Zero.
Hmm. Very interesting indeed. So, what colony are you from?
LOOK AT THEM...
SO MANY KIDS WANT TO BE PILOTS...
...BUT THERE ARE ONLY FIVE INGRIDS AND ONLY FIVE PILOTS.

Kanji: Japanese system of writing based on borrowed or modified Chinese characters.

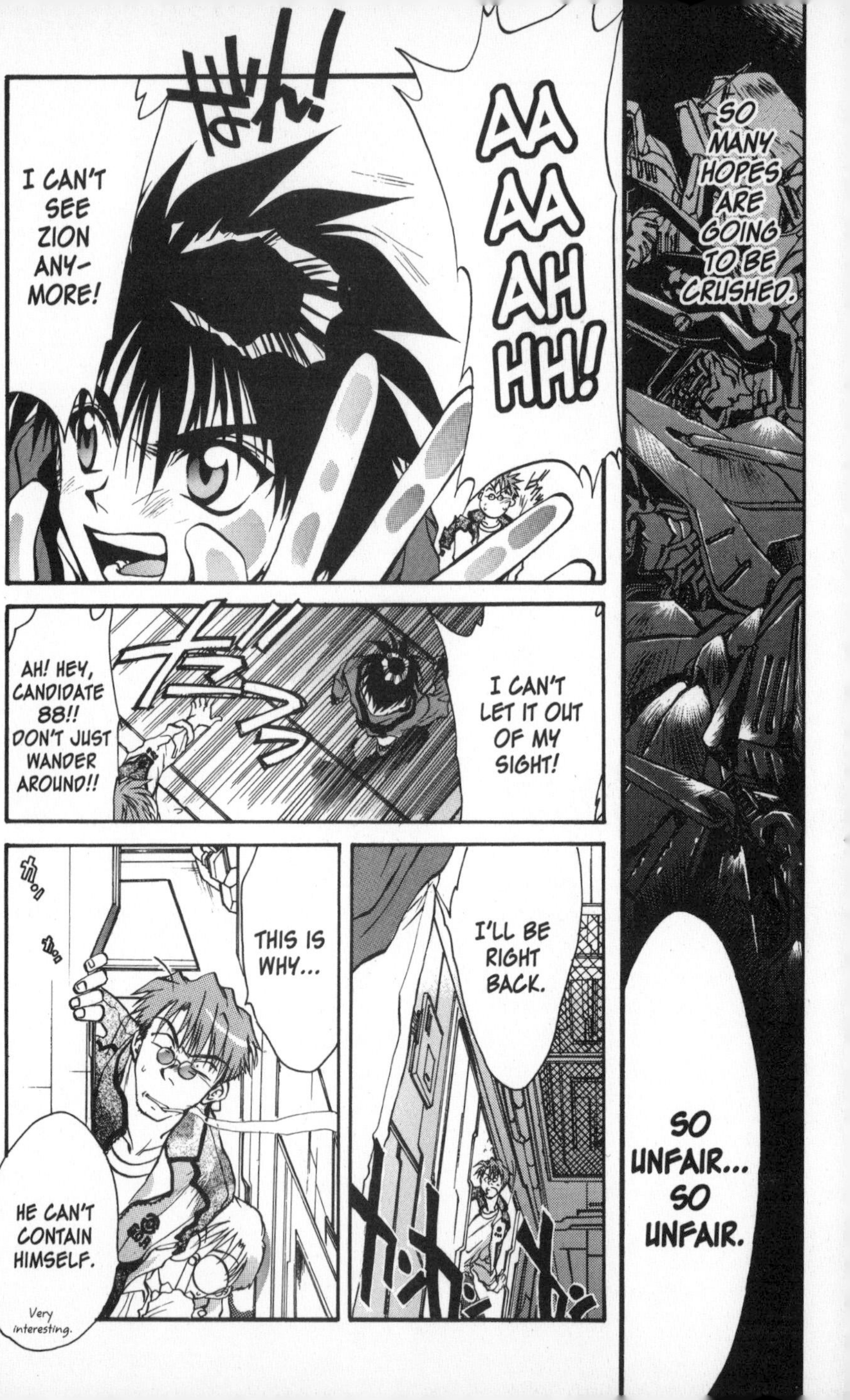
SO MANY HOPES ARE GOING TO BE CRUSHED.
SO UNFAIR... SO UNFAIR.
AAAAAHHH!
I CAN'T SEE ZION ANY-MORE!
I CAN'T LET IT OUT OF MY SIGHT!
AH! HEY, CANDIDATE 88!! DON'T JUST WANDER AROUND!!
I'LL BE RIGHT BACK.
THIS IS WHY...
HE CAN'T CONTAIN HIMSELF.
Very interesting.

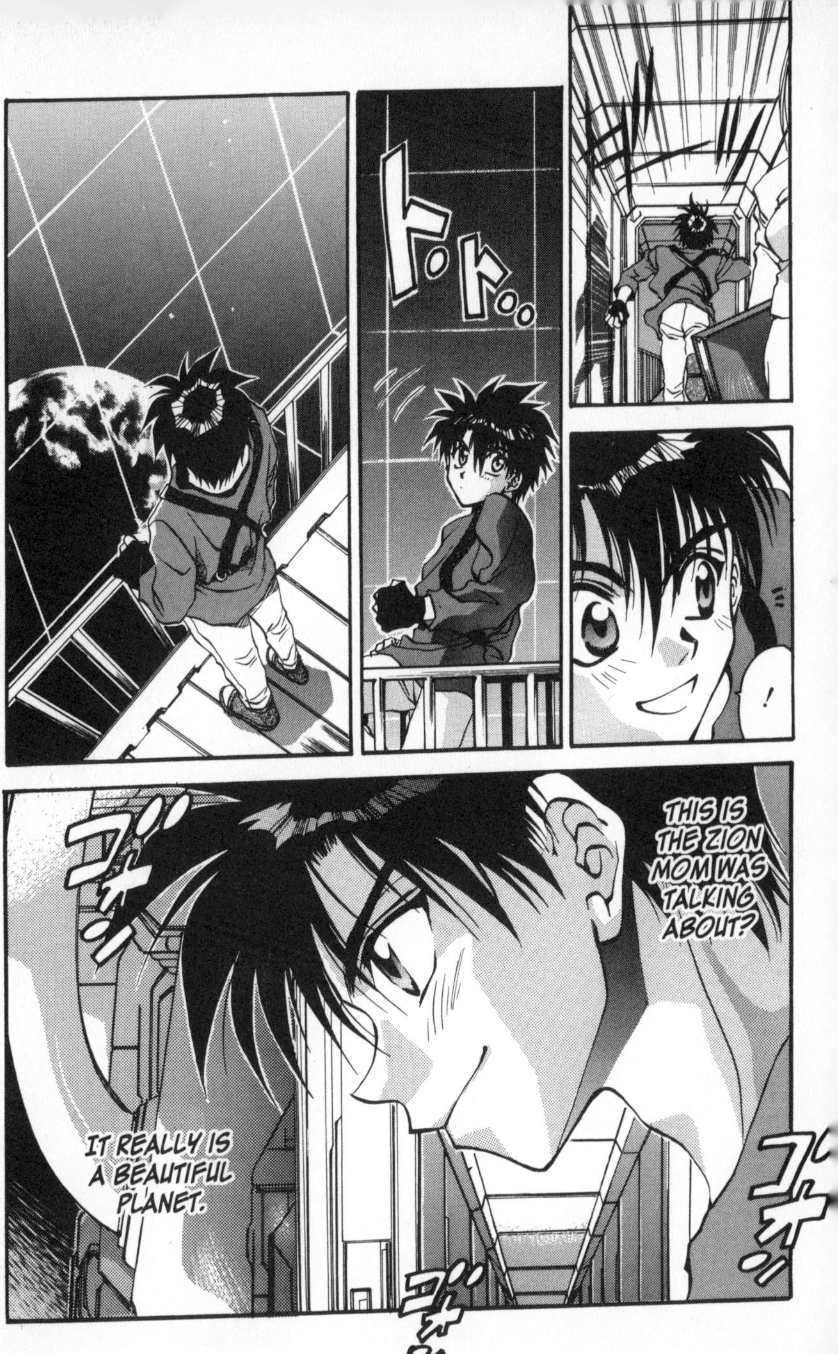
!
THIS IS THE ZION MOM WAS TALKING ABOUT?
IT REALLY IS A BEAUTIFUL PLANET.

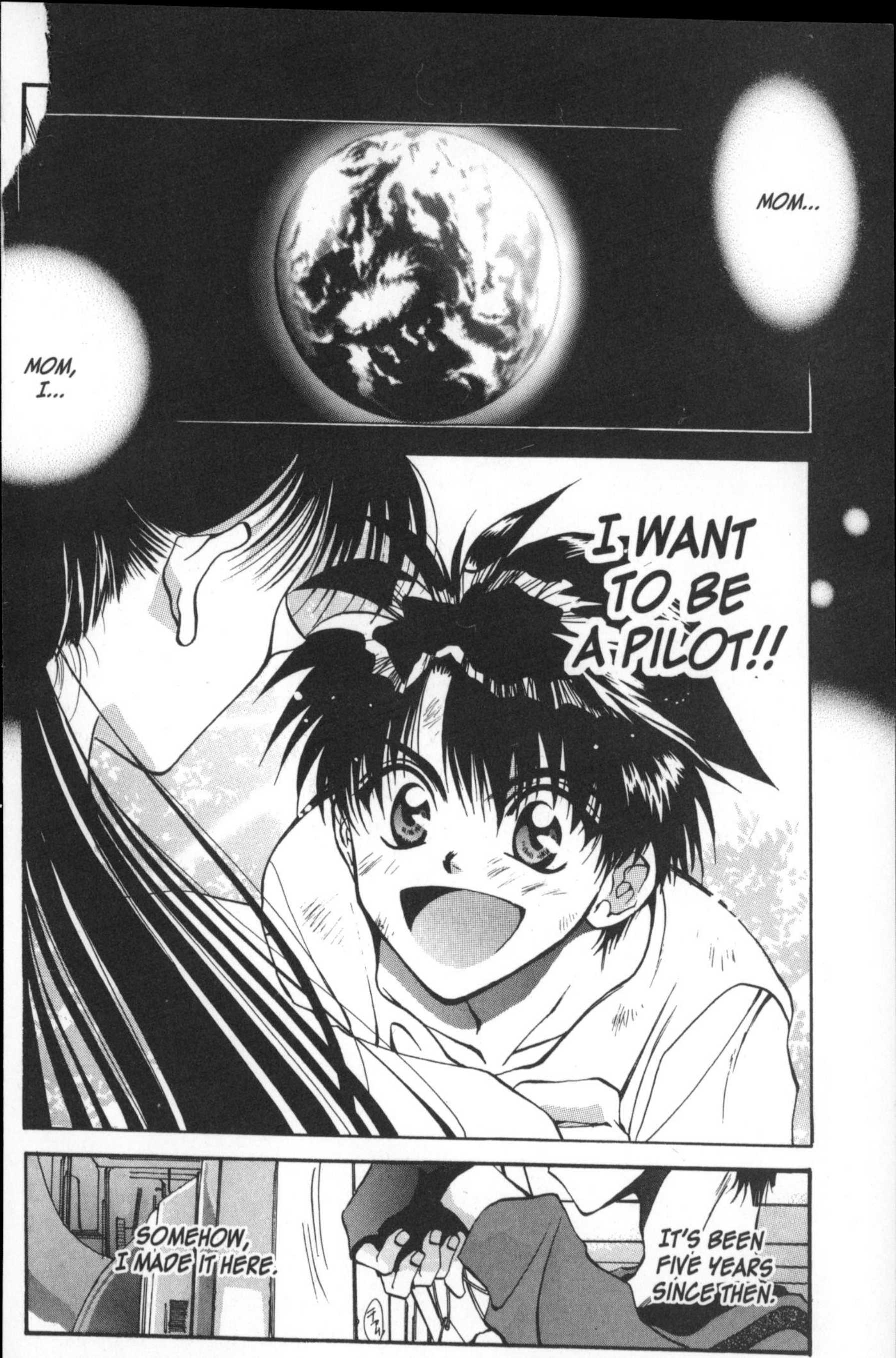
MOM...
MOM, I...
I WANT TO BE A PILOT!!
IT'S BEEN FIVE YEARS SINCE THEN.
SOMEHOW, I MADE IT HERE.

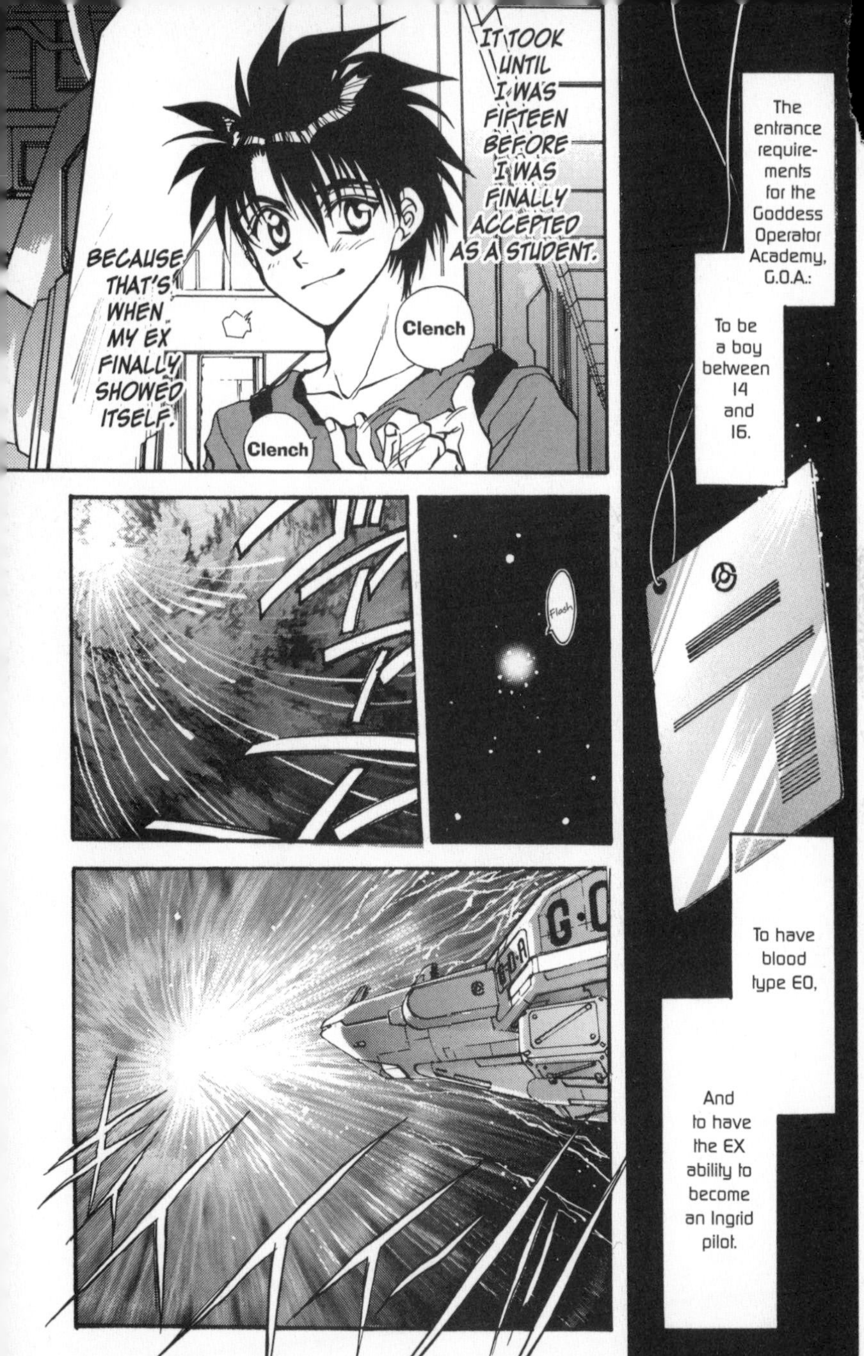
The entrance require-ments for the Goddess Operator Academy, G.O.A.:
To be a boy between 14 and 16.
To have blood type EO,
And to have the EX ability to become an Ingrid pilot.
IT TOOK UNTIL I WAS FIFTEEN BEFORE I WAS FINALLY ACCEPTED AS A STUDENT.
BECAUSE THAT'S WHEN MY EX FINALLY SHOWED ITSELF.
Clench
Clench
Flash
G·O·A
G·O

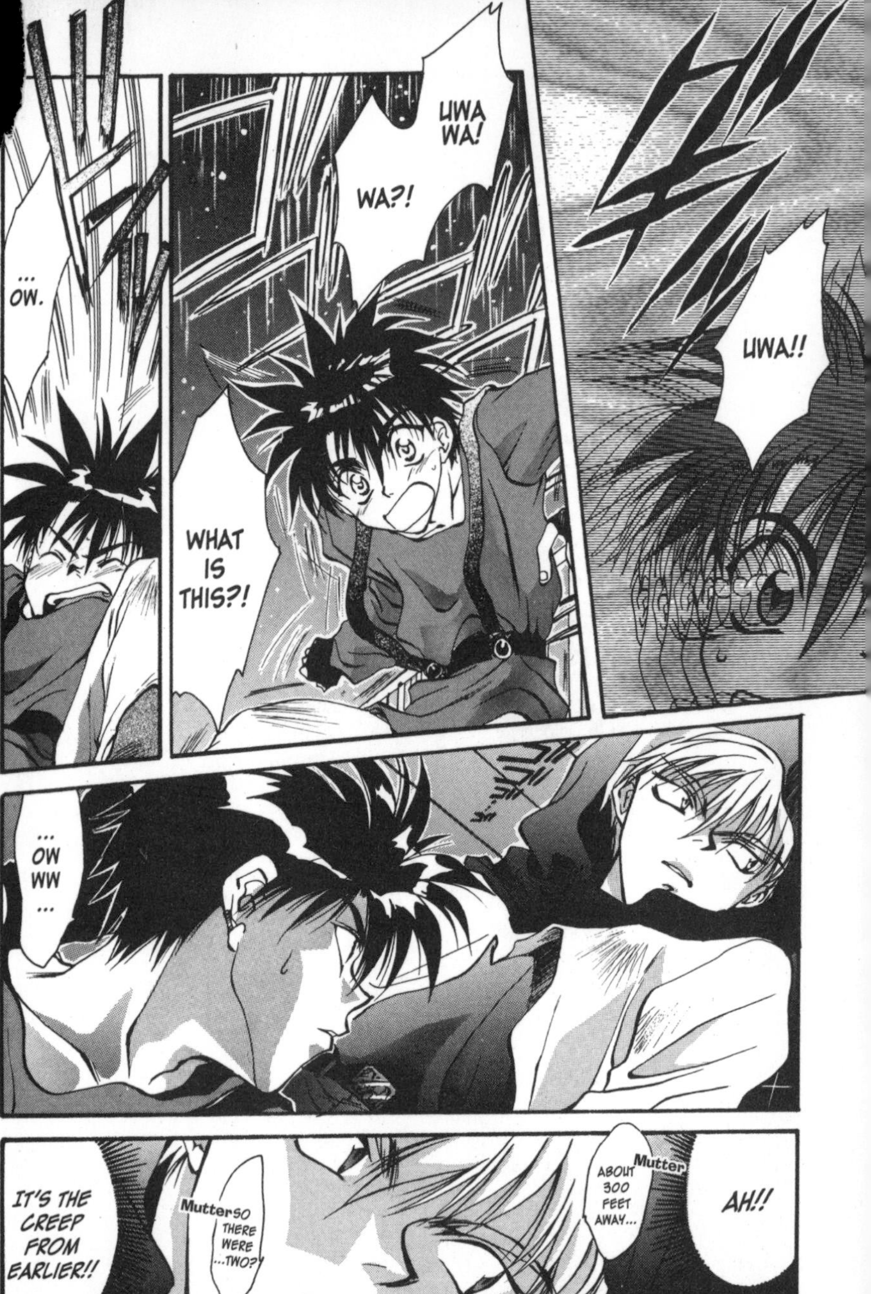
UWA!!
UWA WA!
WA?!
WHAT IS THIS?!
... OW.
... OW WW ...
AH!!
Mutter
ABOUT 300 FEET AWAY...
Mutter
SO THERE WERE ...TWO?
IT'S THE CREEP FROM EARLIER!!

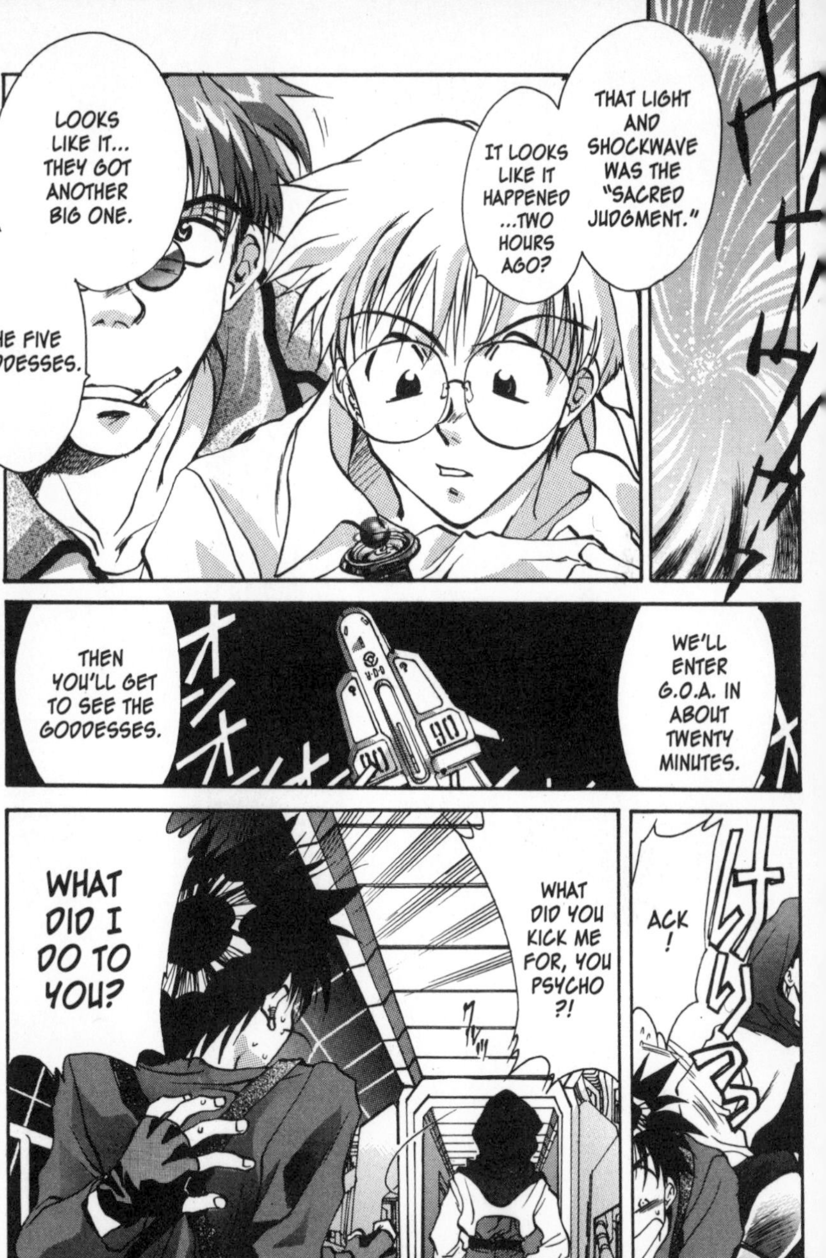
THAT LIGHT AND SHOCKWAVE WAS THE "SACRED JUDGMENT."
IT LOOKS LIKE IT HAPPENED ...TWO HOURS AGO?
LOOKS LIKE IT... THEY GOT ANOTHER BIG ONE.
THE FIVE GODDESSES.
WE'LL ENTER G.O.A. IN ABOUT TWENTY MINUTES.
THEN YOU'LL GET TO SEE THE GODDESSES.
ACK!
WHAT DID YOU KICK ME FOR, YOU PSYCHO?!
WHAT DID I DO TO YOU?

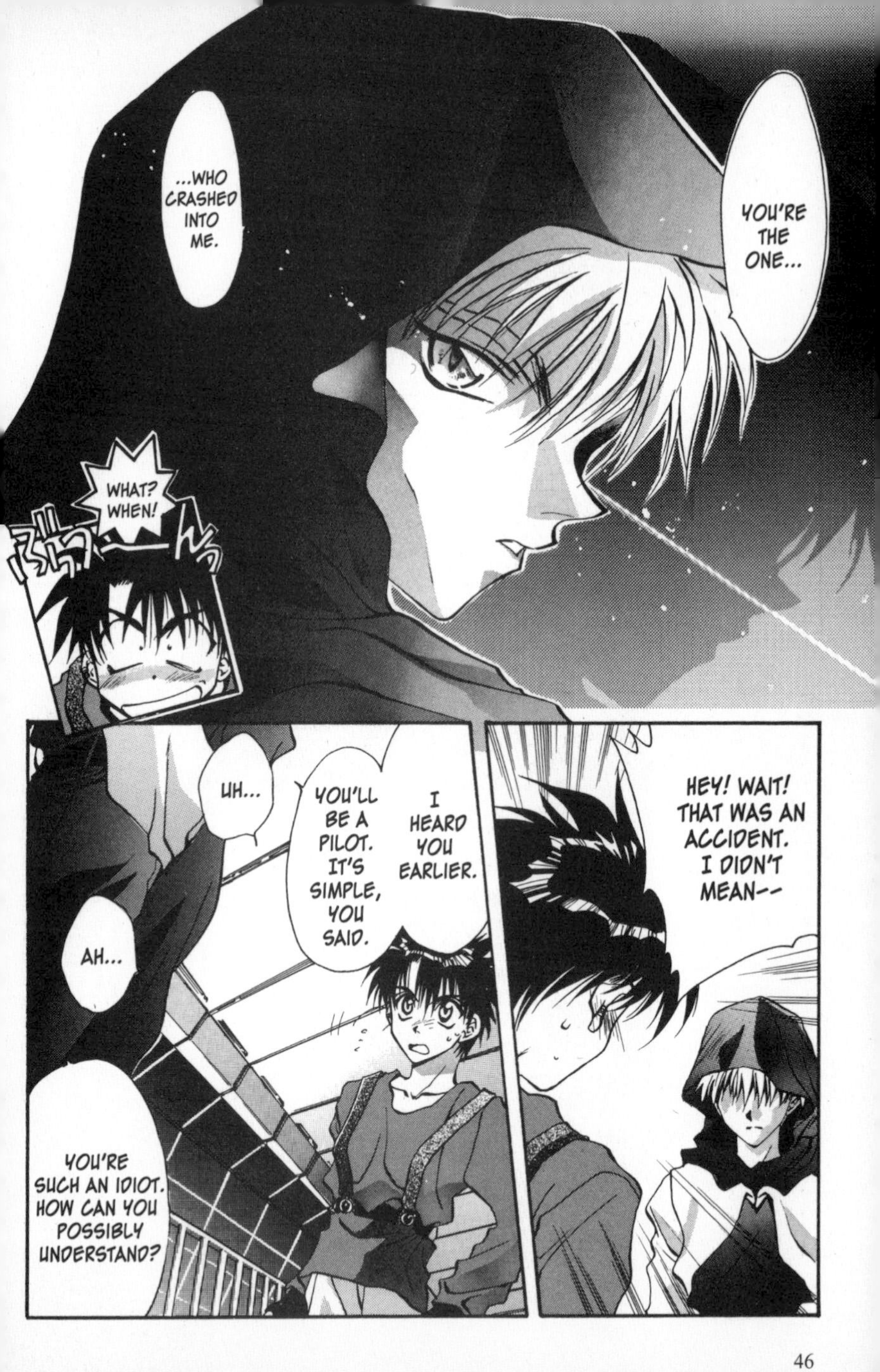
YOU'RE THE ONE...
...WHO CRASHED INTO ME.
WHAT? WHEN!
HEY! WAIT! THAT WAS AN ACCIDENT. I DIDN'T MEAN--
I HEARD YOU EARLIER.
YOU'LL BE A PILOT. IT'S SIMPLE, YOU SAID.
UH...
AH...
YOU'RE SUCH AN IDIOT. HOW CAN YOU POSSIBLY UNDERSTAND?

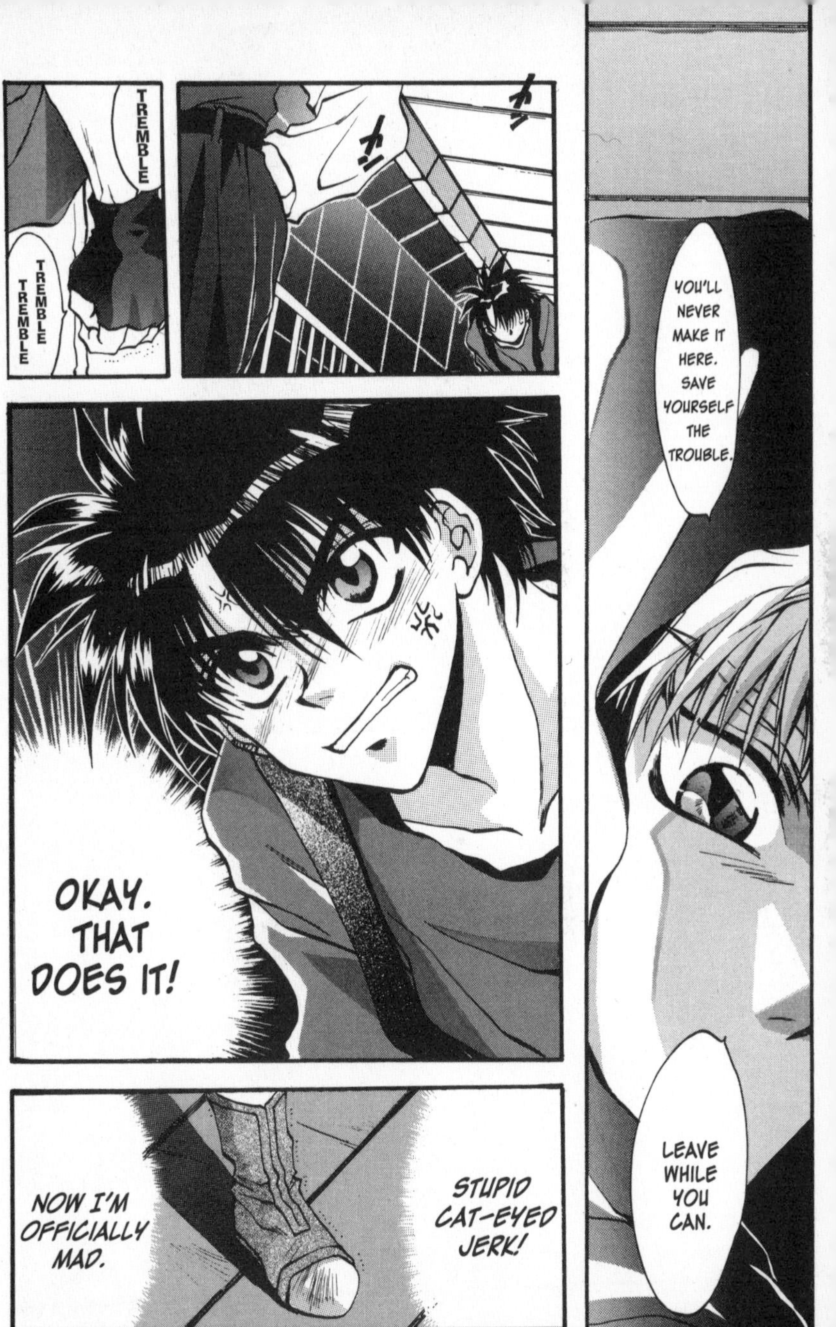

YOU'LL NEVER MAKE IT HERE. SAVE YOURSELF THE TROUBLE.
LEAVE WHILE YOU CAN.
カッ
カッ
TREMBLE
TREMBLE TREMBLE
OKAY. THAT DOES IT!
STUPID CAT-EYED JERK!
NOW I'M OFFICIALLY MAD.

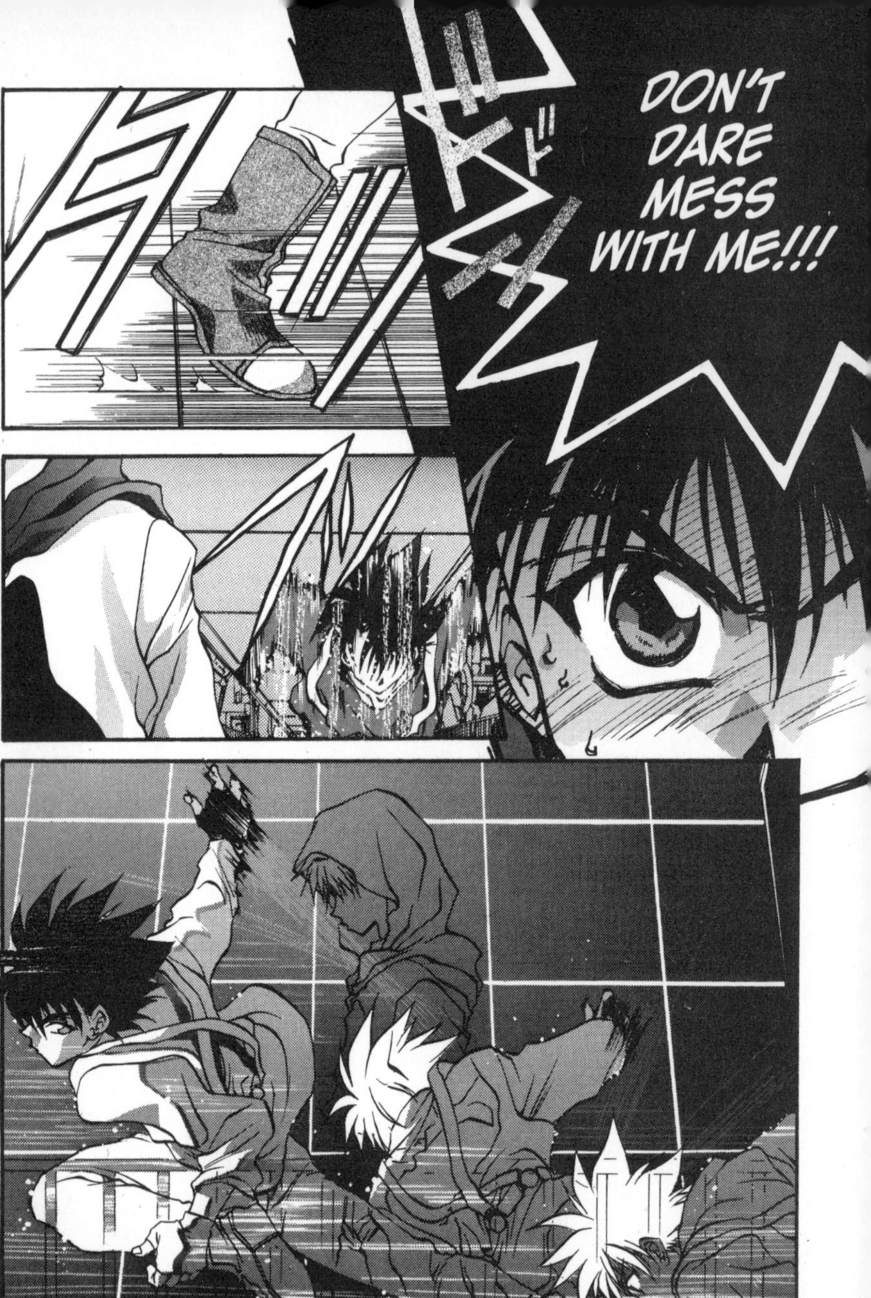

DON'T DARE MESS WITH ME!!!

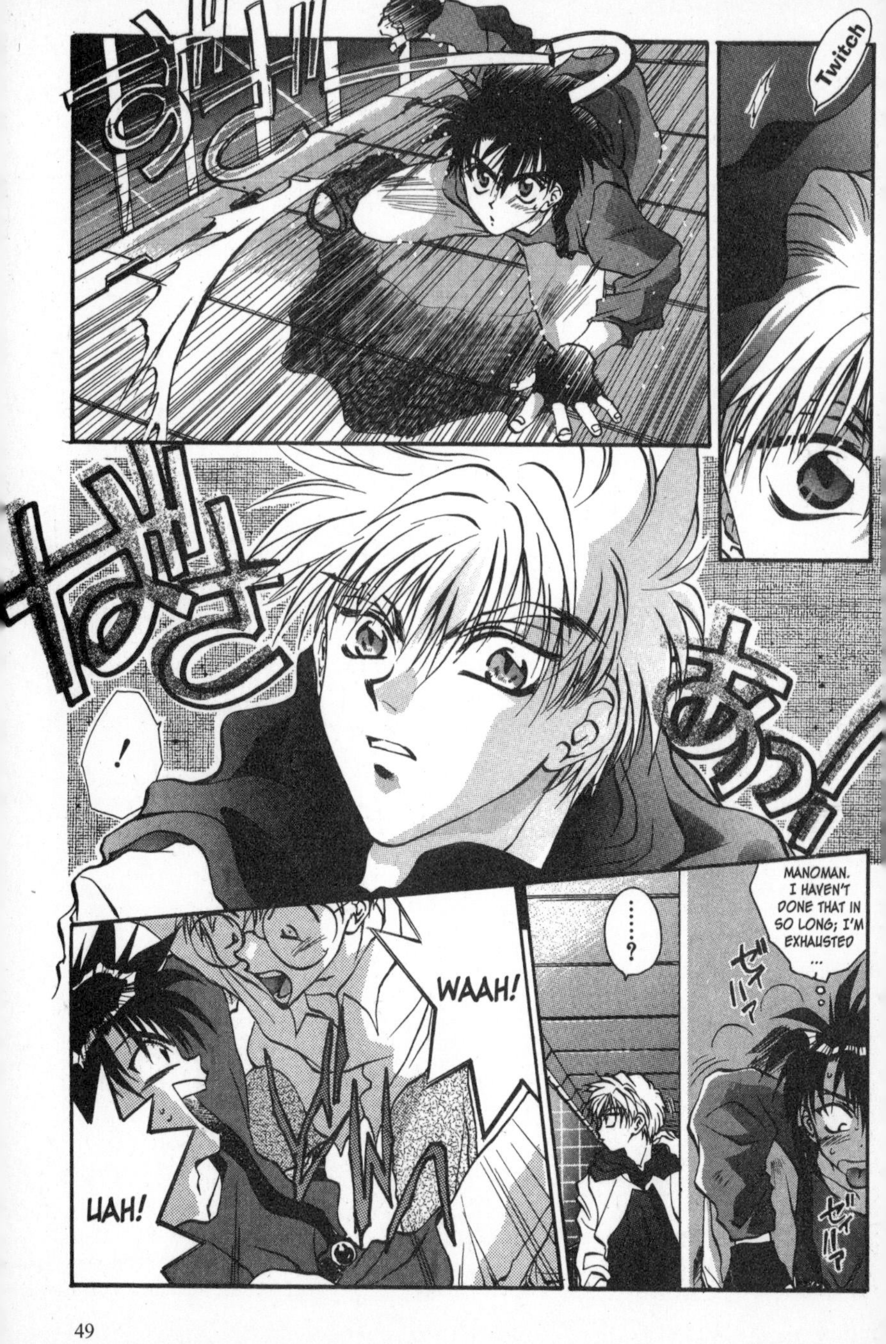
Twitch
!
MANOMAN. I HAVEN'T DONE THAT IN SO LONG; I'M EXHAUSTED ...
.....?
WAAH!
UAH!

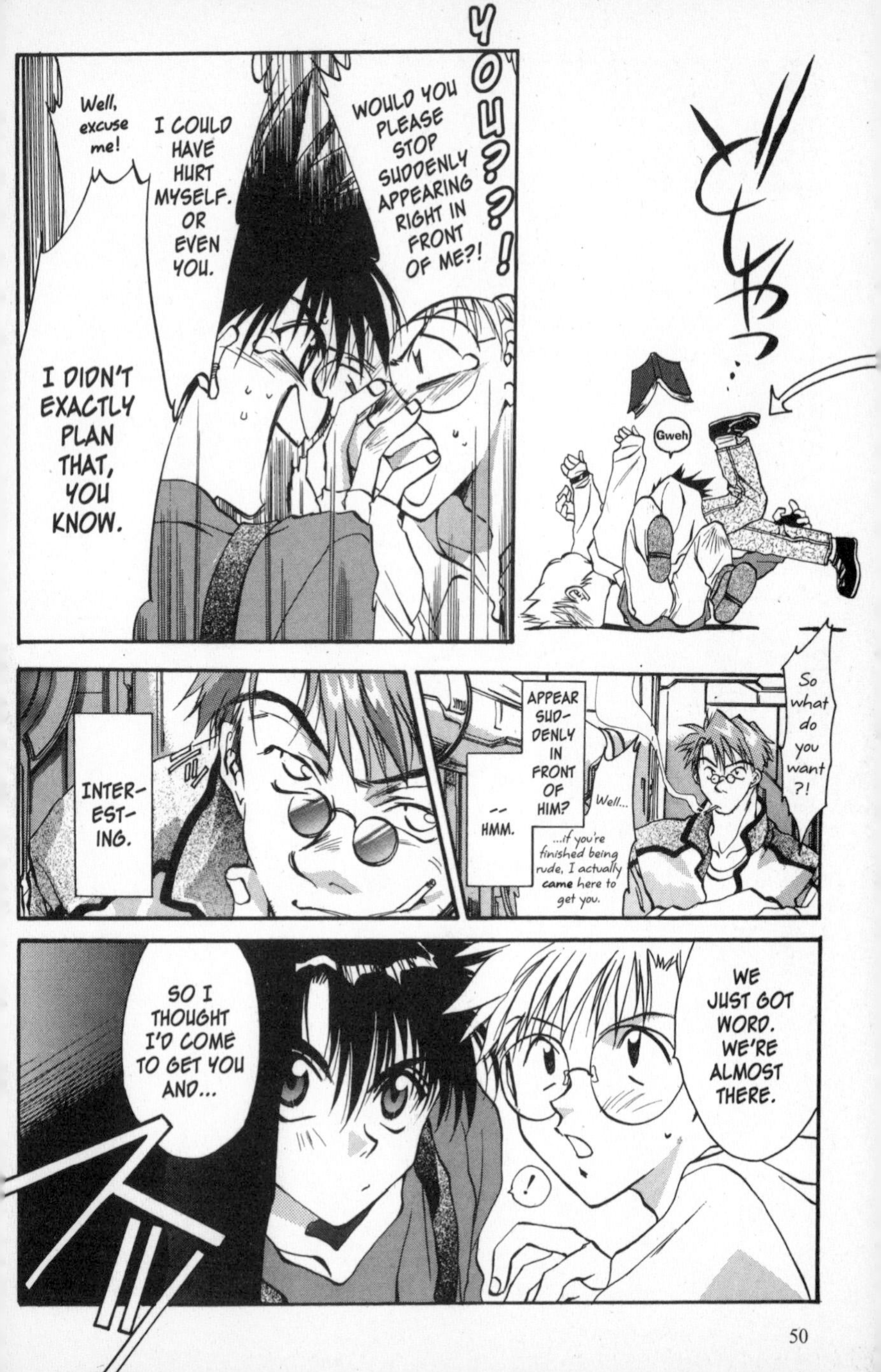
どしゃっ!!
Gweh
YOU?!
WOULD YOU PLEASE STOP SUDDENLY APPEARING RIGHT IN FRONT OF ME?!
I COULD HAVE HURT MYSELF. OR EVEN YOU.
Well, excuse me!
I DIDN'T EXACTLY PLAN THAT, YOU KNOW.
So what do you want?!
APPEAR SUDDENLY IN FRONT OF HIM?
Well...
...if you're finished being rude, I actually came here to get you.
-- HMM.
INTERESTING.
WE JUST GOT WORD. WE'RE ALMOST THERE.
!
SO I THOUGHT I'D COME TO GET YOU AND...

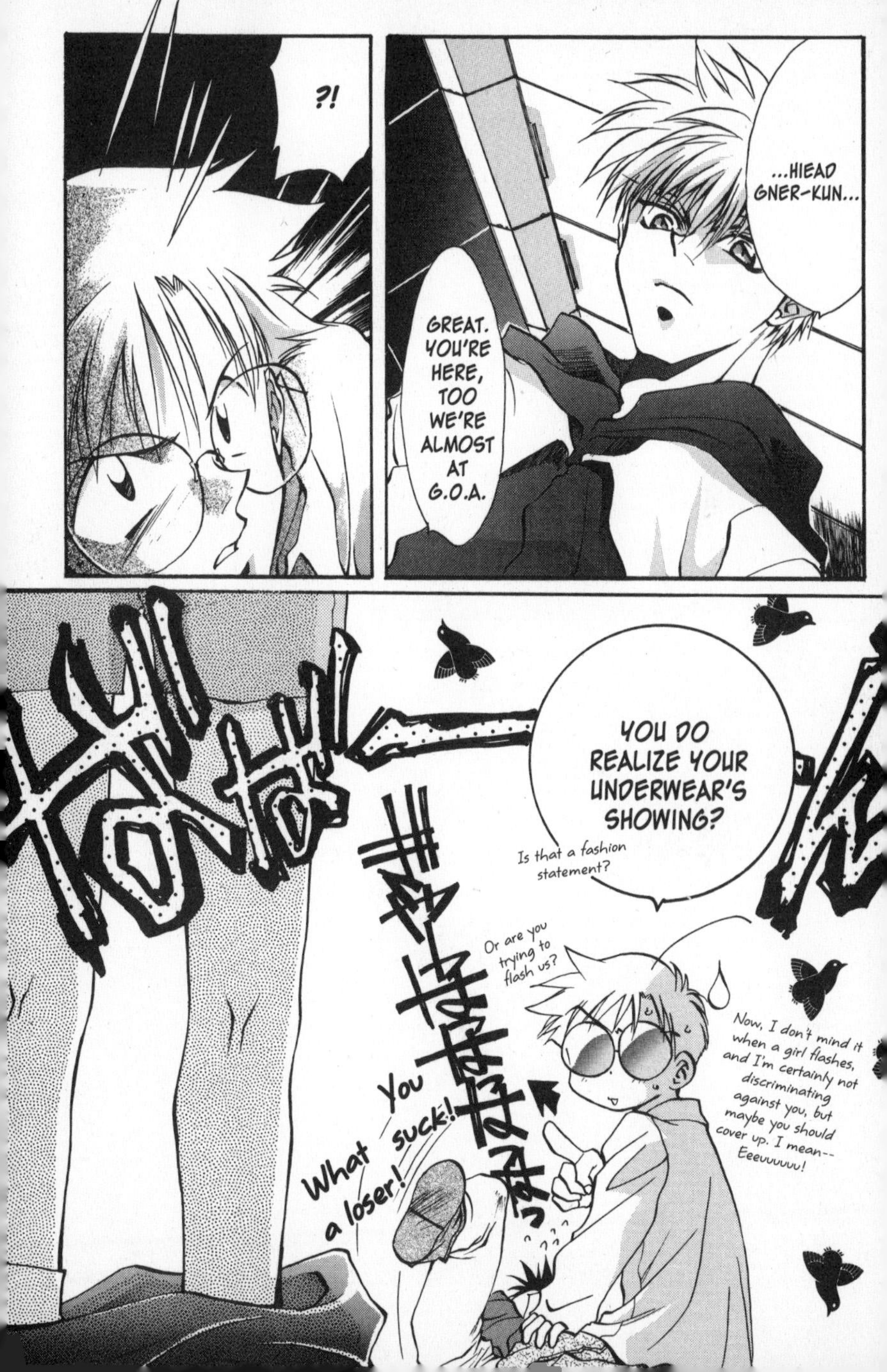
...HIEAD GNER-KUN...
GREAT. YOU'RE HERE, TOO WE'RE ALMOST AT G.O.A.
?!
YOU DO REALIZE YOUR UNDERWEAR'S SHOWING?
Is that a fashion statement?
Or are you trying to flash us?
Now, I don't mind it when a girl flashes, and I'm certainly not discriminating against you, but maybe you should cover up. I mean-- Eeeuuuuuu!
You suck!
What a loser!

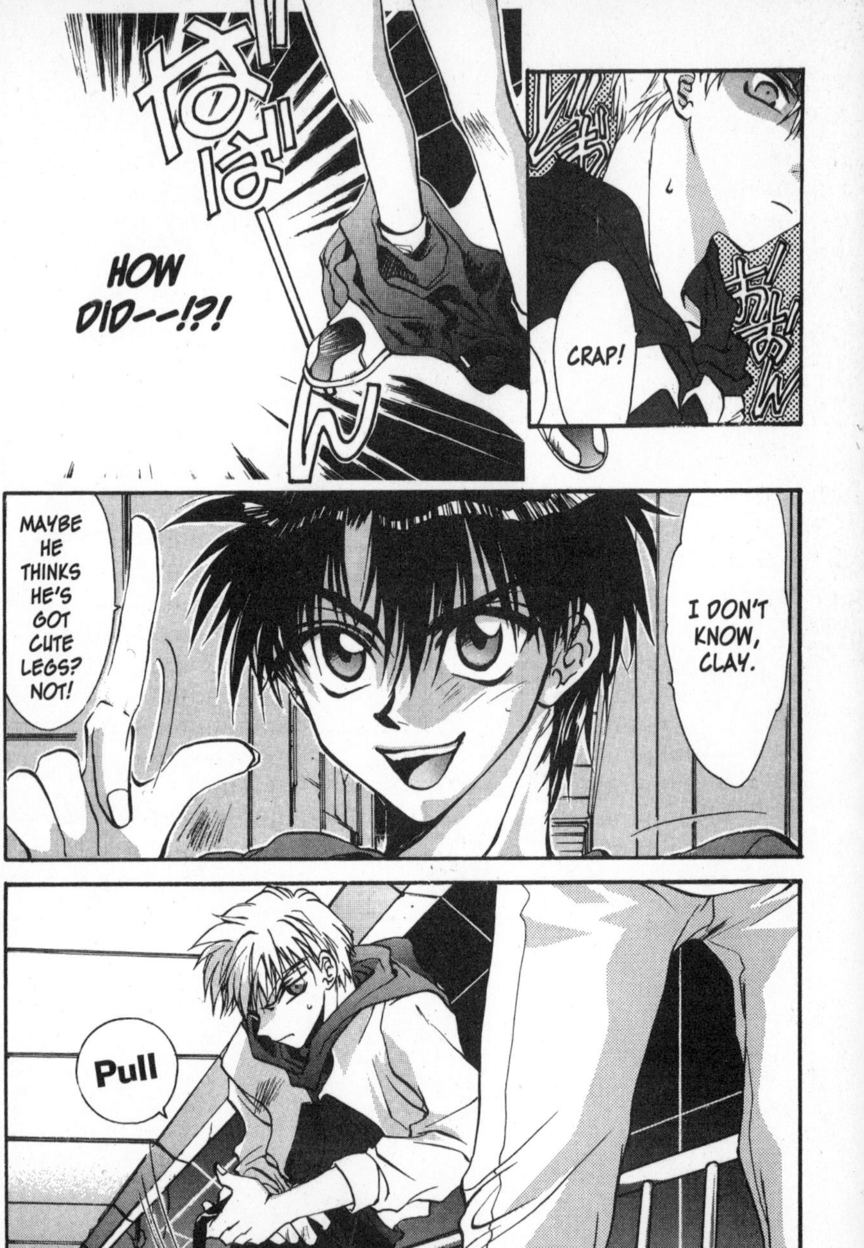
CRAP!
HOW DID--!?!
I DON'T KNOW, CLAY.
MAYBE HE THINKS HE'S GOT CUTE LEGS? NOT!
Pull

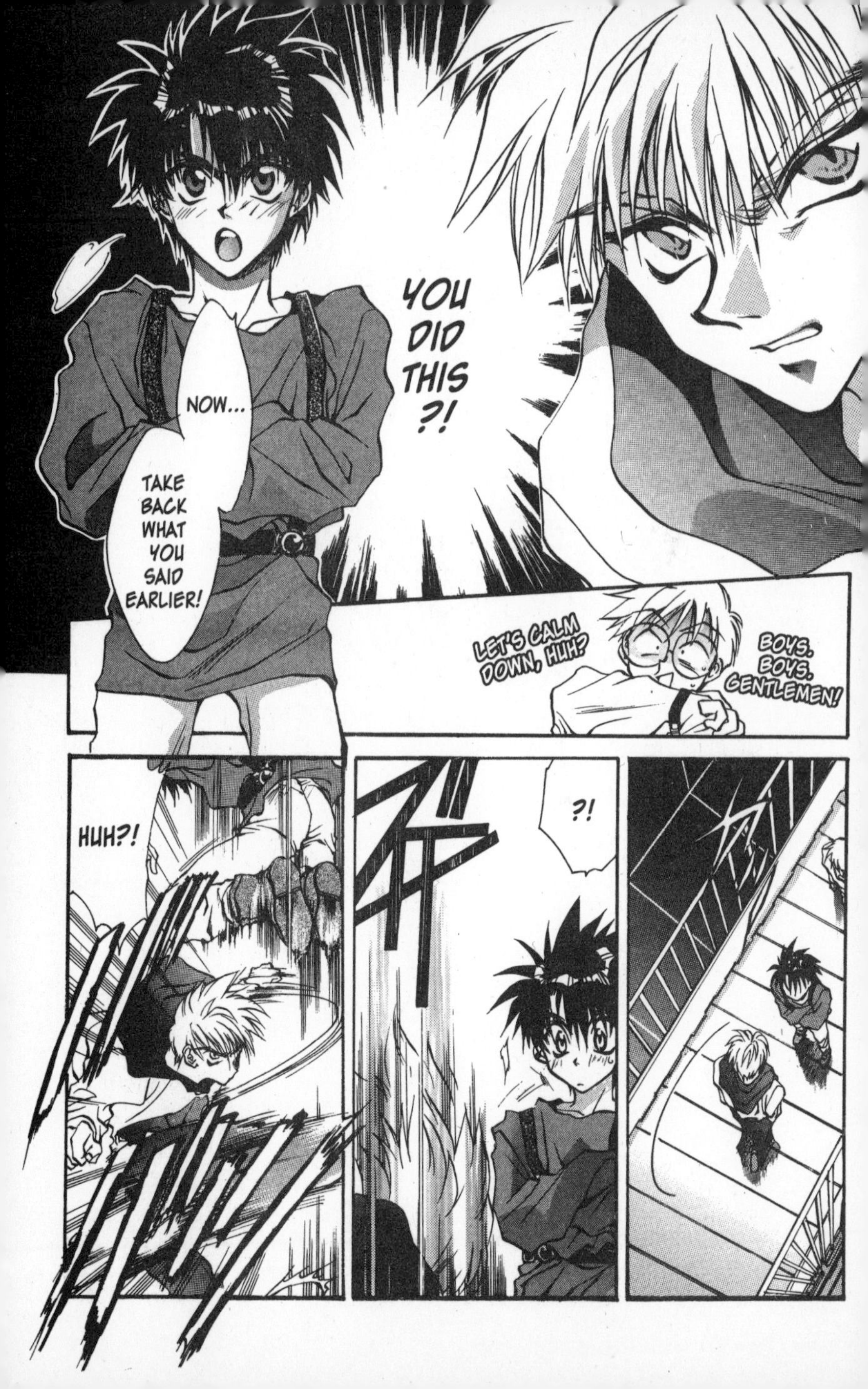
YOU DID THIS ?!
NOW...
TAKE BACK WHAT YOU SAID EARLIER!
BOYS. BOYS. GENTLEMEN!
LET'S CALM DOWN, HUH?
?!
HUH?!

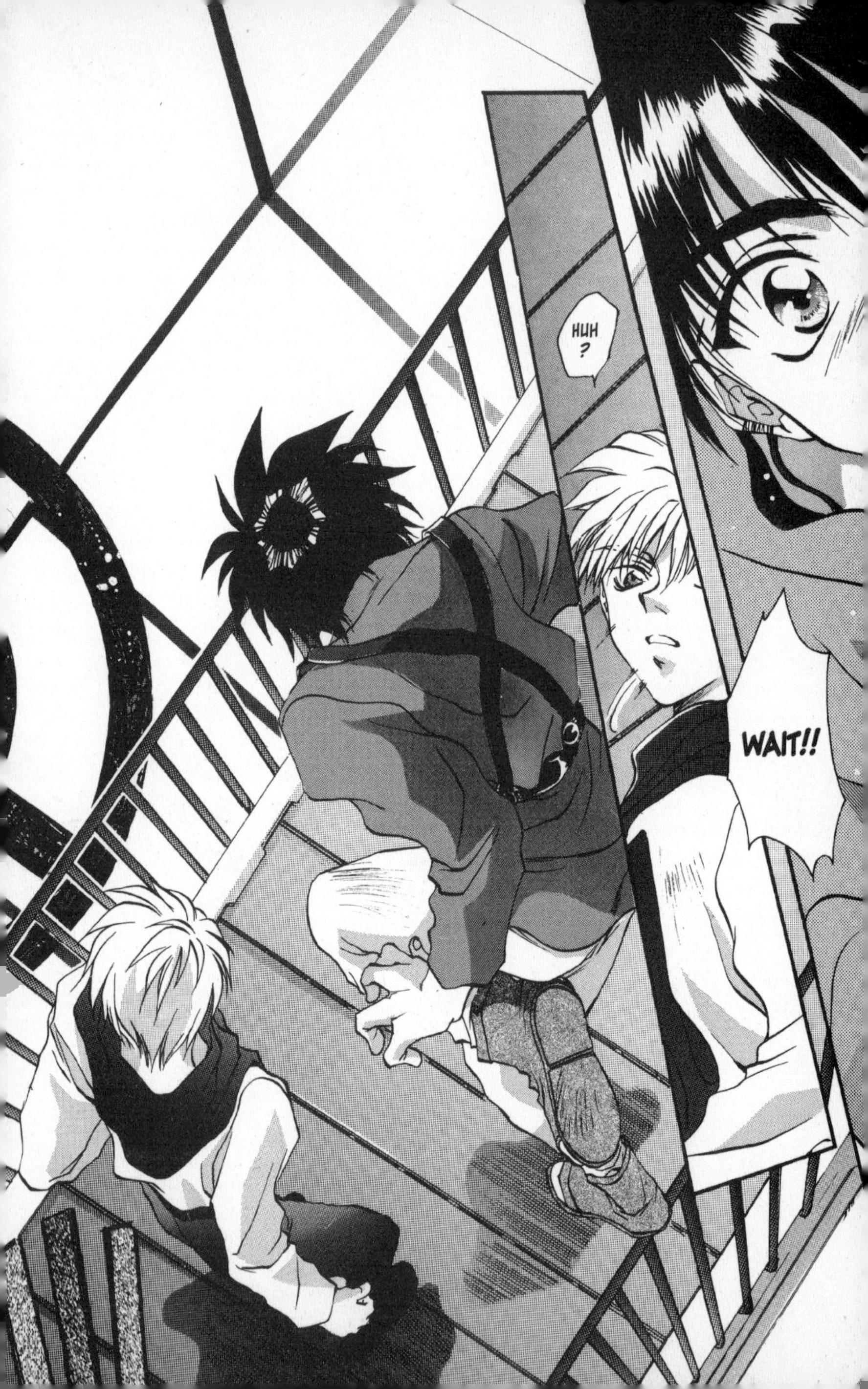
WAIT!!
HUH ?

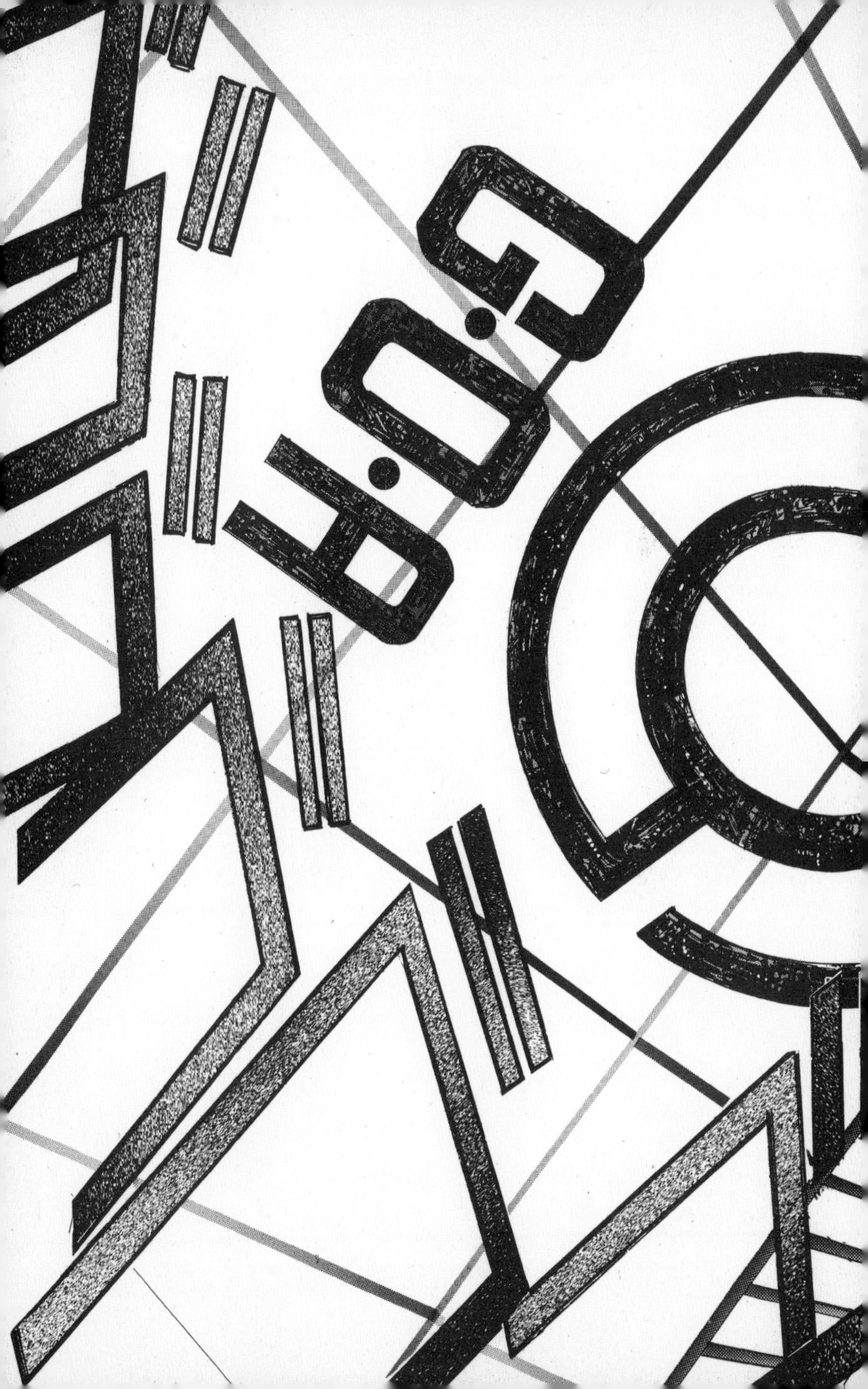

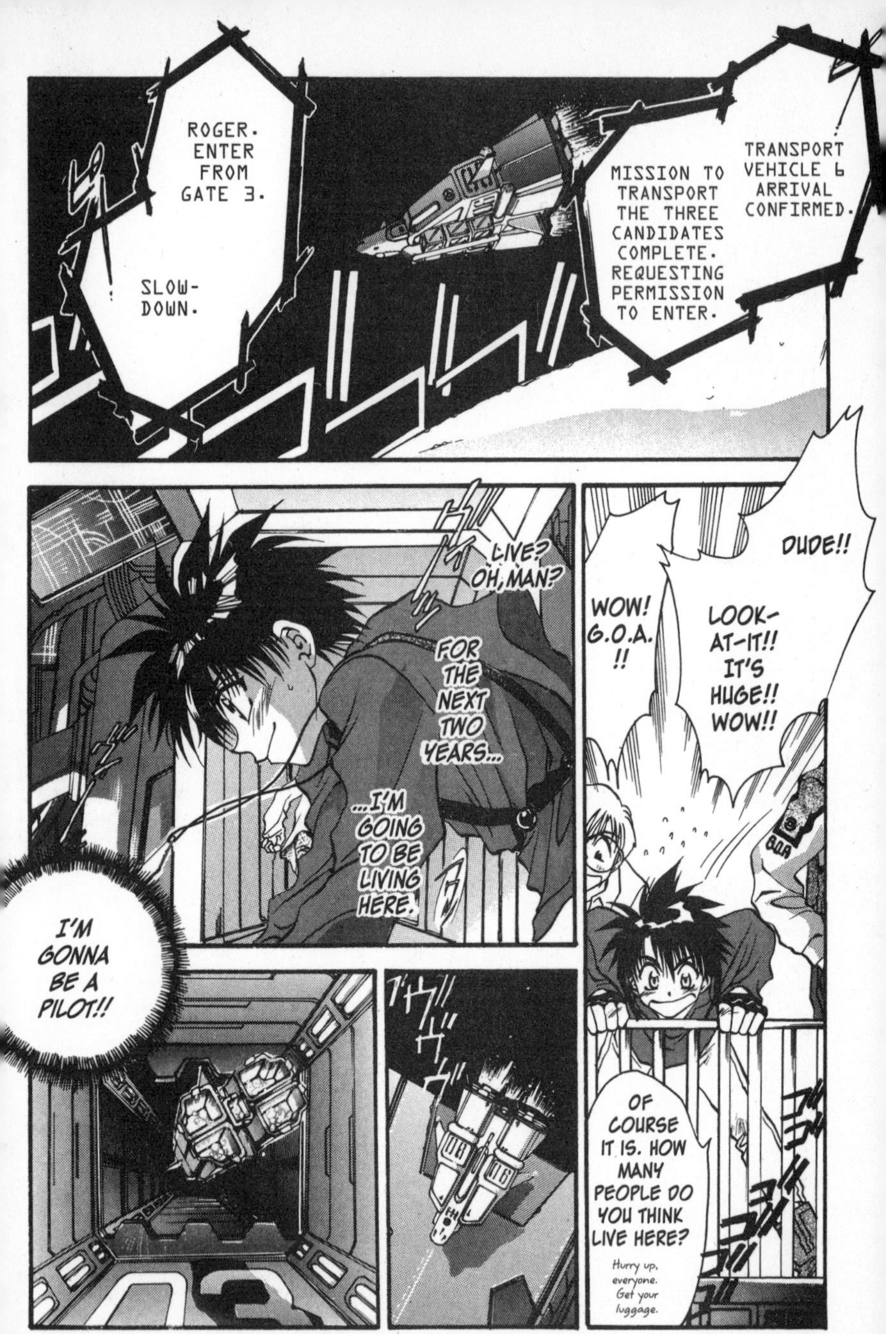
TRANSPORT VEHICLE 6 ARRIVAL CONFIRMED.
MISSION TO TRANSPORT THE THREE CANDIDATES COMPLETE. REQUESTING PERMISSION TO ENTER.
ROGER. ENTER FROM GATE 3.
SLOW-DOWN.
DUDE!!
LOOK-AT-IT!! IT'S HUGE!! WOW!!
WOW! G.O.A. !!
OF COURSE IT IS. HOW MANY PEOPLE DO YOU THINK LIVE HERE?
Hurry up, everyone. Get your luggage.
LIVE? OH, MAN?
FOR THE NEXT TWO YEARS...
...I'M GOING TO BE LIVING HERE.
I'M GONNA BE A PILOT!!

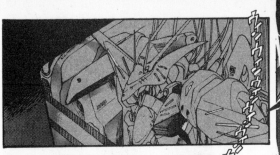

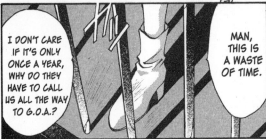

"G.O.A."!! THIS IS AWESOME!
MAN, THIS IS A WASTE OF TIME.
I DON'T CARE IF IT'S ONLY ONCE A YEAR, WHY DO THEY HAVE TO CALL US ALL THE WAY TO G.O.A.?
TELLING YOU, DUDE, THEY LIKE TO PROVE THEY'RE IN CHARGE.
YEAH. GUESS SO. STILL...
......

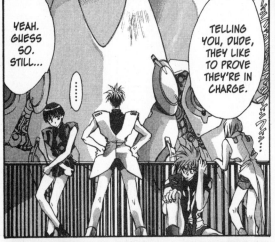

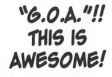

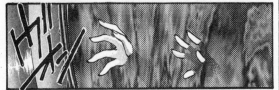

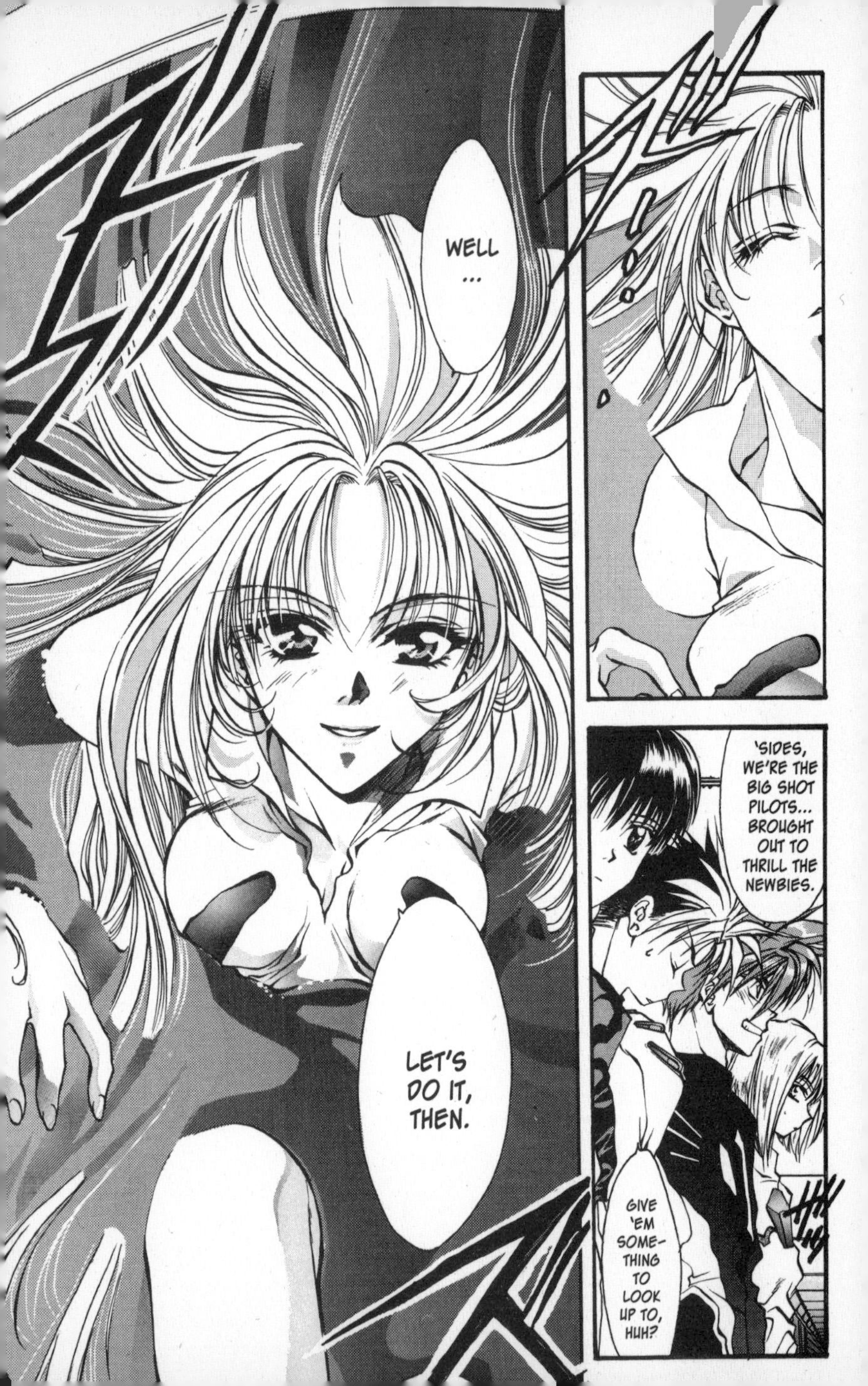
'SIDES, WE'RE THE BIG SHOT PILOTS... BROUGHT OUT TO THRILL THE NEWBIES.
GIVE 'EM SOME-THING TO LOOK UP TO, HUH?
WELL ...
LET'S DO IT, THEN.

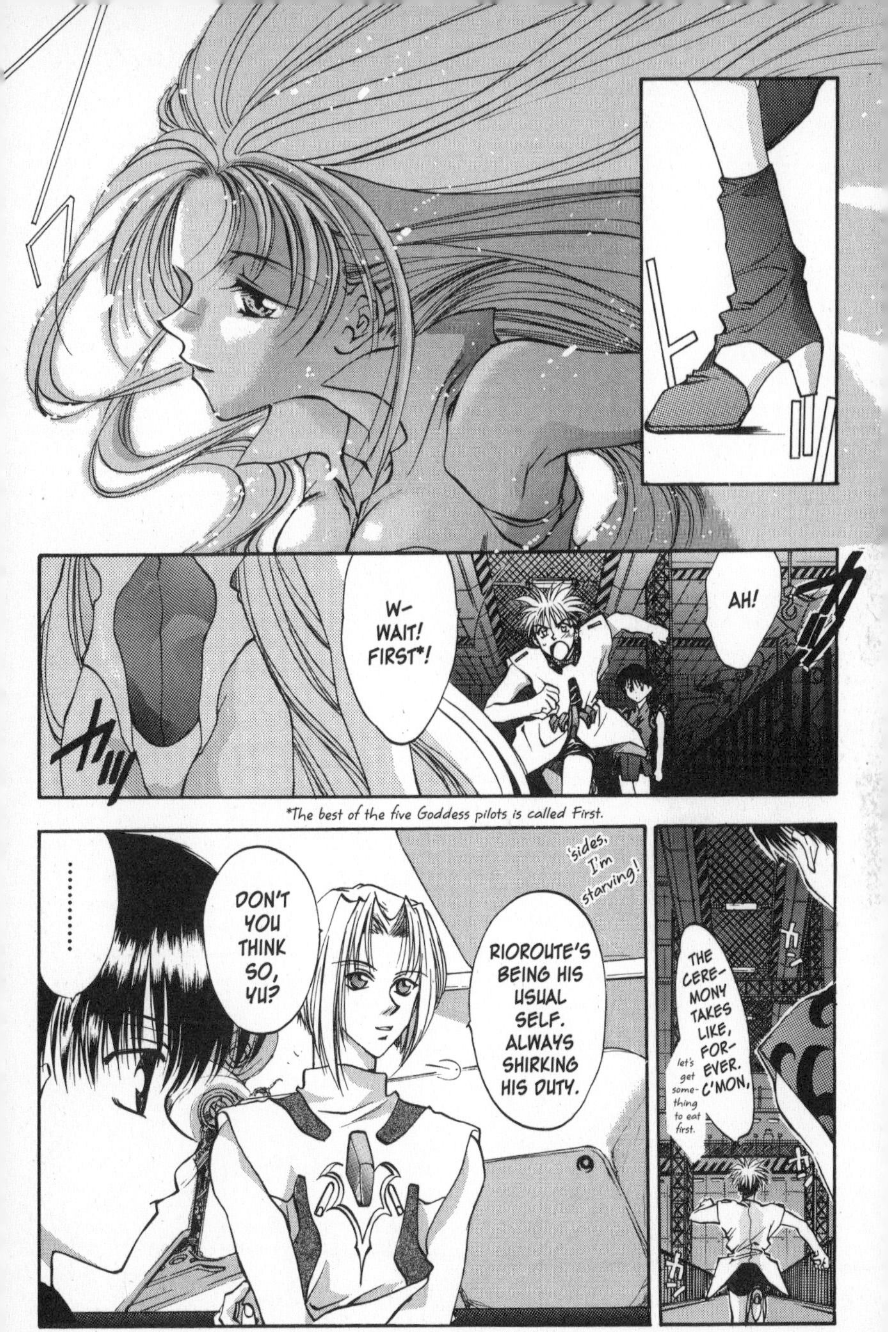
AH!
W-WAIT! FIRST*!
THE CERE-MONY TAKES LIKE, FOR-EVER. C'MON,
let's get some-thing to eat first.
'sides, I'm starving!
RIOROUTE'S BEING HIS USUAL SELF. ALWAYS SHIRKING HIS DUTY.
DON'T YOU THINK SO, YU?
……
*The best of the five Goddess pilots is called First.

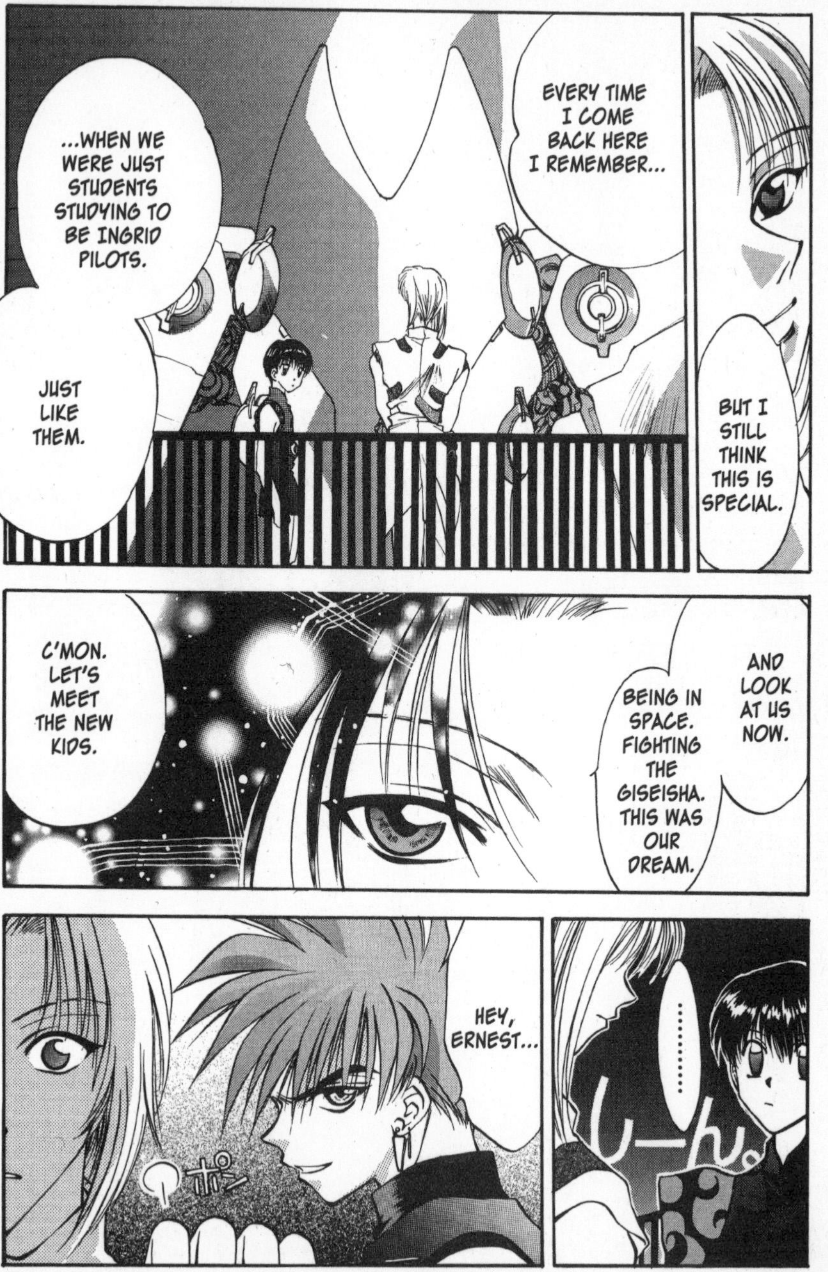
BUT I STILL THINK THIS IS SPECIAL.
EVERY TIME I COME BACK HERE I REMEMBER...
...WHEN WE WERE JUST STUDENTS STUDYING TO BE INGRID PILOTS.
JUST LIKE THEM.
AND LOOK AT US NOW.
BEING IN SPACE. FIGHTING THE GISEISHA. THIS WAS OUR DREAM.
C'MON. LET'S MEET THE NEW KIDS.
....
HEY, ERNEST...
ポン

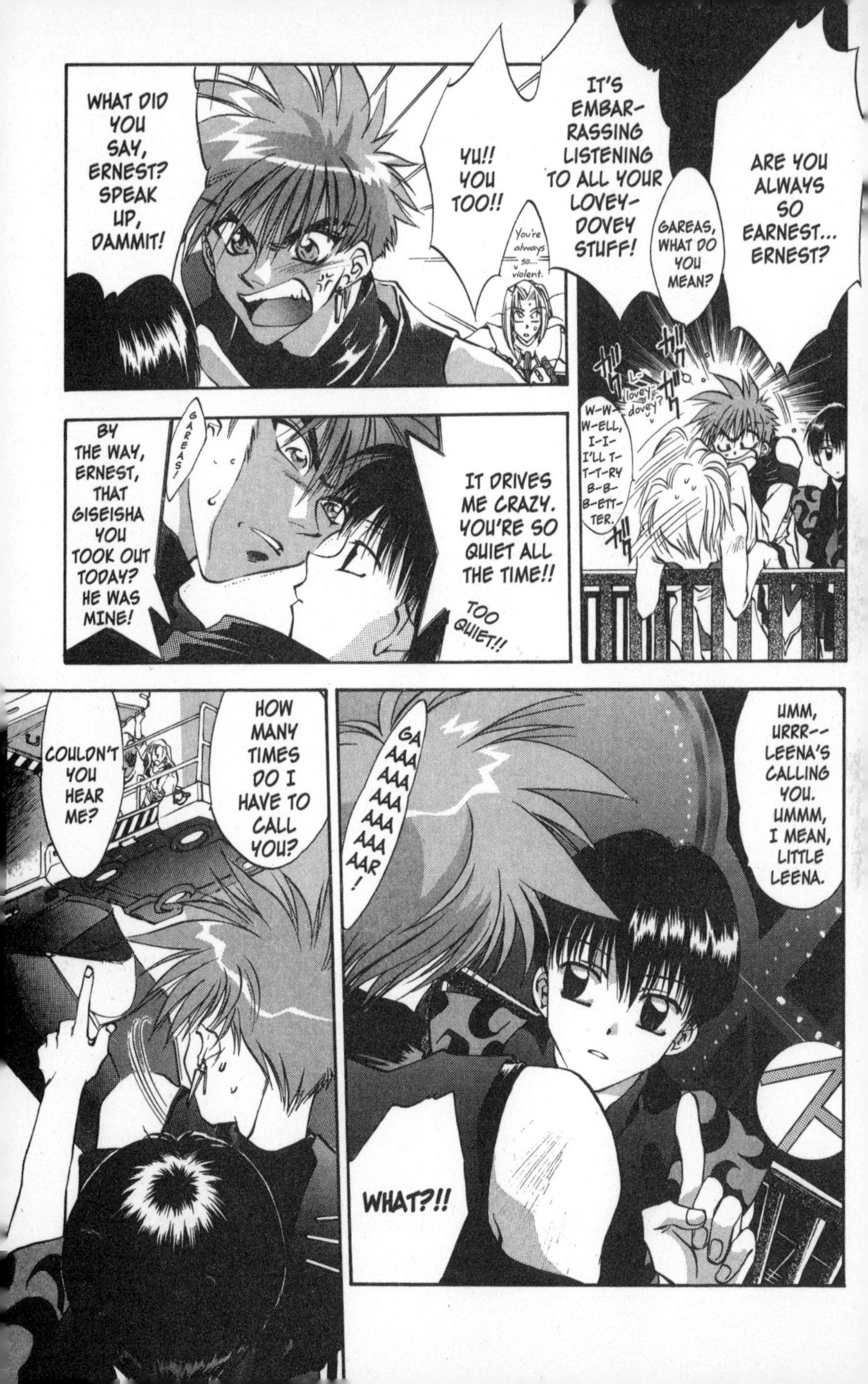
ARE YOU ALWAYS SO EARNEST... ERNEST?
GAREAS, WHAT DO YOU MEAN?
IT'S EMBARRASSING LISTENING TO ALL YOUR LOVEY-DOVEY STUFF!
lovey dovey?
W-W-W-ELL, I-I-I'LL T-T-T-RY B-B-B-ETTTER.
YU!! YOU TOO!!
You're always so... violent.
WHAT DID YOU SAY, ERNEST? SPEAK UP, DAMMIT!
IT DRIVES ME CRAZY. YOU'RE SO QUIET ALL THE TIME!!
TOO QUIET!!
GAREAS!
BY THE WAY, ERNEST, THAT GISEISHA YOU TOOK OUT TODAY? HE WAS MINE!
UMM, URRR-- LEENA'S CALLING YOU. UMMM, I MEAN, LITTLE LEENA.
GAAAAAAAAAAAAAAAAAAR!
WHAT?!!
HOW MANY TIMES DO I HAVE TO CALL YOU?
COULDN'T YOU HEAR ME?

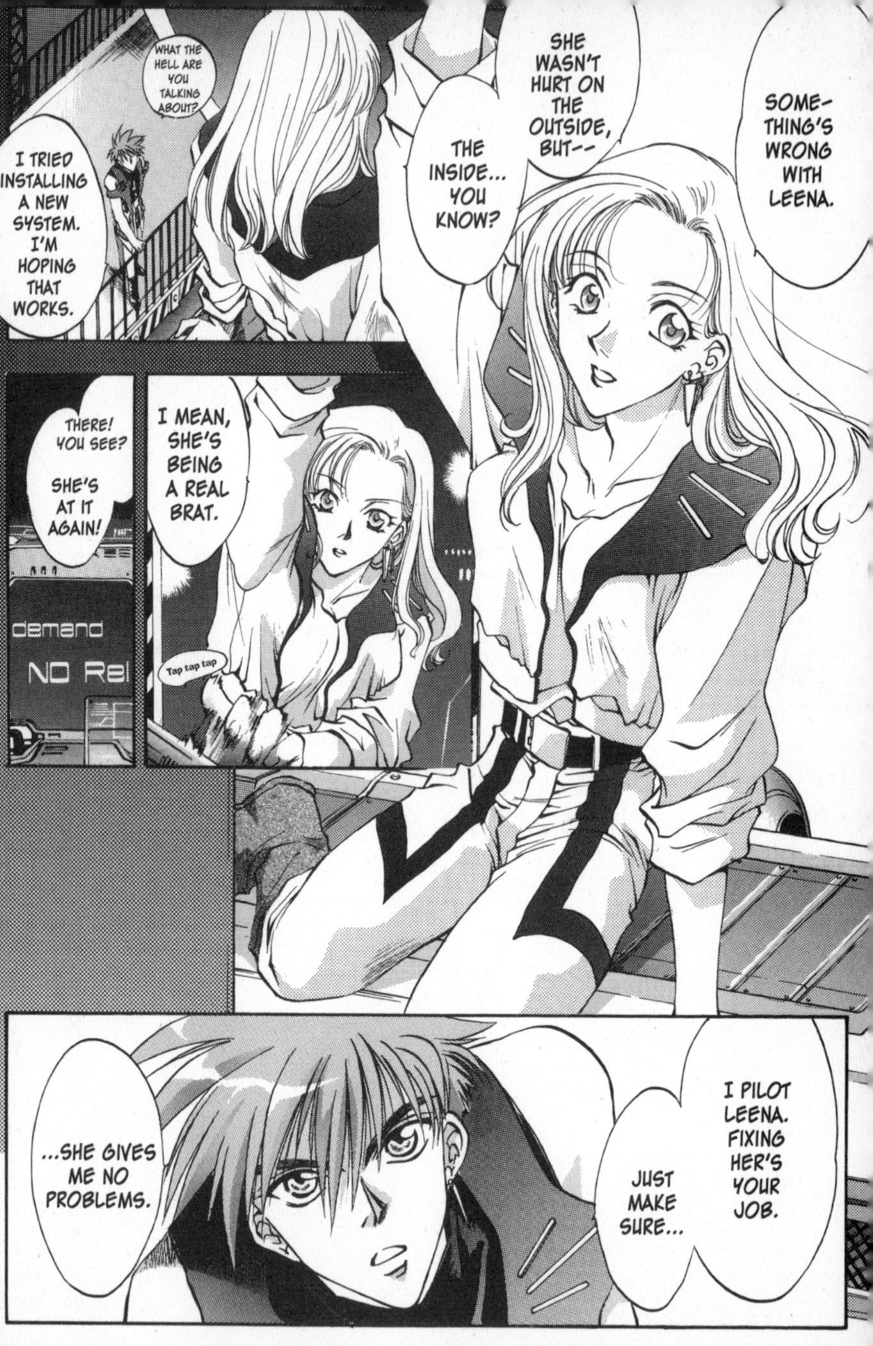
SOMETHING'S WRONG WITH LEENA.
SHE WASN'T HURT ON THE OUTSIDE, BUT--
THE INSIDE... YOU KNOW?
WHAT THE HELL ARE YOU TALKING ABOUT?
I TRIED INSTALLING A NEW SYSTEM. I'M HOPING THAT WORKS.
I MEAN, SHE'S BEING A REAL BRAT.
Tap tap tap
THERE! YOU SEE?
SHE'S AT IT AGAIN!
demand
NO Rel
I PILOT LEENA. FIXING HER'S YOUR JOB.
JUST MAKE SURE...
...SHE GIVES ME NO PROBLEMS.

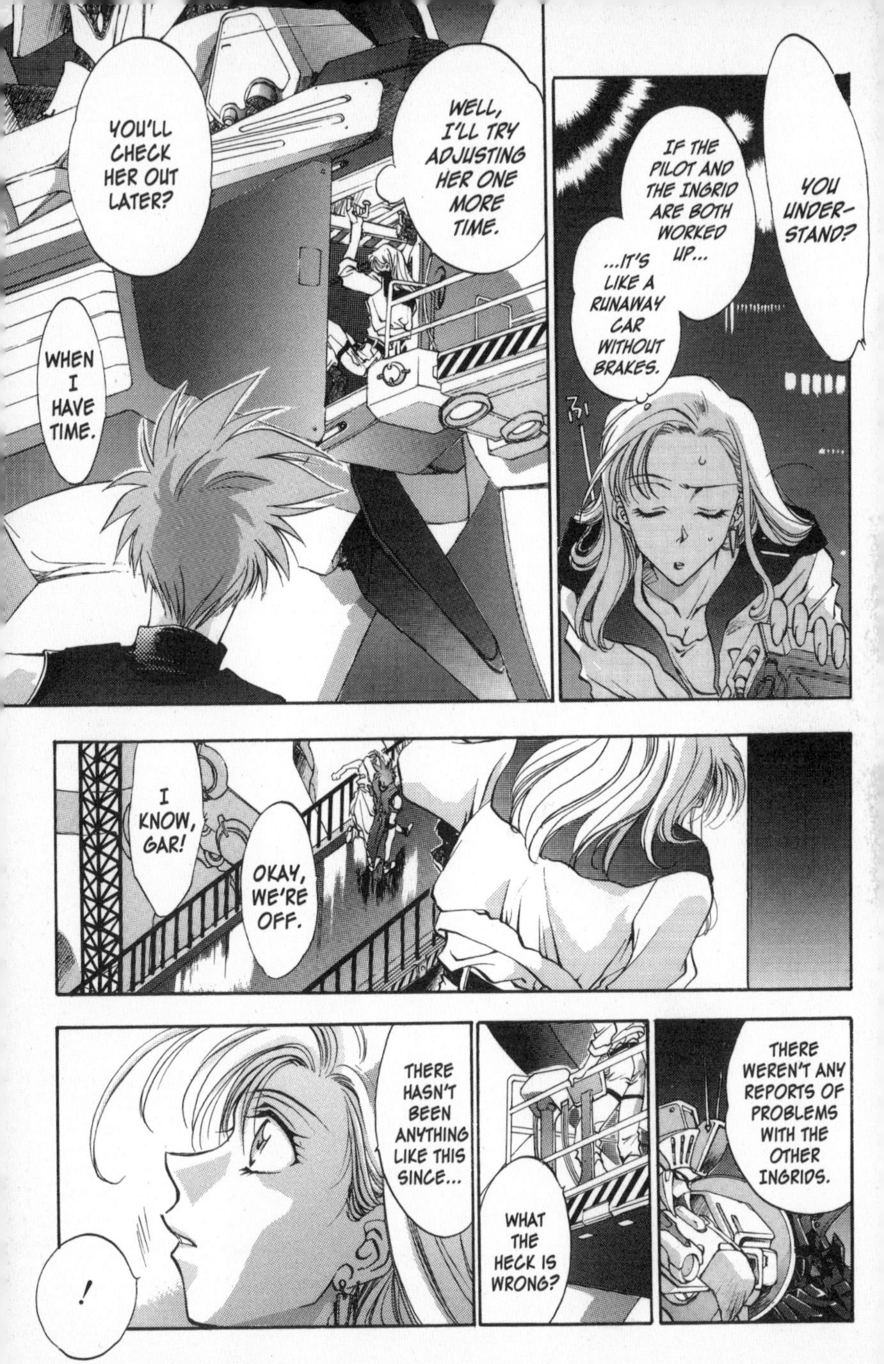
YOU UNDERSTAND?
IF THE PILOT AND THE INGRID ARE BOTH WORKED UP...
...IT'S LIKE A RUNAWAY CAR WITHOUT BRAKES.
WELL, I'LL TRY ADJUSTING HER ONE MORE TIME.
YOU'LL CHECK HER OUT LATER?
WHEN I HAVE TIME.
OKAY, WE'RE OFF.
I KNOW, GAR!
THERE WEREN'T ANY REPORTS OF PROBLEMS WITH THE OTHER INGRIDS.
WHAT THE HECK IS WRONG?
THERE HASN'T BEEN ANYTHING LIKE THIS SINCE...
!

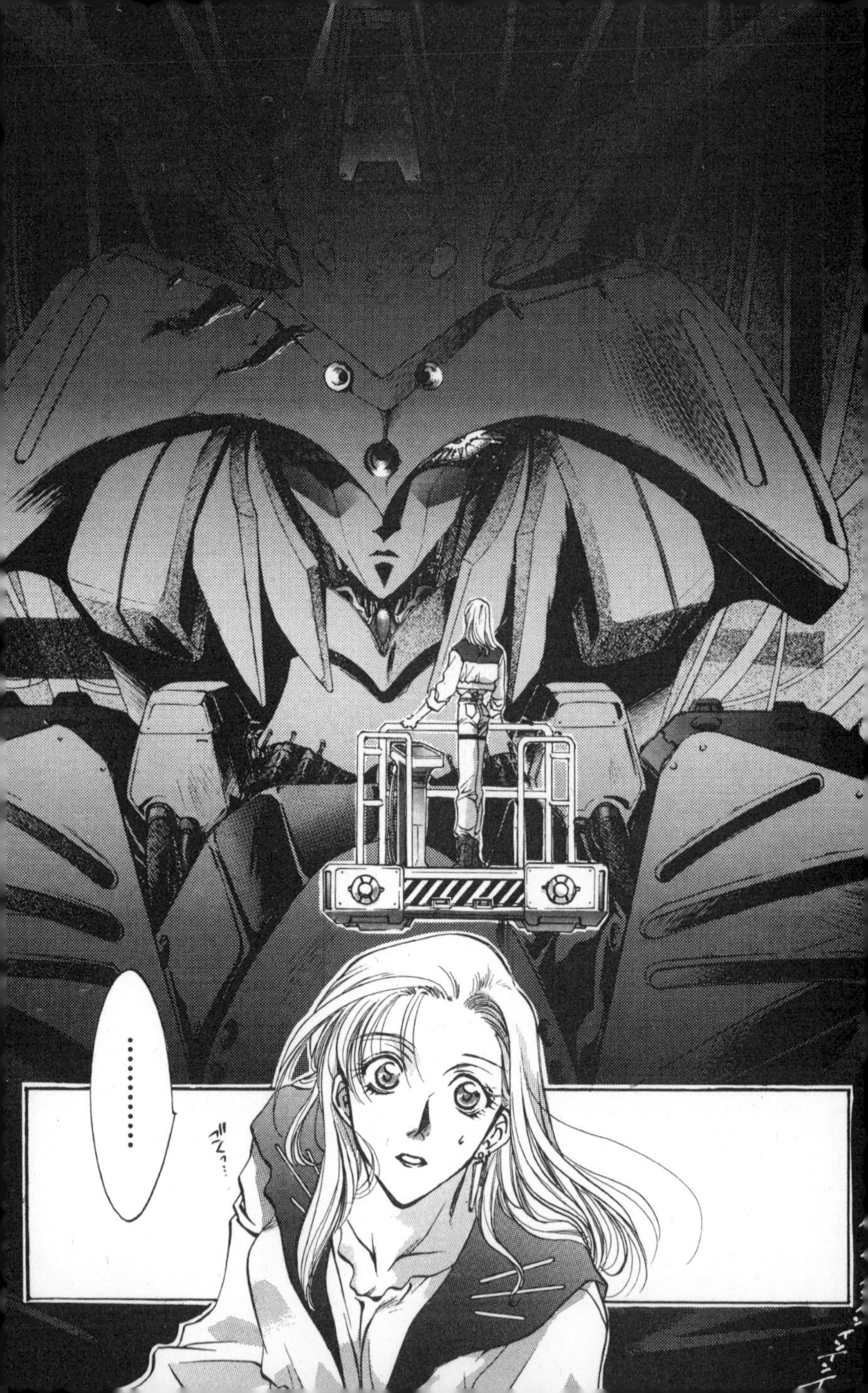
……………
ブルッ…

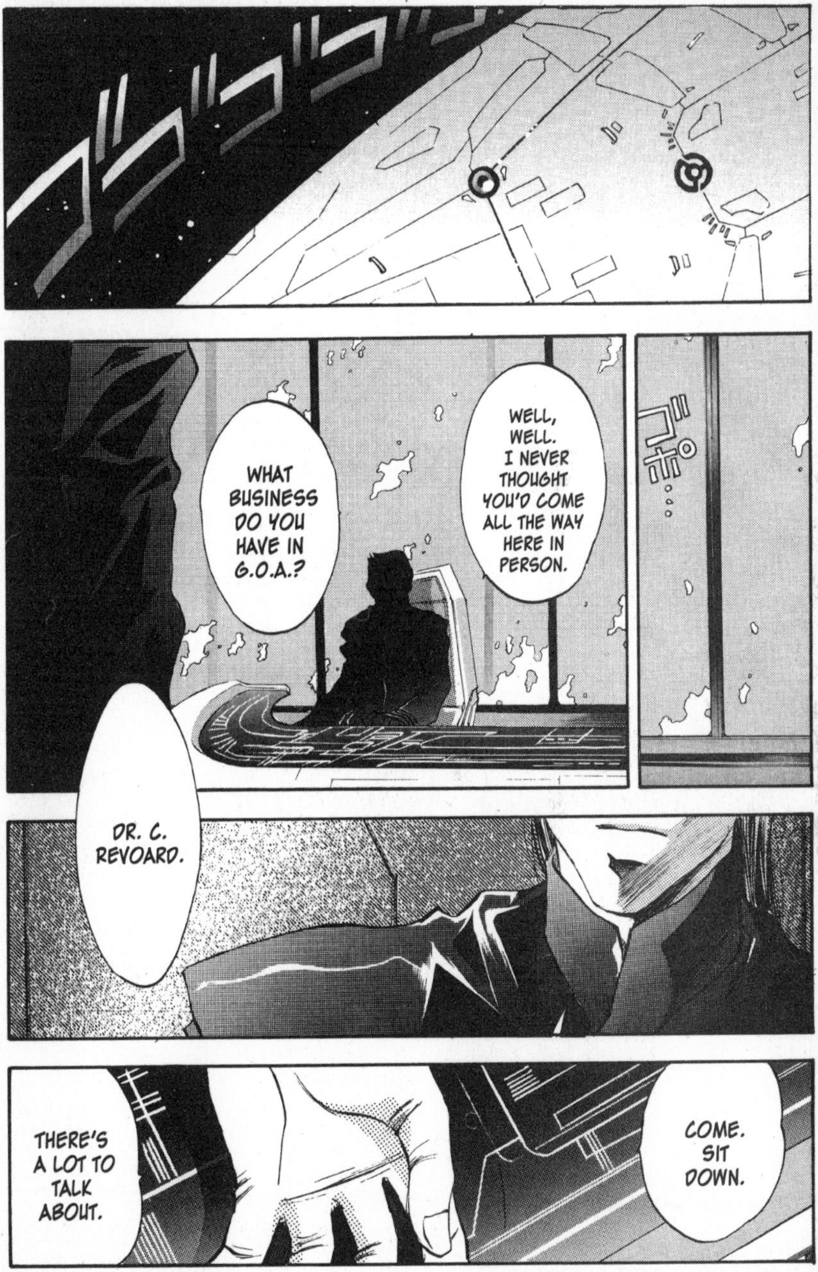
ゴポ
WELL, WELL. I NEVER THOUGHT YOU'D COME ALL THE WAY HERE IN PERSON.
WHAT BUSINESS DO YOU HAVE IN G.O.A.?
DR. C. REVOARD.
COME. SIT DOWN.
THERE'S A LOT TO TALK ABOUT.

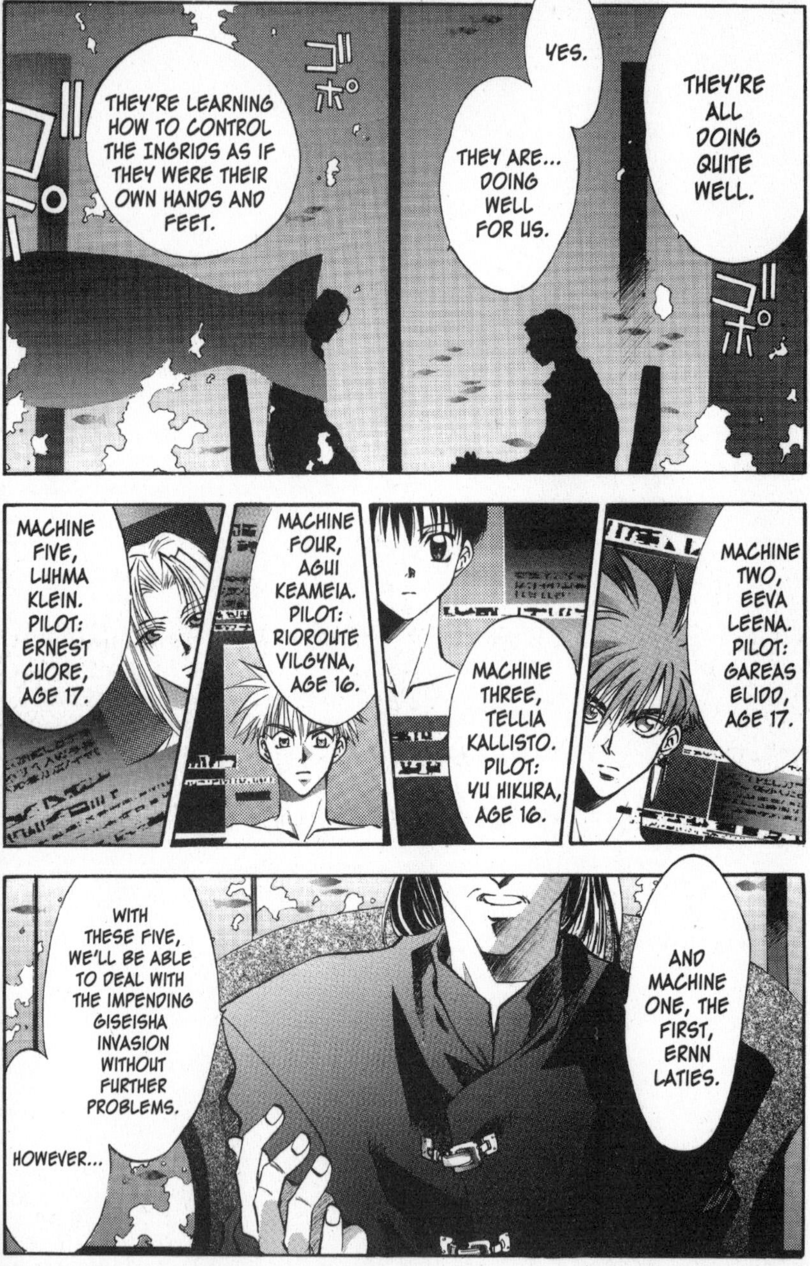
THEY'RE ALL DOING QUITE WELL.
YES.
THEY ARE... DOING WELL FOR US.
ゴポ
ゴポ
THEY'RE LEARNING HOW TO CONTROL THE INGRIDS AS IF THEY WERE THEIR OWN HANDS AND FEET.
MACHINE TWO, EEVA LEENA. PILOT: GAREAS ELIDD, AGE 17.
MACHINE THREE, TELLIA KALLISTO. PILOT: YU HIKURA, AGE 16.
MACHINE FOUR, AGUI KEAMEIA. PILOT: RIOROUTE VILGYNA, AGE 16.
MACHINE FIVE, LUHMA KLEIN. PILOT: ERNEST CUORE, AGE 17.
AND MACHINE ONE, THE FIRST, ERNN LATIES.
WITH THESE FIVE, WE'LL BE ABLE TO DEAL WITH THE IMPENDING GISEISHA INVASION WITHOUT FURTHER PROBLEMS.
HOWEVER...

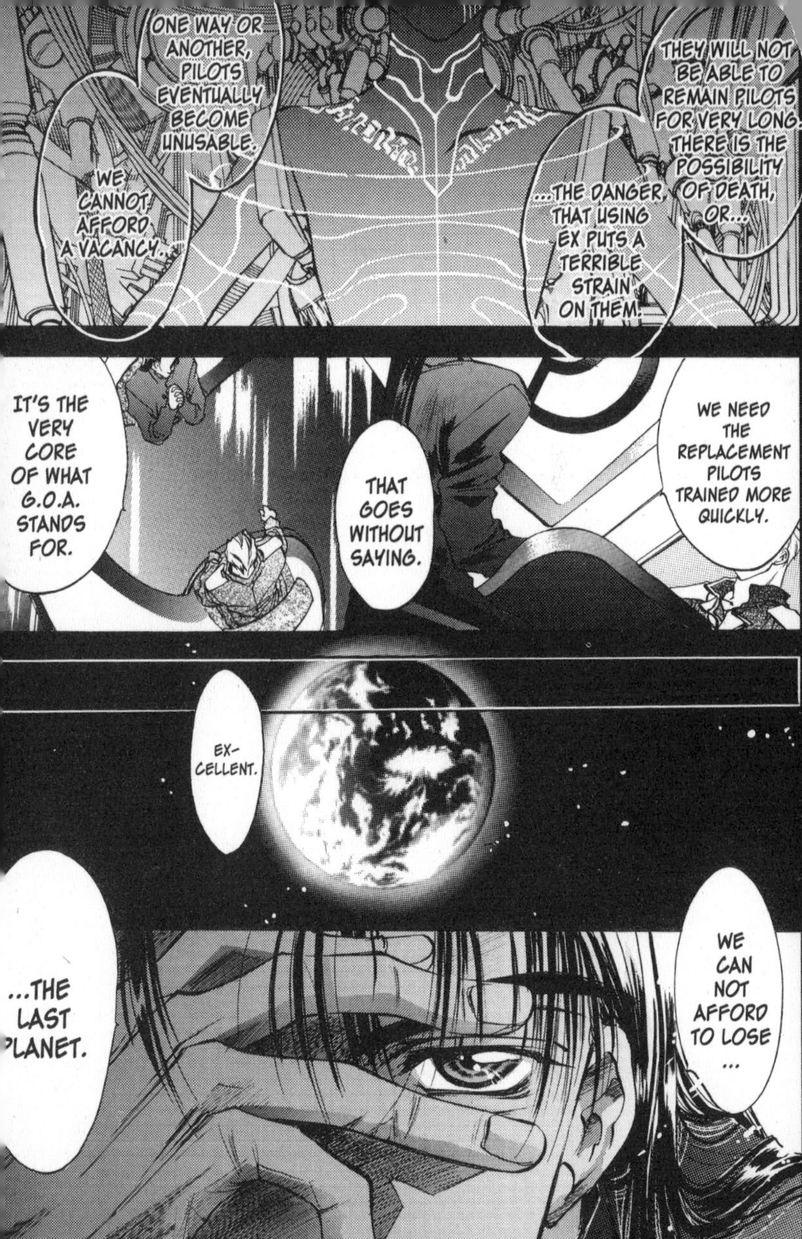
THEY WILL NOT BE ABLE TO REMAIN PILOTS FOR VERY LONG. THERE IS THE POSSIBILITY OF DEATH, OR...
...THE DANGER, THAT USING EX PUTS A TERRIBLE STRAIN ON THEM!
ONE WAY OR ANOTHER, PILOTS EVENTUALLY BECOME UNUSABLE.
WE CANNOT AFFORD A VACANCY...
WE NEED THE REPLACEMENT PILOTS TRAINED MORE QUICKLY.
THAT GOES WITHOUT SAYING.
IT'S THE VERY CORE OF WHAT G.O.A. STANDS FOR.
EX-CELLENT.
WE CAN NOT AFFORD TO LOSE ...
...THE LAST PLANET.

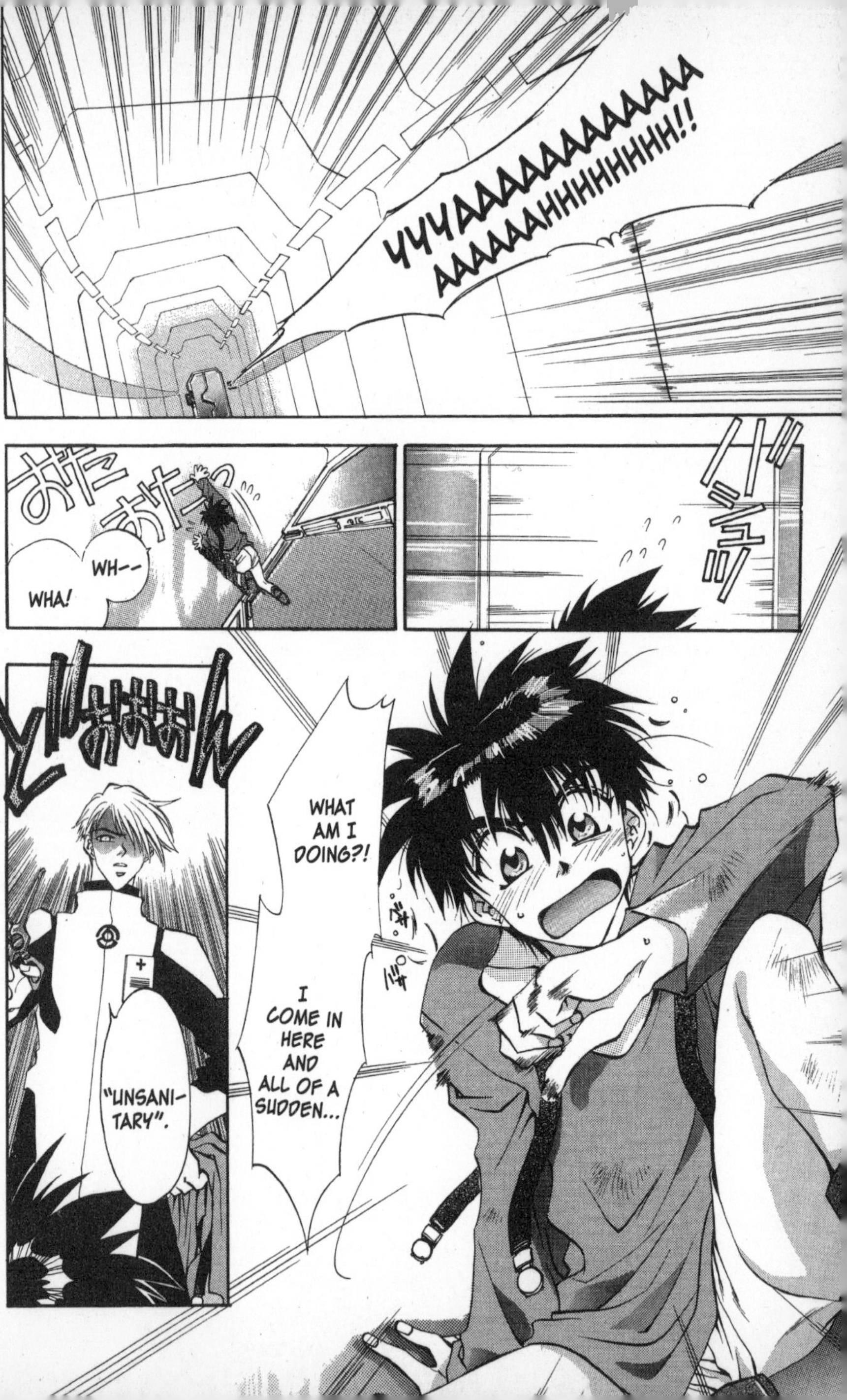
YYYAAAAAAAAAAAAA AAAAAAHHHHHHHH!!
WH-- WHA!
WHAT AM I DOING?!
I COME IN HERE AND ALL OF A SUDDEN...
"UNSANITARY".

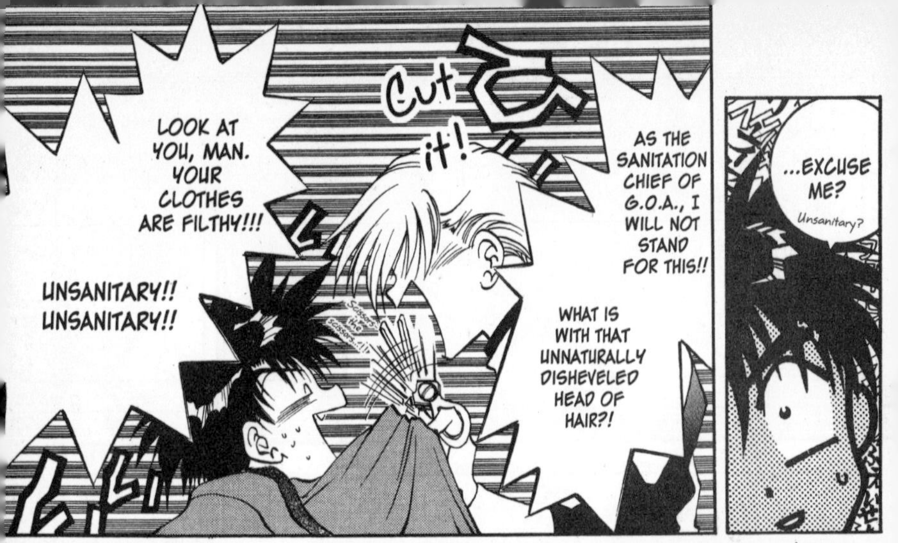
...EXCUSE ME?
Unsanitary?
AS THE SANITATION CHIEF OF G.O.A., I WILL NOT STAND FOR THIS!!
Cut it!
LOOK AT YOU, MAN. YOUR CLOTHES ARE FILTHY!!!
WHAT IS WITH THAT UNNATURALLY DISHEVELED HEAD OF HAIR?!
Scissors the scissors...!!
UNSANITARY!! UNSANITARY!!

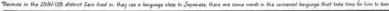

*Because in the ZINN-128 district Zero lived in, they use a language close to Japanese, there are some words in the universal language that take time for him to learn.

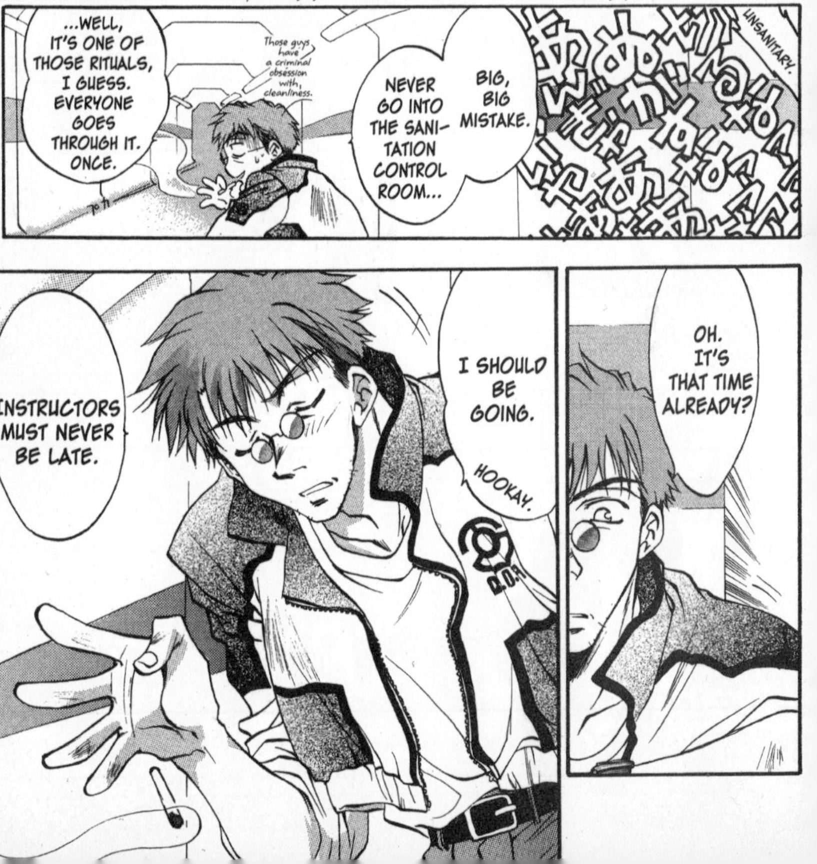
UNSANITARY.
BIG, BIG MISTAKE.
NEVER GO INTO THE SANITATION CONTROL ROOM...
Those guys have a criminal obsession with cleanliness.
...WELL, IT'S ONE OF THOSE RITUALS, I GUESS. EVERYONE GOES THROUGH IT. ONCE.
OH. IT'S THAT TIME ALREADY?
I SHOULD BE GOING.
HOOKAY.
INSTRUCTORS MUST NEVER BE LATE.

the Candidate for goddess™

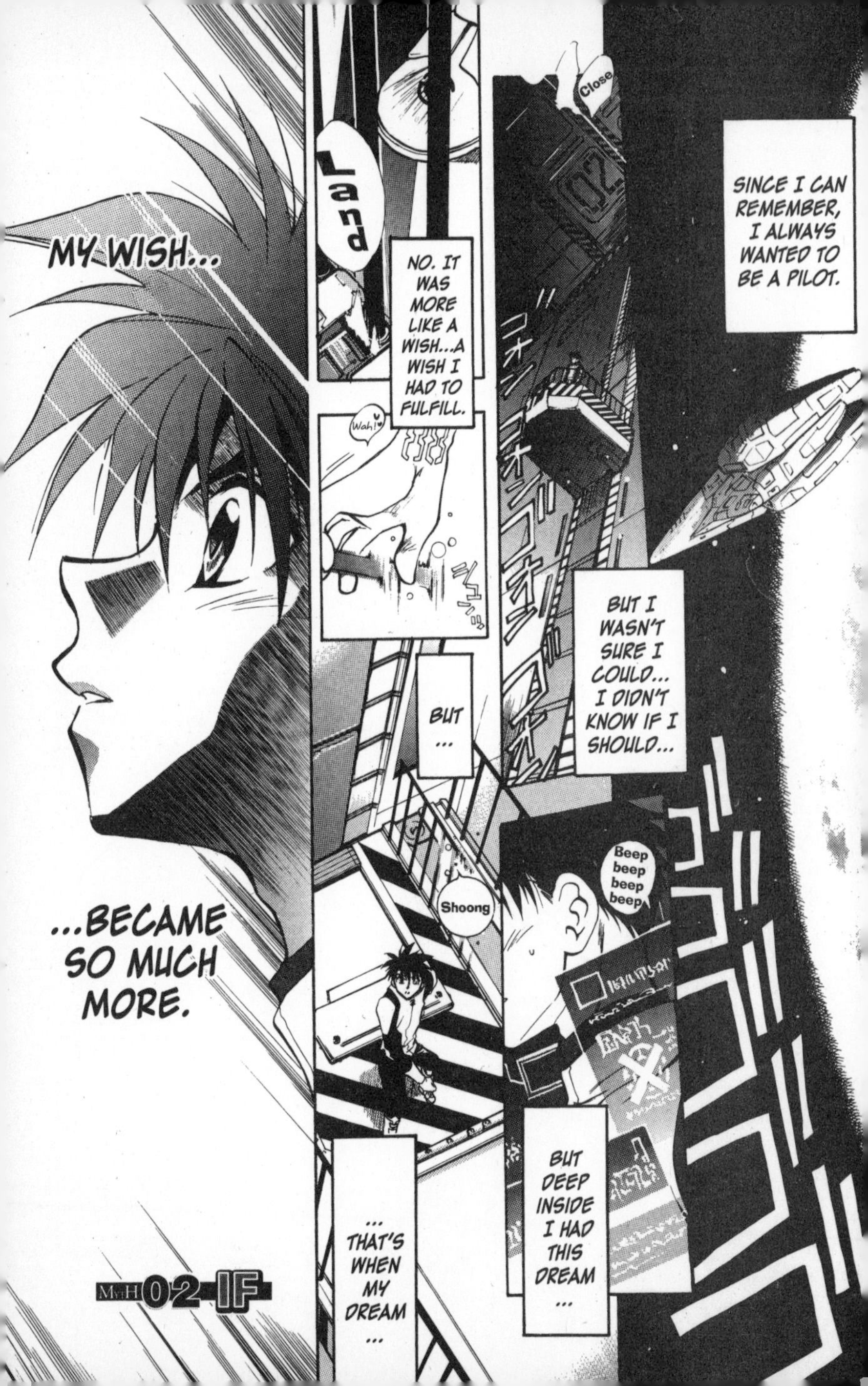
SINCE I CAN REMEMBER, I ALWAYS WANTED TO BE A PILOT.
Close
BUT I WASN'T SURE I COULD... I DIDN'T KNOW IF I SHOULD...
Beep beep beep beep
BUT DEEP INSIDE I HAD THIS DREAM ...
Land
NO. IT WAS MORE LIKE A WISH...A WISH I HAD TO FULFILL.
Wah!
BUT ...
Shoong
... THAT'S WHEN MY DREAM ...
MY WISH...
...BECAME SO MUCH MORE.
MYTH 02 IF

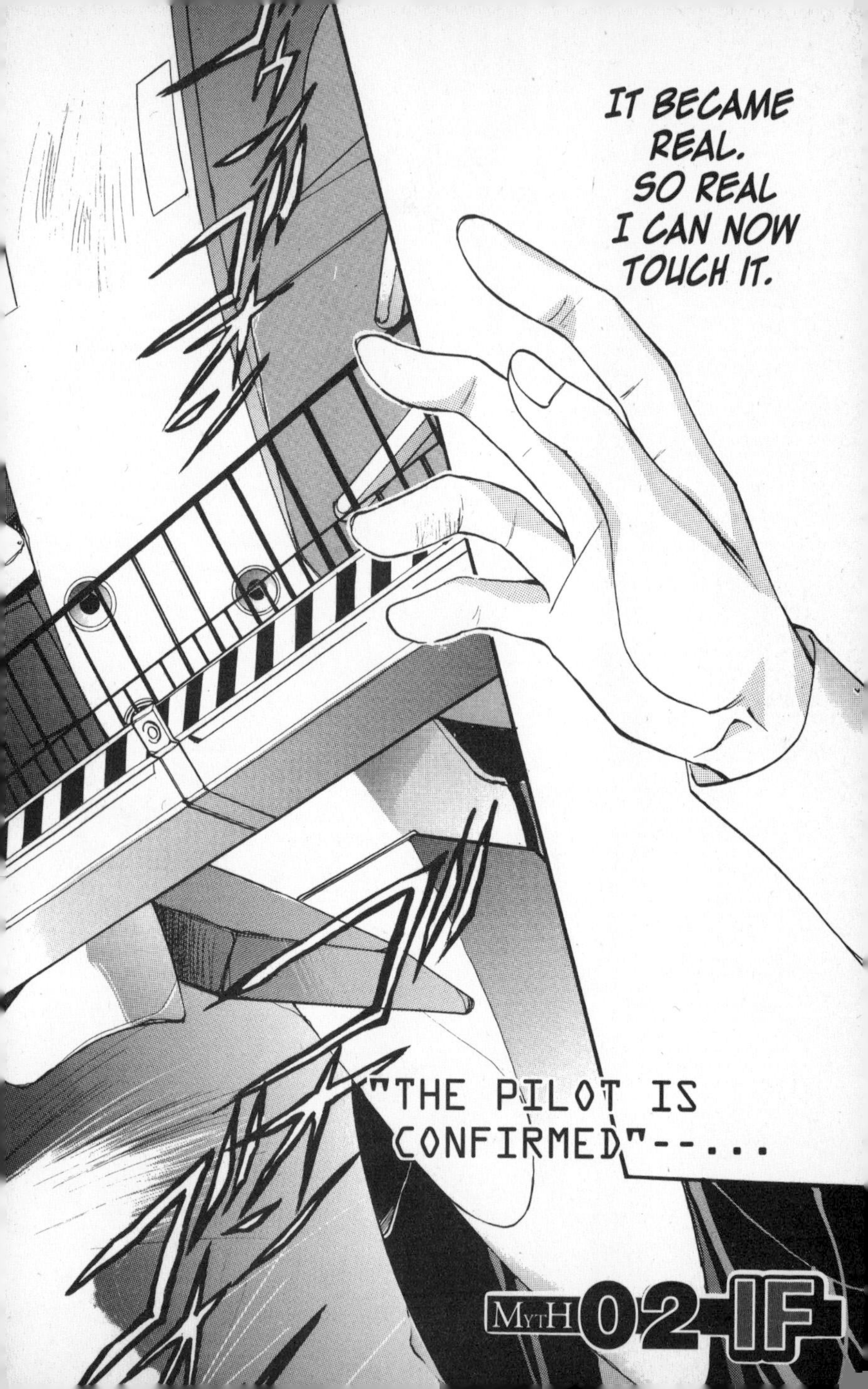
IT BECAME REAL. SO REAL I CAN NOW TOUCH IT.
"THE PILOT IS CONFIRMED"--...
MYTH 02 IF

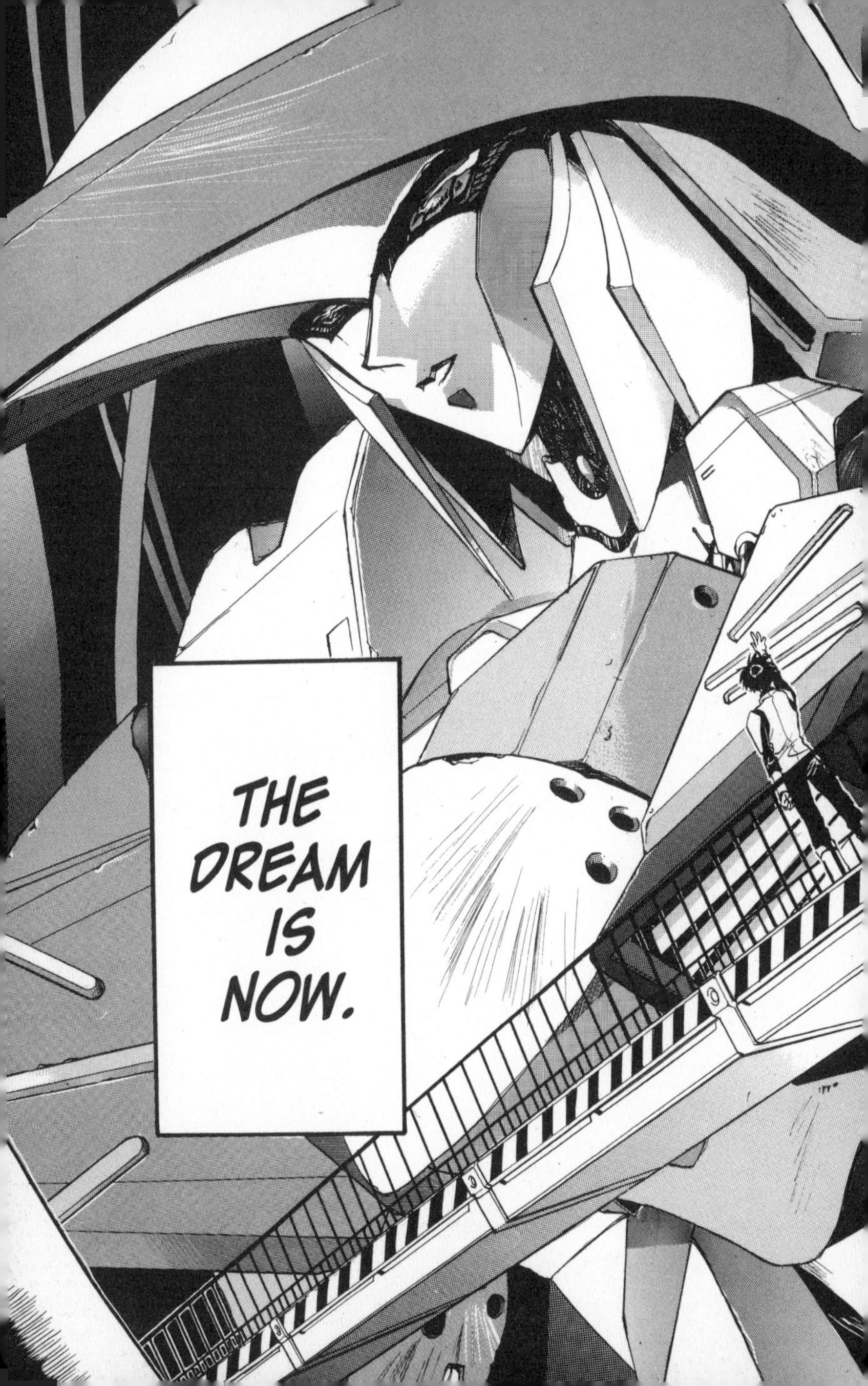
THE DREAM IS NOW.

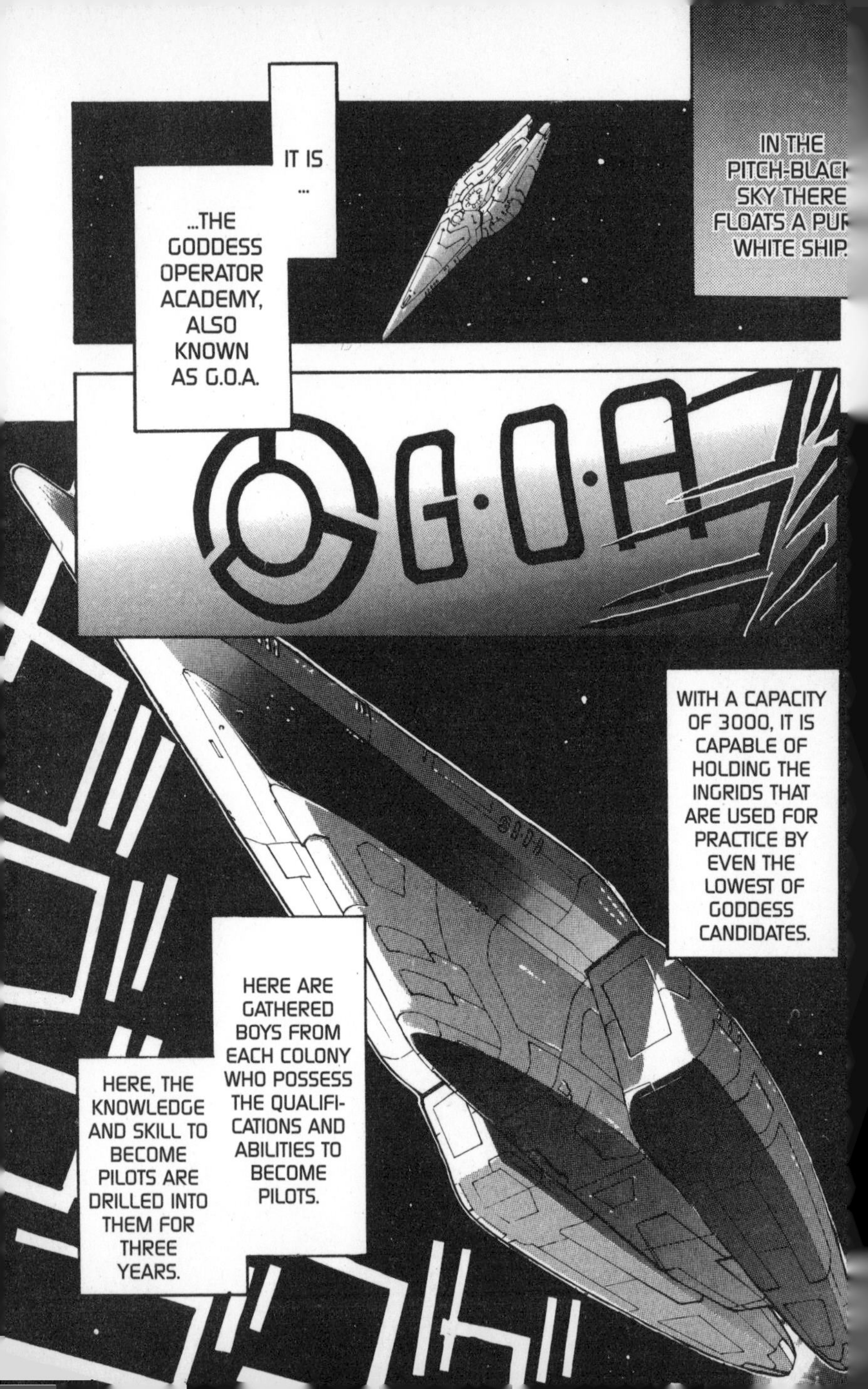
IN THE PITCH-BLACK SKY THERE FLOATS A PUR WHITE SHIP.
IT IS ...
...THE GODDESS OPERATOR ACADEMY, ALSO KNOWN AS G.O.A.
G.O.A
WITH A CAPACITY OF 3000, IT IS CAPABLE OF HOLDING THE INGRIDS THAT ARE USED FOR PRACTICE BY EVEN THE LOWEST OF GODDESS CANDIDATES.
HERE ARE GATHERED BOYS FROM EACH COLONY WHO POSSESS THE QUALIFI-CATIONS AND ABILITIES TO BECOME PILOTS.
HERE, THE KNOWLEDGE AND SKILL TO BECOME PILOTS ARE DRILLED INTO THEM FOR THREE YEARS.

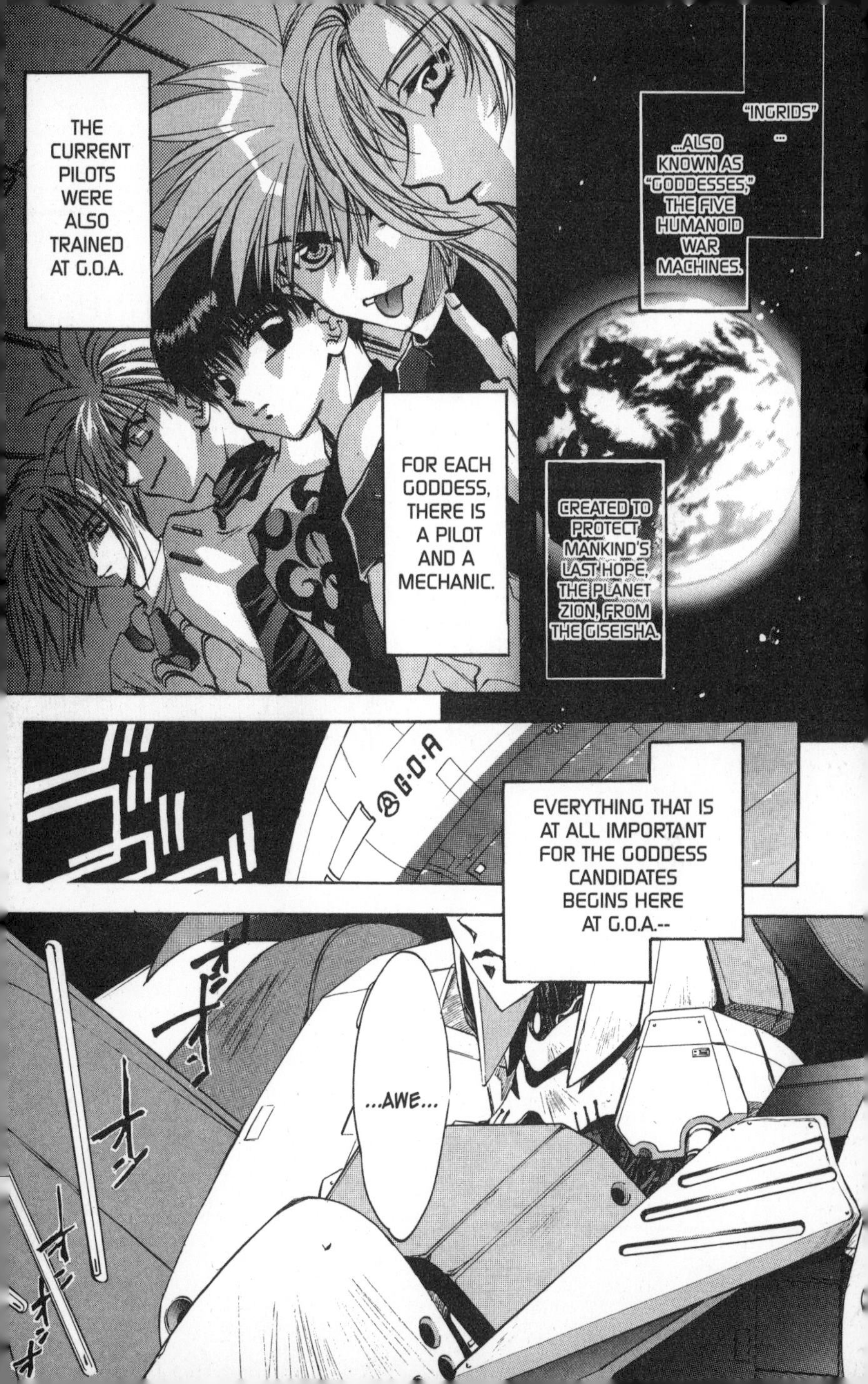
"INGRIDS"...
...ALSO KNOWN AS "GODDESSES," THE FIVE HUMANOID WAR MACHINES.
CREATED TO PROTECT MANKIND'S LAST HOPE, THE PLANET ZION, FROM THE GISEISHA.
THE CURRENT PILOTS WERE ALSO TRAINED AT G.O.A.
FOR EACH GODDESS, THERE IS A PILOT AND A MECHANIC.
G·O·A
EVERYTHING THAT IS AT ALL IMPORTANT FOR THE GODDESS CANDIDATES BEGINS HERE AT G.O.A.--
...AWE...

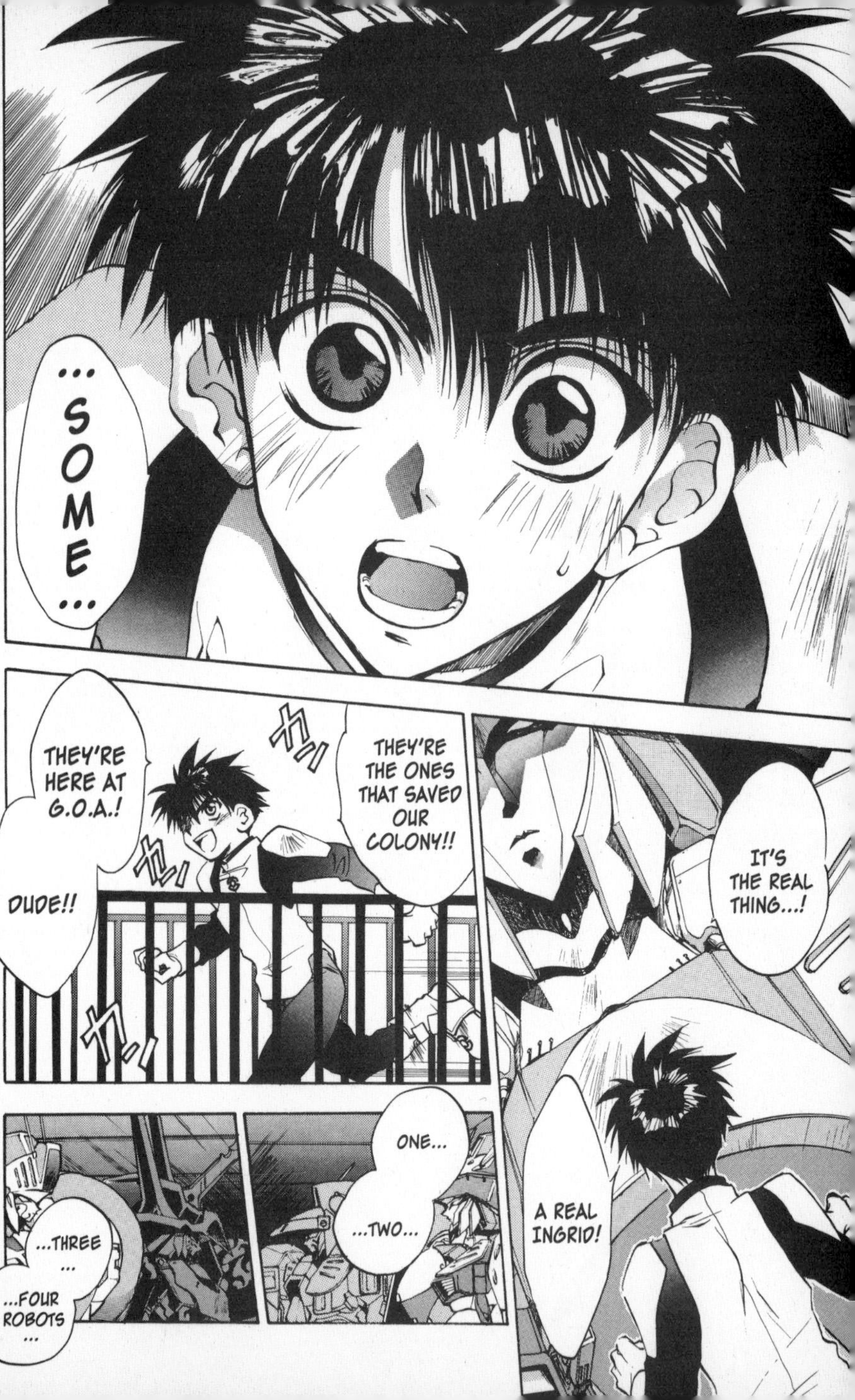
...SOME...
IT'S THE REAL THING...!
A REAL INGRID!
THEY'RE THE ONES THAT SAVED OUR COLONY!!
THEY'RE HERE AT G.O.A.!
DUDE!!
ONE...
...TWO...
...THREE ...
...FOUR ROBOTS ...

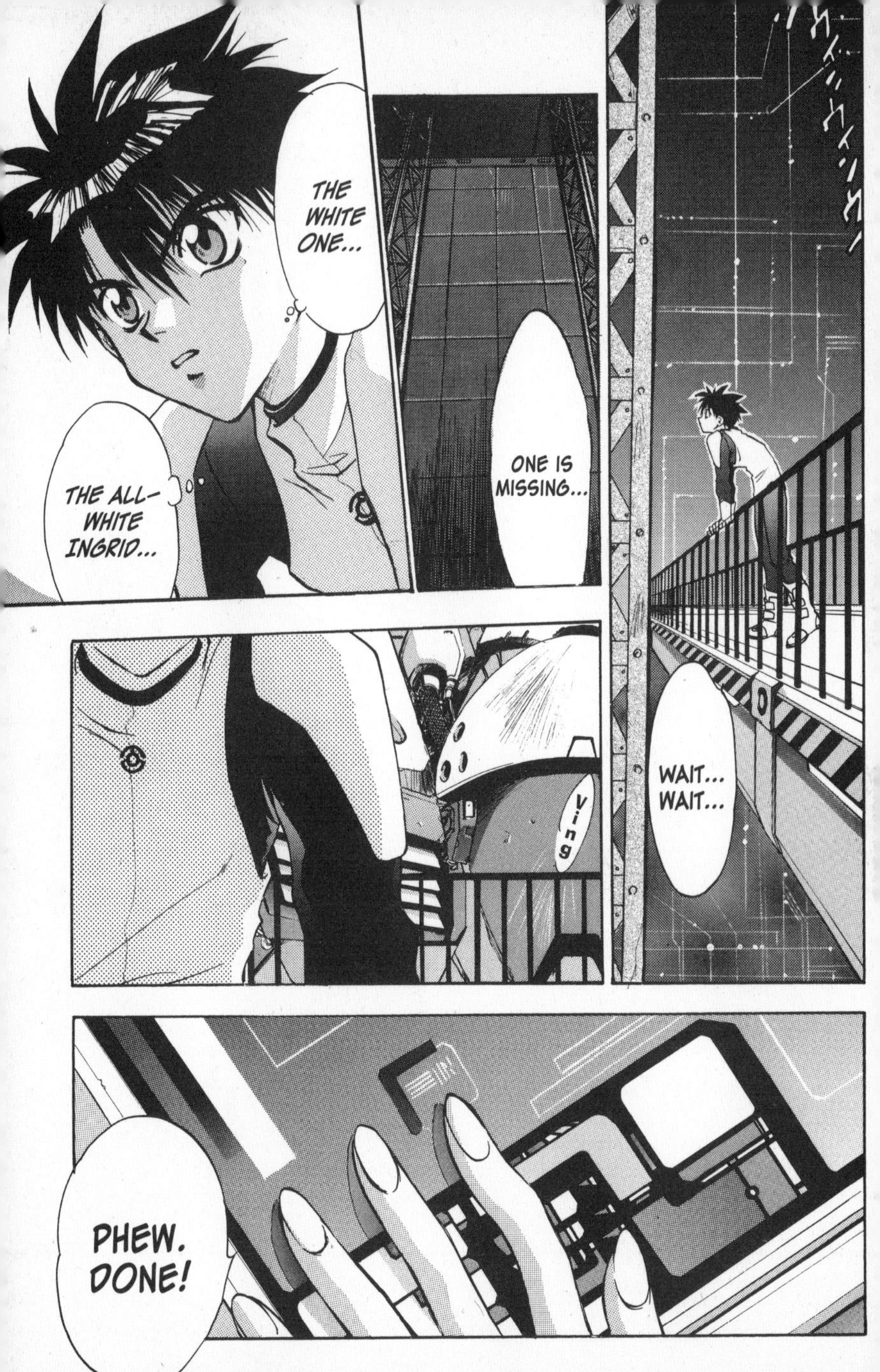
WAIT... WAIT...
ONE IS MISSING...
THE WHITE ONE...
THE ALL-WHITE INGRID...
Ving
PHEW. DONE!

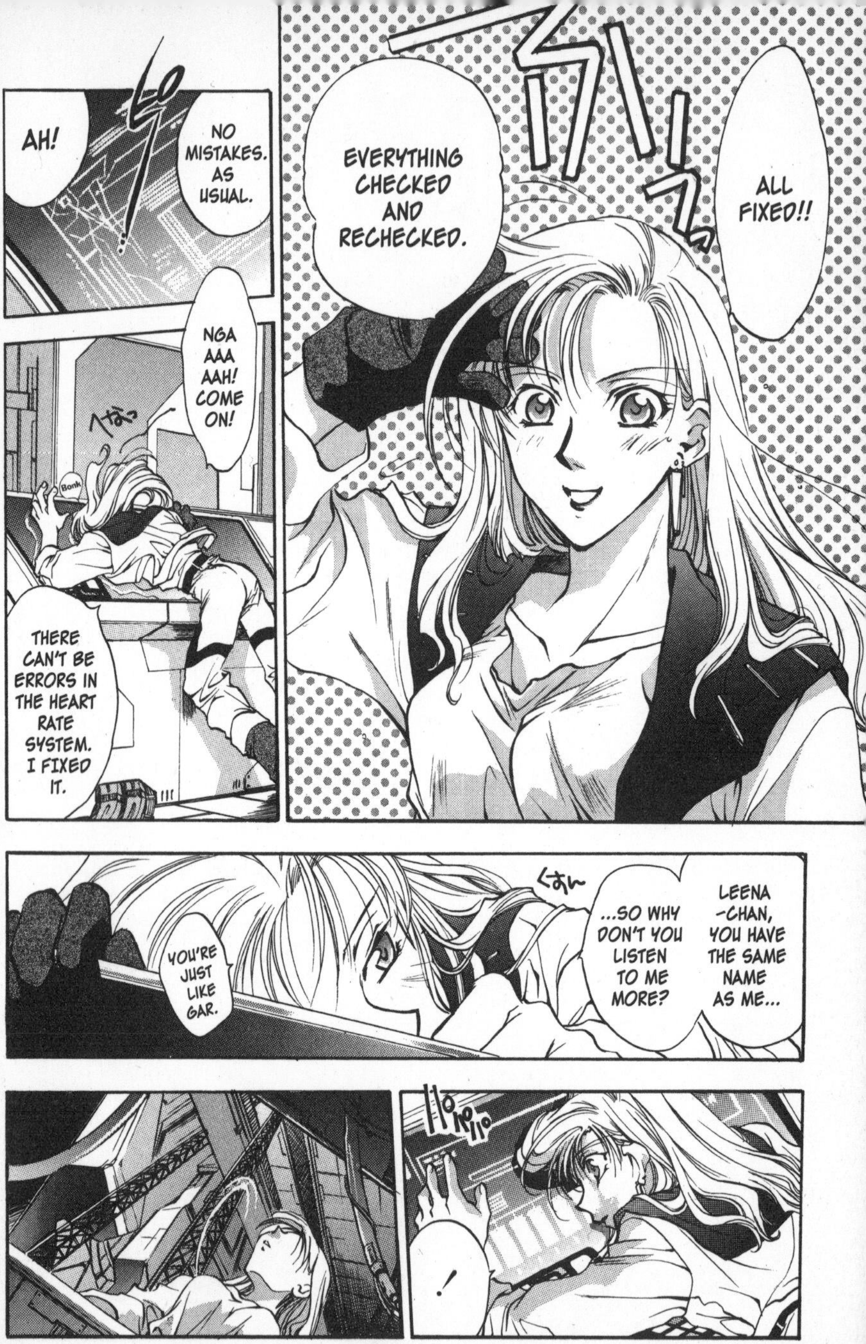
ALL FIXED!!
EVERYTHING CHECKED AND RECHECKED.
NO MISTAKES. AS USUAL.
AH!
NGA AAA AAH! COME ON!
Bonk
THERE CAN'T BE ERRORS IN THE HEART RATE SYSTEM. I FIXED IT.
LEENA-CHAN, YOU HAVE THE SAME NAME AS ME...
...SO WHY DON'T YOU LISTEN TO ME MORE?
YOU'RE JUST LIKE GAR.
!

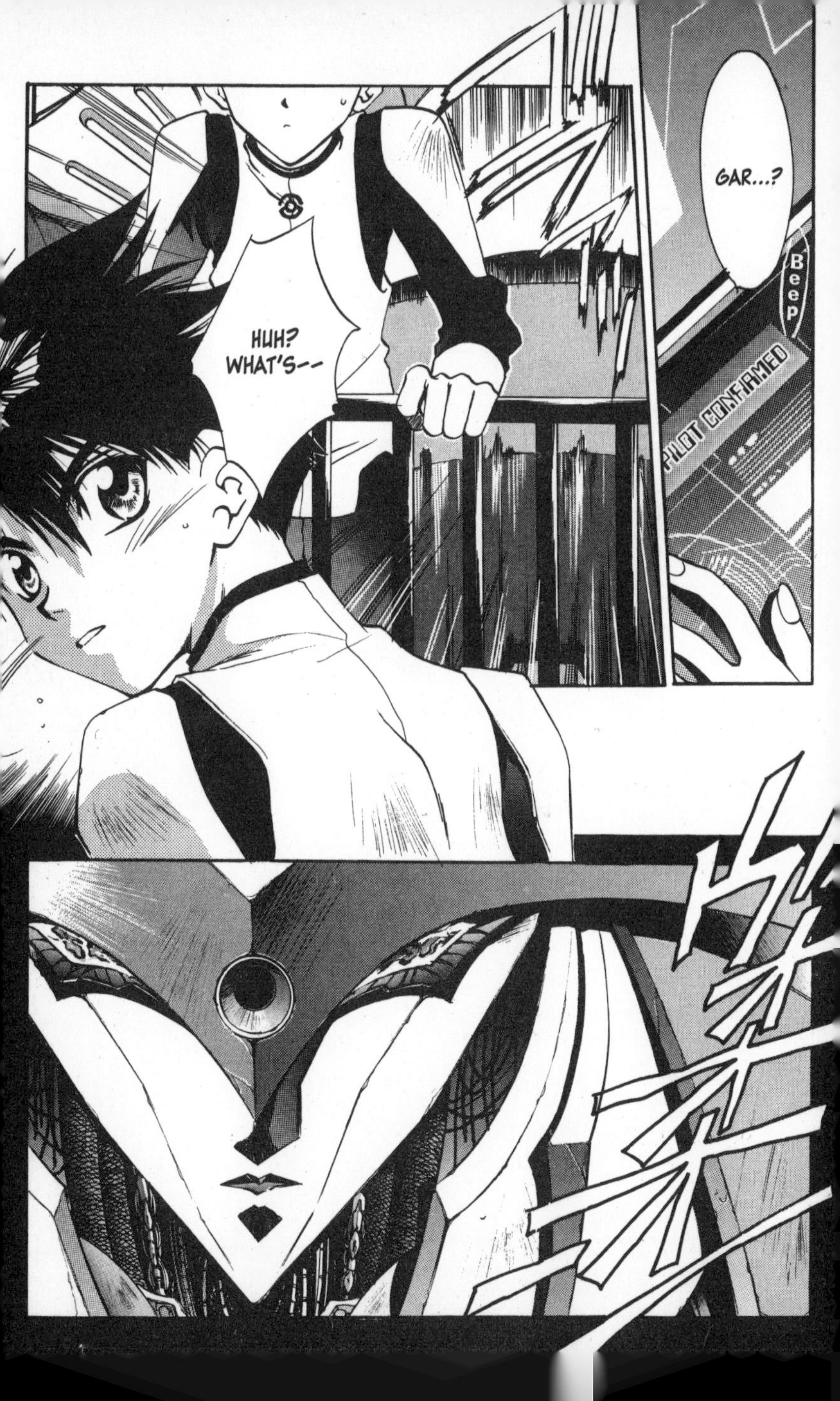
GAR...?
BeeP
PILOT CONFIRMED
HUH? WHAT'S--

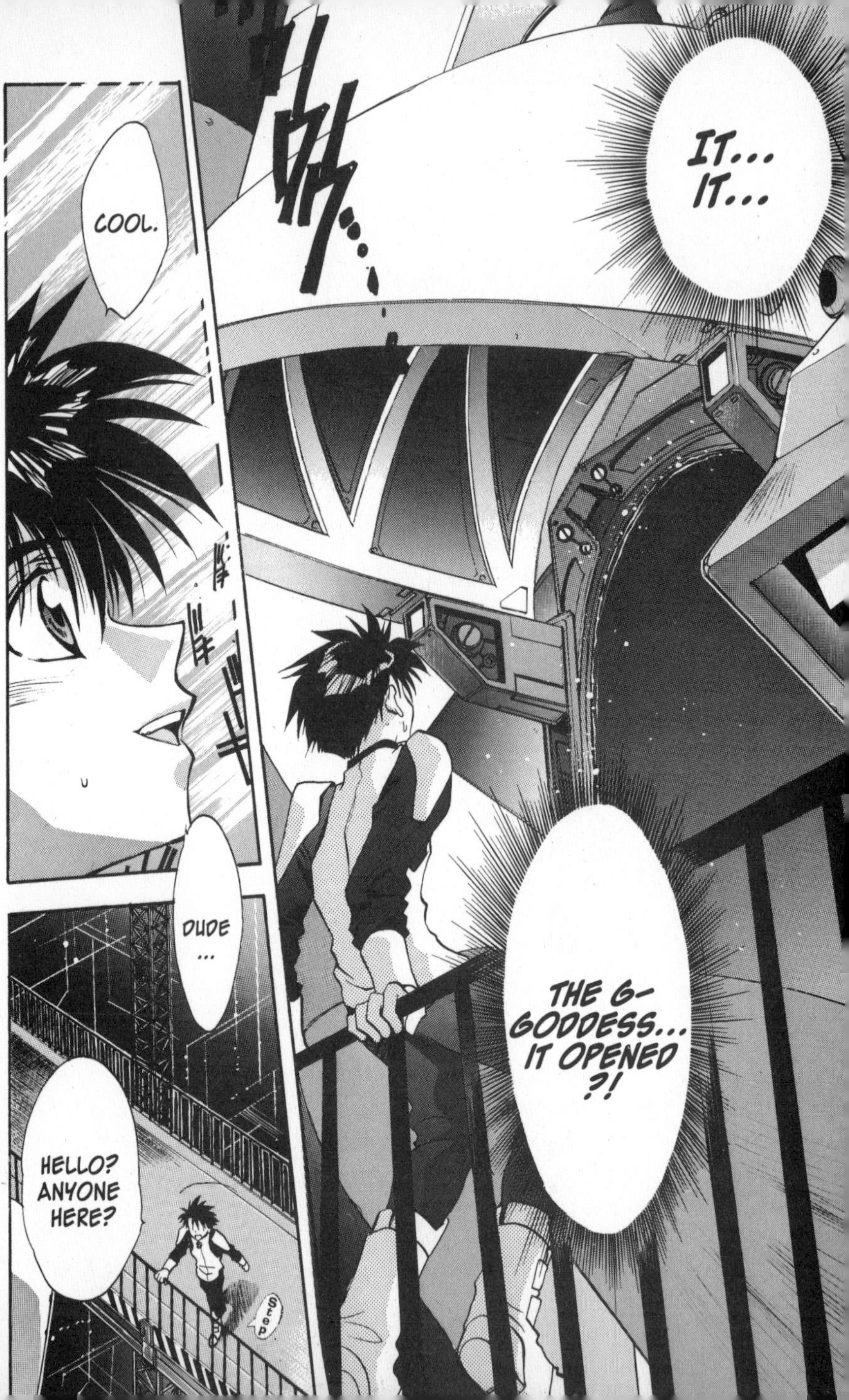
IT... IT...
THE G-GODDESS... IT OPENED?!
COOL.
DUDE ...
HELLO? ANYONE HERE?
step

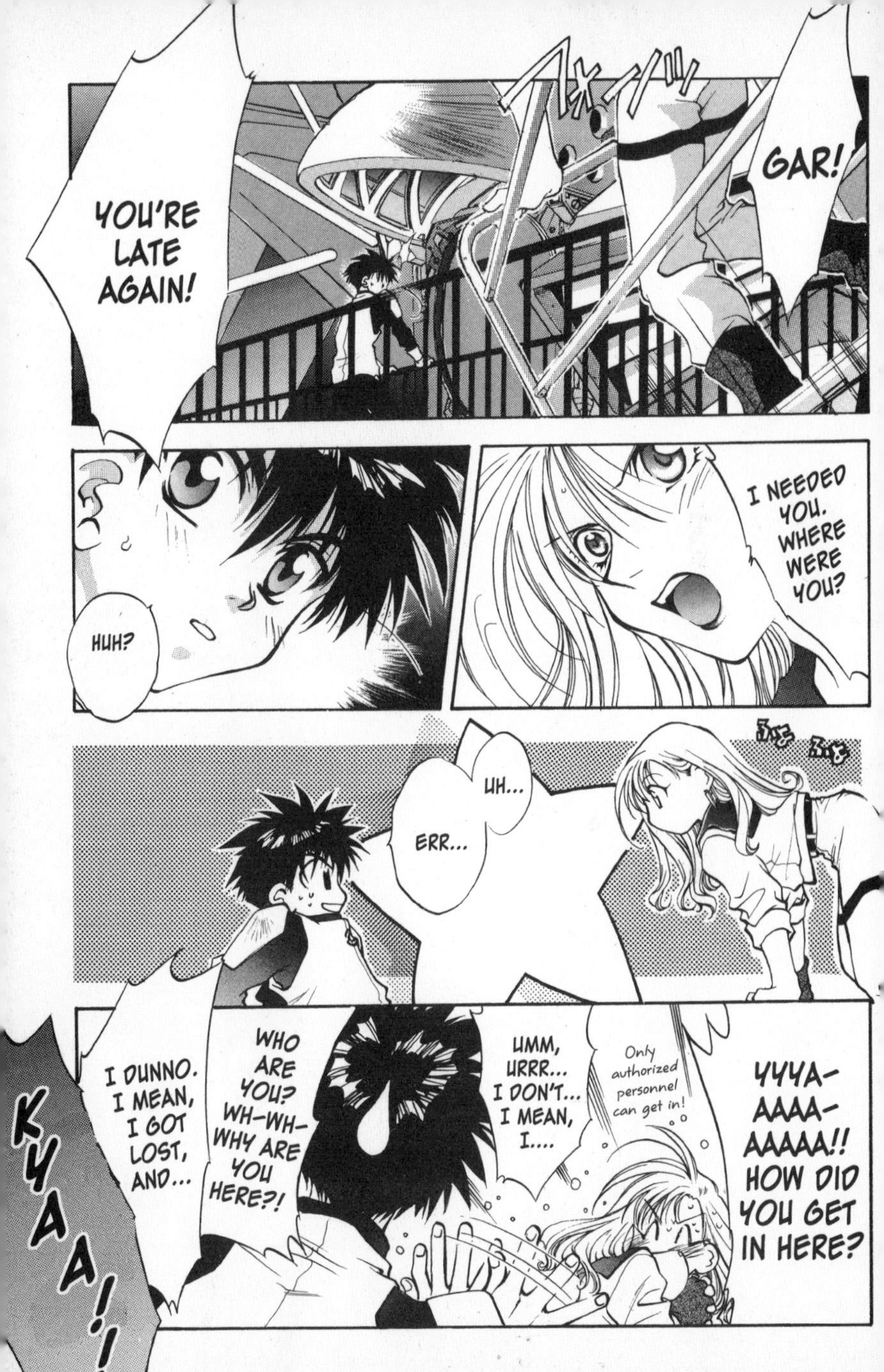
GAR!
YOU'RE LATE AGAIN!
I NEEDED YOU. WHERE WERE YOU?
HUH?
UH...
ERR...
YYYA-AAAA-AAAAA!! HOW DID YOU GET IN HERE?
Only authorized personnel can get in!
UMM, URRR... I DON'T... I MEAN, I....
WHO ARE YOU? WH-WH-WHY ARE YOU HERE?!
I DUNNO. I MEAN, I GOT LOST, AND...
KYAAA!!

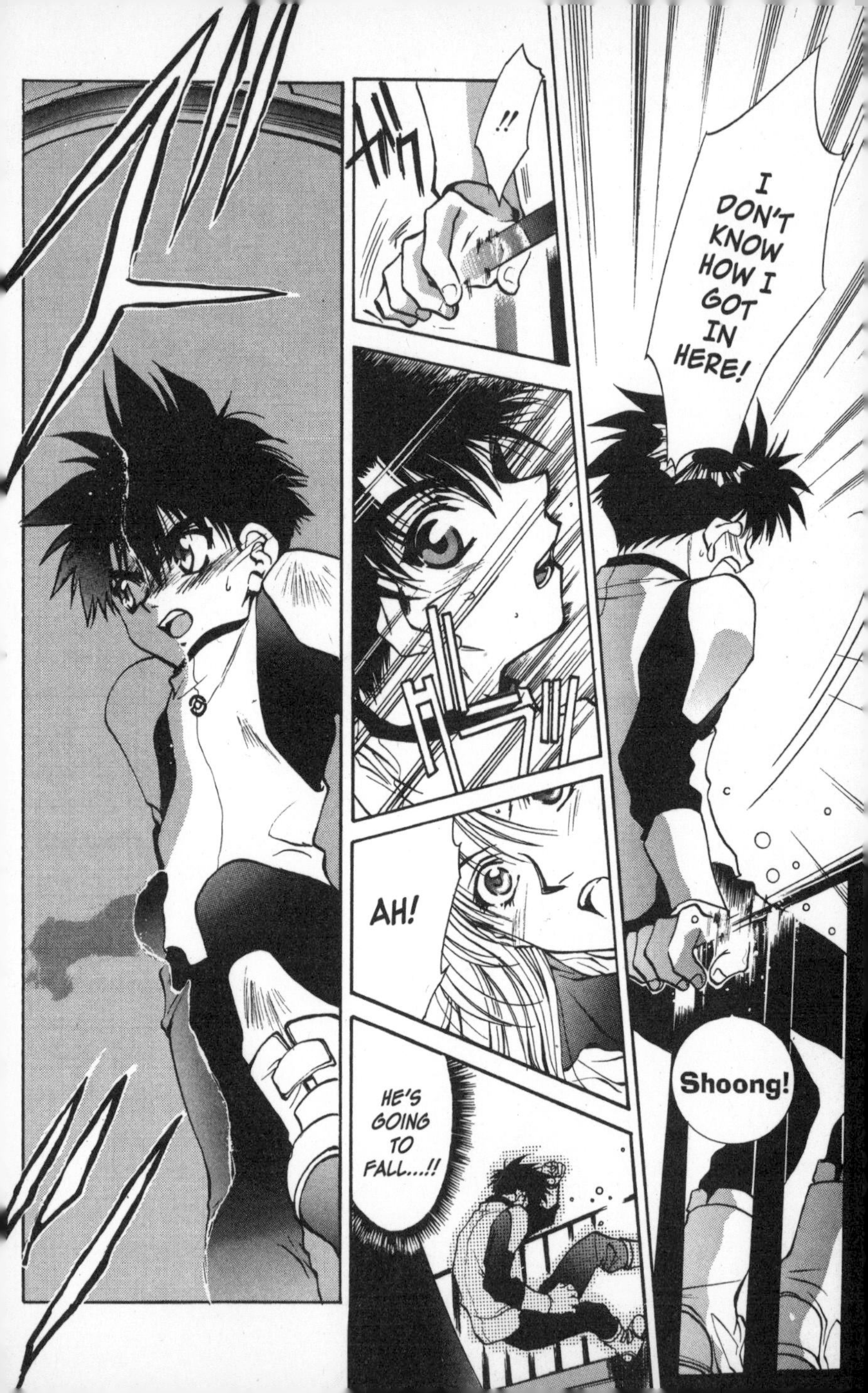
I DON'T KNOW HOW I GOT IN HERE!
Shoong!
!!
AH!
HE'S GOING TO FALL...!!

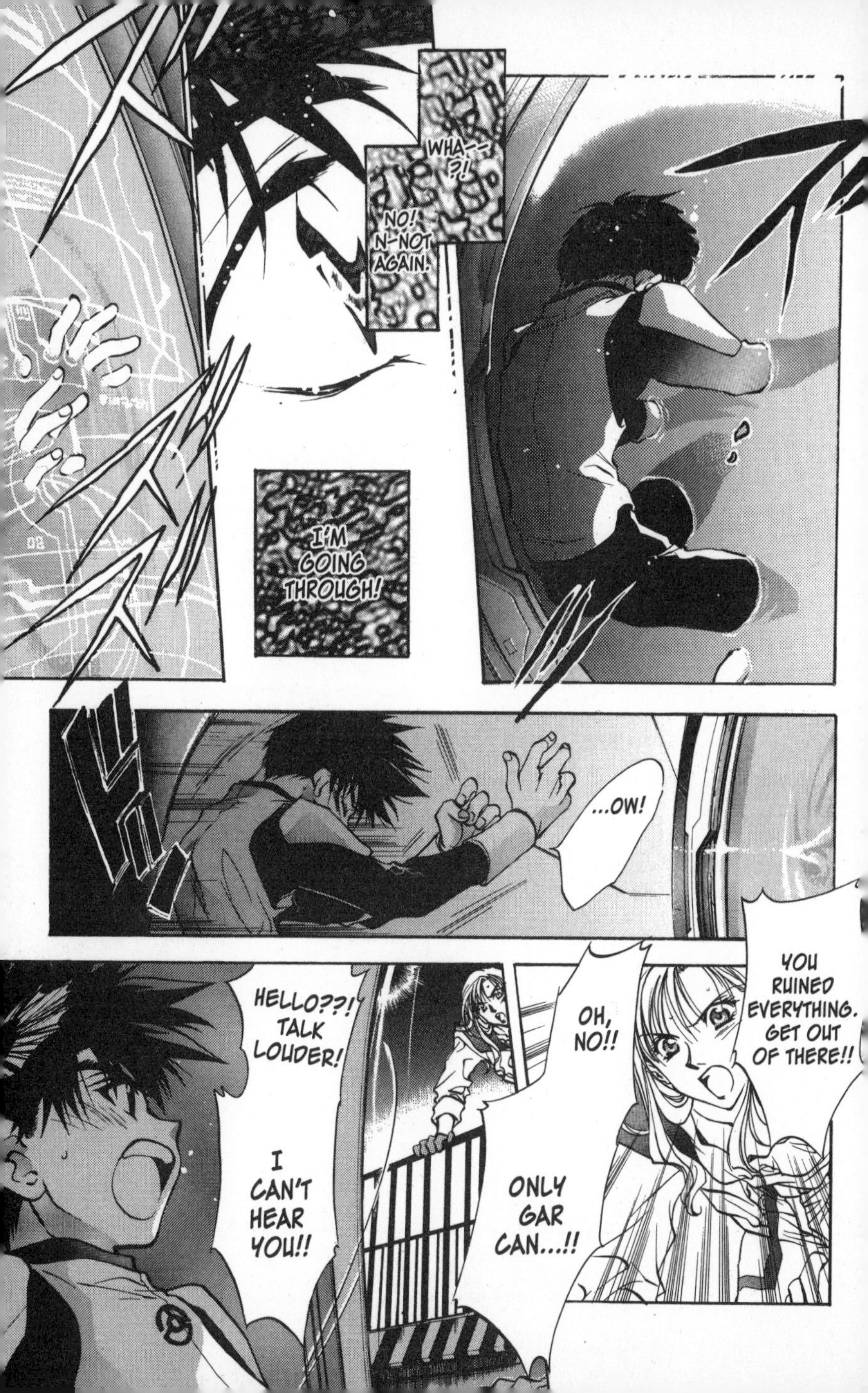
WHA--?!
NO! N-NOT AGAIN.
I'M GOING THROUGH!
...OW!
YOU RUINED EVERYTHING. GET OUT OF THERE!!
OH, NO!!
ONLY GAR CAN...!!
HELLO??! TALK LOUDER!
I CAN'T HEAR YOU!!

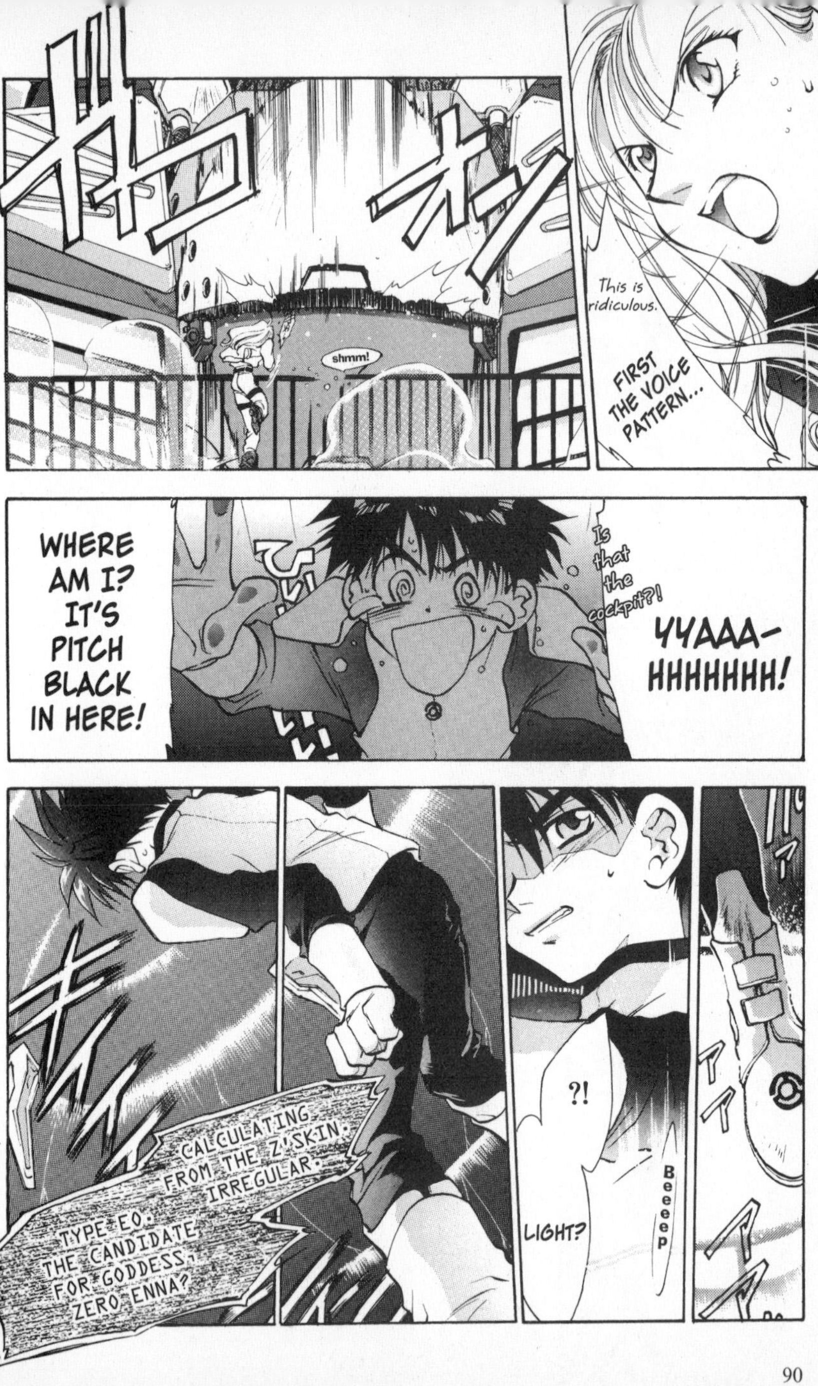
This is ridiculous.
FIRST THE VOICE PATTERN...
shmm!
Is that the cockpit?!
YYAAA-HHHHHHH!
WHERE AM I? IT'S PITCH BLACK IN HERE!
?!
Beeeep
LIGHT?
CALCULATING FROM THE Z'SKIN. IRREGULAR.
TYPE EO. THE CANDIDATE FOR GODDESS, ZERO ENNA?

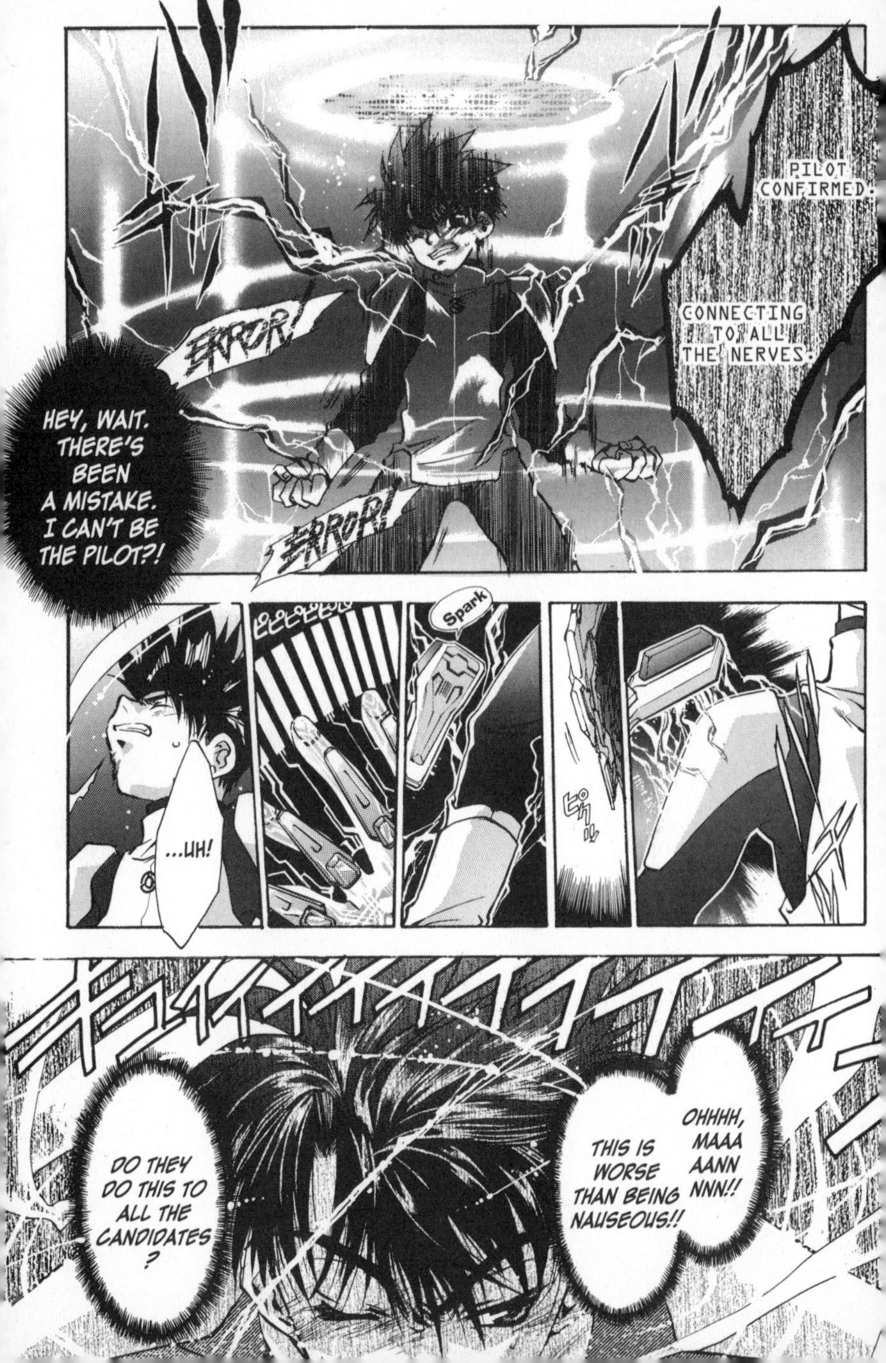
PILOT CONFIRMED.
CONNECTING TO ALL THE NERVES.
ERROR!
ERROR!
HEY, WAIT. THERE'S BEEN A MISTAKE. I CAN'T BE THE PILOT?!
Spark
...UH!
OHHHH, MAAA AANN NNN!!
THIS IS WORSE THAN BEING NAUSEOUS!!
DO THEY DO THIS TO ALL THE CANDIDATES?

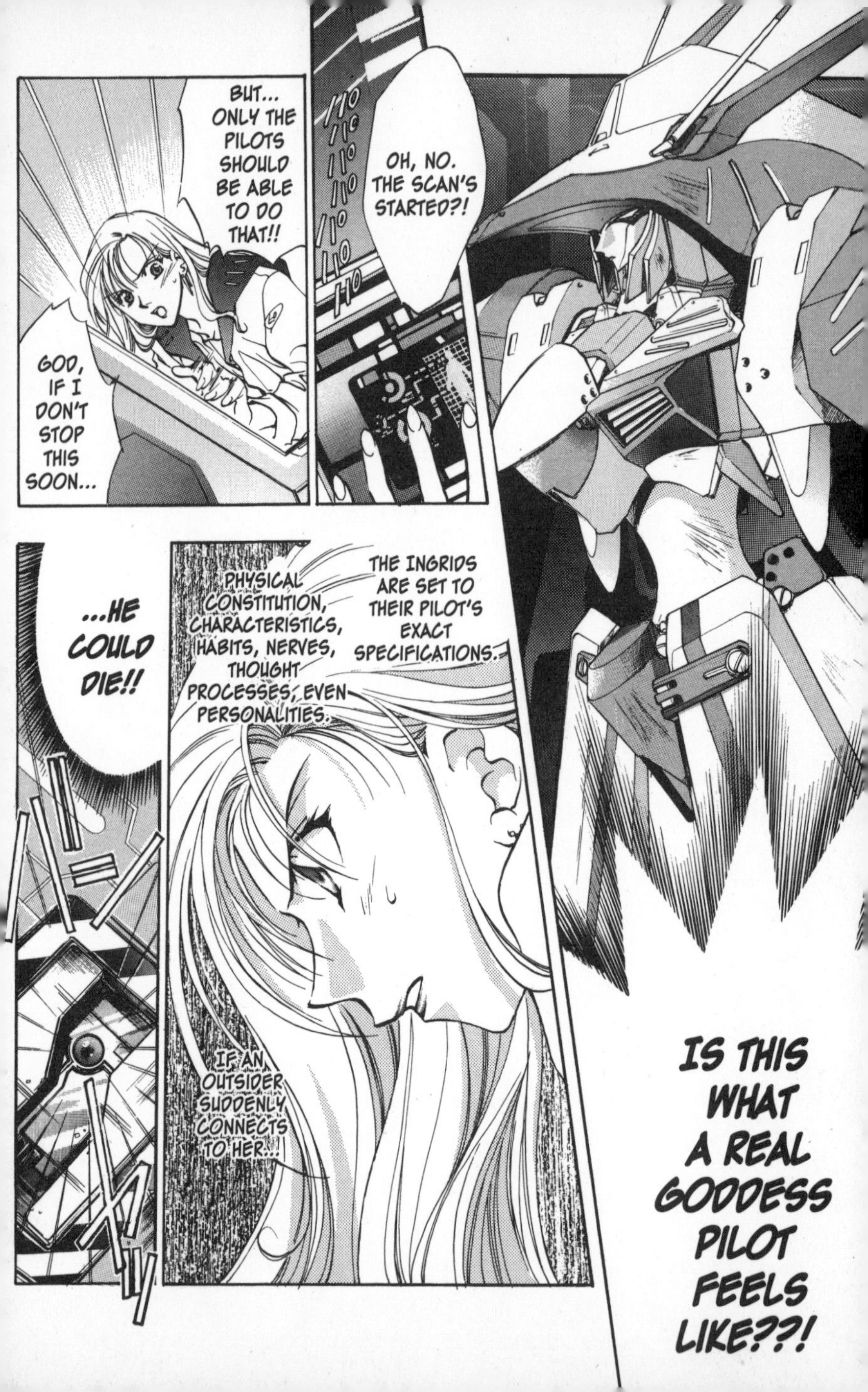
IS THIS WHAT A REAL GODDESS PILOT FEELS LIKE??!
OH, NO. THE SCAN'S STARTED?!
BUT... ONLY THE PILOTS SHOULD BE ABLE TO DO THAT!!
GOD, IF I DON'T STOP THIS SOON...
THE INGRIDS ARE SET TO THEIR PILOT'S EXACT SPECIFICATIONS.
PHYSICAL CONSTITUTION, CHARACTERISTICS, HABITS, NERVES, THOUGHT PROCESSES, EVEN PERSONALITIES.
IF AN OUTSIDER SUDDENLY CONNECTS TO HER...
...HE COULD DIE!!

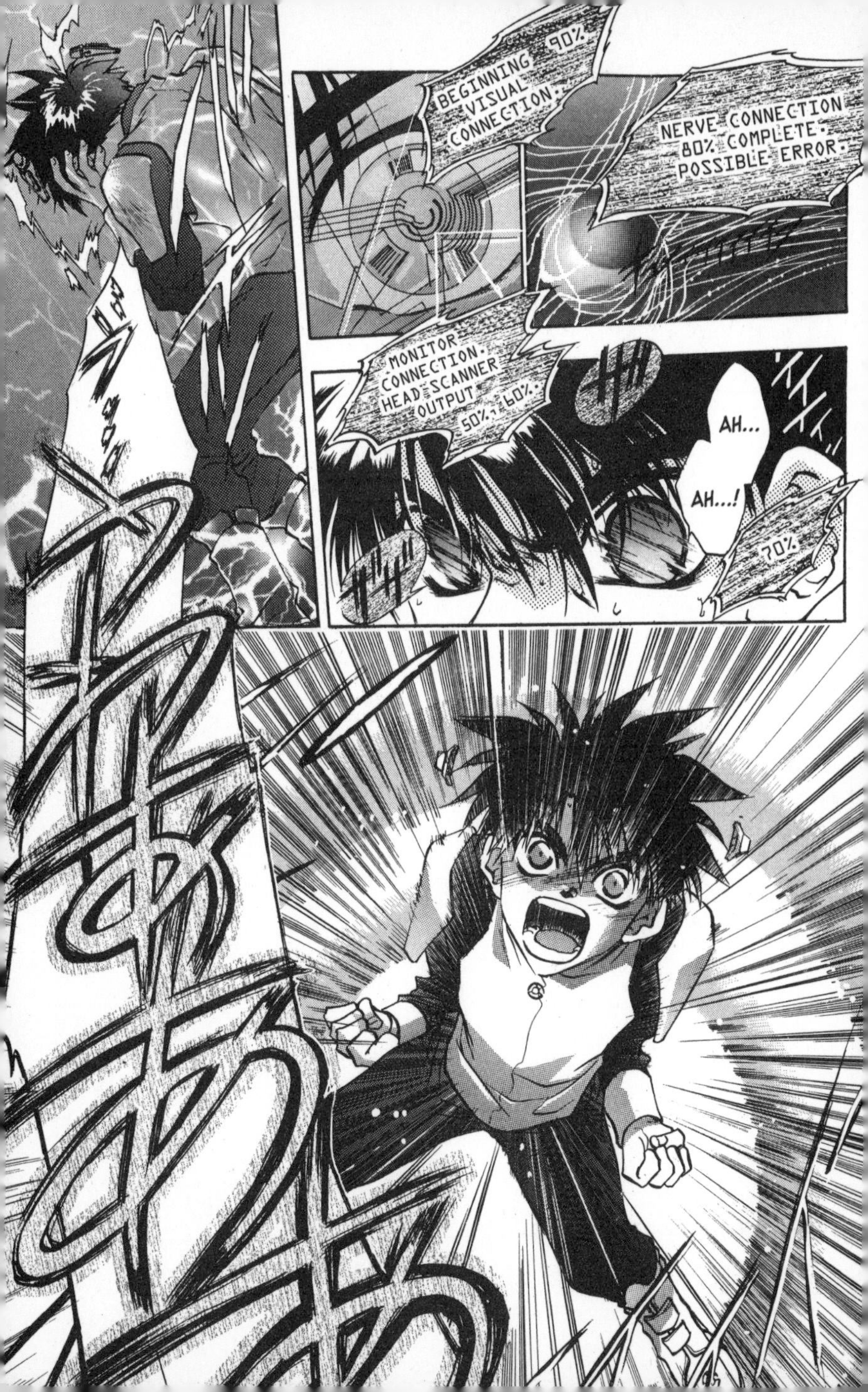
BEGINNING VISUAL CONNECTION. 90%
NERVE CONNECTION 80% COMPLETE. POSSIBLE ERROR.
MONITOR CONNECTION. HEAD SCANNER OUTPUT 50%, 60%.
AH...
AH...!
70%

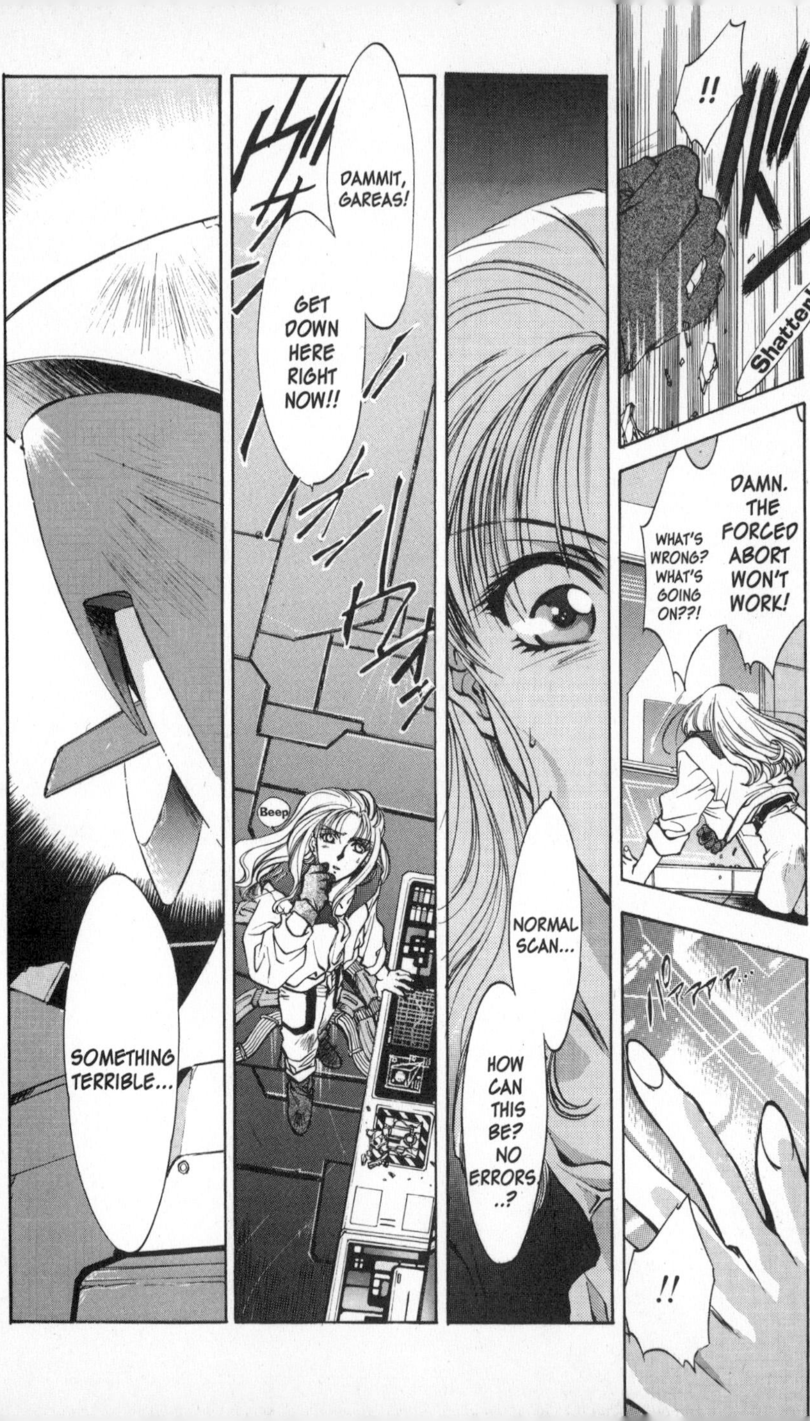
!!
Shatter!
DAMN. THE FORCED ABORT WON'T WORK!
WHAT'S WRONG? WHAT'S GOING ON??!
!!
NORMAL SCAN...
HOW CAN THIS BE? NO ERRORS ..?
DAMMIT, GAREAS!
GET DOWN HERE RIGHT NOW!!
Beep
SOMETHING TERRIBLE...

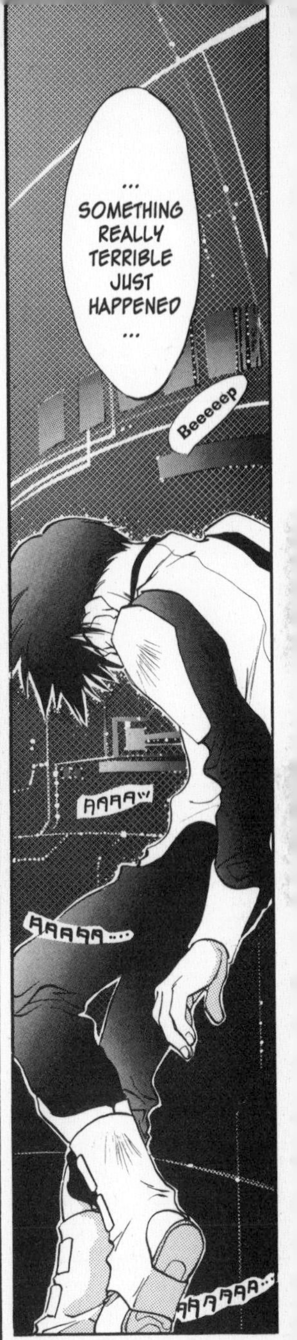
... SOMETHING REALLY TERRIBLE JUST HAPPENED ...
Beeeeep
AAAAW
AAAAA...
AAAAAA...

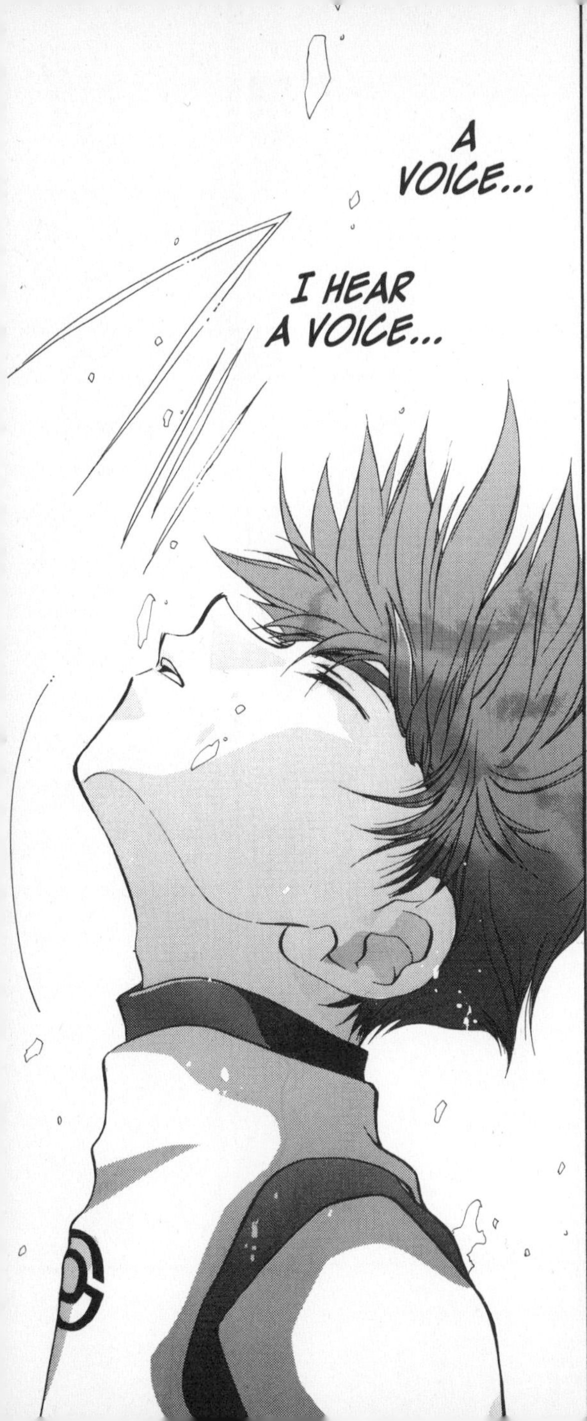
A VOICE...
I HEAR A VOICE...

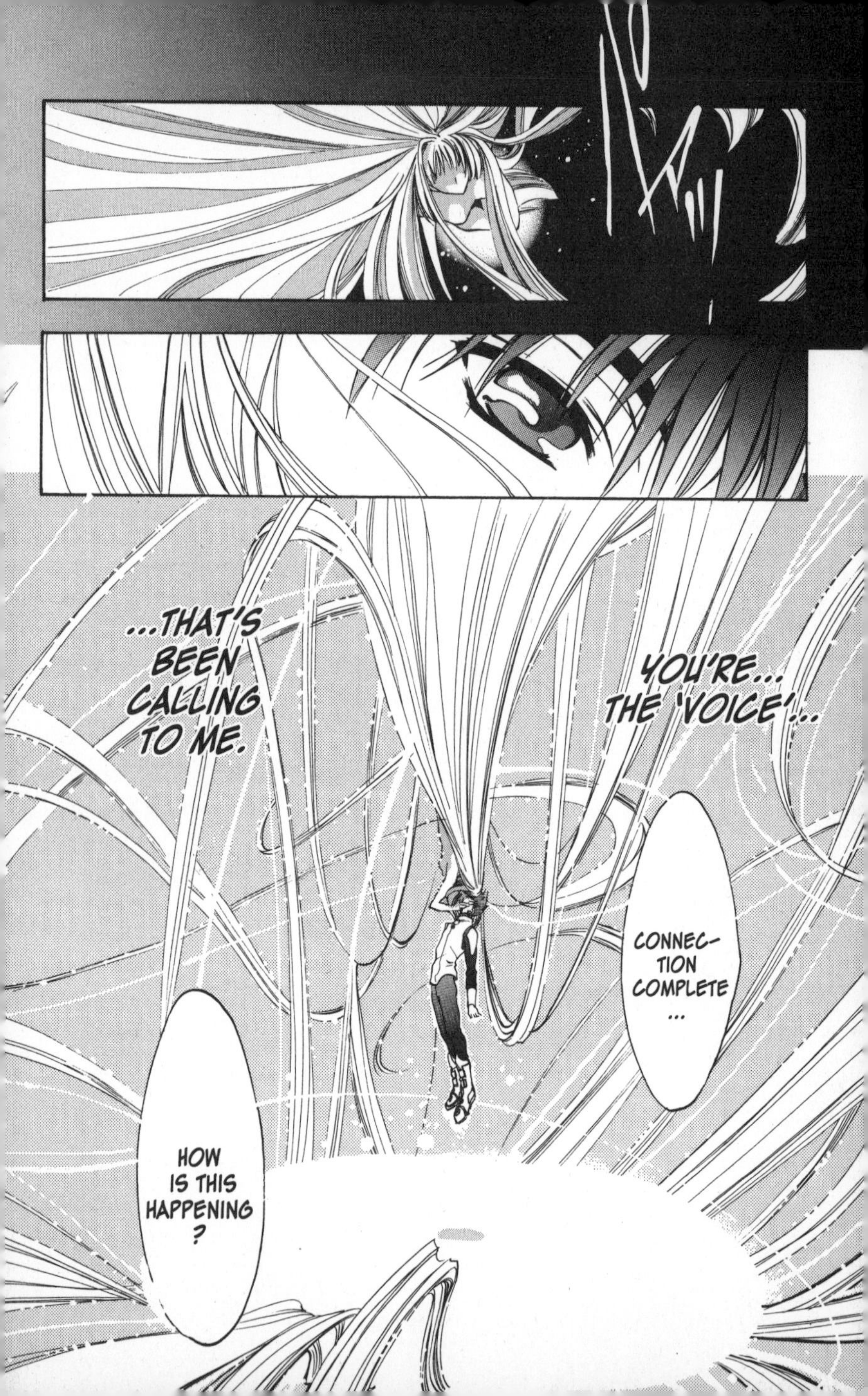
YOU'RE... THE 'VOICE'...
...THAT'S BEEN CALLING TO ME.
CONNEC-TION COMPLETE...
HOW IS THIS HAPPENING?

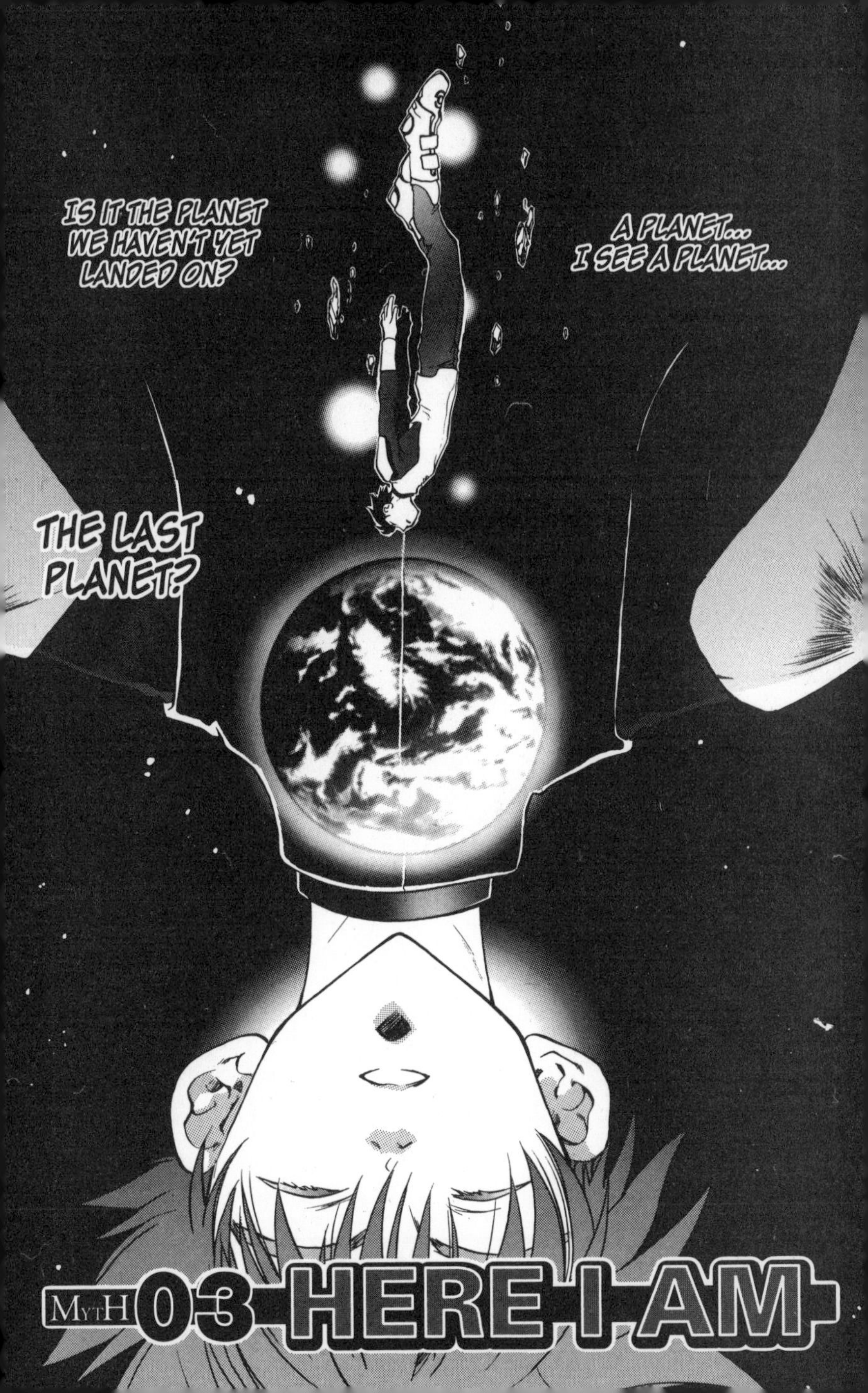
A PLANET... I SEE A PLANET...
IS IT THE PLANET WE HAVEN'T YET LANDED ON?
THE LAST PLANET?
MYTH 03 HERE I AM

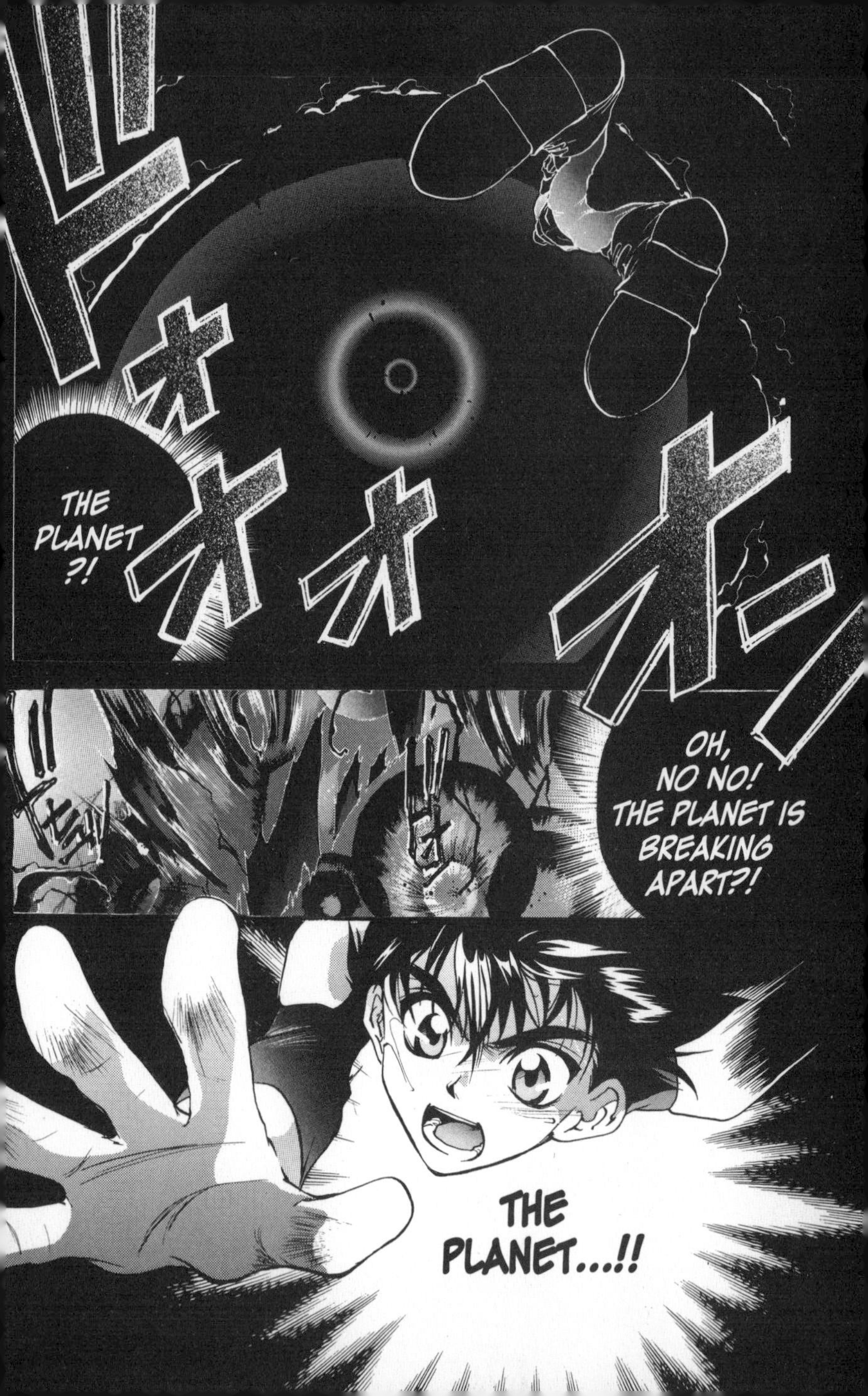
THE PLANET ?!
OH, NO NO! THE PLANET IS BREAKING APART?!
THE PLANET...!!

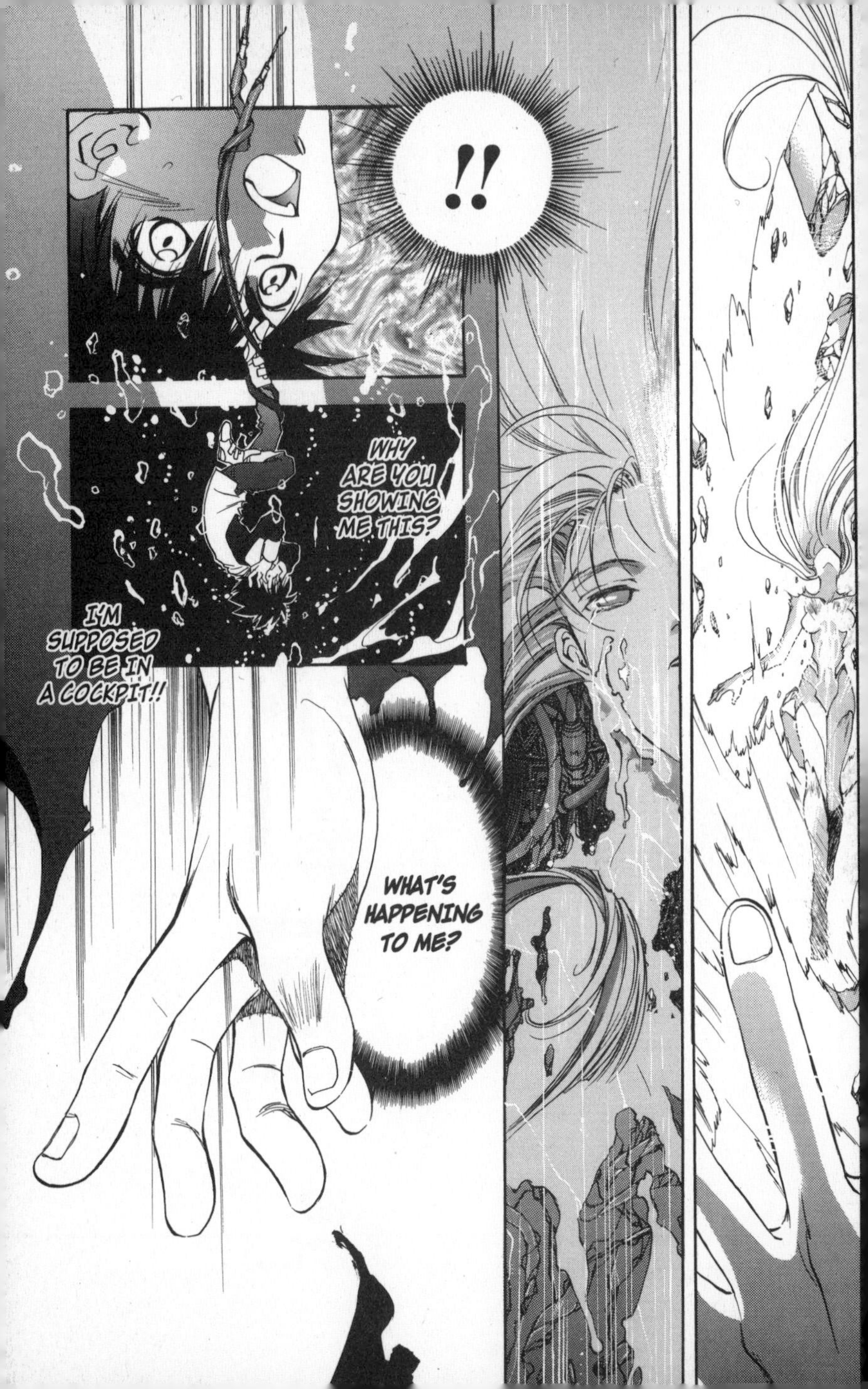
!!
WHY ARE YOU SHOWING ME THIS?
I'M SUPPOSED TO BE IN A COCKPIT!!
WHAT'S HAPPENING TO ME?

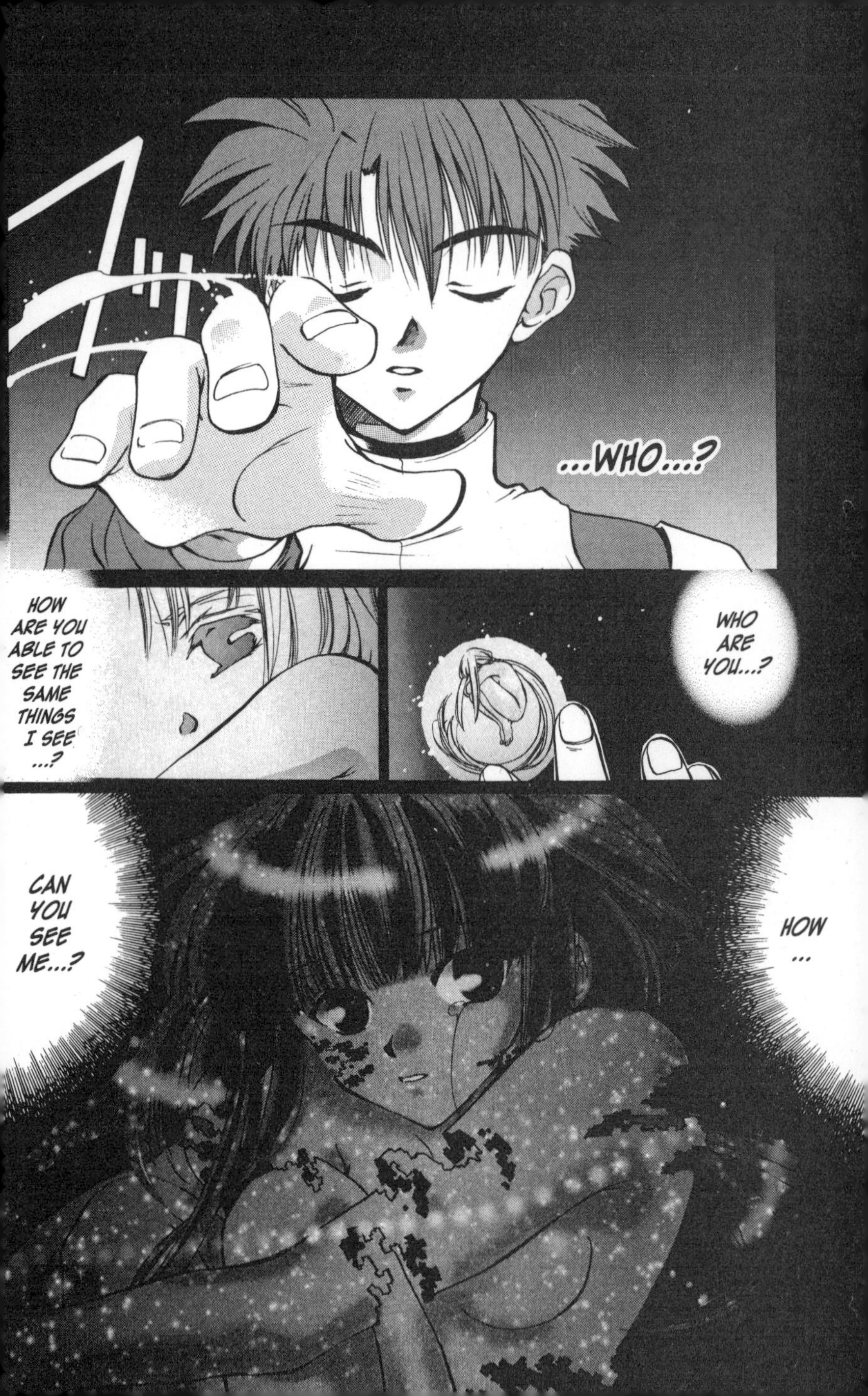
...WHO...?
WHO ARE YOU...?
HOW ARE YOU ABLE TO SEE THE SAME THINGS I SEE ...?
HOW ...
CAN YOU SEE ME...?

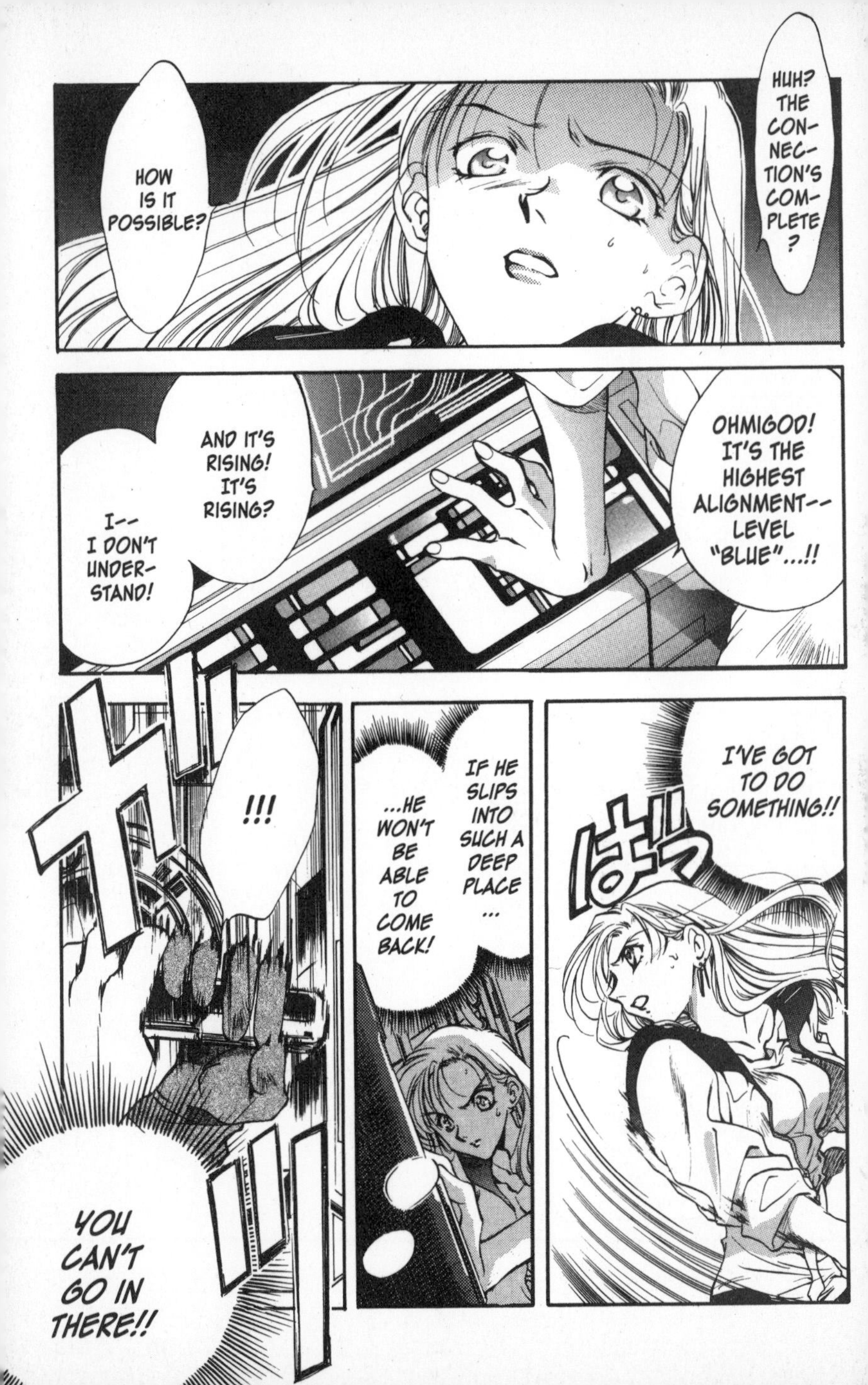
HUH? THE CON-NEC-TION'S COM-PLETE?
HOW IS IT POSSIBLE?
OHMIGOD! IT'S THE HIGHEST ALIGNMENT--LEVEL "BLUE"...!!
AND IT'S RISING! IT'S RISING?
I-- I DON'T UNDER-STAND!
I'VE GOT TO DO SOMETHING!!
はっ
IF HE SLIPS INTO SUCH A DEEP PLACE ...
...HE WON'T BE ABLE TO COME BACK!
!!!
YOU CAN'T GO IN THERE!!

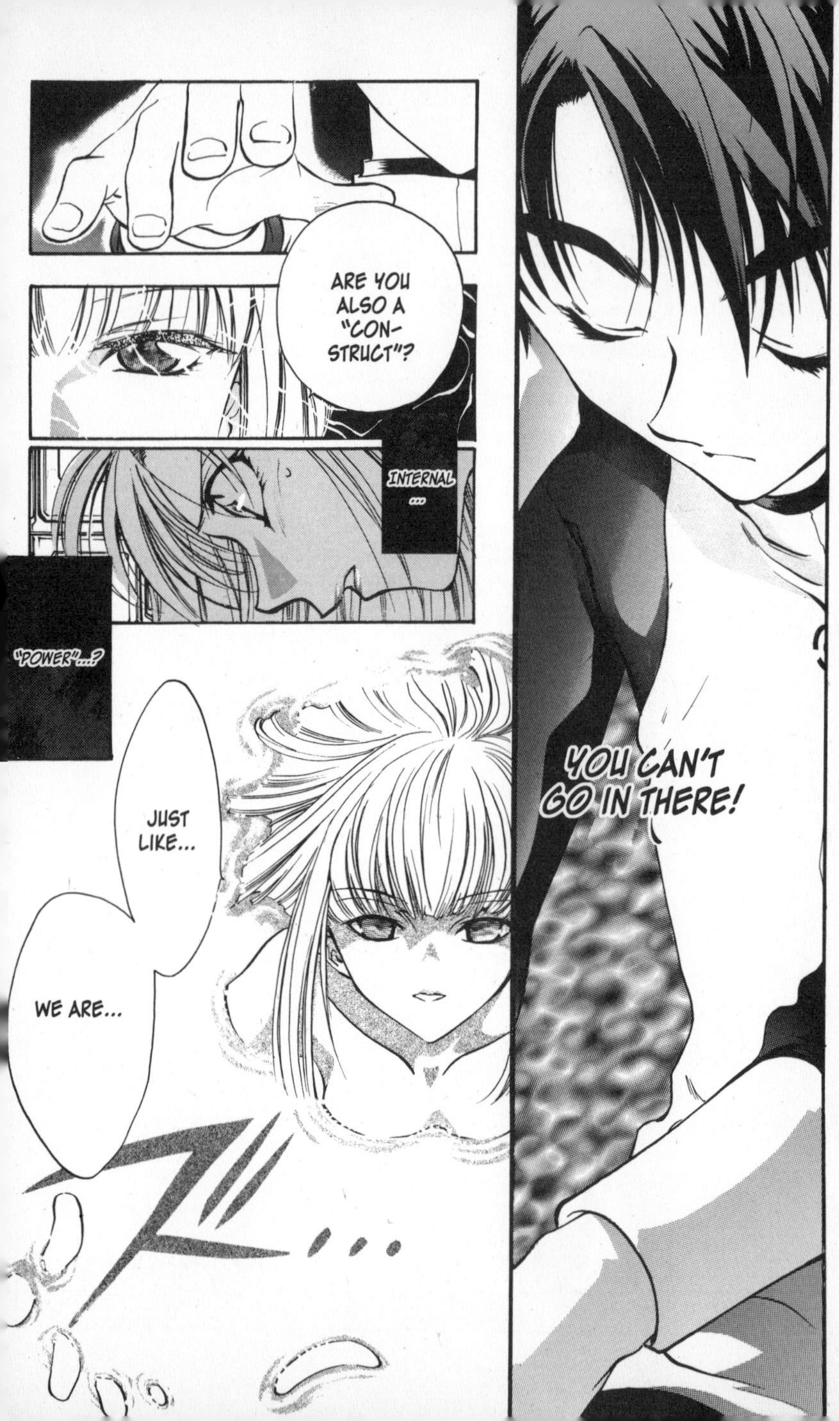
YOU CAN'T GO IN THERE!
ARE YOU ALSO A "CON-STRUCT"?
INTERNAL ...
"POWER"...?
JUST LIKE...
WE ARE...
Z'...

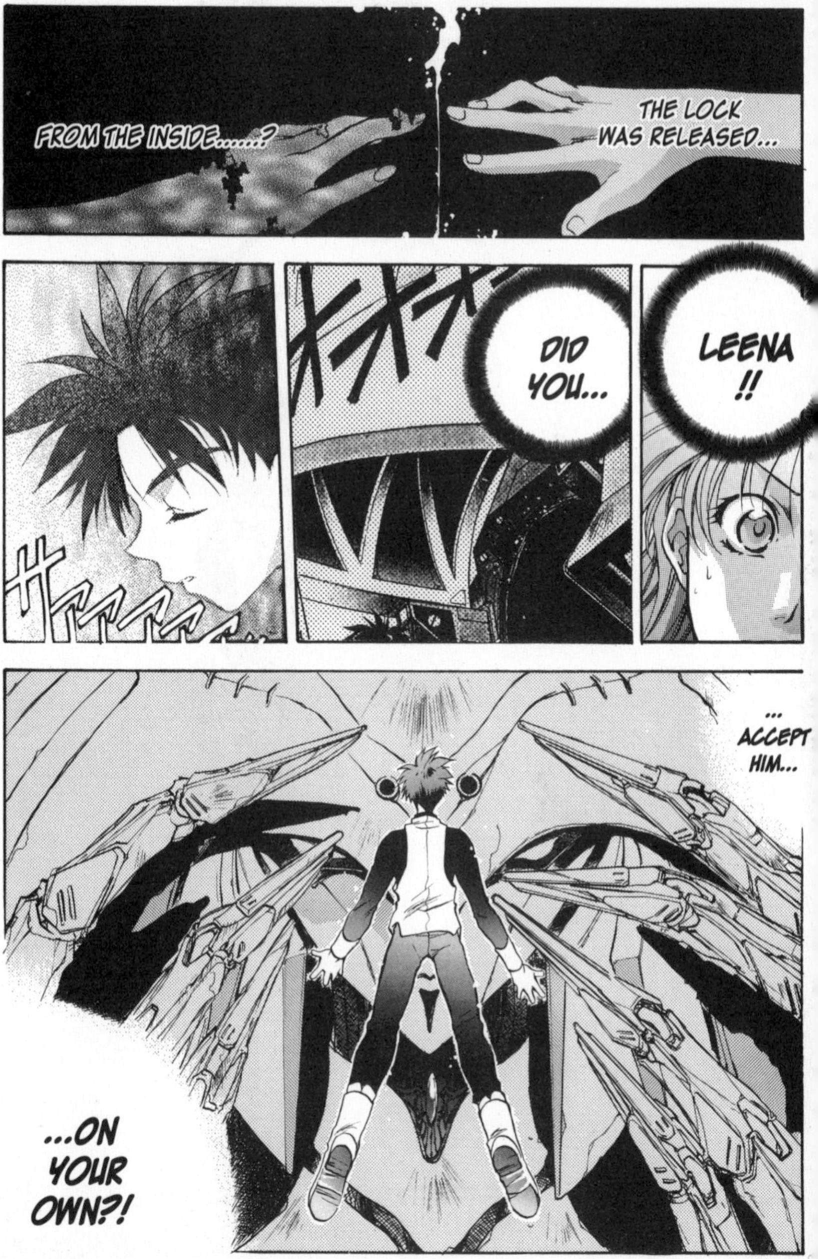
THE LOCK WAS RELEASED...
FROM THE INSIDE......?
LEENA !!
DID YOU...
...ACCEPT HIM...
...ON YOUR OWN?!

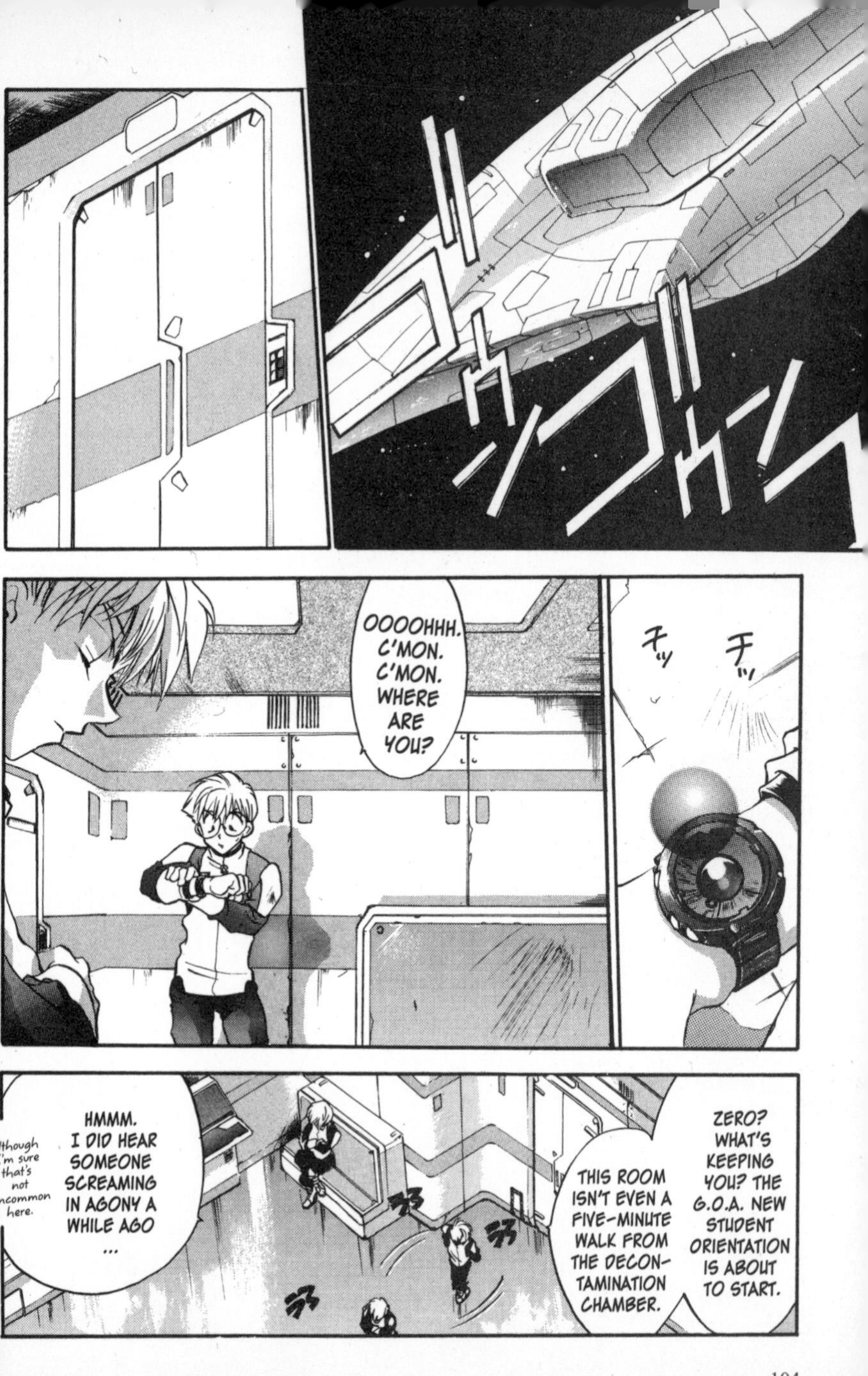
チッ
チッ
OOOOHHH. C'MON. C'MON. WHERE ARE YOU?
ZERO? WHAT'S KEEPING YOU? THE G.O.A. NEW STUDENT ORIENTATION IS ABOUT TO START.
THIS ROOM ISN'T EVEN A FIVE-MINUTE WALK FROM THE DECON-TAMINATION CHAMBER.
HMMM. I DID HEAR SOMEONE SCREAMING IN AGONY A WHILE AGO ...
Although I'm sure that's not uncommon here.

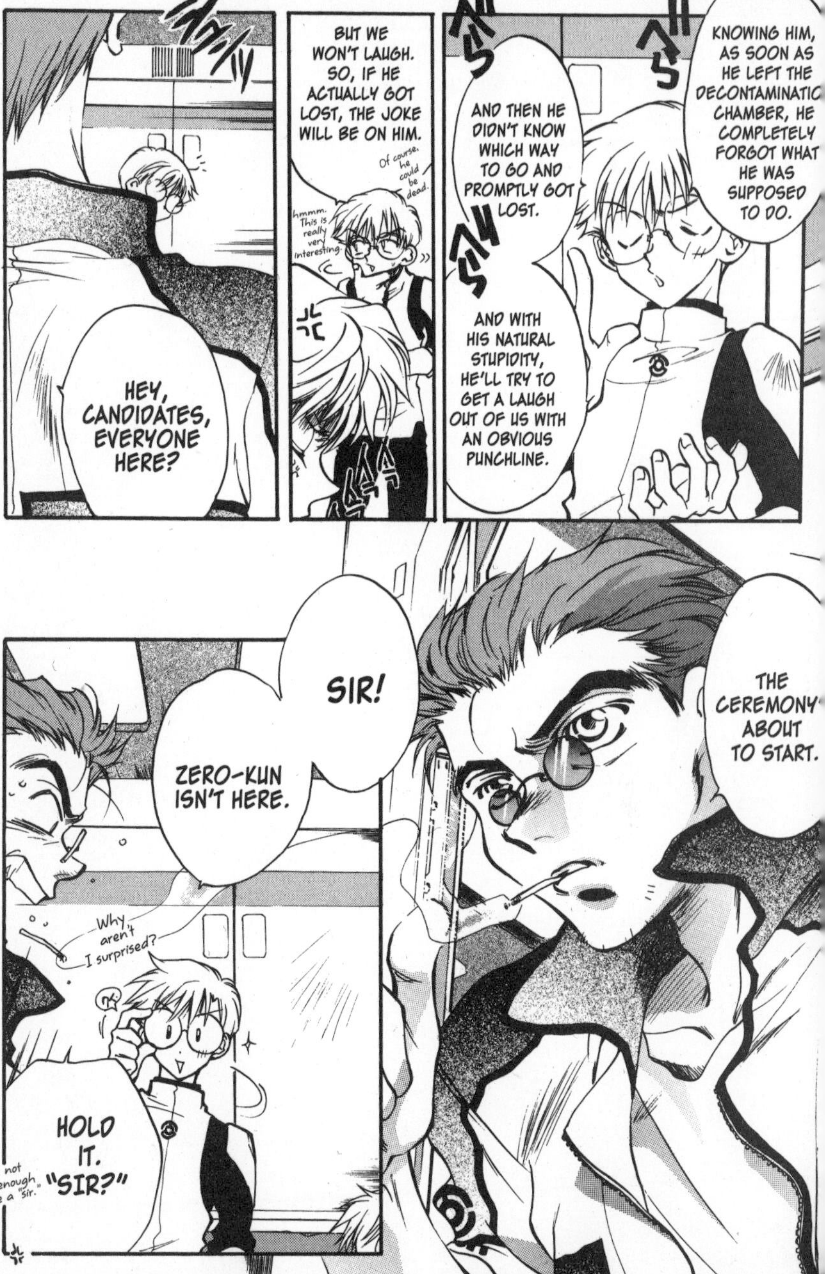
KNOWING HIM, AS SOON AS HE LEFT THE DECONTAMINATIC CHAMBER, HE COMPLETELY FORGOT WHAT HE WAS SUPPOSED TO DO.
AND THEN HE DIDN'T KNOW WHICH WAY TO GO AND PROMPTLY GOT LOST.
AND WITH HIS NATURAL STUPIDITY, HE'LL TRY TO GET A LAUGH OUT OF US WITH AN OBVIOUS PUNCHLINE.
BUT WE WON'T LAUGH. SO, IF HE ACTUALLY GOT LOST, THE JOKE WILL BE ON HIM.
Of course, he could be dead.
hmmm. This is really very interesting.
HEY, CANDIDATES, EVERYONE HERE?
THE CEREMONY ABOUT TO START.
SIR!
ZERO-KUN ISN'T HERE.
Why aren't I surprised?
HOLD IT. "SIR?"
I'm not old enough to be a "sir."

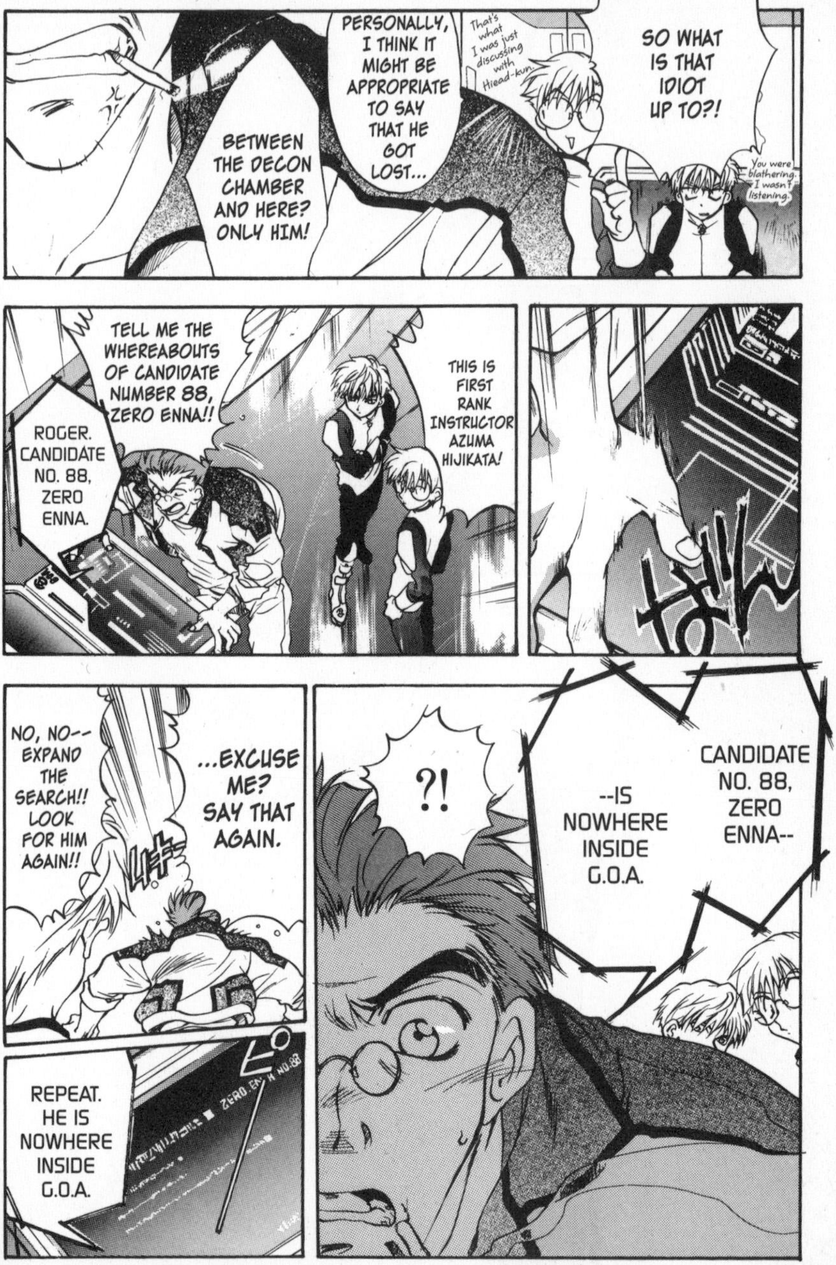
SO WHAT IS THAT IDIOT UP TO?!
You were blathering. I wasn't listening.
That's what I was just discussing with Hiead-kun.
PERSONALLY, I THINK IT MIGHT BE APPROPRIATE TO SAY THAT HE GOT LOST...
BETWEEN THE DECON CHAMBER AND HERE? ONLY HIM!
THIS IS FIRST RANK INSTRUCTOR AZUMA HIJIKATA!
TELL ME THE WHEREABOUTS OF CANDIDATE NUMBER 88, ZERO ENNA!!
ROGER. CANDIDATE NO. 88, ZERO ENNA.
CANDIDATE NO. 88, ZERO ENNA--
--IS NOWHERE INSIDE G.O.A.
?!
...EXCUSE ME? SAY THAT AGAIN.
NO, NO-- EXPAND THE SEARCH!! LOOK FOR HIM AGAIN!!
REPEAT. HE IS NOWHERE INSIDE G.O.A.

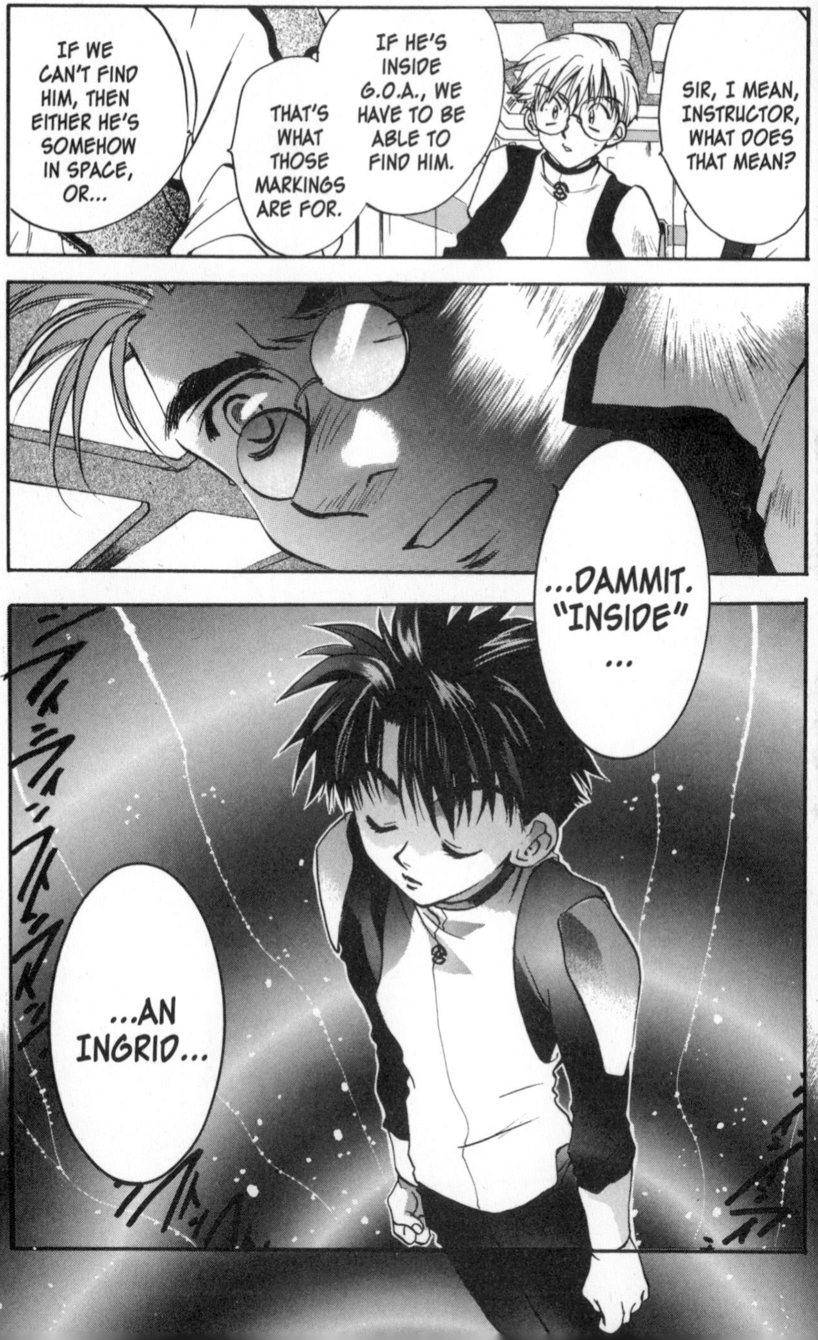
SIR, I MEAN, INSTRUCTOR, WHAT DOES THAT MEAN?
IF HE'S INSIDE G.O.A., WE HAVE TO BE ABLE TO FIND HIM.
THAT'S WHAT THOSE MARKINGS ARE FOR.
IF WE CAN'T FIND HIM, THEN EITHER HE'S SOMEHOW IN SPACE, OR...
...DAMMIT. "INSIDE" ...
...AN INGRID...

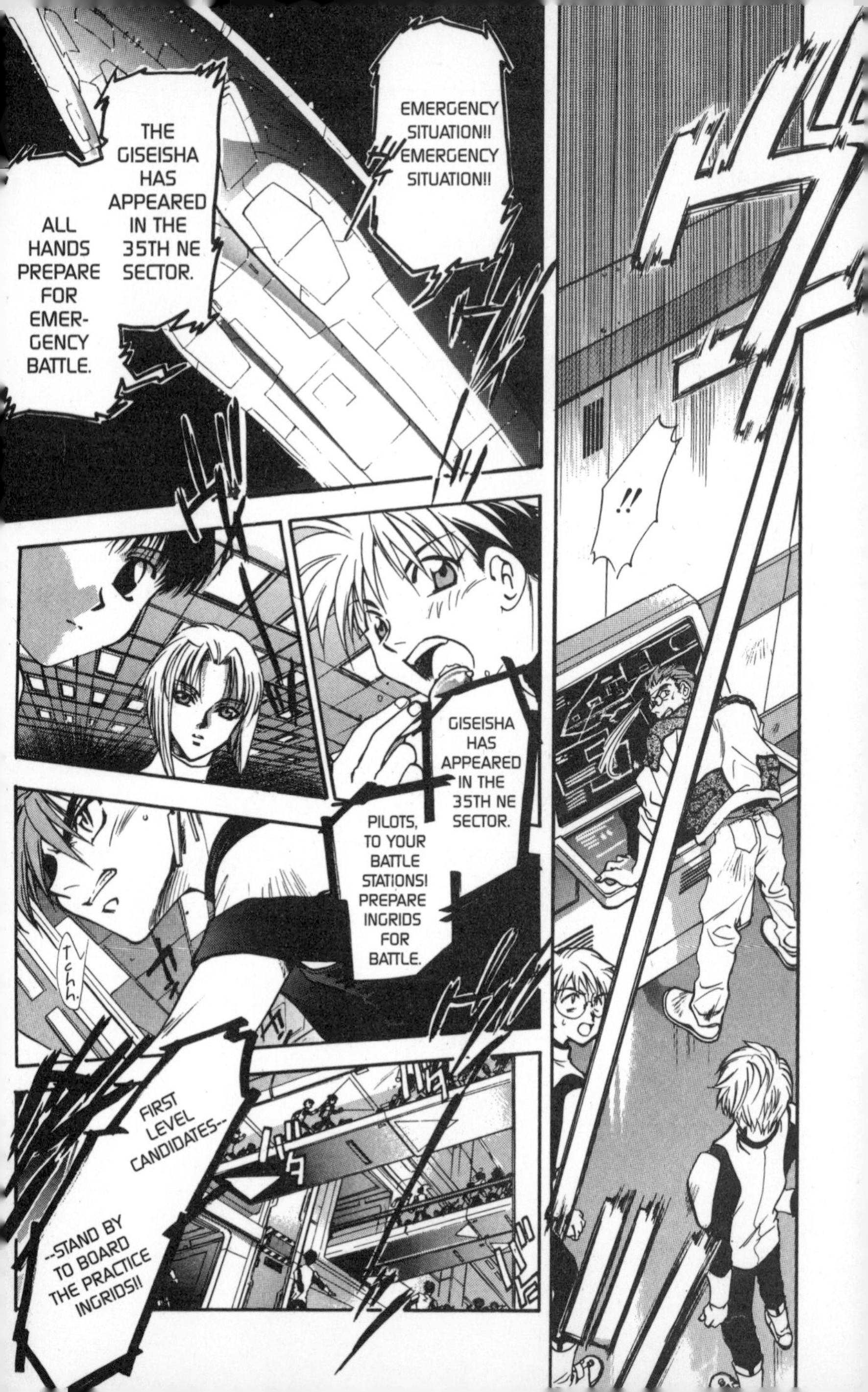
!!
EMERGENCY SITUATION!! EMERGENCY SITUATION!!
THE GISEISHA HAS APPEARED IN THE 35TH NE SECTOR.
ALL HANDS PREPARE FOR EMER-GENCY BATTLE.
GISEISHA HAS APPEARED IN THE 35TH NE SECTOR.
PILOTS, TO YOUR BATTLE STATIONS! PREPARE INGRIDS FOR BATTLE.
Tchh.
FIRST LEVEL CANDIDATES--
--STAND BY TO BOARD THE PRACTICE INGRIDS!!

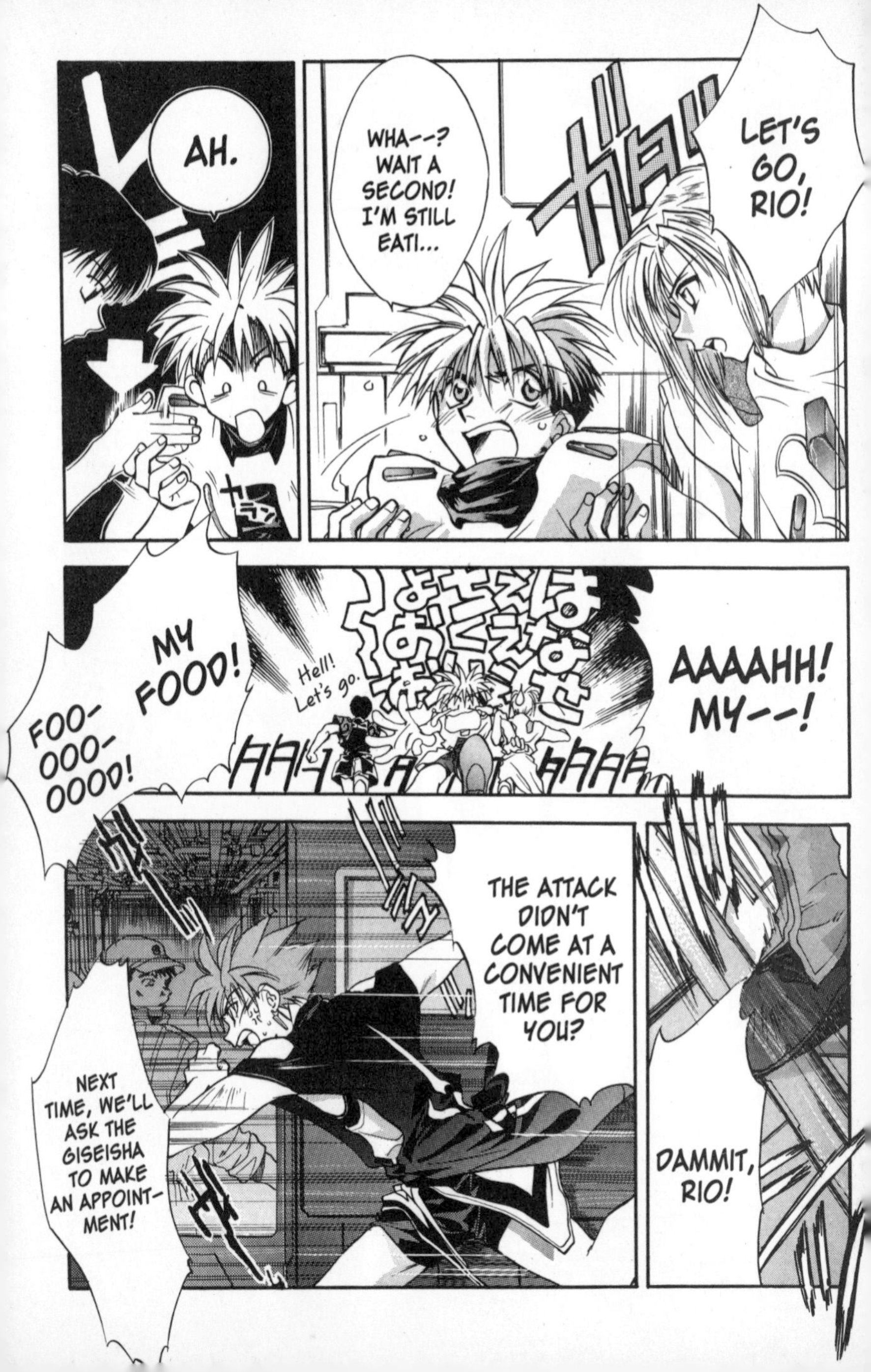
LET'S GO, RIO!
WHA--? WAIT A SECOND! I'M STILL EATI...
AH.
AAAAHH! MY--!
Hell! Let's go.
MY FOOD!
FOO-OOO-OOOD!
DAMMIT, RIO!
THE ATTACK DIDN'T COME AT A CONVENIENT TIME FOR YOU?
NEXT TIME, WE'LL ASK THE GISEISHA TO MAKE AN APPOINTMENT!

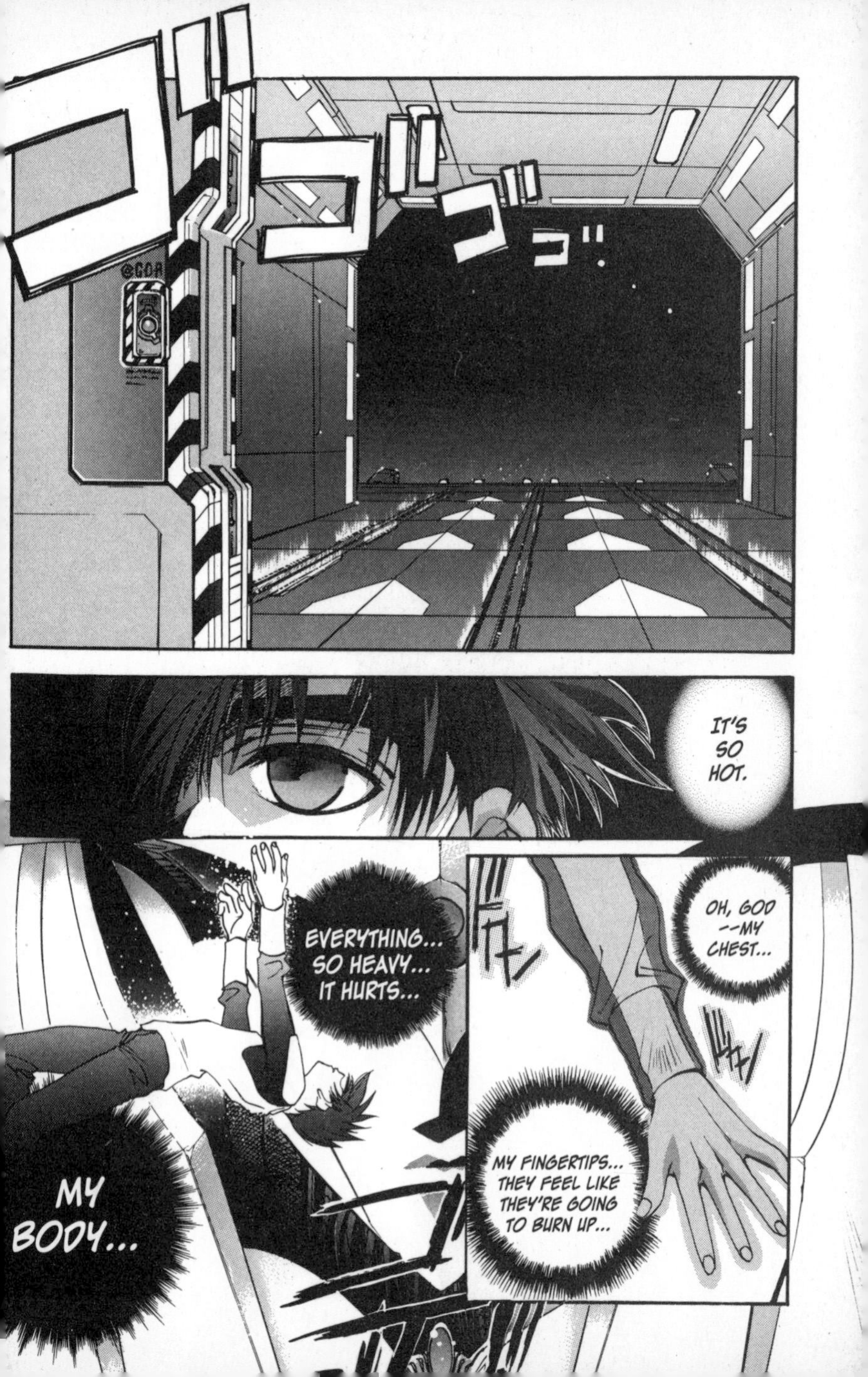
ゴゴゴゴ
IT'S SO HOT.
OH, GOD --MY CHEST...
MY FINGERTIPS... THEY FEEL LIKE THEY'RE GOING TO BURN UP...
EVERYTHING... SO HEAVY... IT HURTS...
MY BODY...

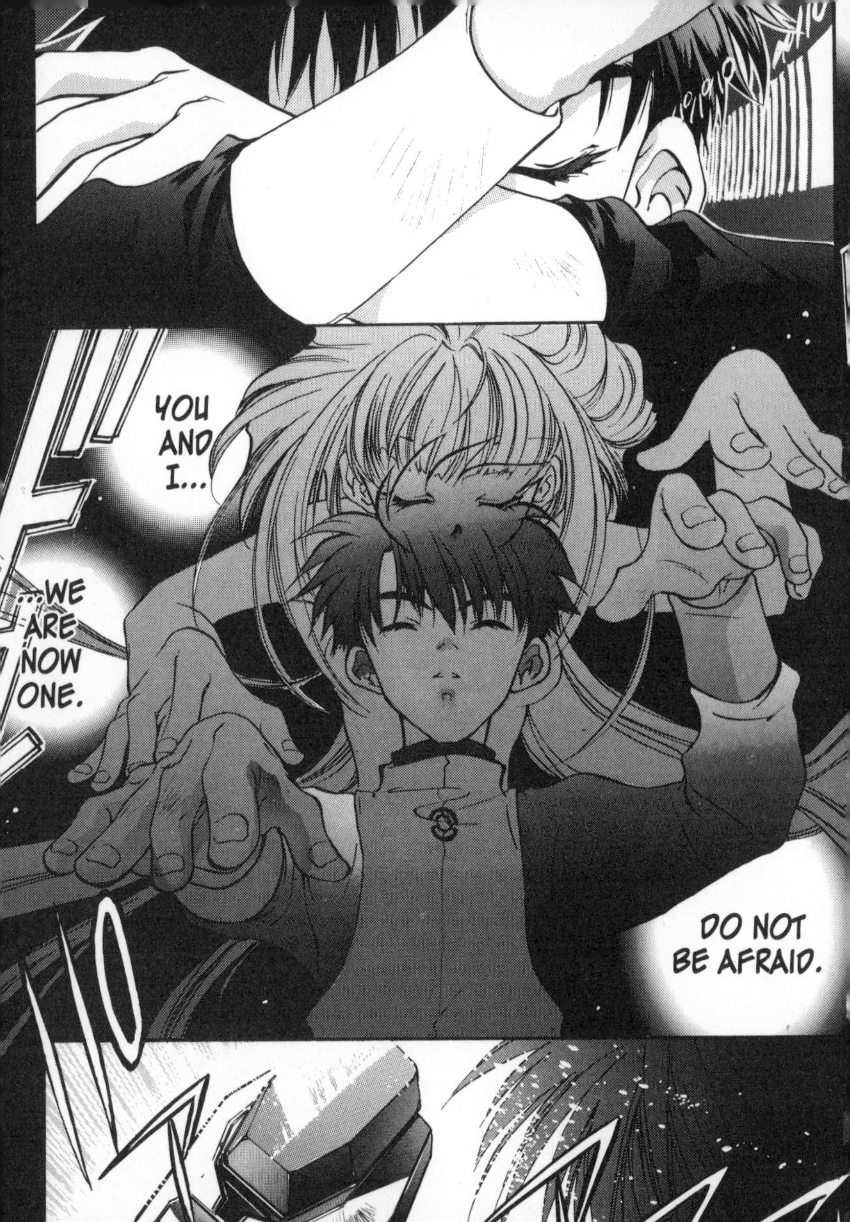
YOU AND I...
...WE ARE NOW ONE.
DO NOT BE AFRAID.

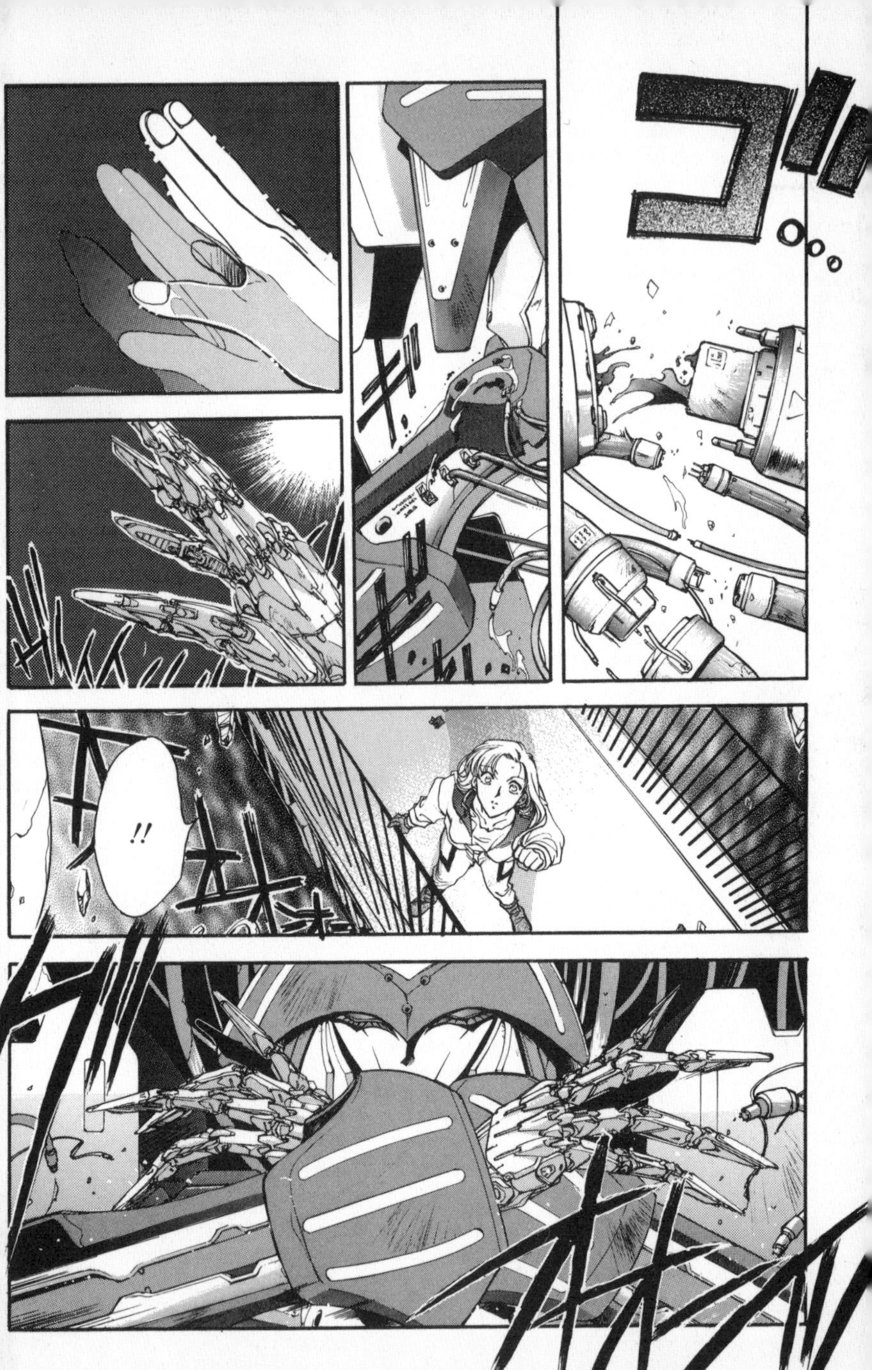
!!

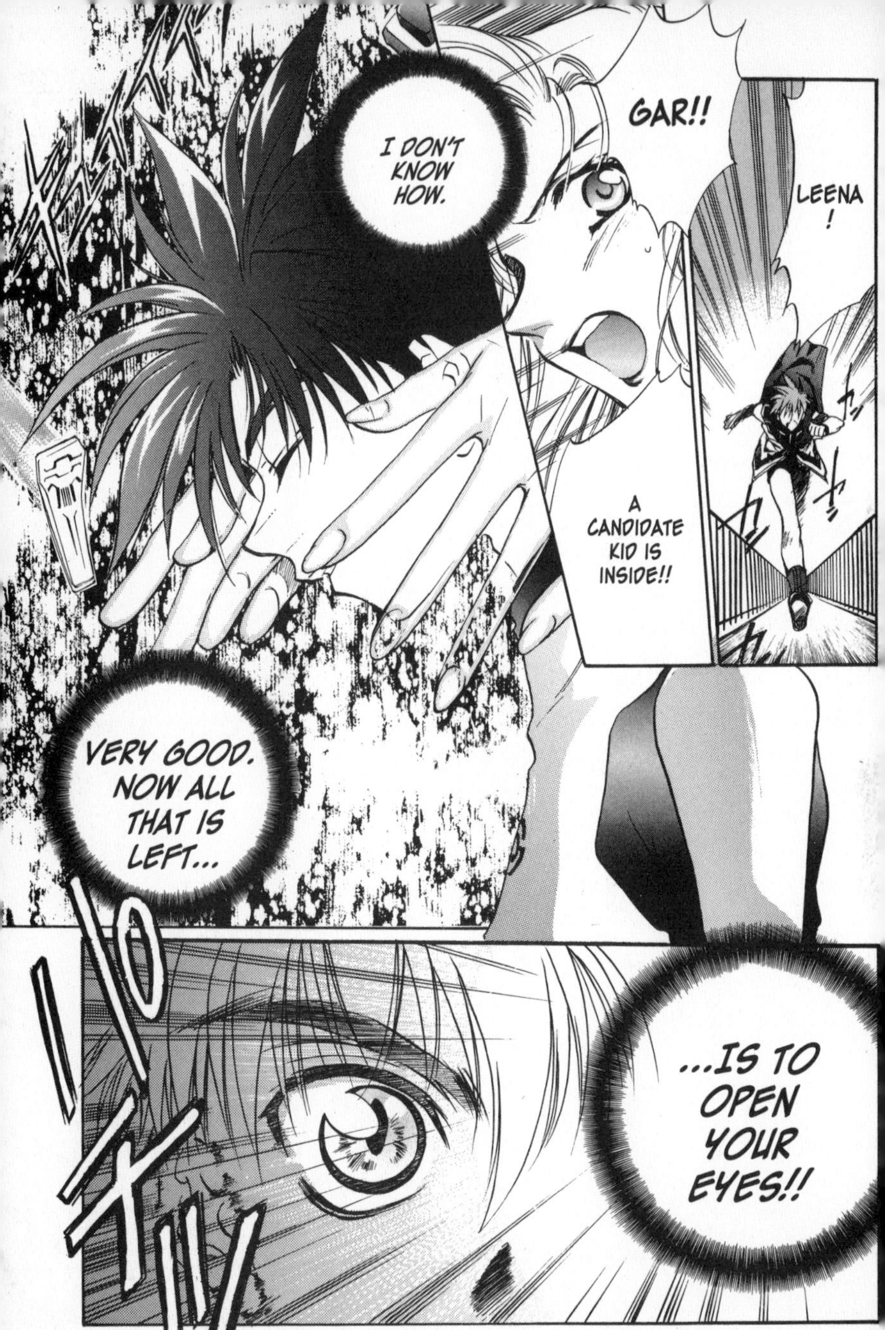
LEENA !
GAR!!
A CANDIDATE KID IS INSIDE!!
I DON'T KNOW HOW.
VERY GOOD. NOW ALL THAT IS LEFT...
...IS TO OPEN YOUR EYES!!

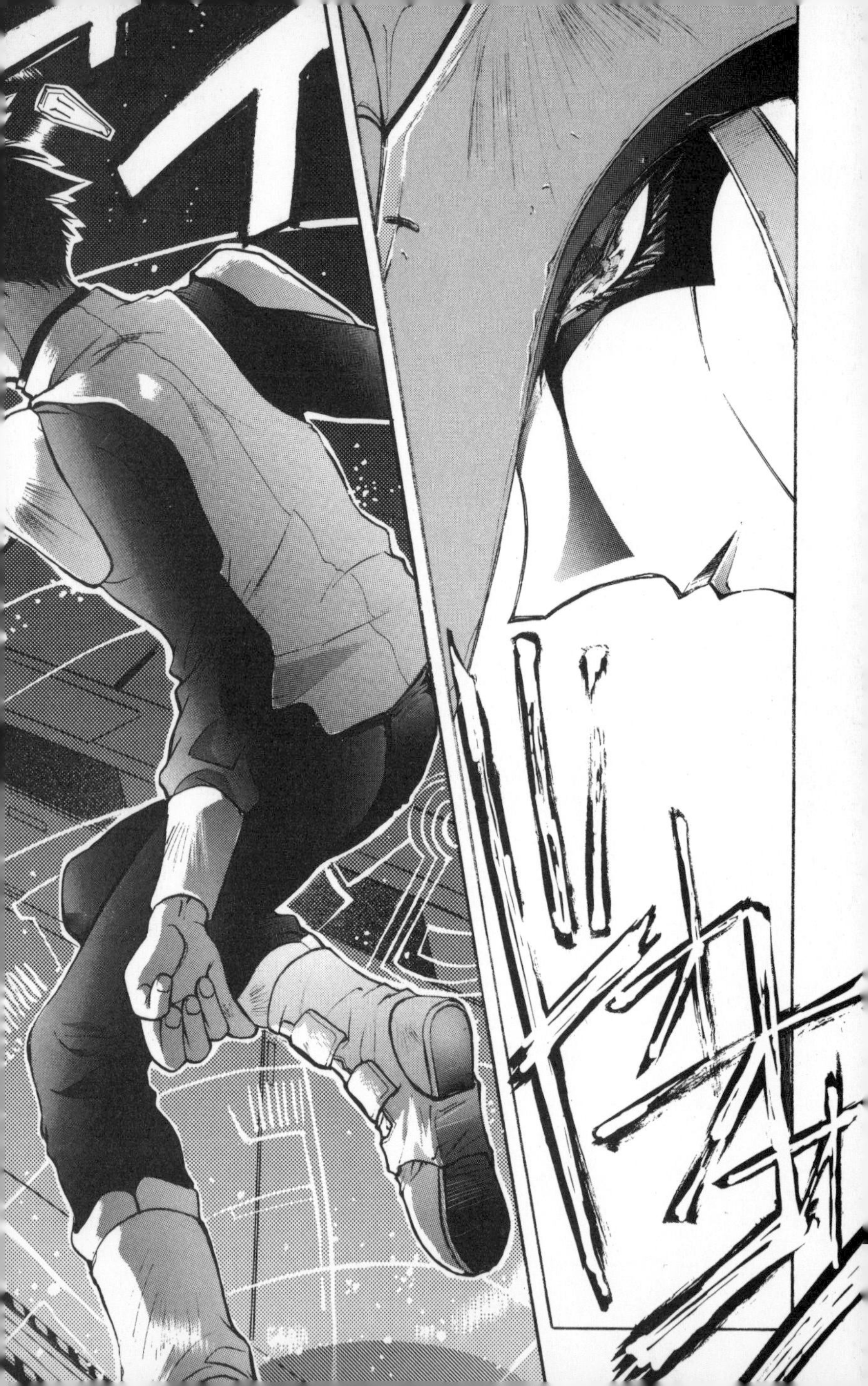

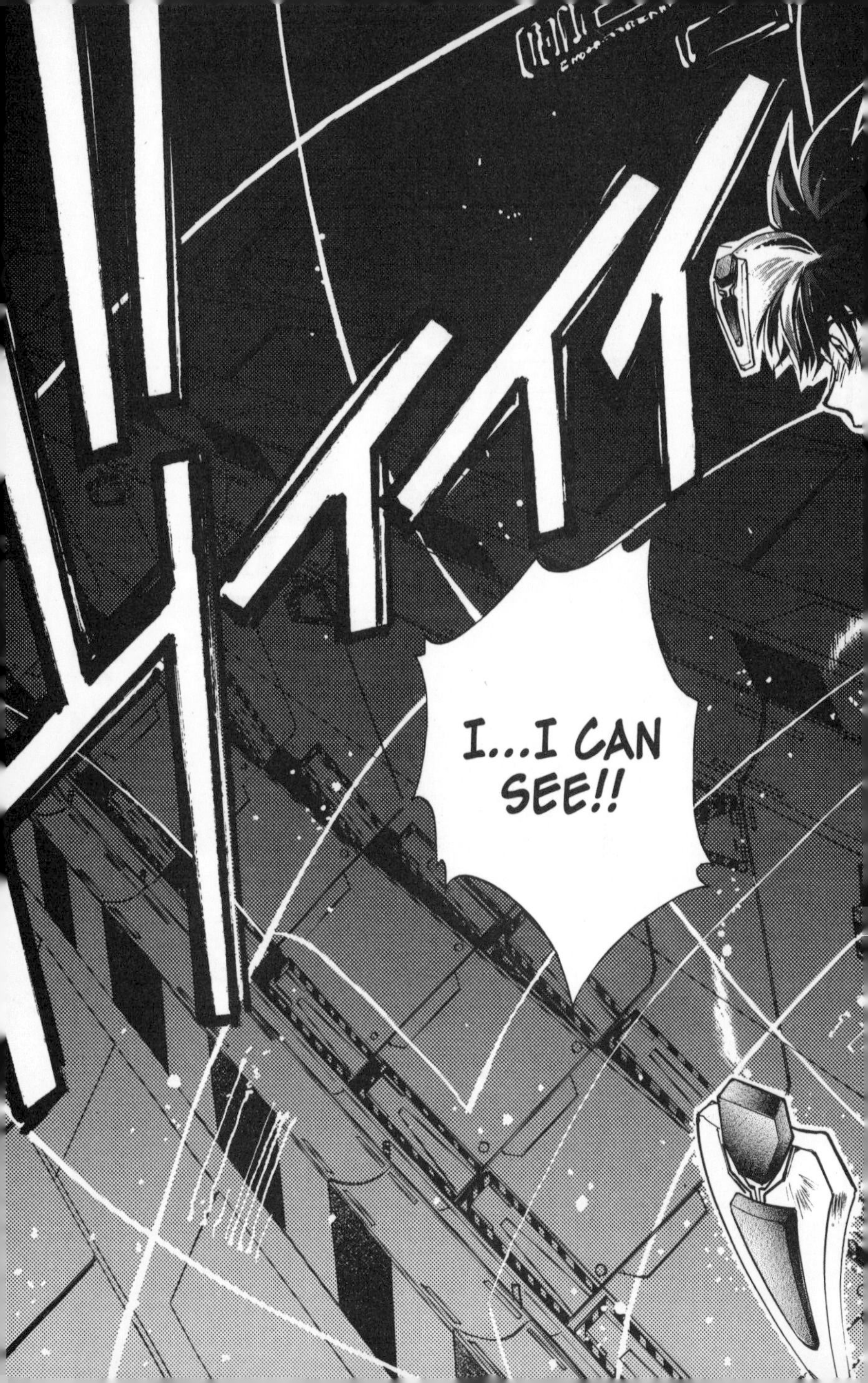
I...I CAN SEE!!

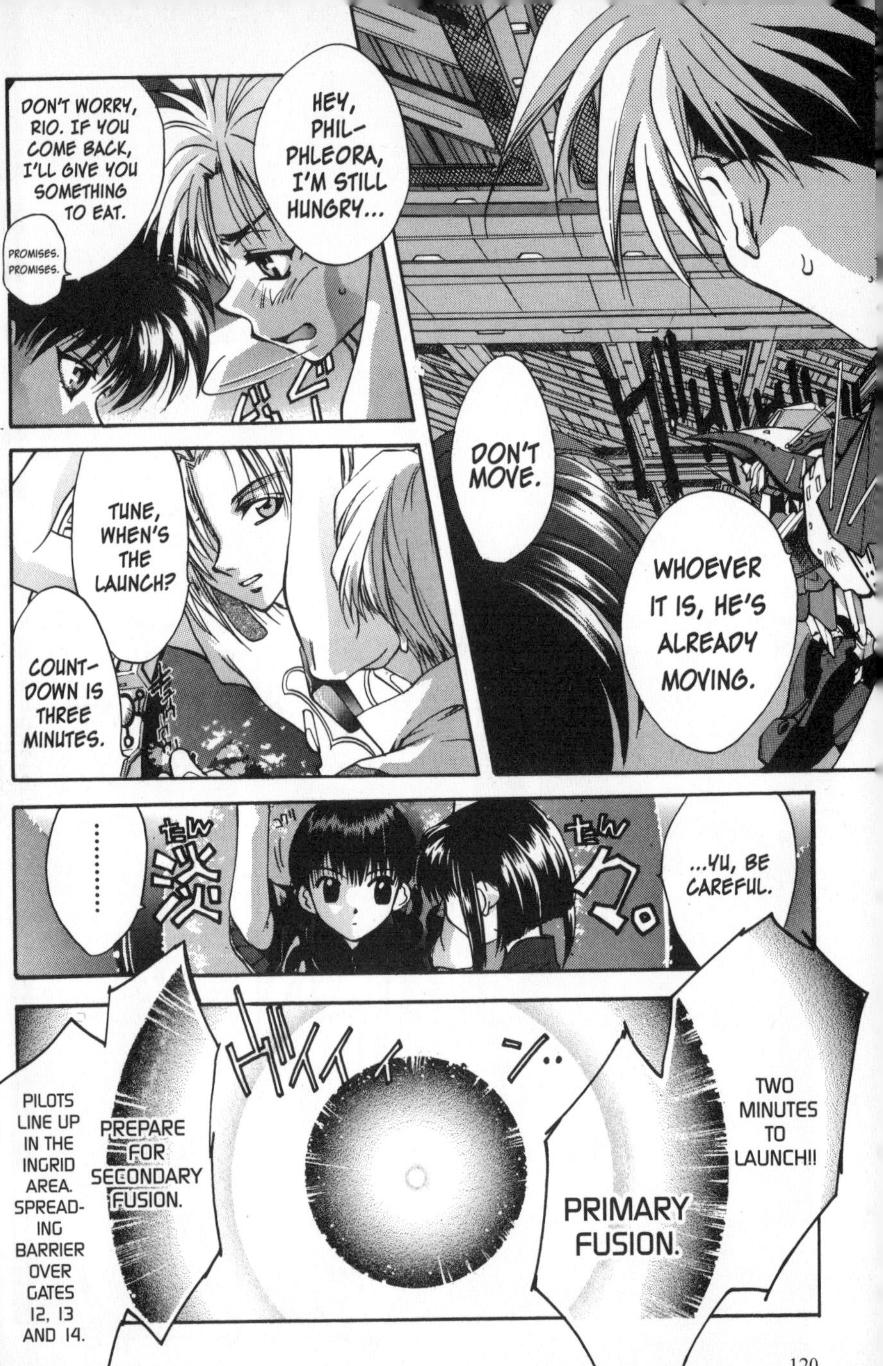
DON'T MOVE.
WHOEVER IT IS, HE'S ALREADY MOVING.
HEY, PHIL-PHLEORA, I'M STILL HUNGRY...
DON'T WORRY, RIO. IF YOU COME BACK, I'LL GIVE YOU SOMETHING TO EAT.
PROMISES. PROMISES.
TUNE, WHEN'S THE LAUNCH?
COUNT-DOWN IS THREE MINUTES.
...YU, BE CAREFUL.
....
TWO MINUTES TO LAUNCH!!
PRIMARY FUSION.
PREPARE FOR SECONDARY FUSION.
PILOTS LINE UP IN THE INGRID AREA. SPREAD-ING BARRIER OVER GATES 12, 13 AND 14.

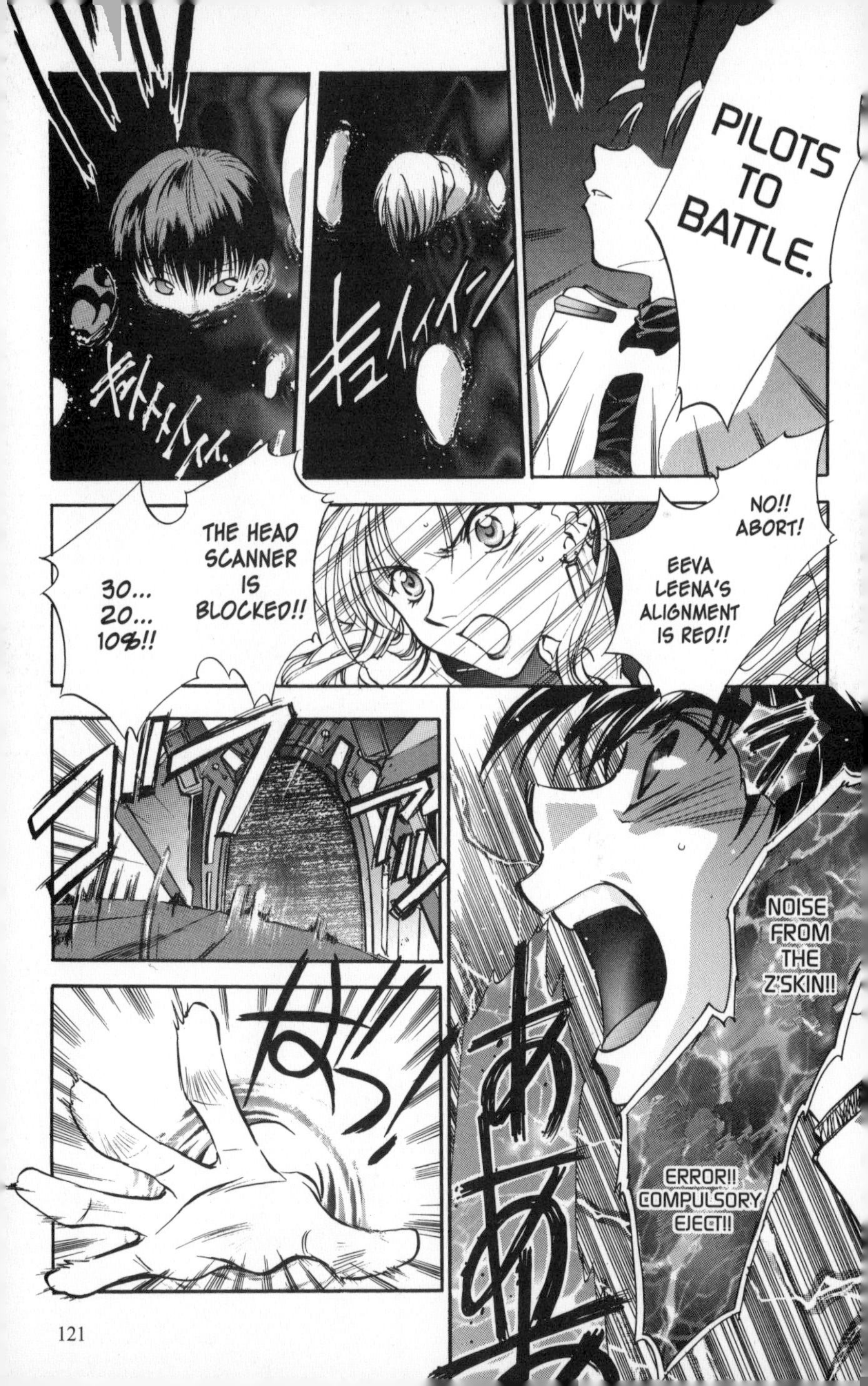
PILOTS TO BATTLE.
NO!! ABORT!
EEVA LEENA'S ALIGNMENT IS RED!!
THE HEAD SCANNER IS BLOCKED!!
30... 20... 10%!!
NOISE FROM THE Z'SKIN!!
ERROR!! COMPULSORY EJECT!!

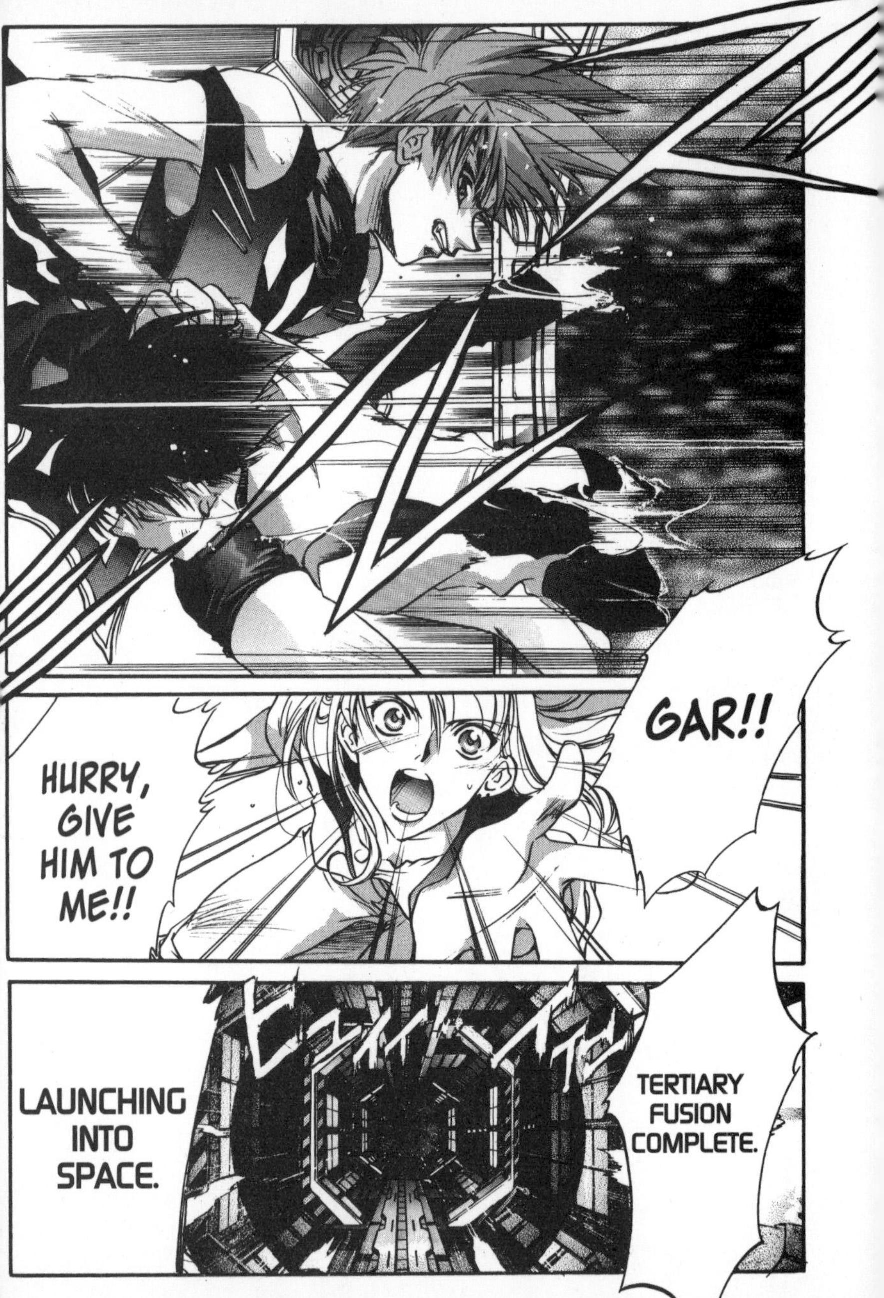

GAR!!
HURRY, GIVE HIM TO ME!!
TERTIARY FUSION COMPLETE.
LAUNCHING INTO SPACE.

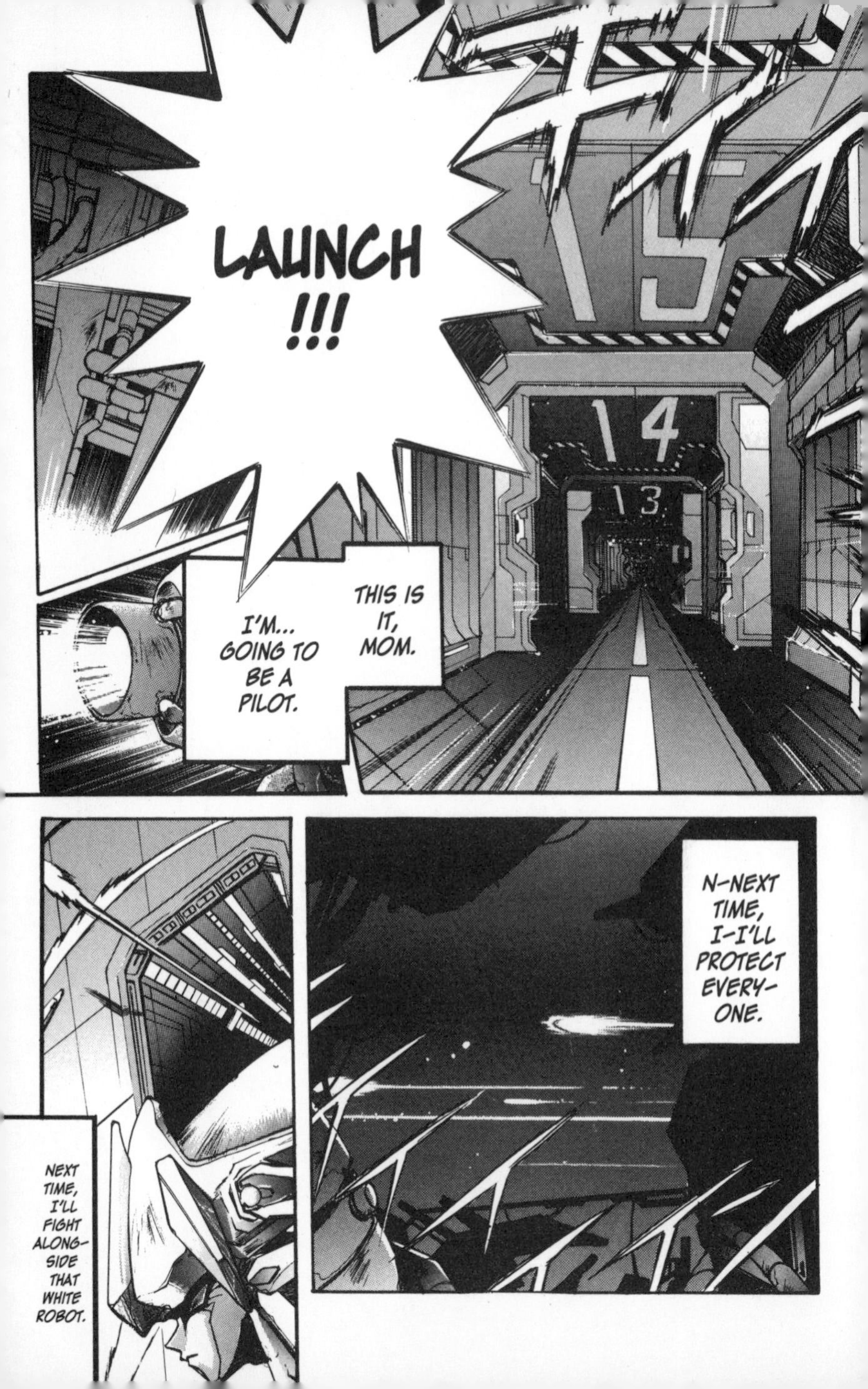
LAUNCH !!!
THIS IS IT, MOM.
I'M... GOING TO BE A PILOT.
N-NEXT TIME, I-I'LL PROTECT EVERY-ONE.
NEXT TIME, I'LL FIGHT ALONG-SIDE THAT WHITE ROBOT.

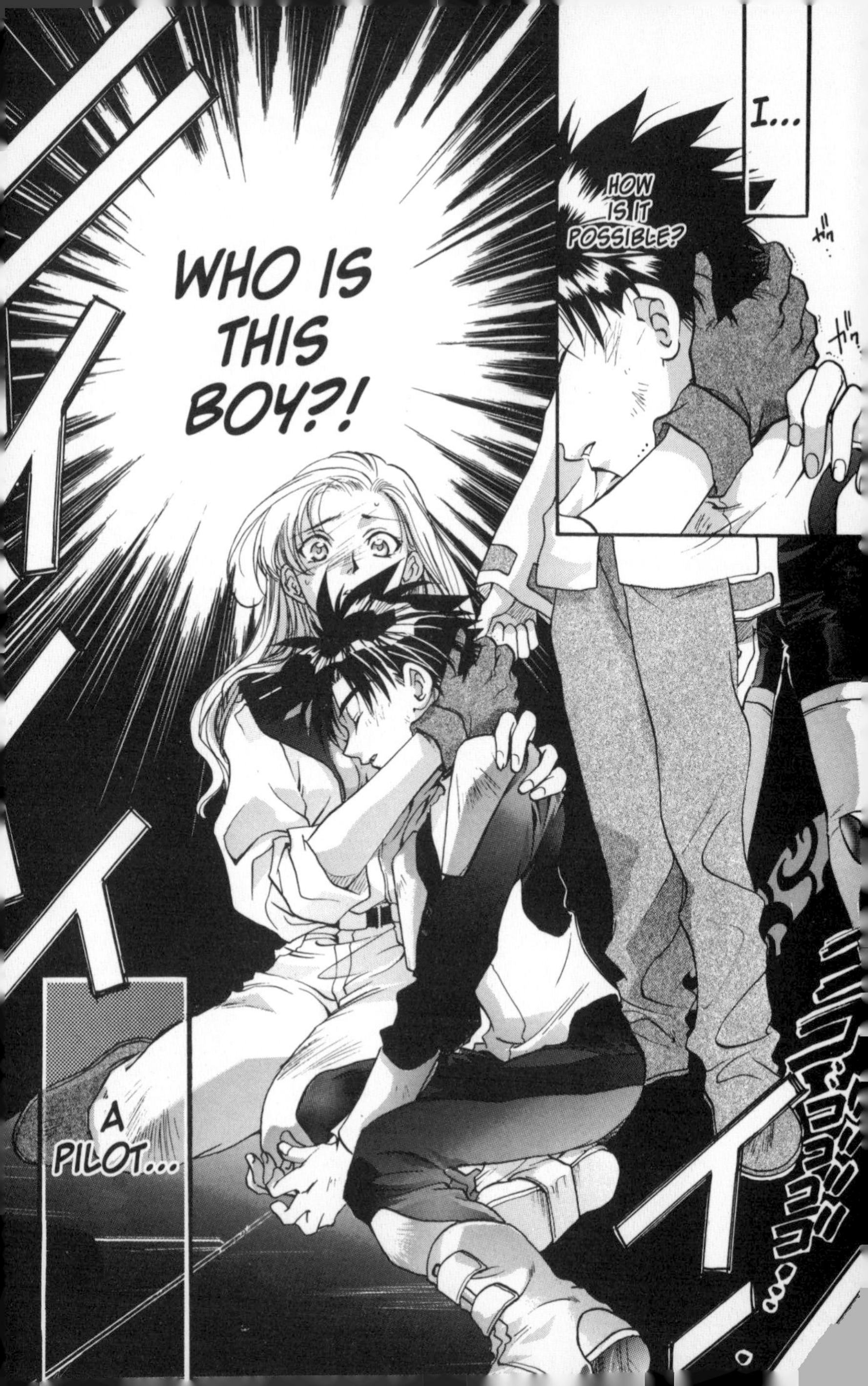
I...
HOW IS IT POSSIBLE?
WHO IS THIS BOY?!
A PILOT...

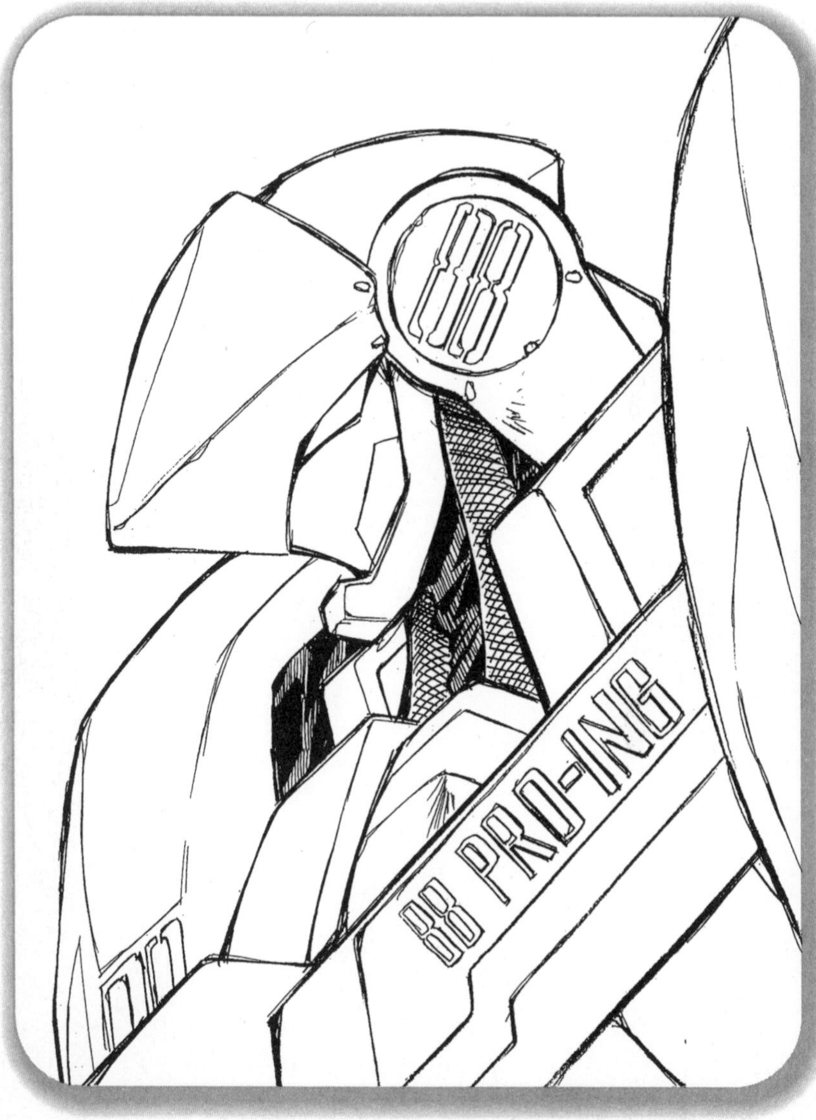
88
88 PRO-ING

the Candidate for goddess

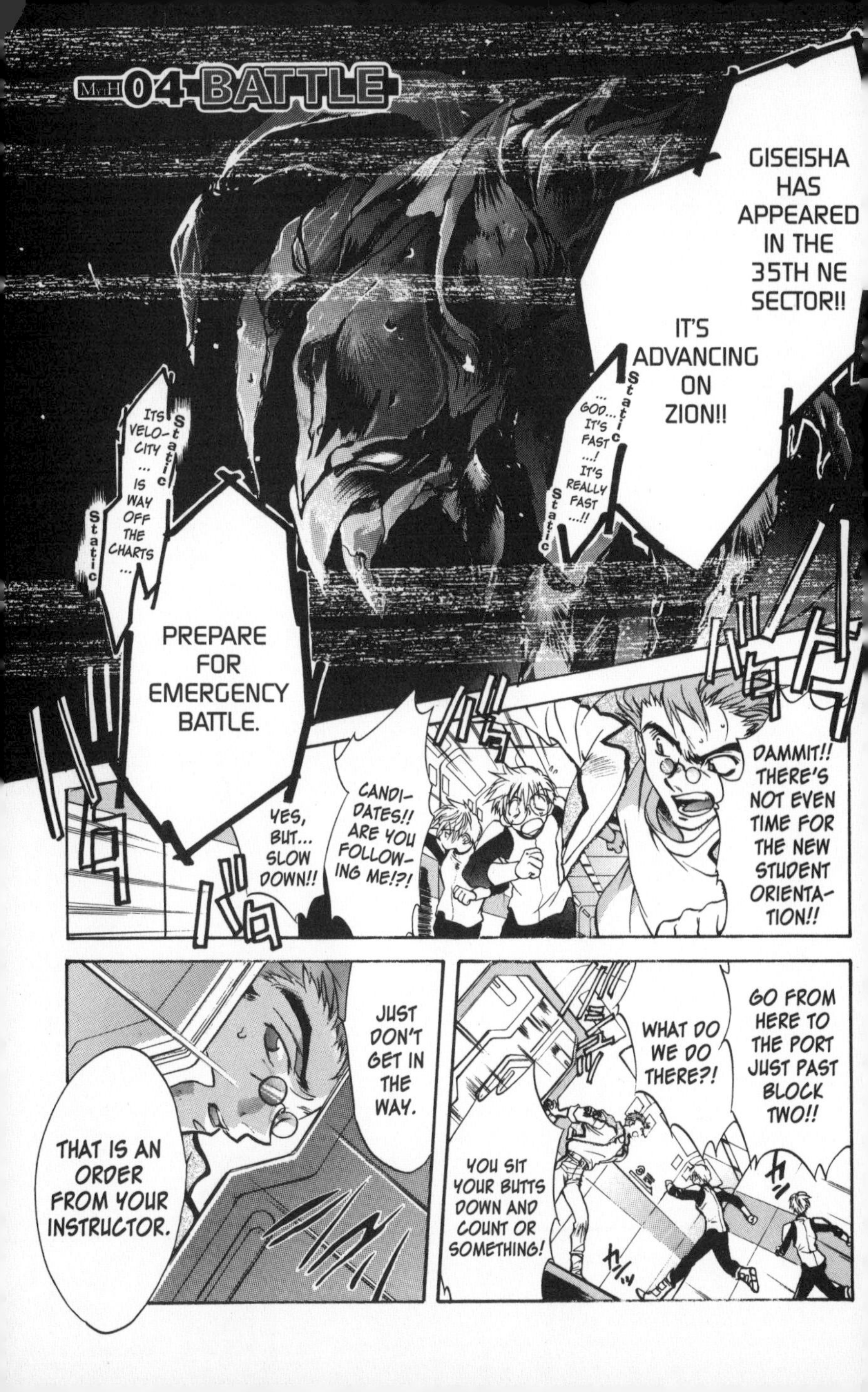
MyH 04 BATTLE
GISEISHA HAS APPEARED IN THE 35TH NE SECTOR!!
IT'S ADVANCING ON ZION!!
Static
... GOD... IT'S FAST ...! IT'S REALLY FAST ...!!
Static
Static
ITS VELOCITY ... IS WAY OFF THE CHARTS ...
Static
PREPARE FOR EMERGENCY BATTLE.
DAMMIT!! THERE'S NOT EVEN TIME FOR THE NEW STUDENT ORIENTATION!!
CANDIDATES!! ARE YOU FOLLOWING ME!?!
YES, BUT... SLOW DOWN!!
GO FROM HERE TO THE PORT JUST PAST BLOCK TWO!!
WHAT DO WE DO THERE?!
YOU SIT YOUR BUTTS DOWN AND COUNT OR SOMETHING!
JUST DON'T GET IN THE WAY.
THAT IS AN ORDER FROM YOUR INSTRUCTOR.

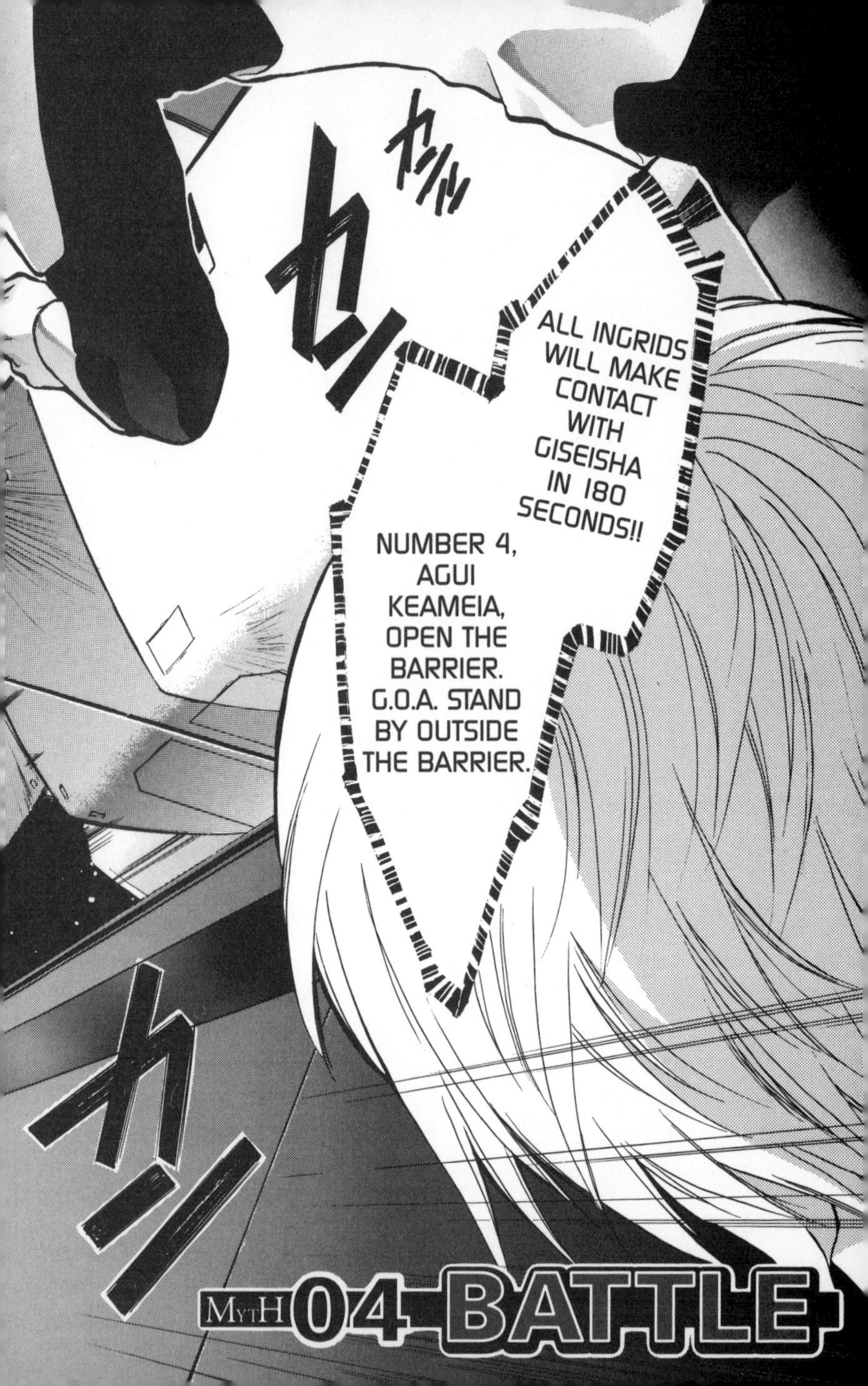
カシャン
ガシャ
ガシャ
ALL INGRIDS WILL MAKE CONTACT WITH GISEISHA IN 180 SECONDS!!
NUMBER 4, AGUI KEAMEIA, OPEN THE BARRIER. G.O.A. STAND BY OUTSIDE THE BARRIER.
MYTH 04 BATTLE

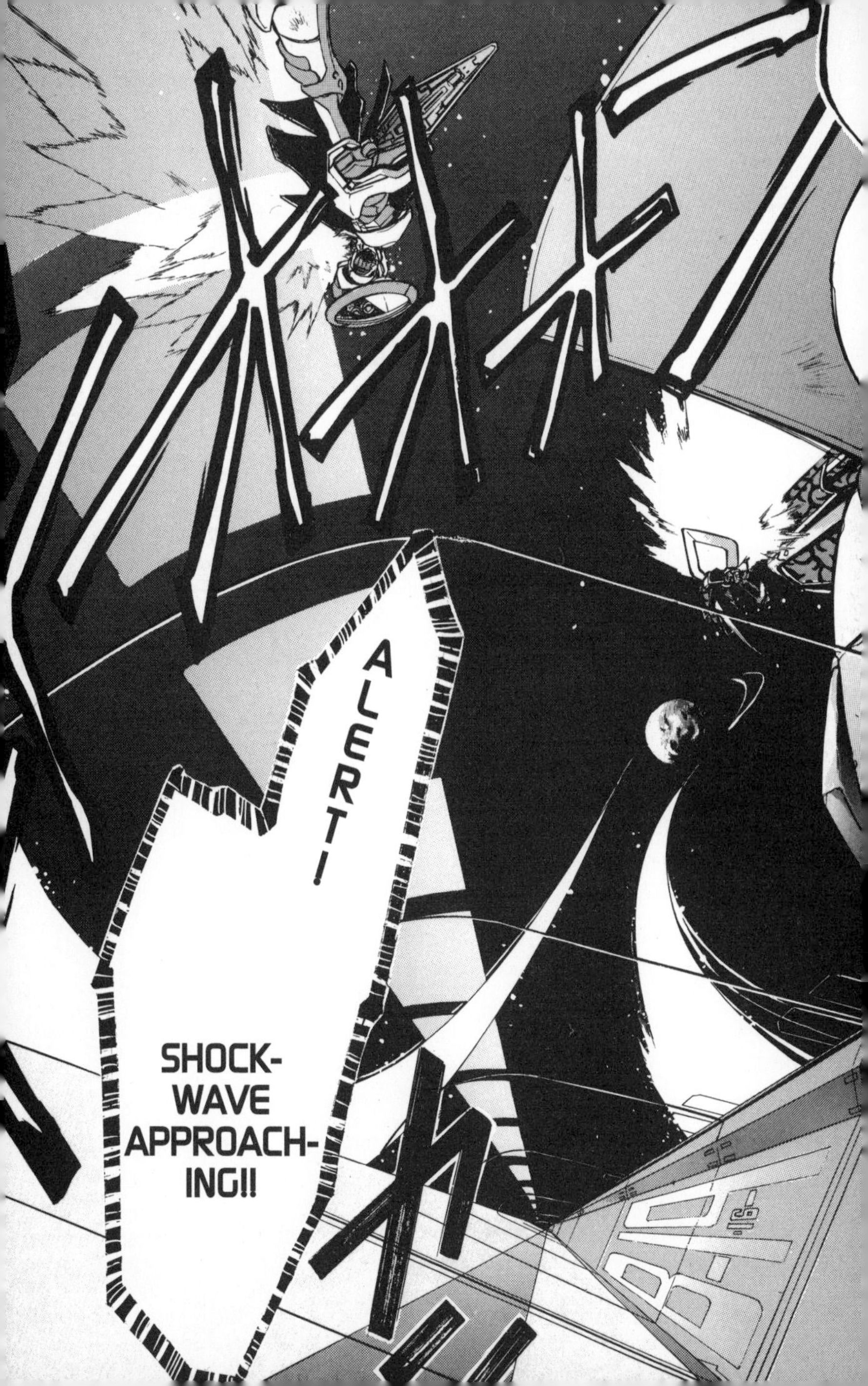
ALERT!
SHOCK-
WAVE
APPROACH-
ING!!

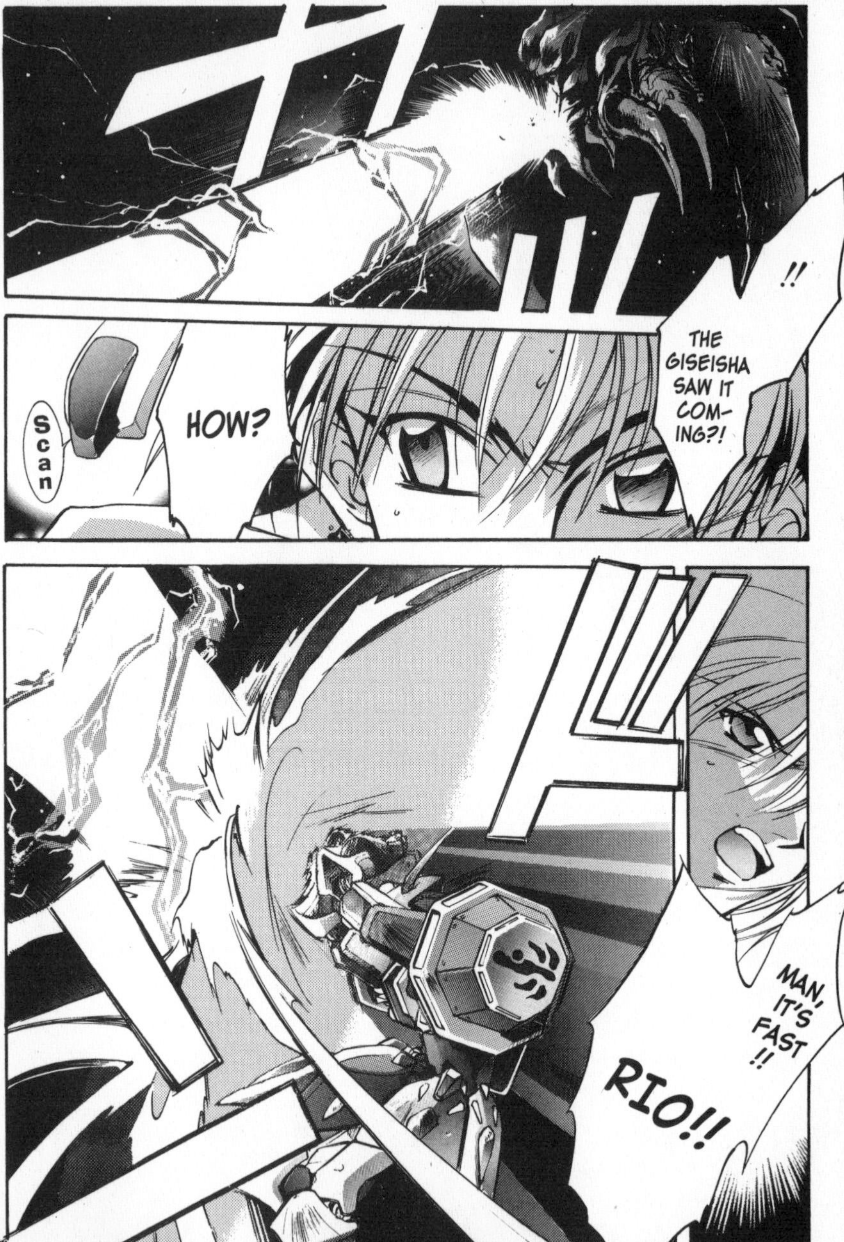
!!
THE GISEISHA SAW IT COMING?!
HOW?
Scan
MAN, IT'S FAST!!
RIO!!

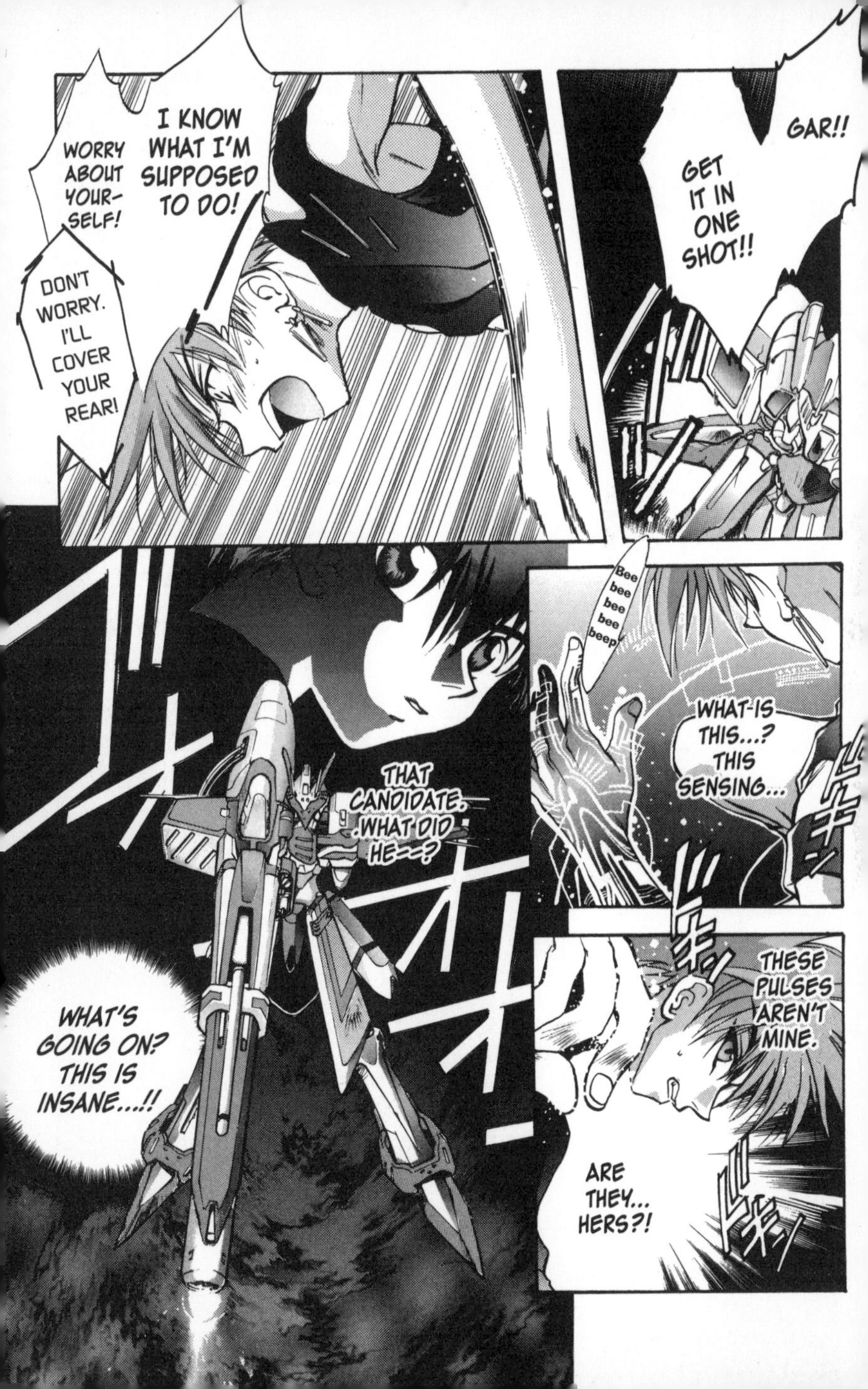
GAR!!
GET IT IN ONE SHOT!!
I KNOW WHAT I'M SUPPOSED TO DO!
WORRY ABOUT YOUR-SELF!
DON'T WORRY. I'LL COVER YOUR REAR!
Bee bee bee bee beep
WHAT-IS THIS...? THIS SENSING...
THESE PULSES AREN'T MINE.
ARE THEY... HERS?!
THAT CANDIDATE. .WHAT DID HE--?
WHAT'S GOING ON? THIS IS INSANE...!!

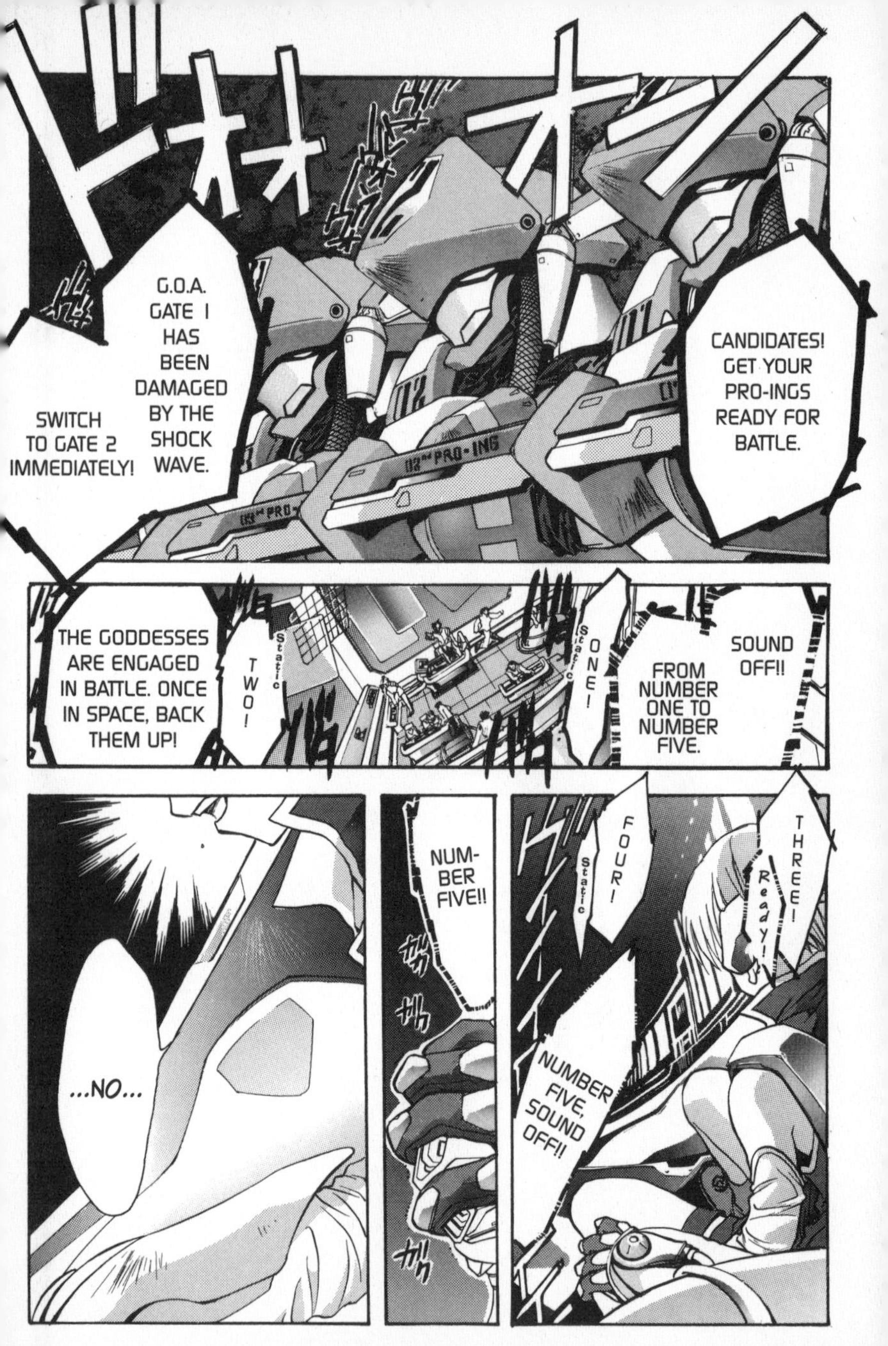
CANDIDATES! GET YOUR PRO-INGS READY FOR BATTLE.
G.O.A. GATE 1 HAS BEEN DAMAGED BY THE SHOCK WAVE.
SWITCH TO GATE 2 IMMEDIATELY!
SOUND OFF!!
FROM NUMBER ONE TO NUMBER FIVE.
Static
ONE!
Static
TWO!
THE GODDESSES ARE ENGAGED IN BATTLE. ONCE IN SPACE, BACK THEM UP!
THREE!
Ready!
Static
FOUR!
NUMBER FIVE, SOUND OFF!!
NUM-BER FIVE!!
...NO...

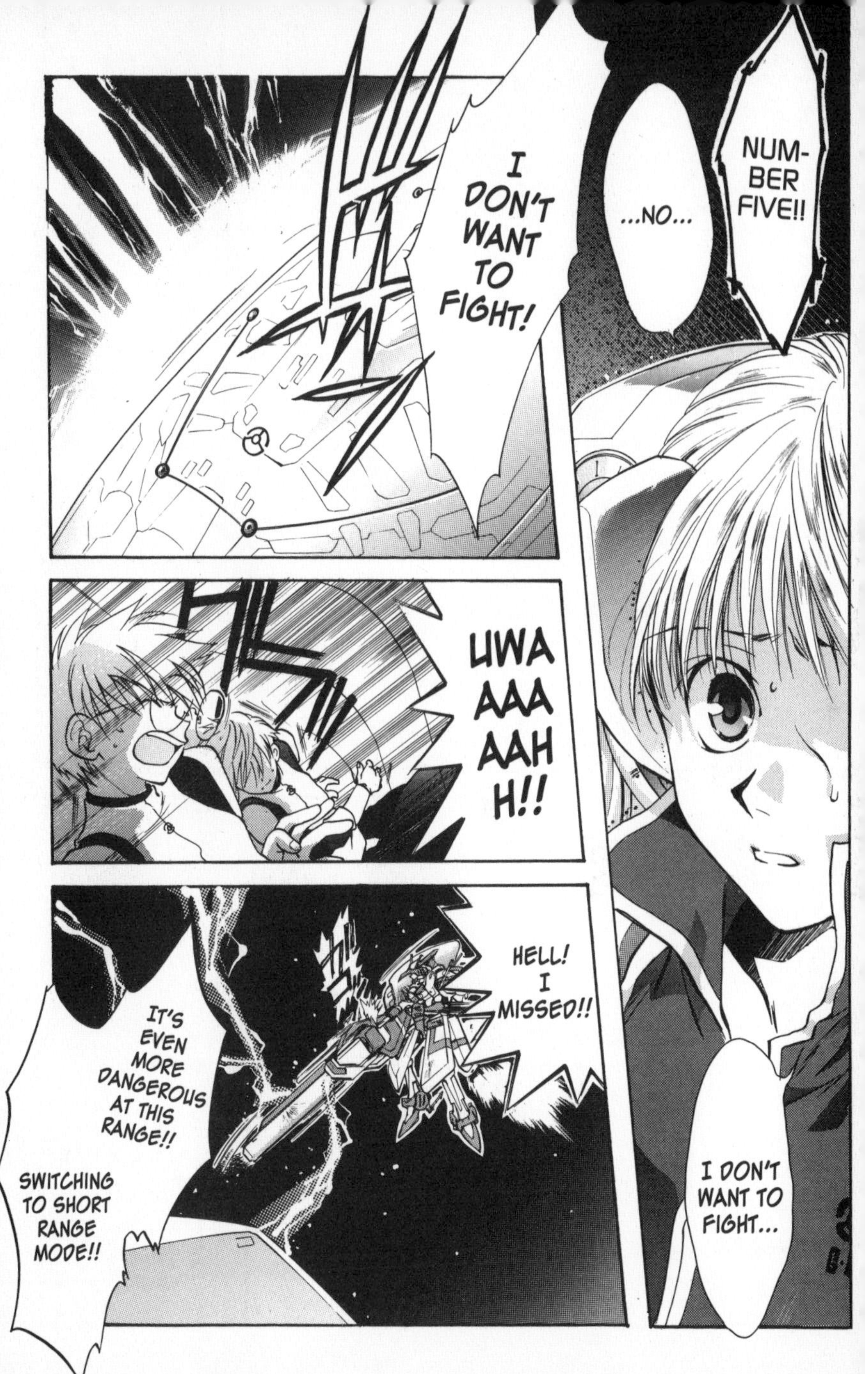
NUMBER FIVE!!
...NO...
I DON'T WANT TO FIGHT...
I DON'T WANT TO FIGHT!
UWAAAAAAHH!!
HELL! I MISSED!!
IT'S EVEN MORE DANGEROUS AT THIS RANGE!!
SWITCHING TO SHORT RANGE MODE!!

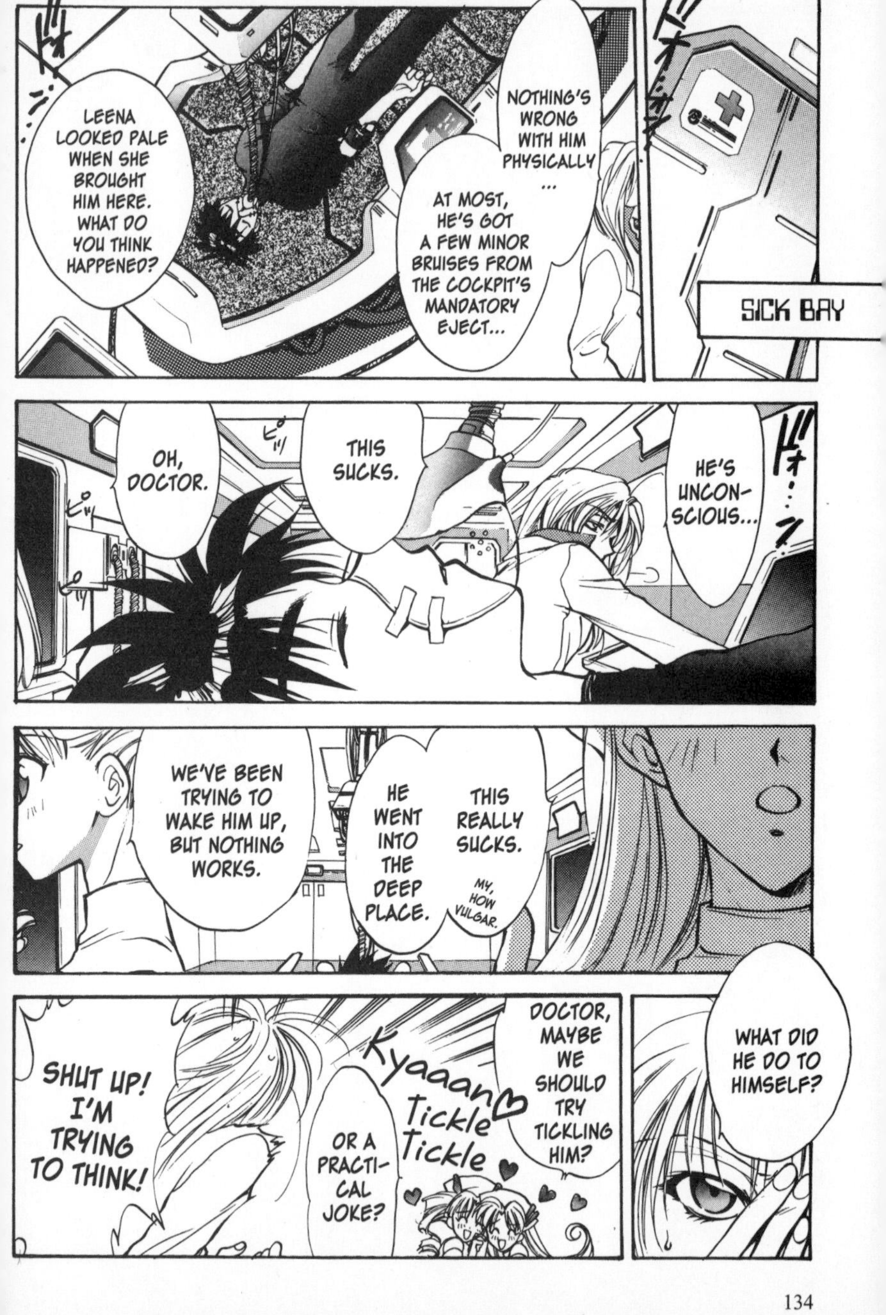
SICK BAY
NOTHING'S WRONG WITH HIM PHYSICALLY...
AT MOST, HE'S GOT A FEW MINOR BRUISES FROM THE COCKPIT'S MANDATORY EJECT...
LEENA LOOKED PALE WHEN SHE BROUGHT HIM HERE. WHAT DO YOU THINK HAPPENED?
HE'S UNCON-SCIOUS...
THIS SUCKS.
OH, DOCTOR.
THIS REALLY SUCKS.
MY, HOW VULGAR.
HE WENT INTO THE DEEP PLACE.
WE'VE BEEN TRYING TO WAKE HIM UP, BUT NOTHING WORKS.
WHAT DID HE DO TO HIMSELF?
DOCTOR, MAYBE WE SHOULD TRY TICKLING HIM?
Kyaaan
Tickle Tickle
OR A PRACTI-CAL JOKE?
SHUT UP! I'M TRYING TO THINK!

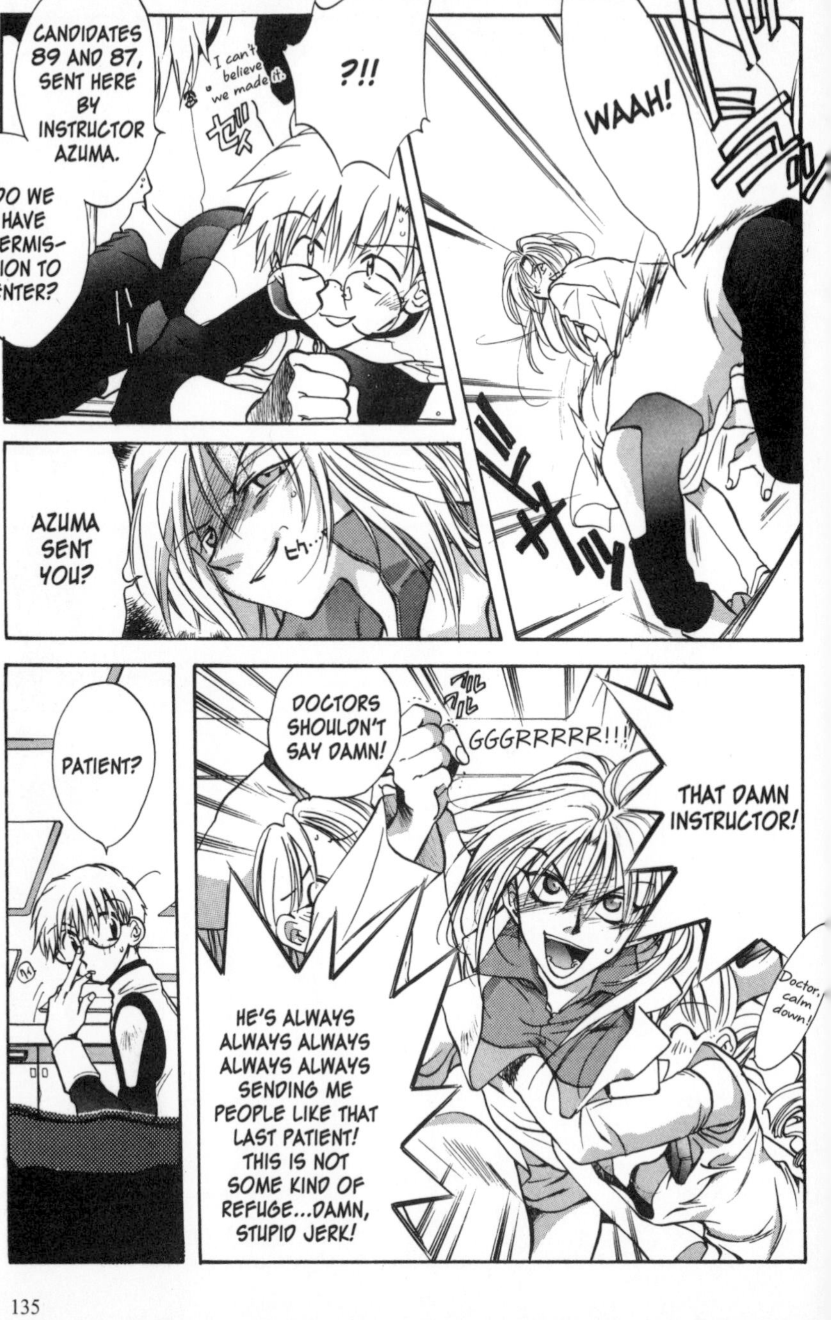
WAAH!
?!!
I can't believe we made it.
CANDIDATES 89 AND 87, SENT HERE BY INSTRUCTOR AZUMA.
DO WE HAVE PERMIS-SION TO ENTER?
AZUMA SENT YOU?
THAT DAMN INSTRUCTOR!
GGGRRRRR!!!
DOCTORS SHOULDN'T SAY DAMN!
Doctor, calm down!
HE'S ALWAYS ALWAYS ALWAYS ALWAYS ALWAYS SENDING ME PEOPLE LIKE THAT LAST PATIENT! THIS IS NOT SOME KIND OF REFUGE...DAMN, STUPID JERK!
PATIENT?

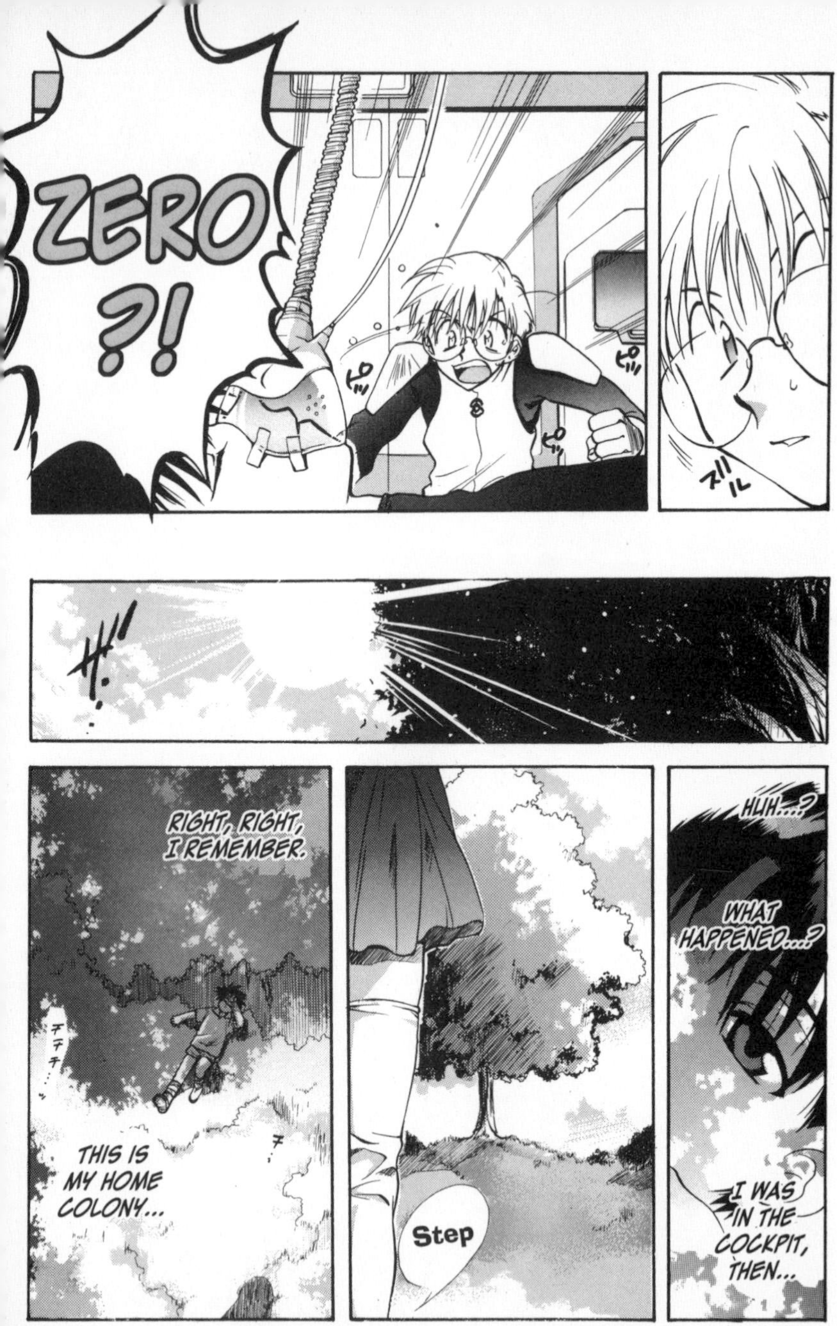
ズル
ZERO ?!
ピッ
ピッ
ピッ
HUH...?
WHAT HAPPENED...?
I WAS IN THE COCKPIT, THEN...
Step
RIGHT, RIGHT, I REMEMBER.
チチチ...
THIS IS MY HOME COLONY...
チ...

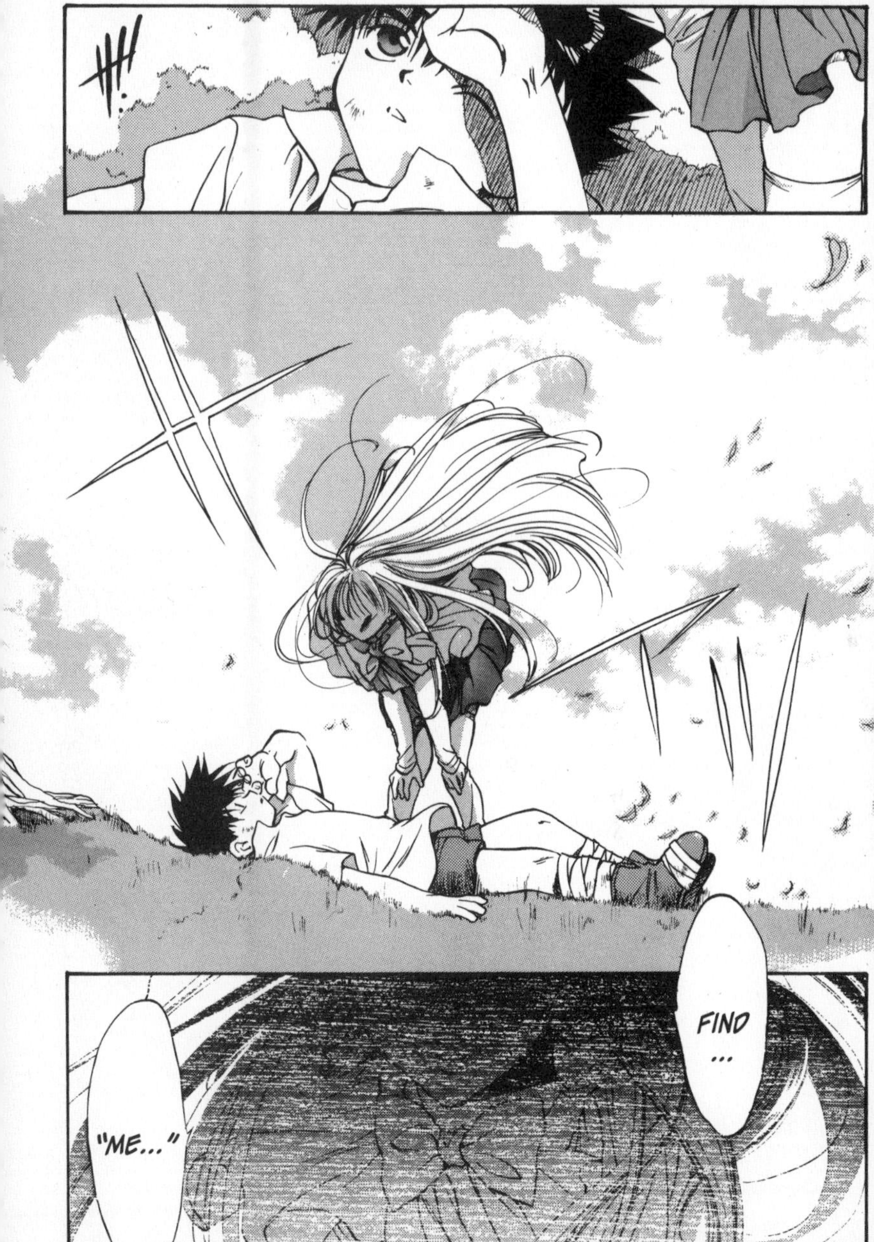
FIND ...
"ME..."

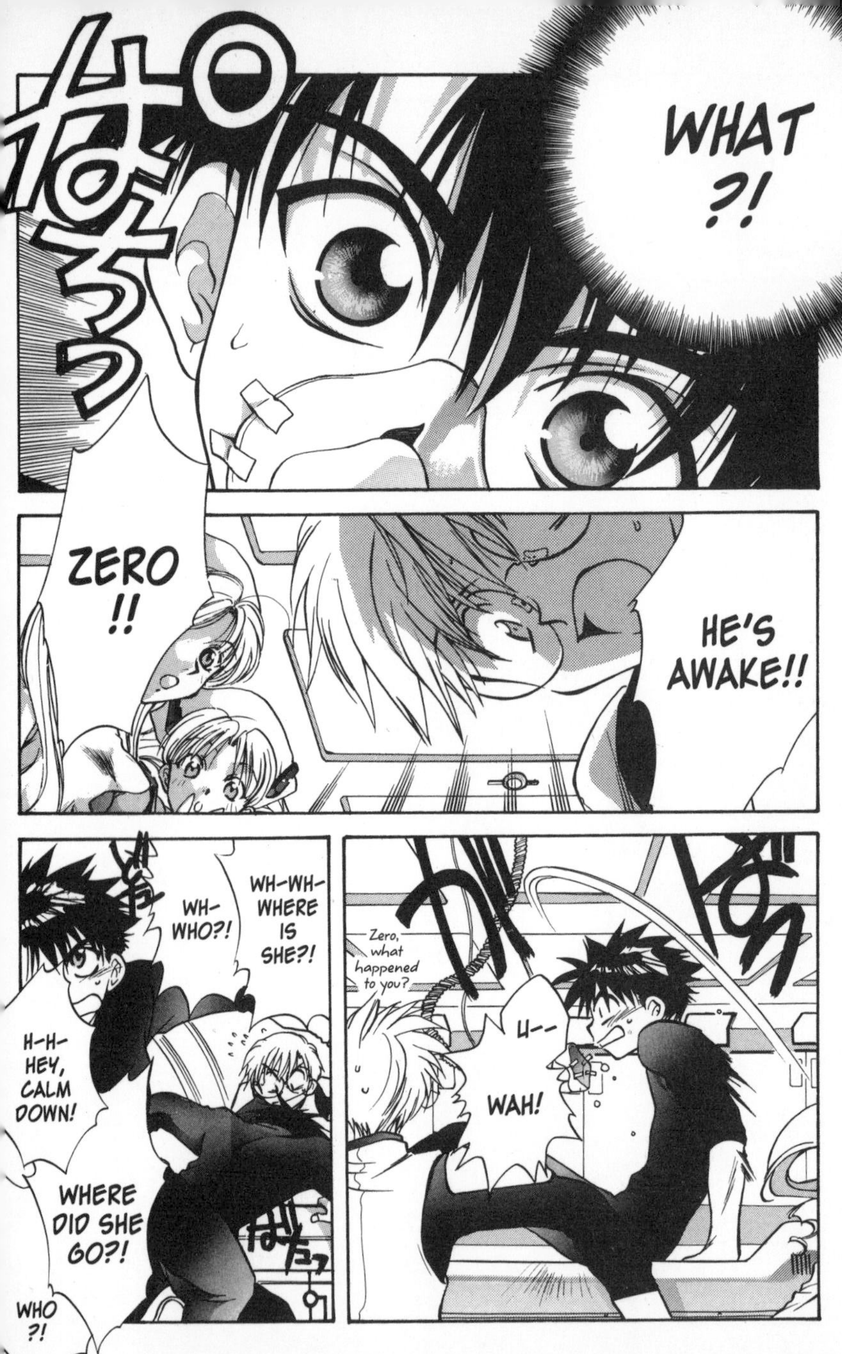
WHAT ?!
HE'S AWAKE!!
ZERO !!
Zero, what happened to you?
U--
WAH!
WH-WH-WHERE IS SHE?!
WH-WHO?!
H-H-HEY, CALM DOWN!
WHERE DID SHE GO?!
WHO ?!

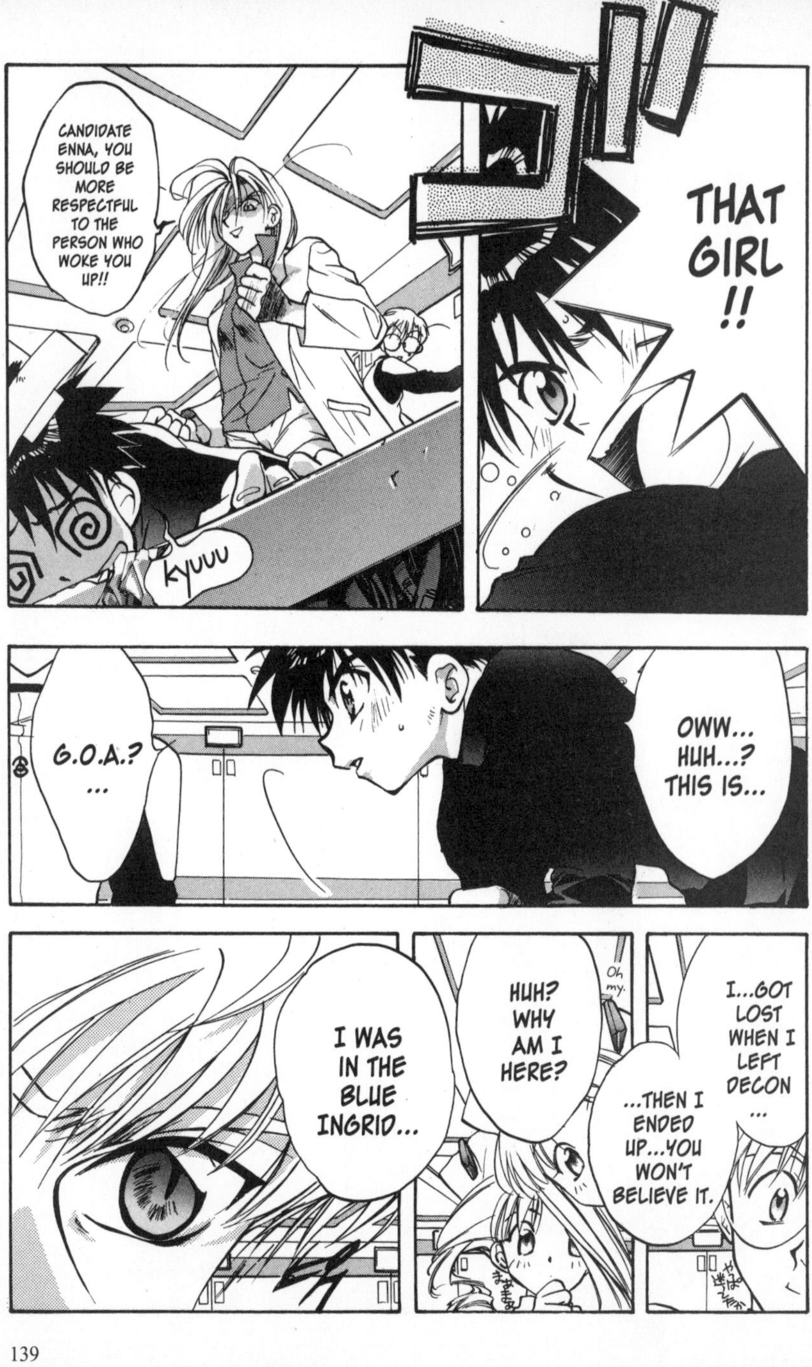
THAT GIRL!!
CANDIDATE ENNA, YOU SHOULD BE MORE RESPECTFUL TO THE PERSON WHO WOKE YOU UP!!
kyuuu
OWW... HUH...? THIS IS...
G.O.A.? ...
I...GOT LOST WHEN I LEFT DECON ...
...THEN I ENDED UP...YOU WON'T BELIEVE IT.
Oh my.
HUH? WHY AM I HERE?
I WAS IN THE BLUE INGRID...

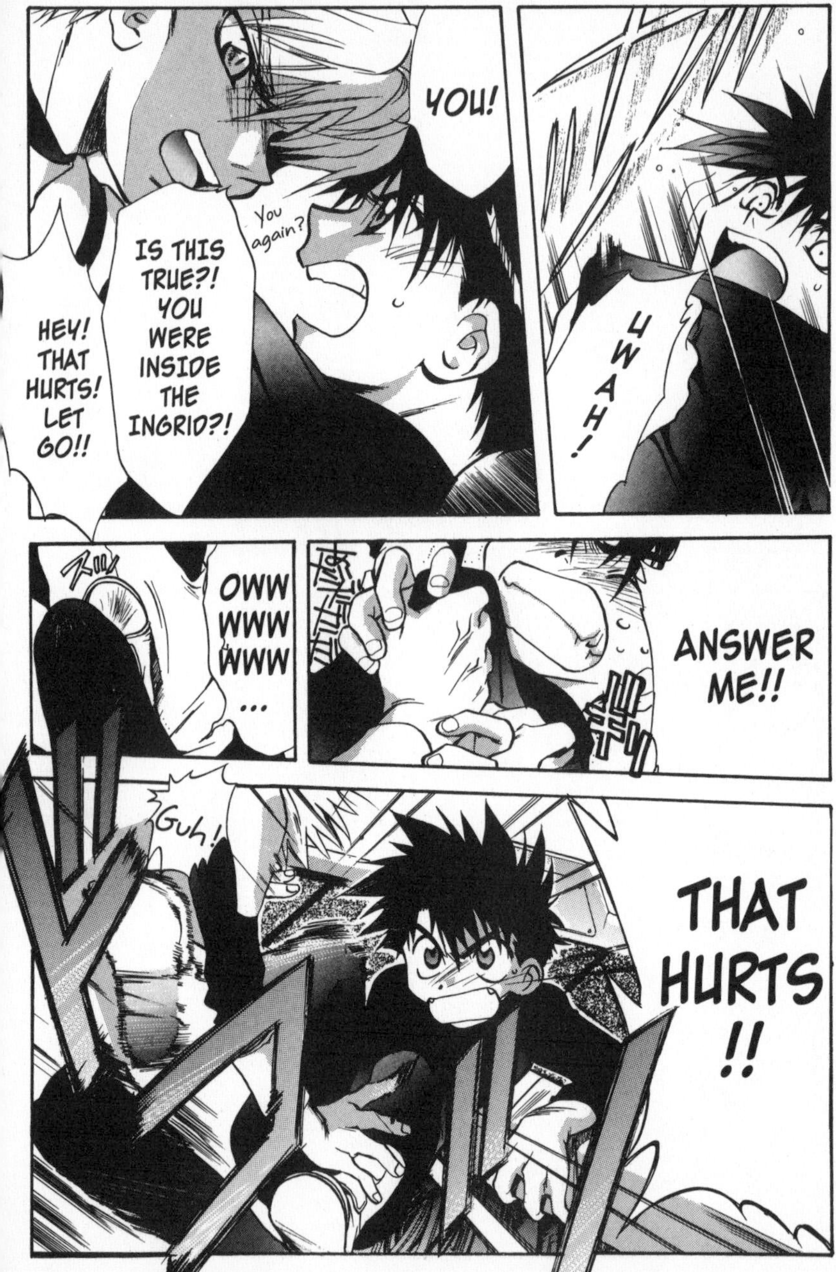
UWAH!
YOU!
You again?
IS THIS TRUE?! YOU WERE INSIDE THE INGRID?!
HEY! THAT HURTS! LET GO!!
ANSWER ME!!
OWW WWW WWW ...
THAT HURTS!!
Guh!

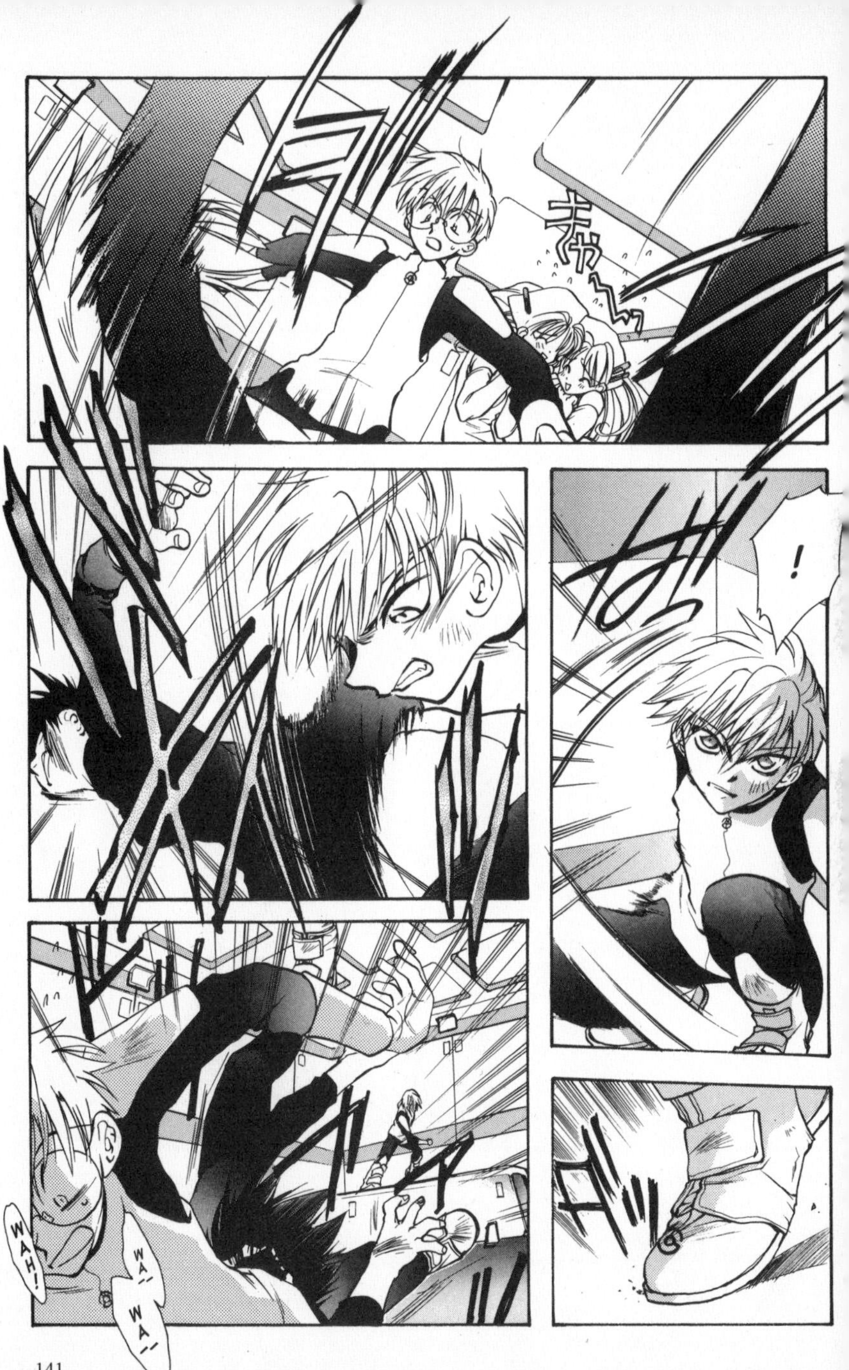
きゃ〜
!
WAH!
WA- WA-

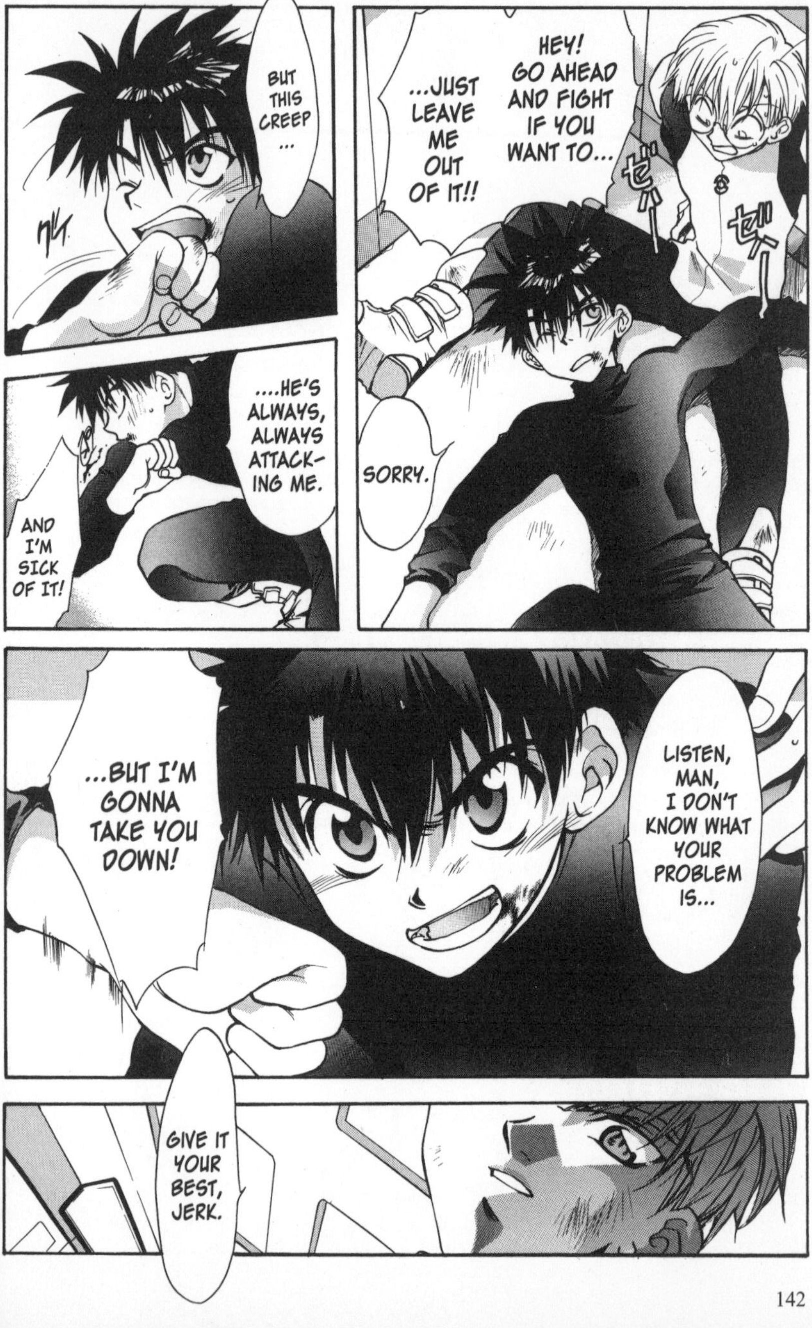
HEY! GO AHEAD AND FIGHT IF YOU WANT TO...
...JUST LEAVE ME OUT OF IT!!
ゼハー
ゼハー
SORRY.
BUT THIS CREEP ...
グイ
....HE'S ALWAYS, ALWAYS ATTACKING ME.
AND I'M SICK OF IT!
LISTEN, MAN, I DON'T KNOW WHAT YOUR PROBLEM IS...
...BUT I'M GONNA TAKE YOU DOWN!
GIVE IT YOUR BEST, JERK.

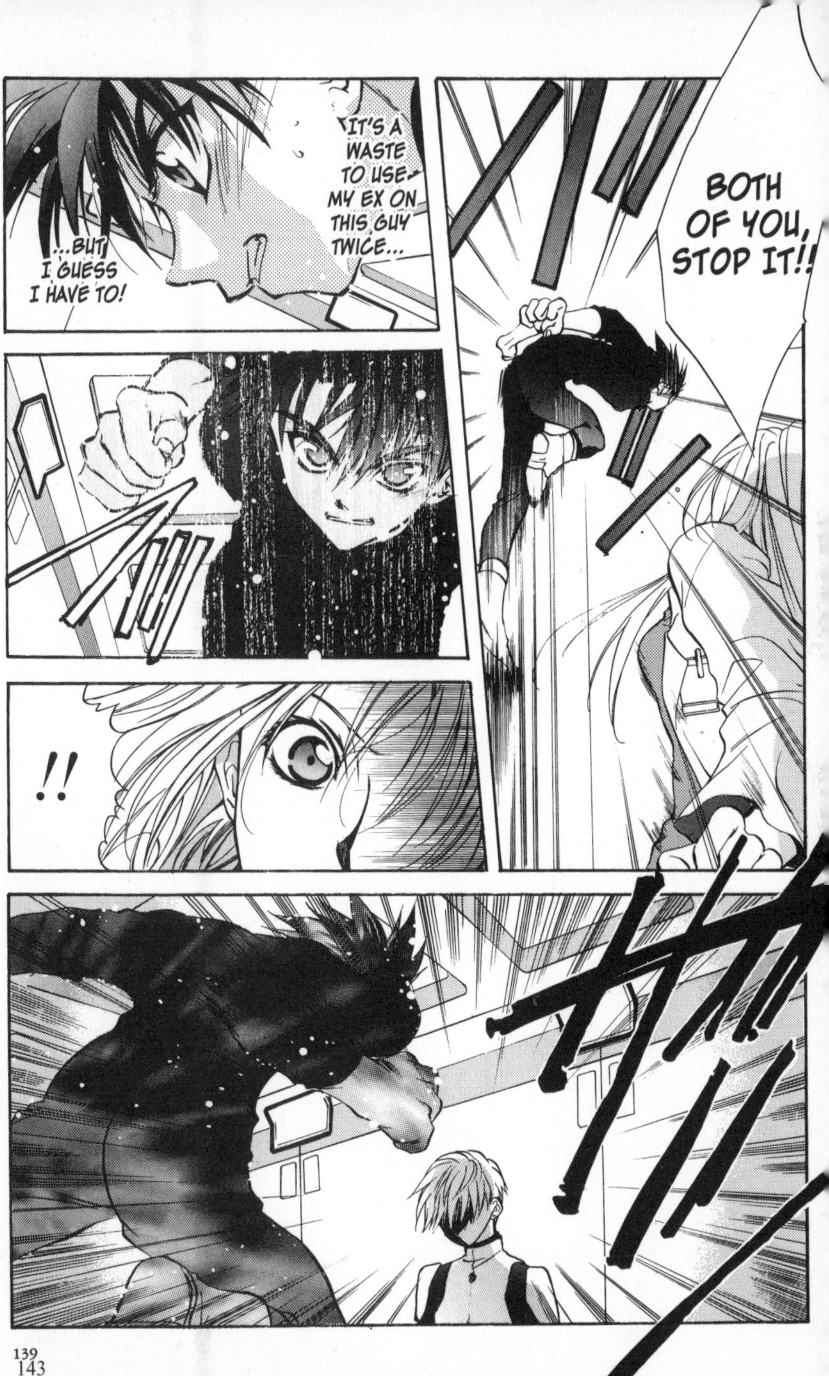
BOTH OF YOU, STOP IT!!
IT'S A WASTE TO USE MY EX ON THIS GUY TWICE...
...BUT I GUESS I HAVE TO!
!!

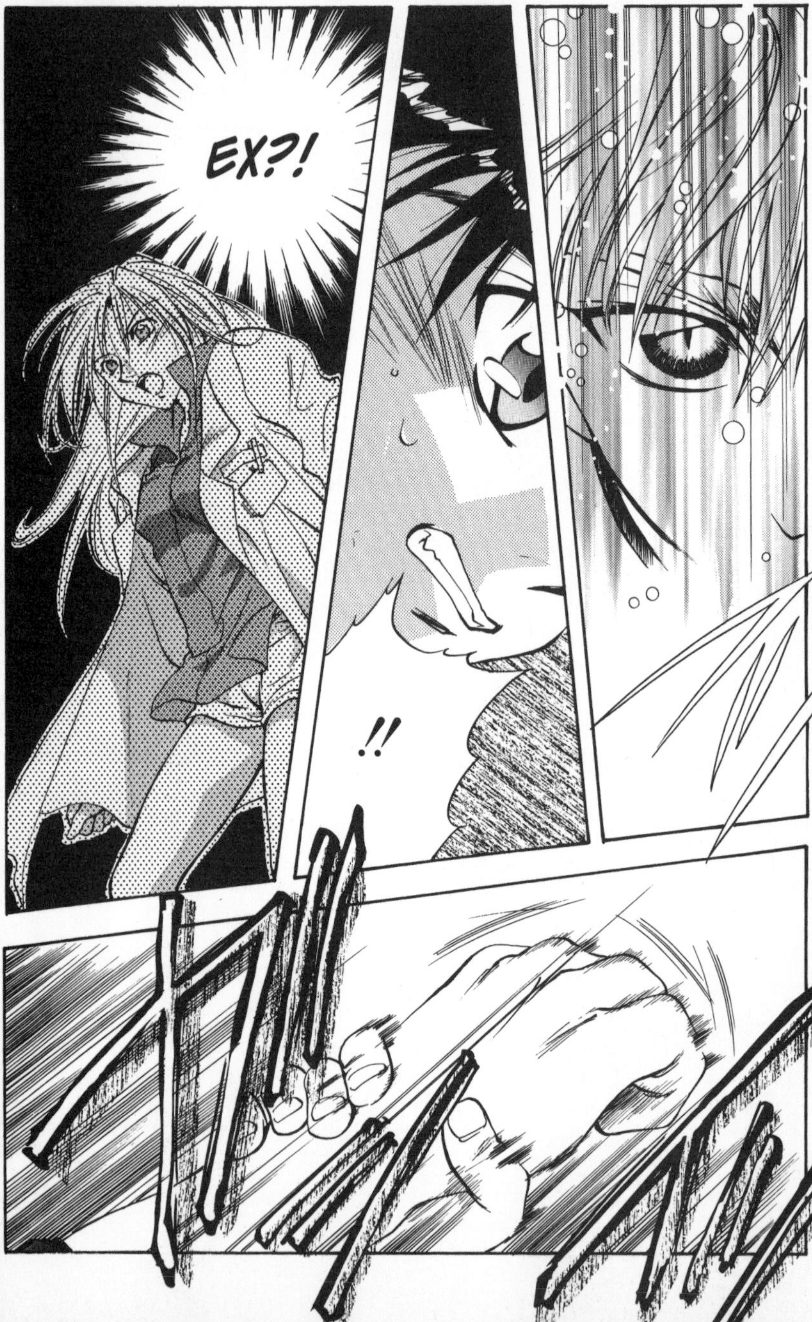
!!
EX?!

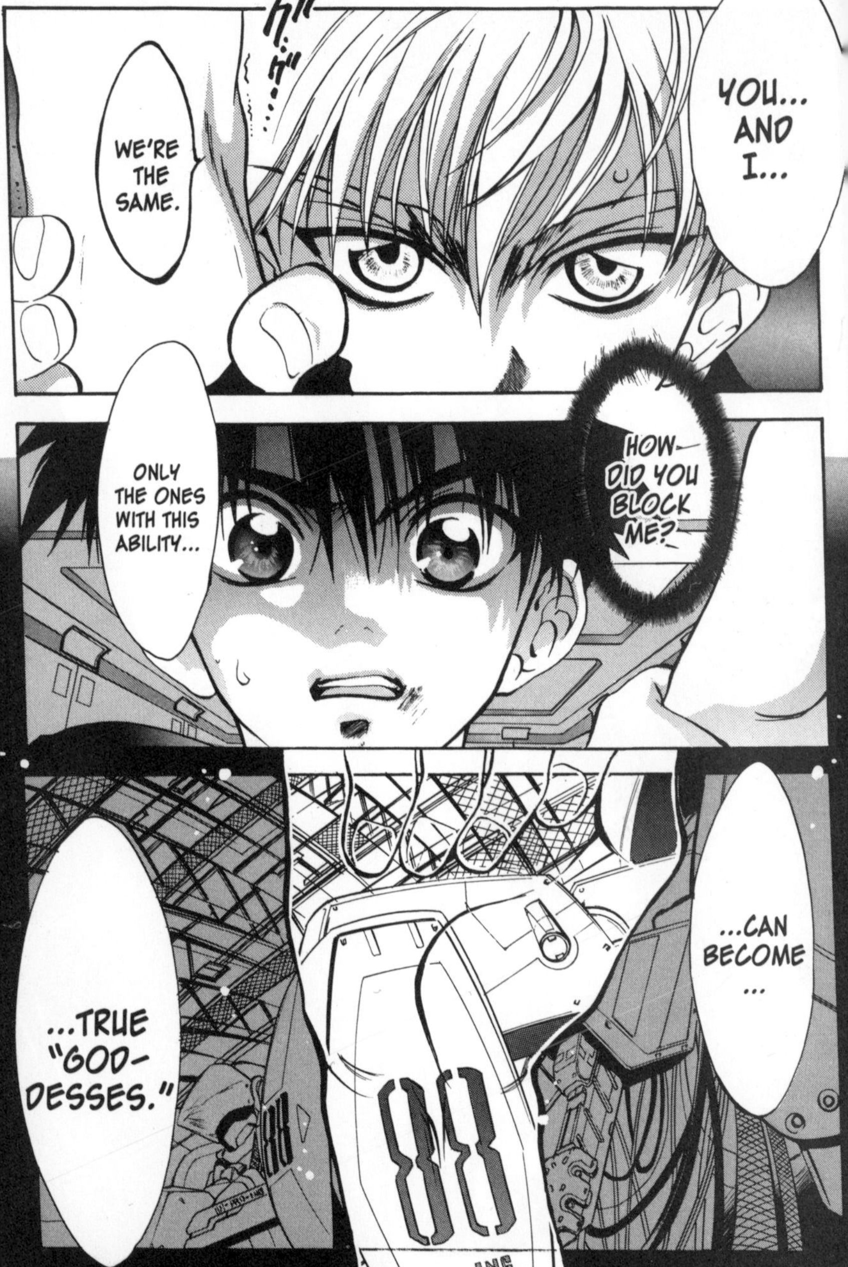
YOU... AND I...
WE'RE THE SAME.
HOW DID YOU BLOCK ME?
ONLY THE ONES WITH THIS ABILITY...
...CAN BECOME ...
...TRUE "GOD-DESSES."
PRO-ING

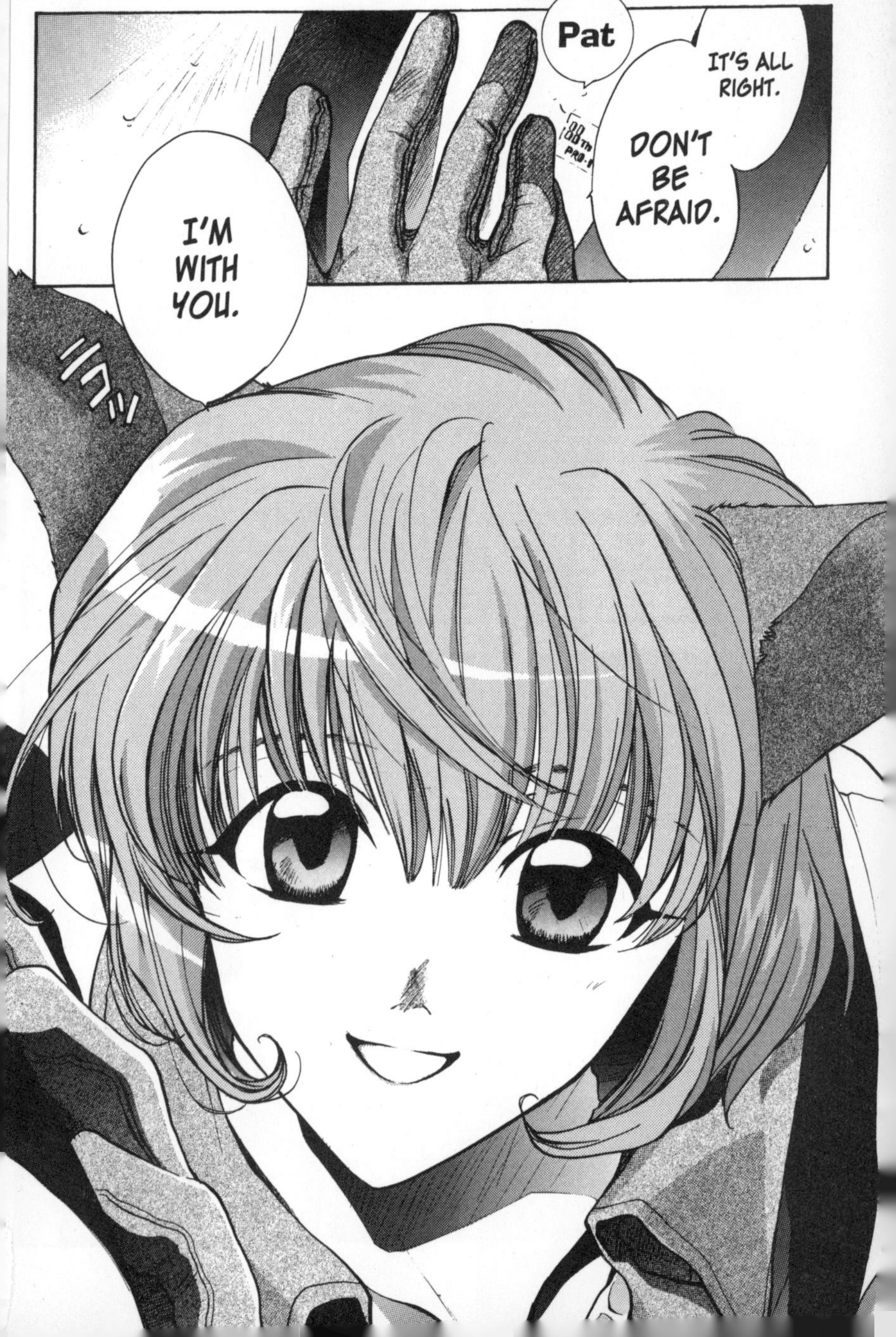
Pat
IT'S ALL RIGHT.
DON'T BE AFRAID.
I'M WITH YOU.

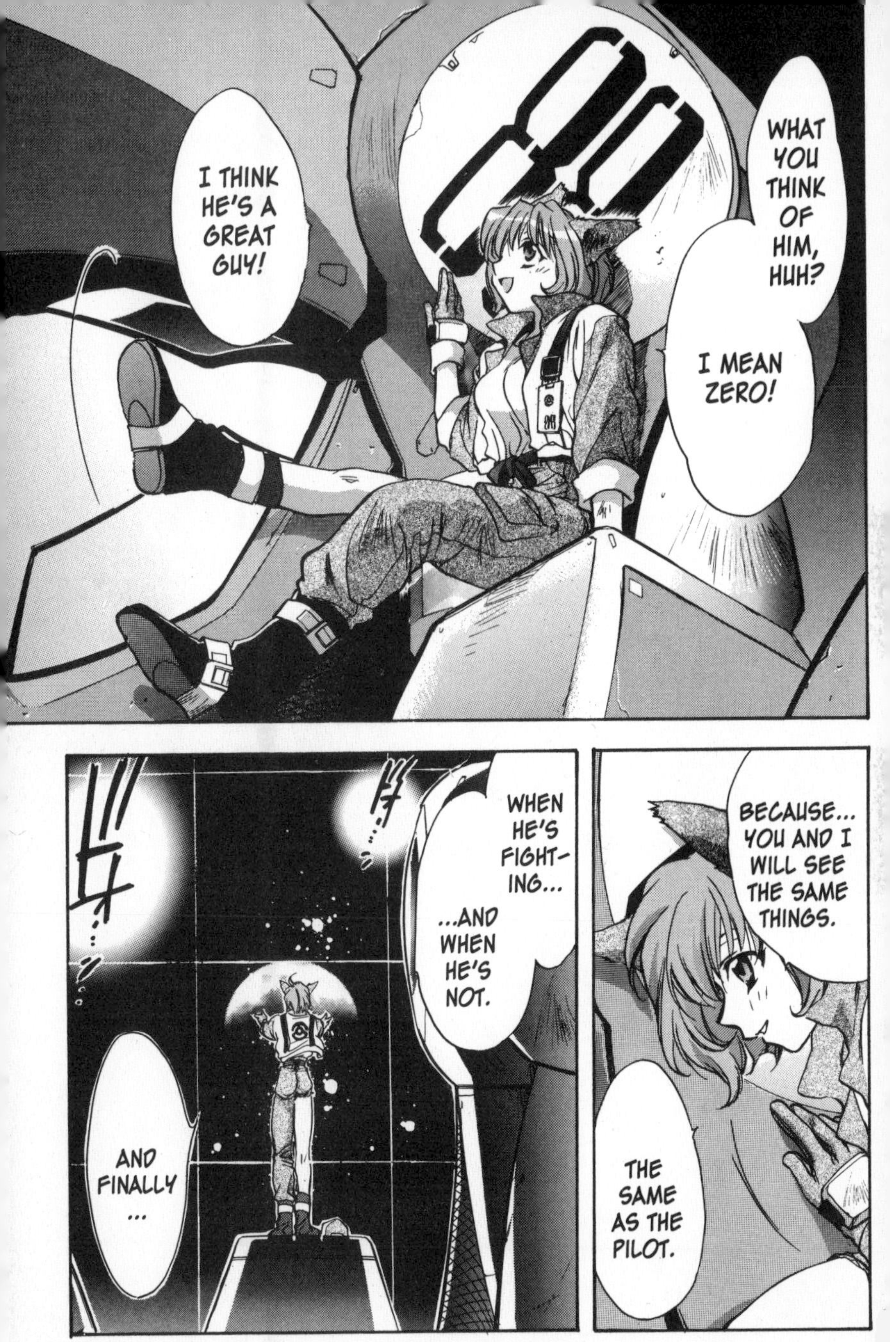
WHAT YOU THINK OF HIM, HUH?
I MEAN ZERO!
I THINK HE'S A GREAT GUY!
BECAUSE... YOU AND I WILL SEE THE SAME THINGS.
THE SAME AS THE PILOT.
WHEN HE'S FIGHTING...
...AND WHEN HE'S NOT.
AND FINALLY...

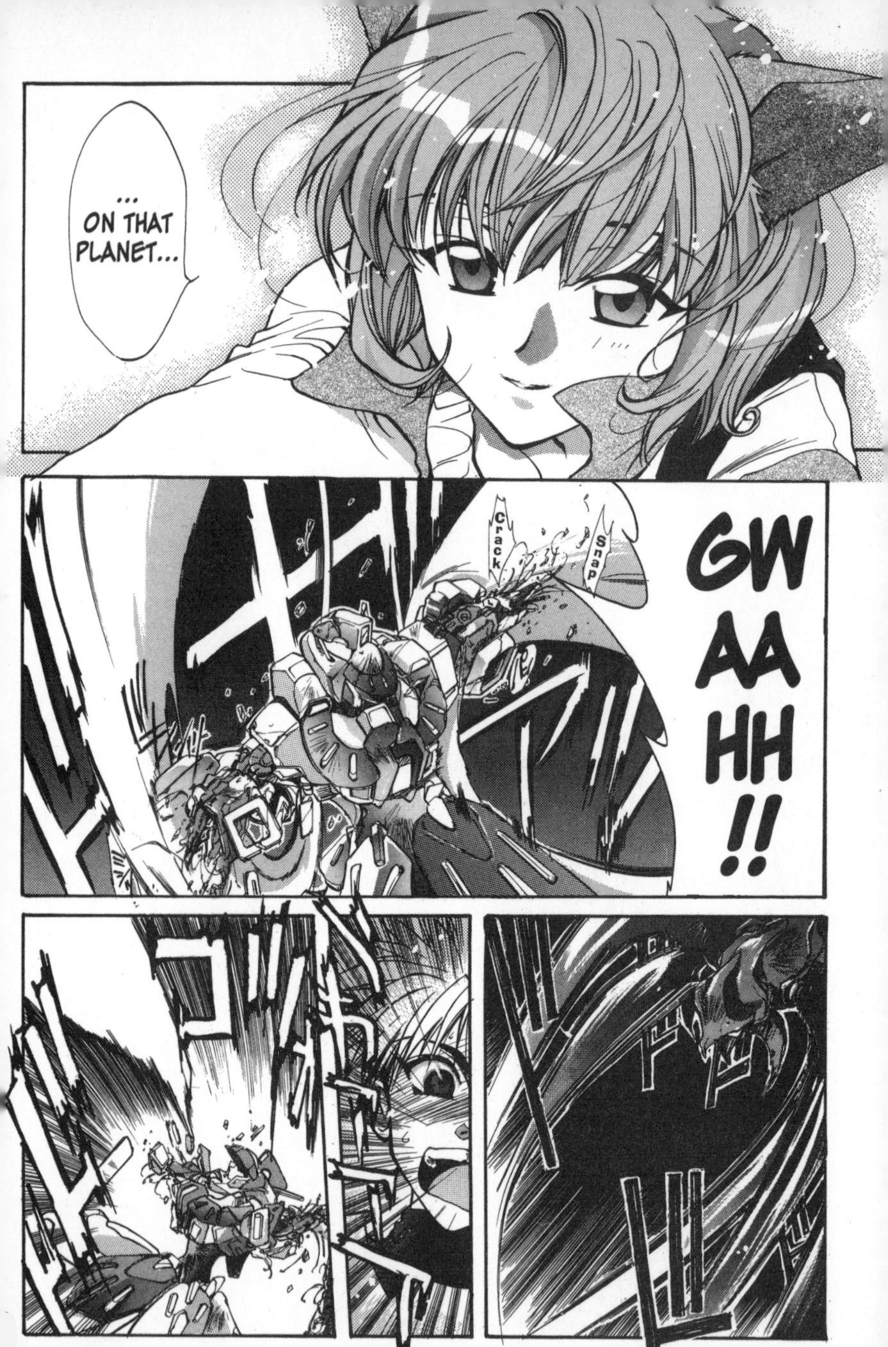

... ON THAT PLANET...
Crack
Snap
GWAAHH!!

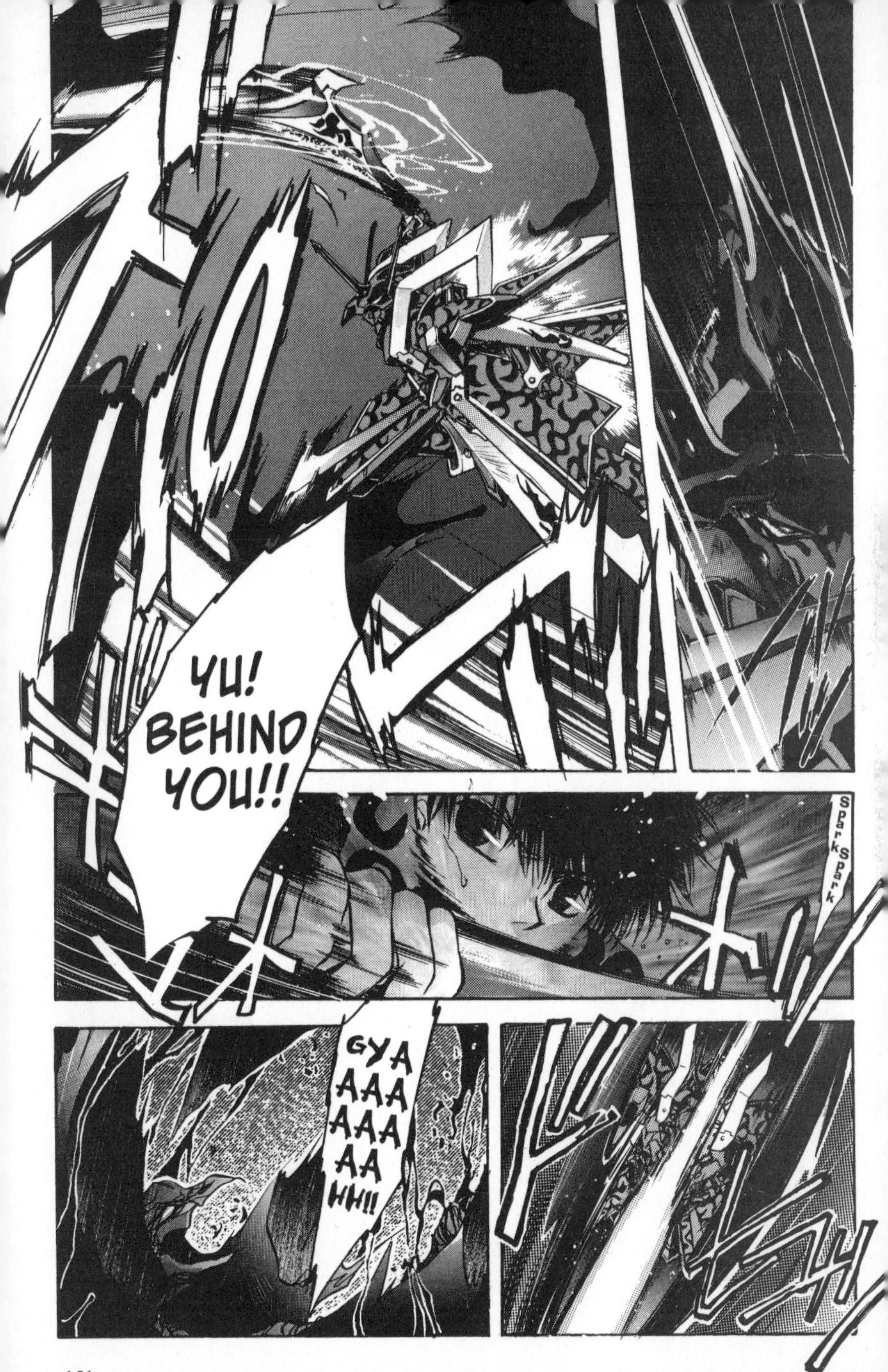
YU! BEHIND YOU!!
Spark Spark
GYAAAAAAAAAAAHH!!

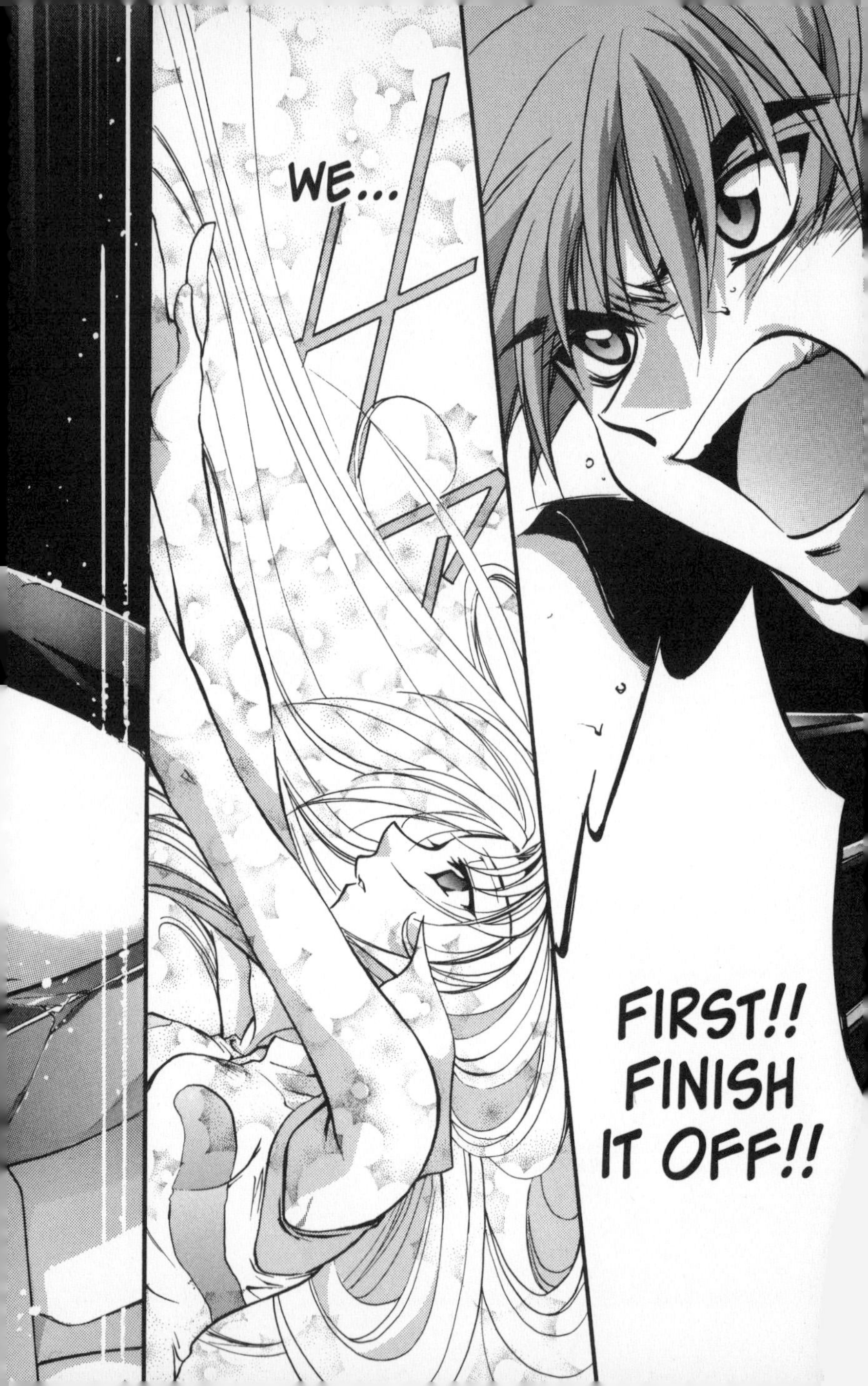
FIRST!! FINISH IT OFF!!
WE...

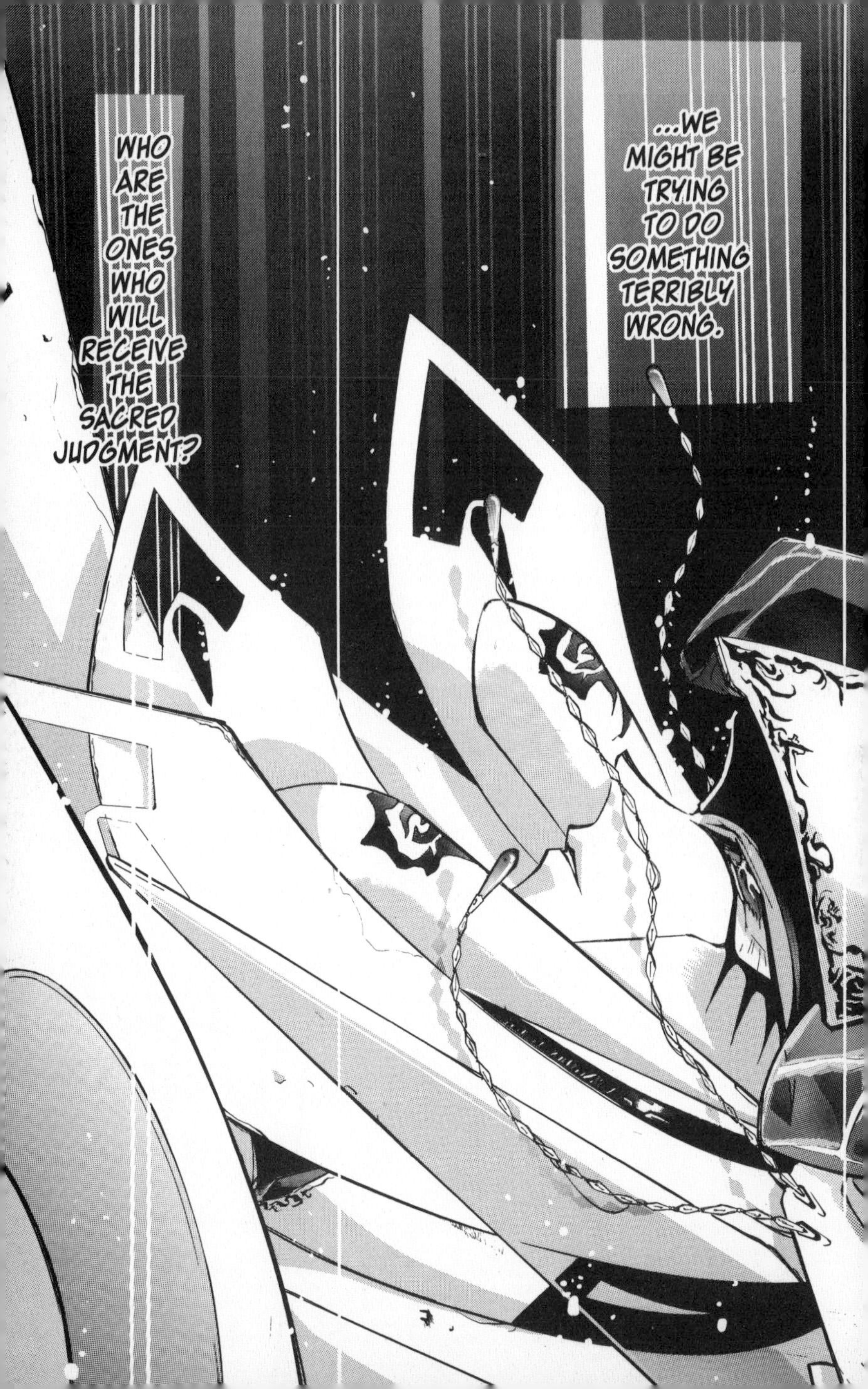
...WE MIGHT BE TRYING TO DO SOMETHING TERRIBLY WRONG.
WHO ARE THE ONES WHO WILL RECEIVE THE SACRED JUDGMENT?

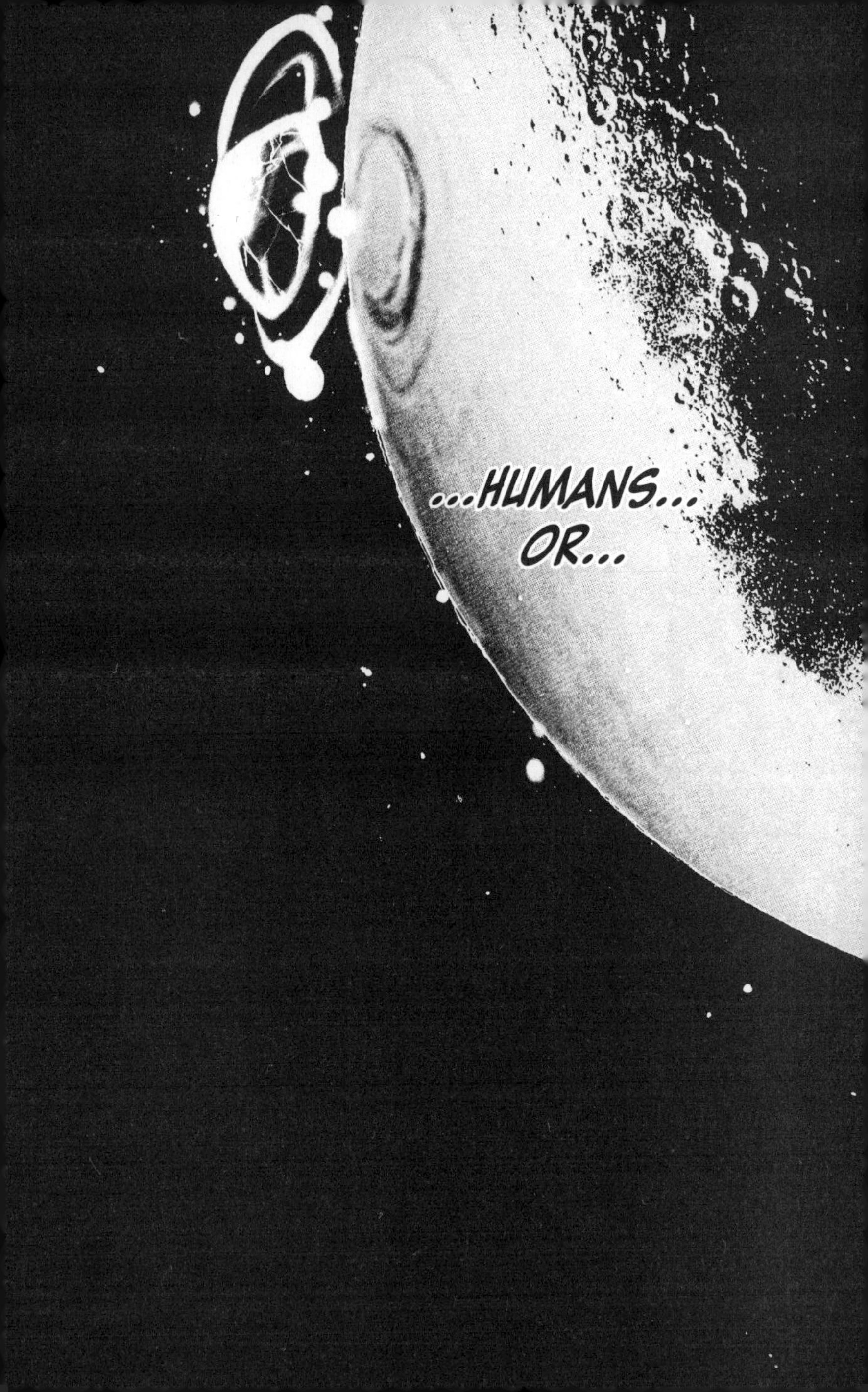
...HUMANS... OR...

US....?

To Be Continued Next Volume

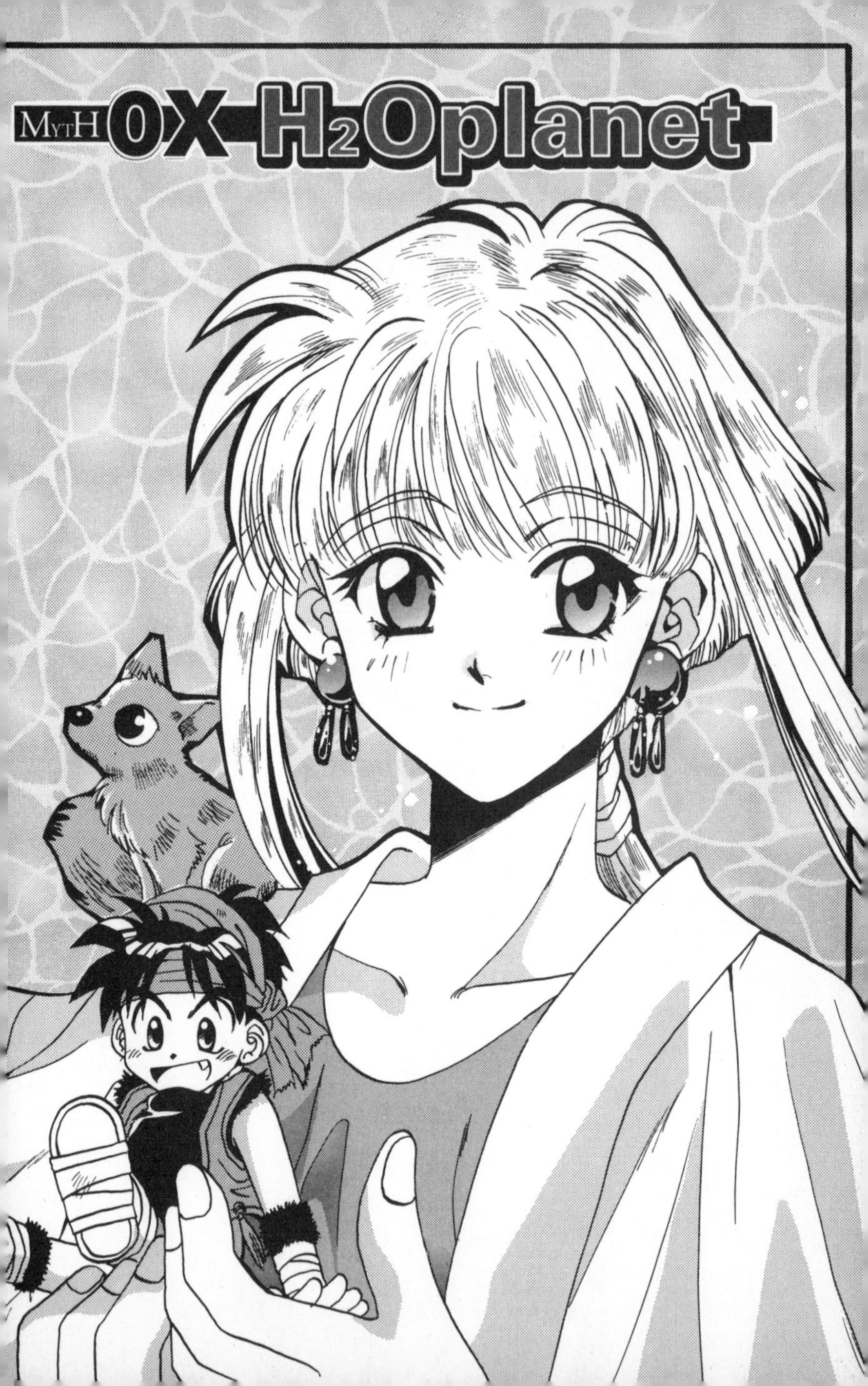
MYTH 0X
H2Oplanet

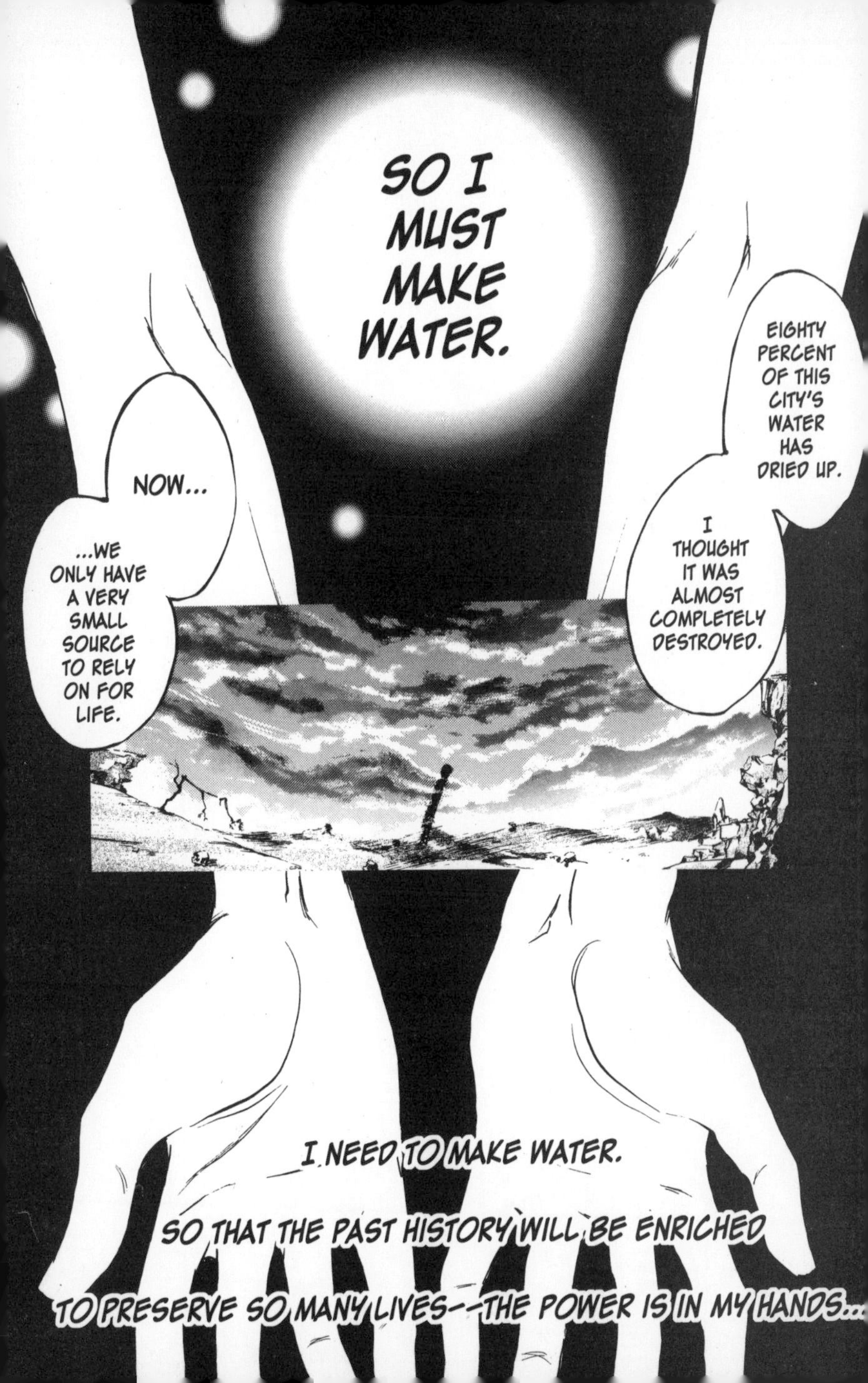
SO I MUST MAKE WATER.
EIGHTY PERCENT OF THIS CITY'S WATER HAS DRIED UP.
I THOUGHT IT WAS ALMOST COMPLETELY DESTROYED.
NOW...
...WE ONLY HAVE A VERY SMALL SOURCE TO RELY ON FOR LIFE.
I NEED TO MAKE WATER.
SO THAT THE PAST HISTORY WILL BE ENRICHED
TO PRESERVE SO MANY LIVES--THE POWER IS IN MY HANDS...

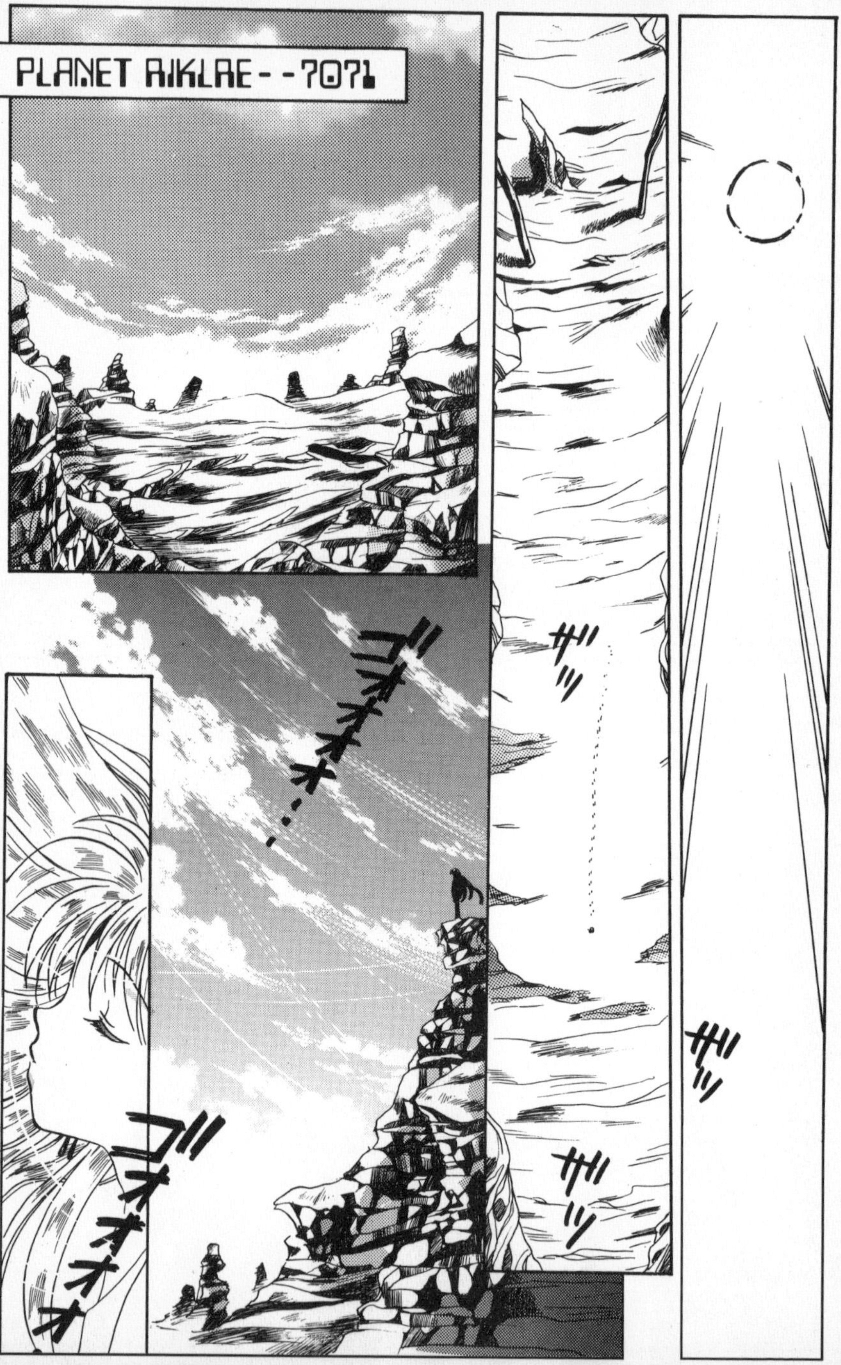
ザッ
ザッ
ザッ
PLANET AIKLAE--7071
ゴオオオ…
ゴオオオオ

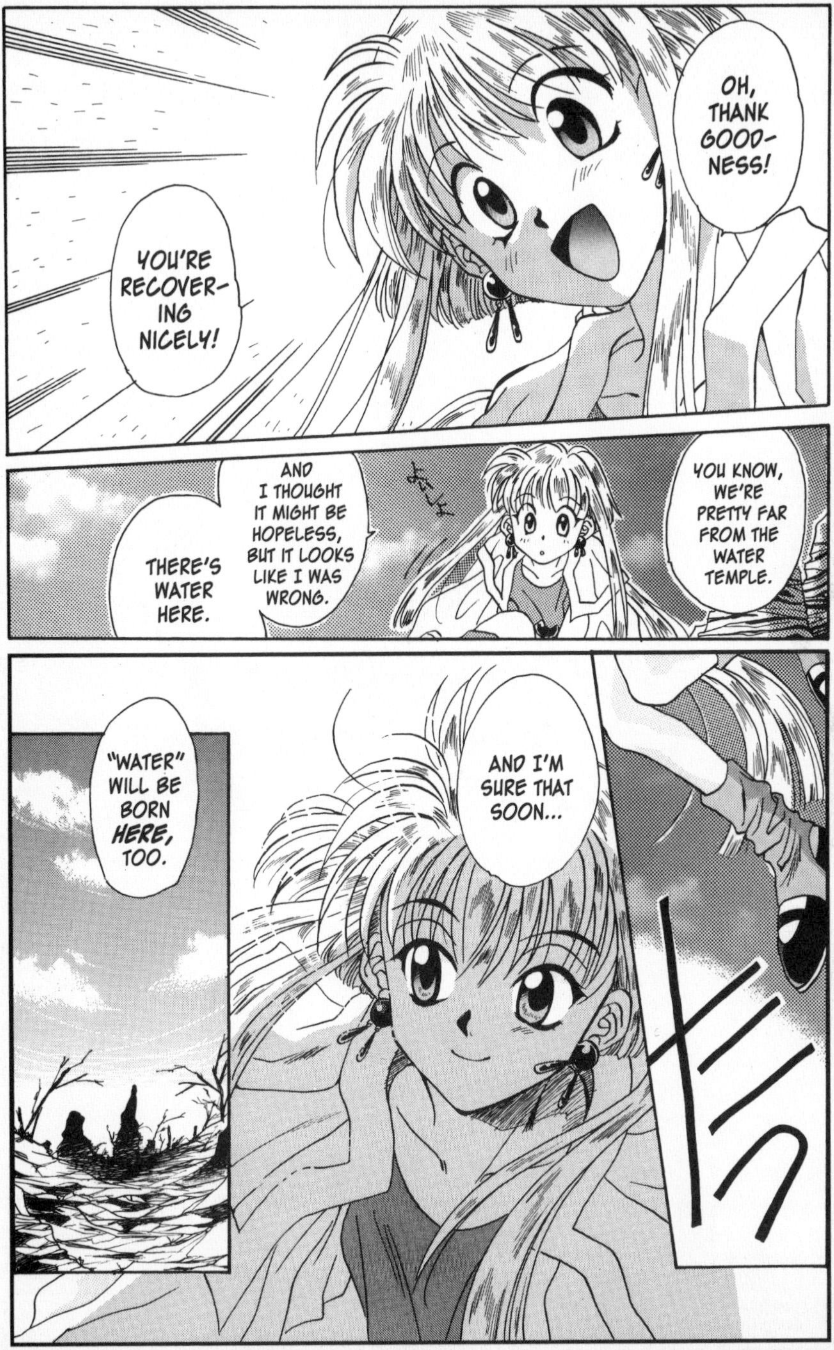
OH, THANK GOOD-NESS!
YOU'RE RECOVER-ING NICELY!
YOU KNOW, WE'RE PRETTY FAR FROM THE WATER TEMPLE.
AND I THOUGHT IT MIGHT BE HOPELESS, BUT IT LOOKS LIKE I WAS WRONG.
THERE'S WATER HERE.
AND I'M SURE THAT SOON...
"WATER" WILL BE BORN HERE, TOO.

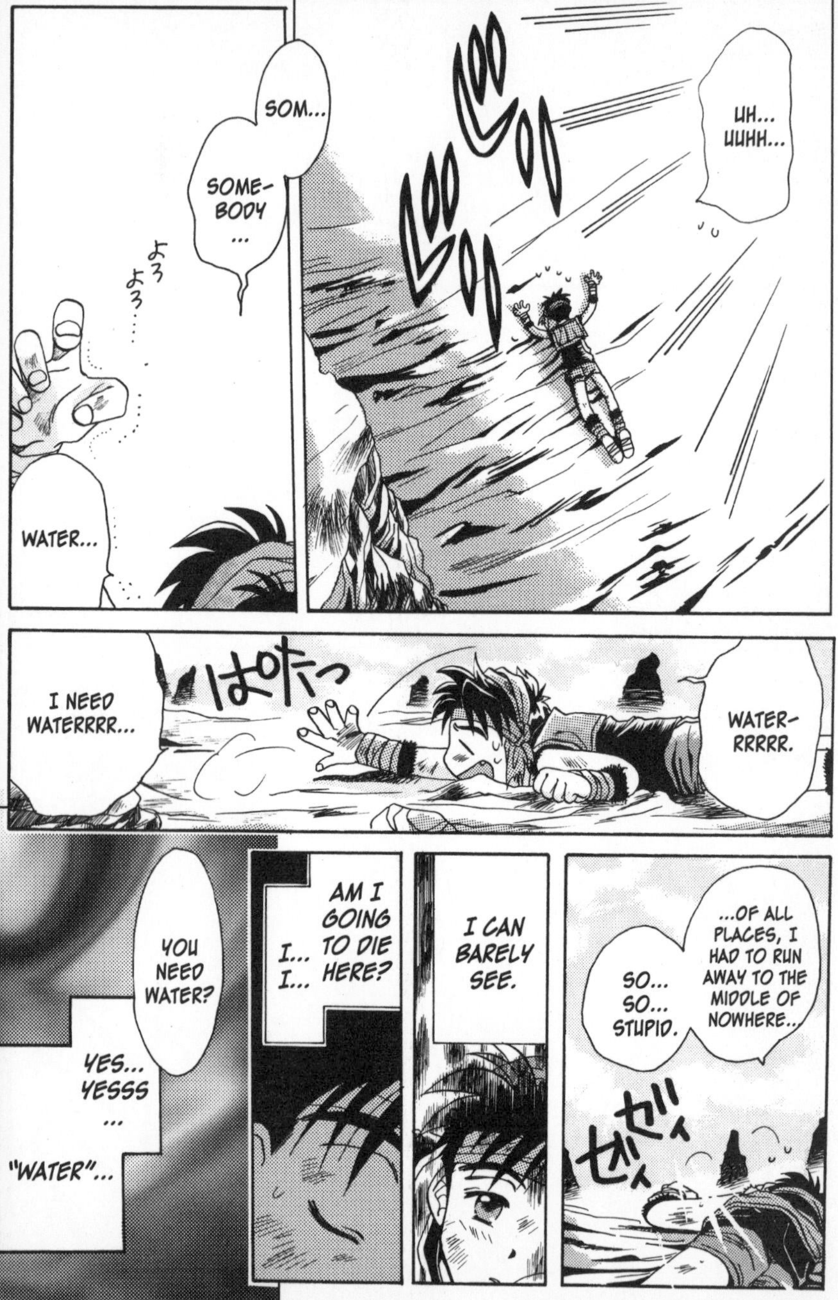
UH... UUHH...
SOM...
SOME-BODY ...
よろよろ
WATER...
WATER-RRRRR.
はたっ
I NEED WATERRRR...
...OF ALL PLACES, I HAD TO RUN AWAY TO THE MIDDLE OF NOWHERE..
SO... SO... STUPID.
ゼィゼィ
I CAN BARELY SEE.
AM I GOING TO DIE HERE?
I... I...
YOU NEED WATER?
YES... YESSS ...
"WATER"...

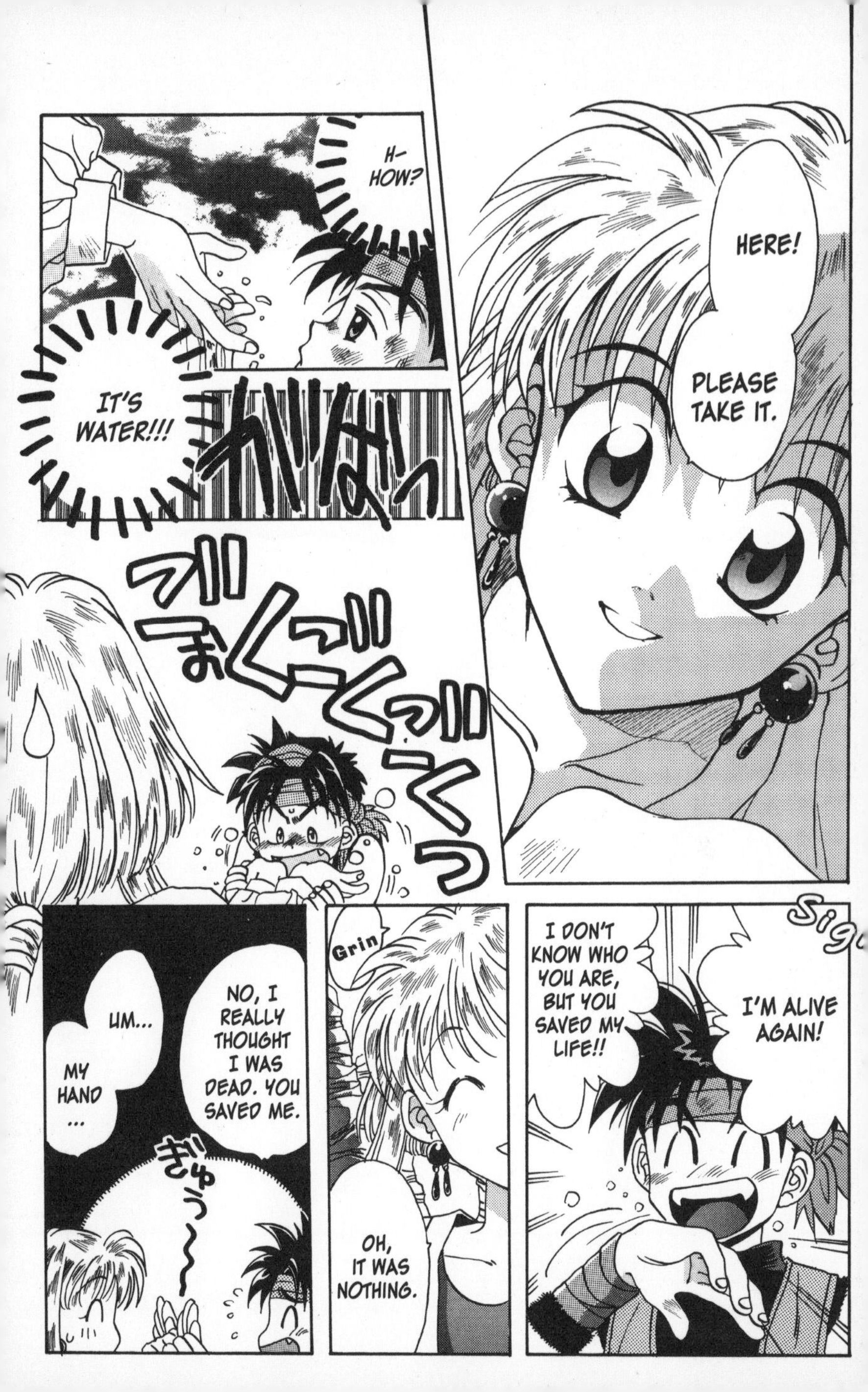
HERE!
PLEASE TAKE IT.
H-HOW?
IT'S WATER!!!
がばっ
I'M ALIVE AGAIN!
I DON'T KNOW WHO YOU ARE, BUT YOU SAVED MY LIFE!!
Grin
OH, IT WAS NOTHING.
NO, I REALLY THOUGHT I WAS DEAD. YOU SAVED ME.
UM...
MY HAND...
ぎゅう～

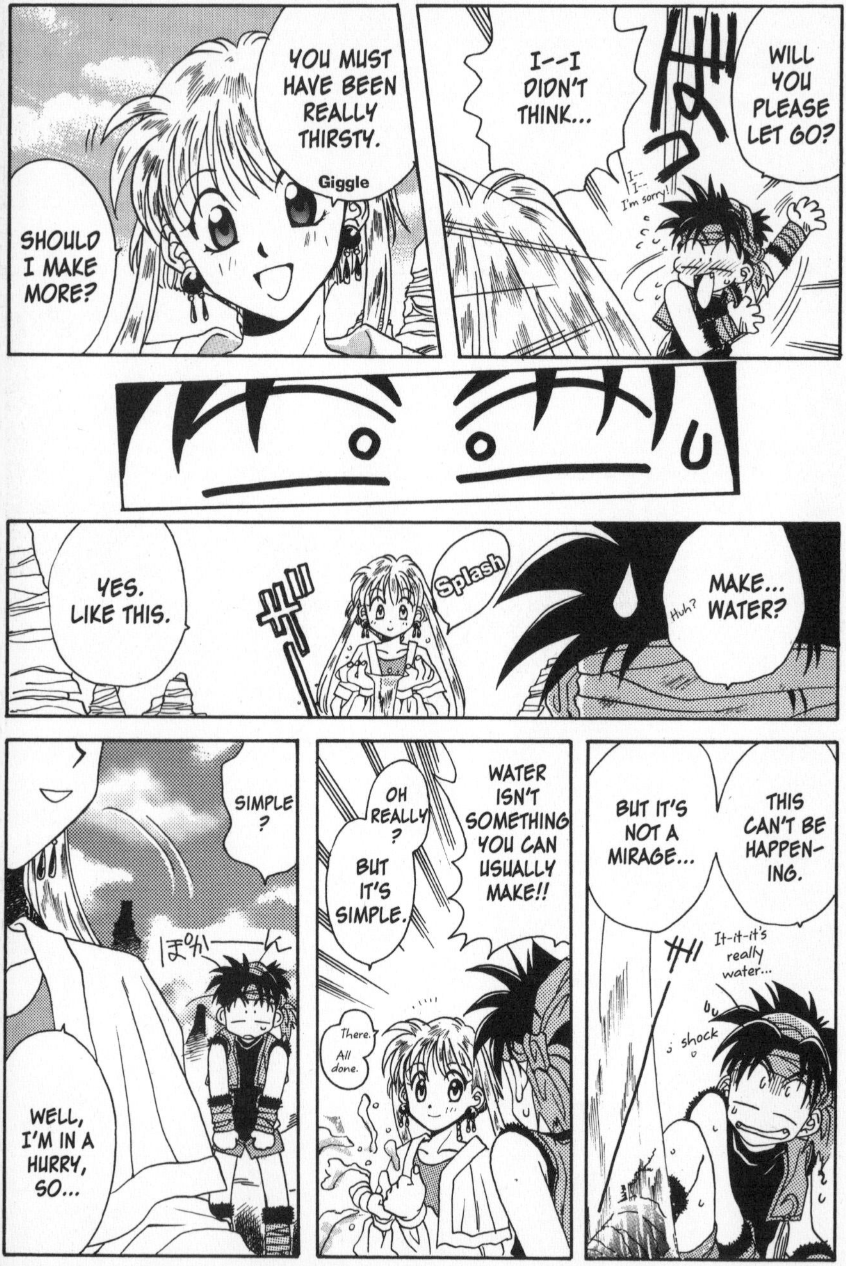
WILL YOU PLEASE LET GO?
I--I DIDN'T THINK...
I-- I-- I'm sorry!
YOU MUST HAVE BEEN REALLY THIRSTY.
Giggle
SHOULD I MAKE MORE?
MAKE... WATER?
Huh?
Splash
YES. LIKE THIS.
THIS CAN'T BE HAPPEN-ING.
BUT IT'S NOT A MIRAGE...
It-it-it's really water...
shock
WATER ISN'T SOMETHING YOU CAN USUALLY MAKE!!
OH REALLY? BUT IT'S SIMPLE.
There. All done.
SIMPLE?
ぽかーーん
WELL, I'M IN A HURRY, SO...

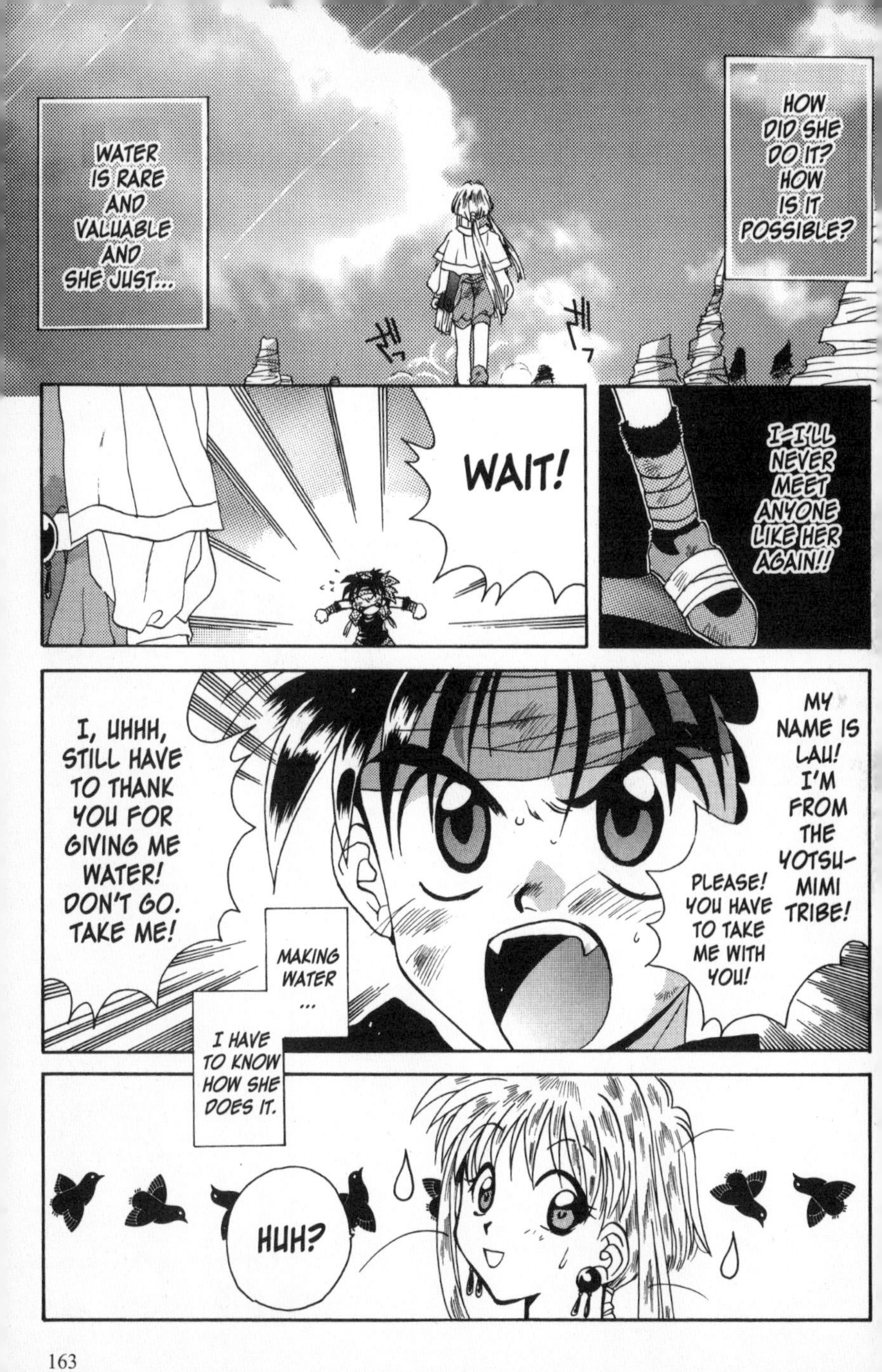
HOW DID SHE DO IT? HOW IS IT POSSIBLE?
WATER IS RARE AND VALUABLE AND SHE JUST...
I-I'LL NEVER MEET ANYONE LIKE HER AGAIN!!
WAIT!
MY NAME IS LAU! I'M FROM THE YOTSU-MIMI TRIBE!
PLEASE! YOU HAVE TO TAKE ME WITH YOU!
I, UHHH, STILL HAVE TO THANK YOU FOR GIVING ME WATER! DON'T GO. TAKE ME!
MAKING WATER ...
I HAVE TO KNOW HOW SHE DOES IT.
HUH?

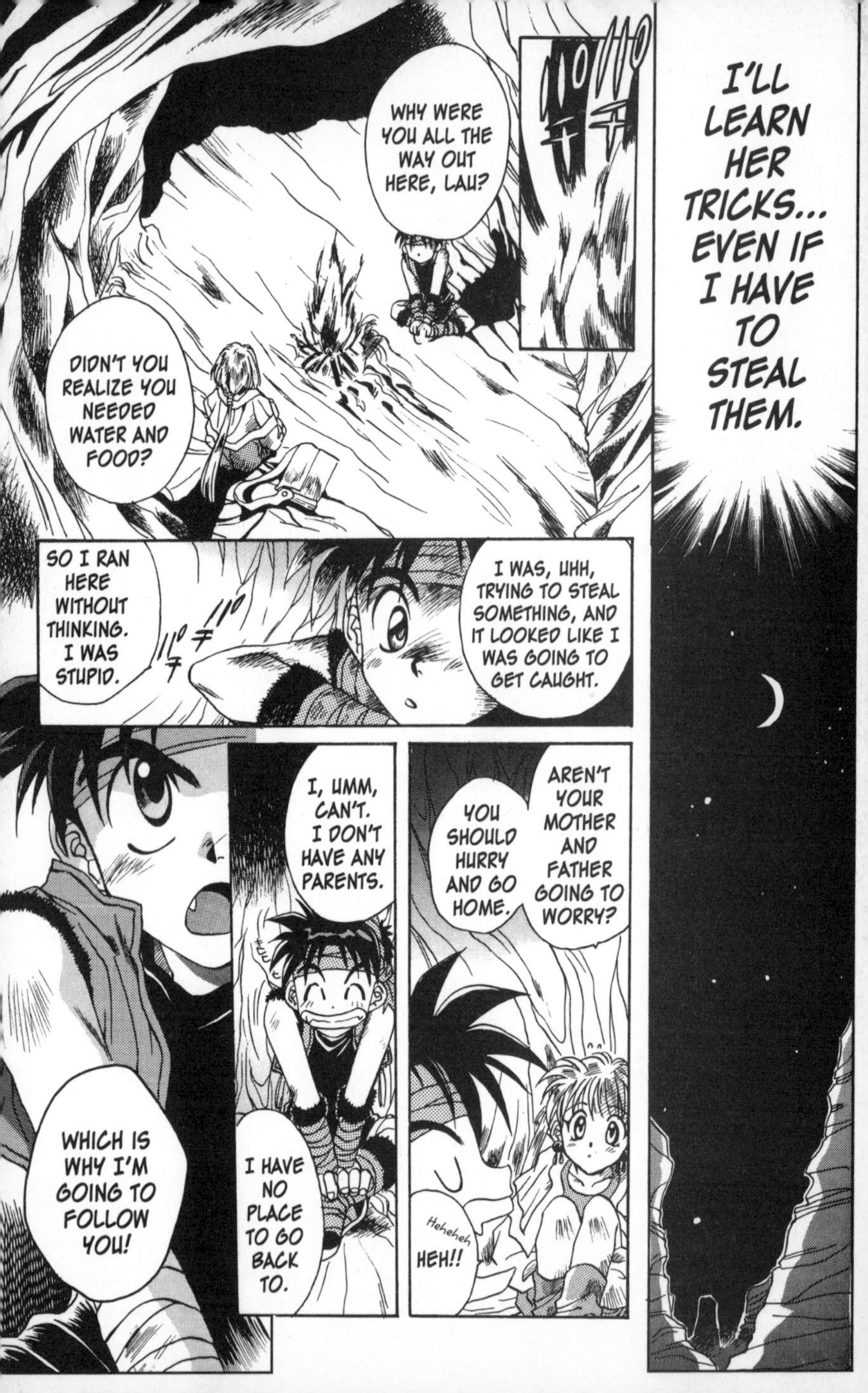
I'LL LEARN HER TRICKS... EVEN IF I HAVE TO STEAL THEM.
WHY WERE YOU ALL THE WAY OUT HERE, LAU?
DIDN'T YOU REALIZE YOU NEEDED WATER AND FOOD?
I WAS, UHH, TRYING TO STEAL SOMETHING, AND IT LOOKED LIKE I WAS GOING TO GET CAUGHT.
SO I RAN HERE WITHOUT THINKING. I WAS STUPID.
AREN'T YOUR MOTHER AND FATHER GOING TO WORRY?
YOU SHOULD HURRY AND GO HOME.
Heheheh
HEH!!
I, UMM, CAN'T. I DON'T HAVE ANY PARENTS.
I HAVE NO PLACE TO GO BACK TO.
WHICH IS WHY I'M GOING TO FOLLOW YOU!

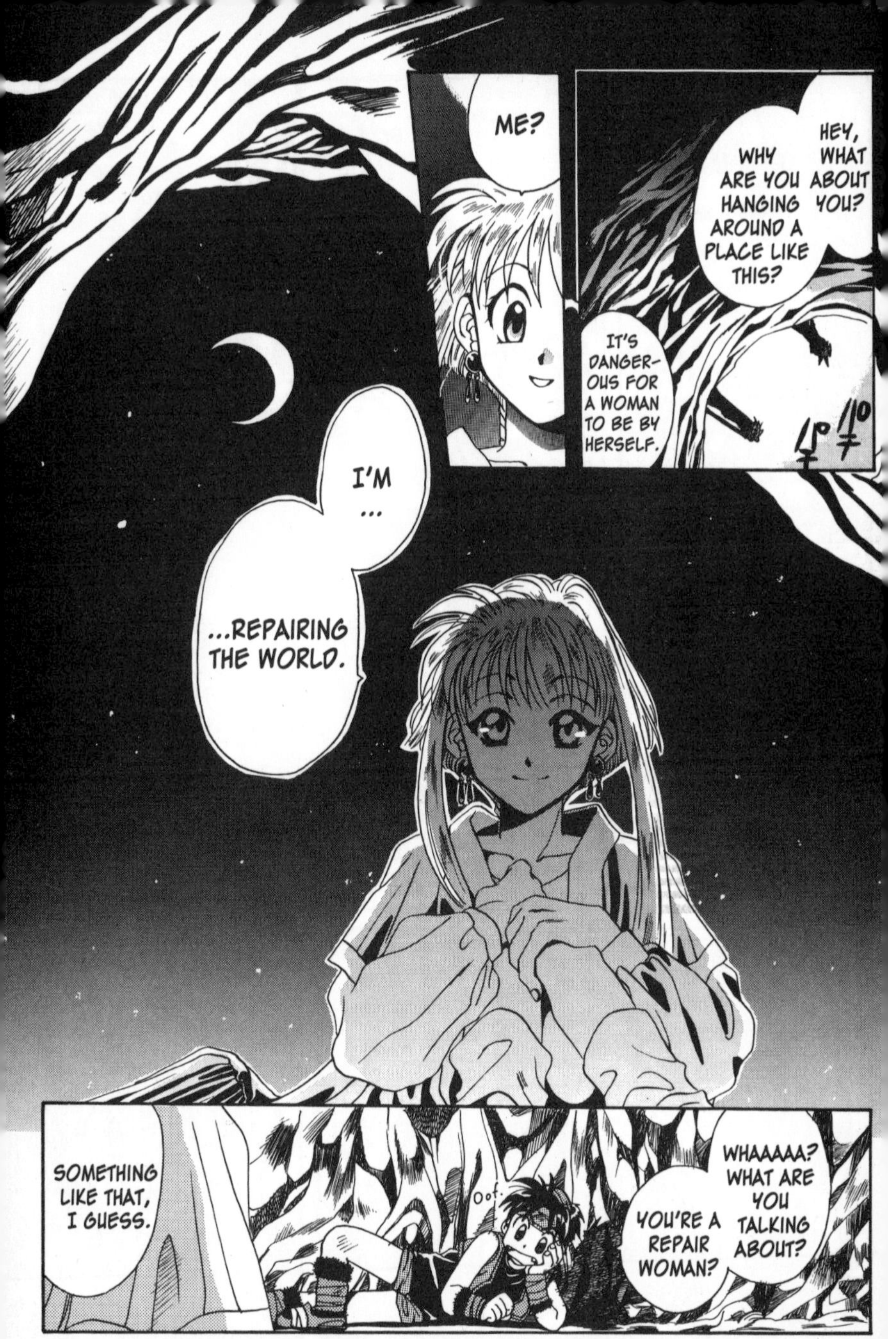
HEY, WHAT ABOUT YOU? WHY ARE YOU HANGING AROUND A PLACE LIKE THIS?
IT'S DANGER-OUS FOR A WOMAN TO BE BY HERSELF.
ME?
I'M ...
...REPAIRING THE WORLD.
WHAAAAA? WHAT ARE YOU TALKING ABOUT?
YOU'RE A REPAIR WOMAN?
Oof.
SOMETHING LIKE THAT, I GUESS.

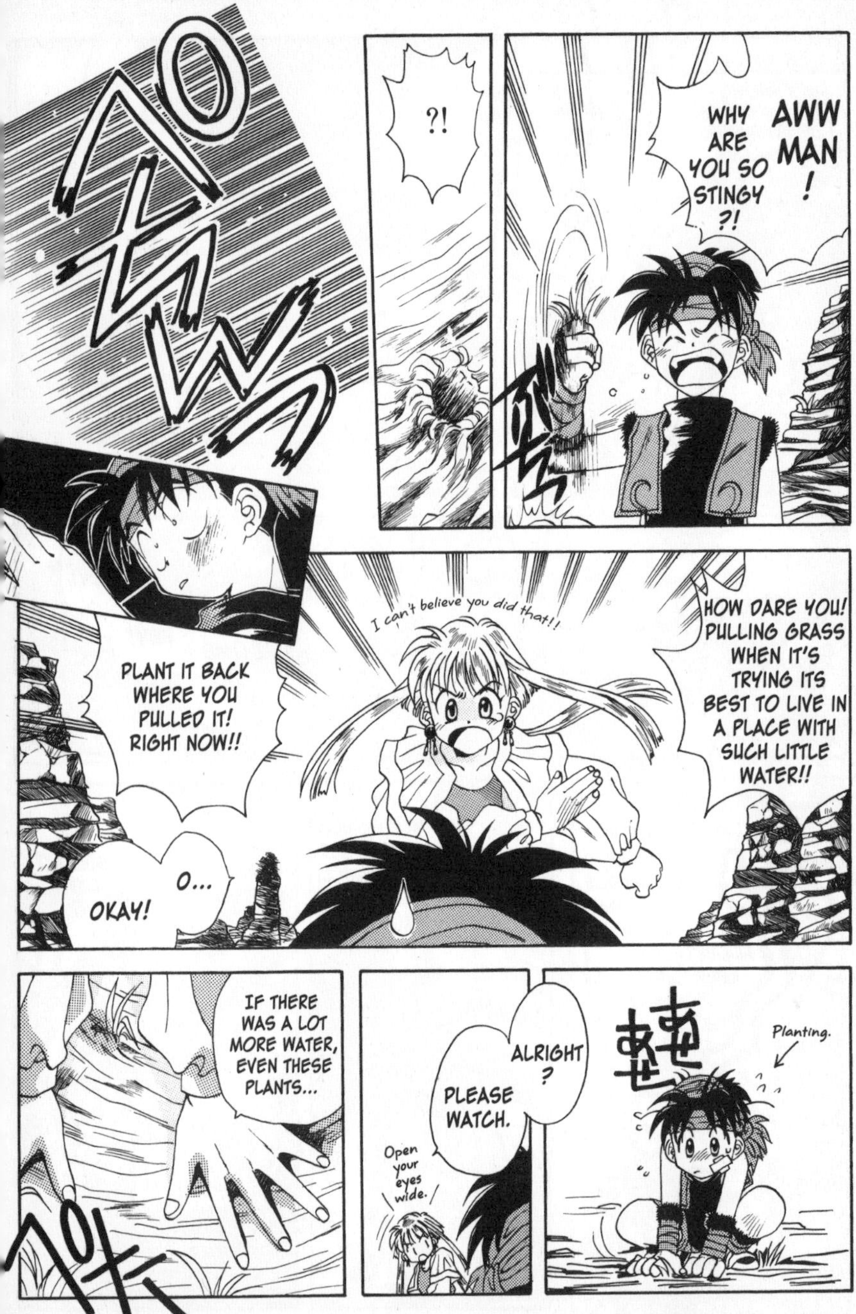
AWW MAN!
WHY ARE YOU SO STINGY?!
?!
HOW DARE YOU! PULLING GRASS WHEN IT'S TRYING ITS BEST TO LIVE IN A PLACE WITH SUCH LITTLE WATER!!
I can't believe you did that!!
PLANT IT BACK WHERE YOU PULLED IT! RIGHT NOW!!
O... OKAY!
Planting.
ALRIGHT?
PLEASE WATCH.
Open your eyes wide.
IF THERE WAS A LOT MORE WATER, EVEN THESE PLANTS...

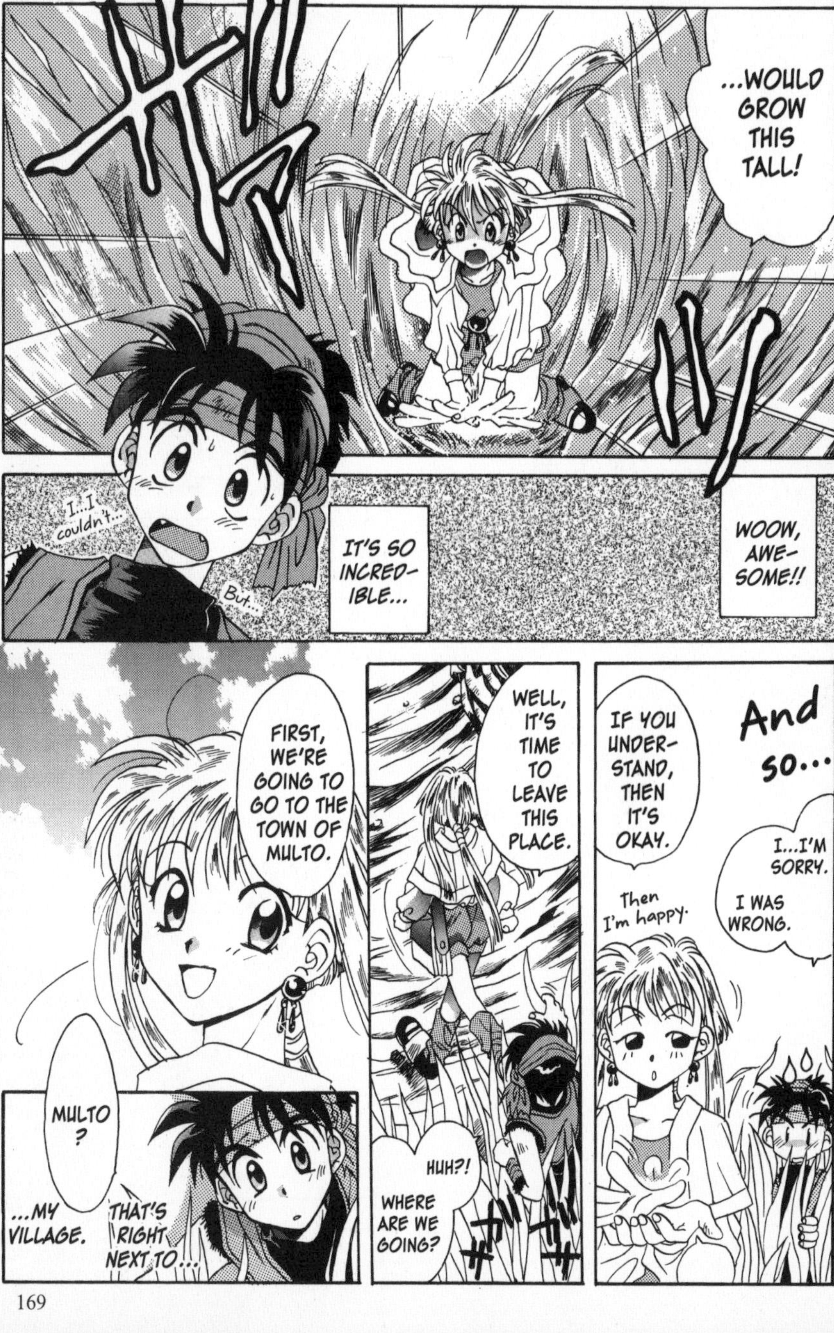
...WOULD GROW THIS TALL!
WOOW, AWE-SOME!!
IT'S SO INCRED-IBLE...
I...I couldn't...
But...
And so...
I...I'M SORRY.
I WAS WRONG.
IF YOU UNDER-STAND, THEN IT'S OKAY.
Then I'm happy.
WELL, IT'S TIME TO LEAVE THIS PLACE.
HUH?!
WHERE ARE WE GOING?
FIRST, WE'RE GOING TO GO TO THE TOWN OF MULTO.
MULTO?
THAT'S RIGHT NEXT TO...
...MY VILLAGE.

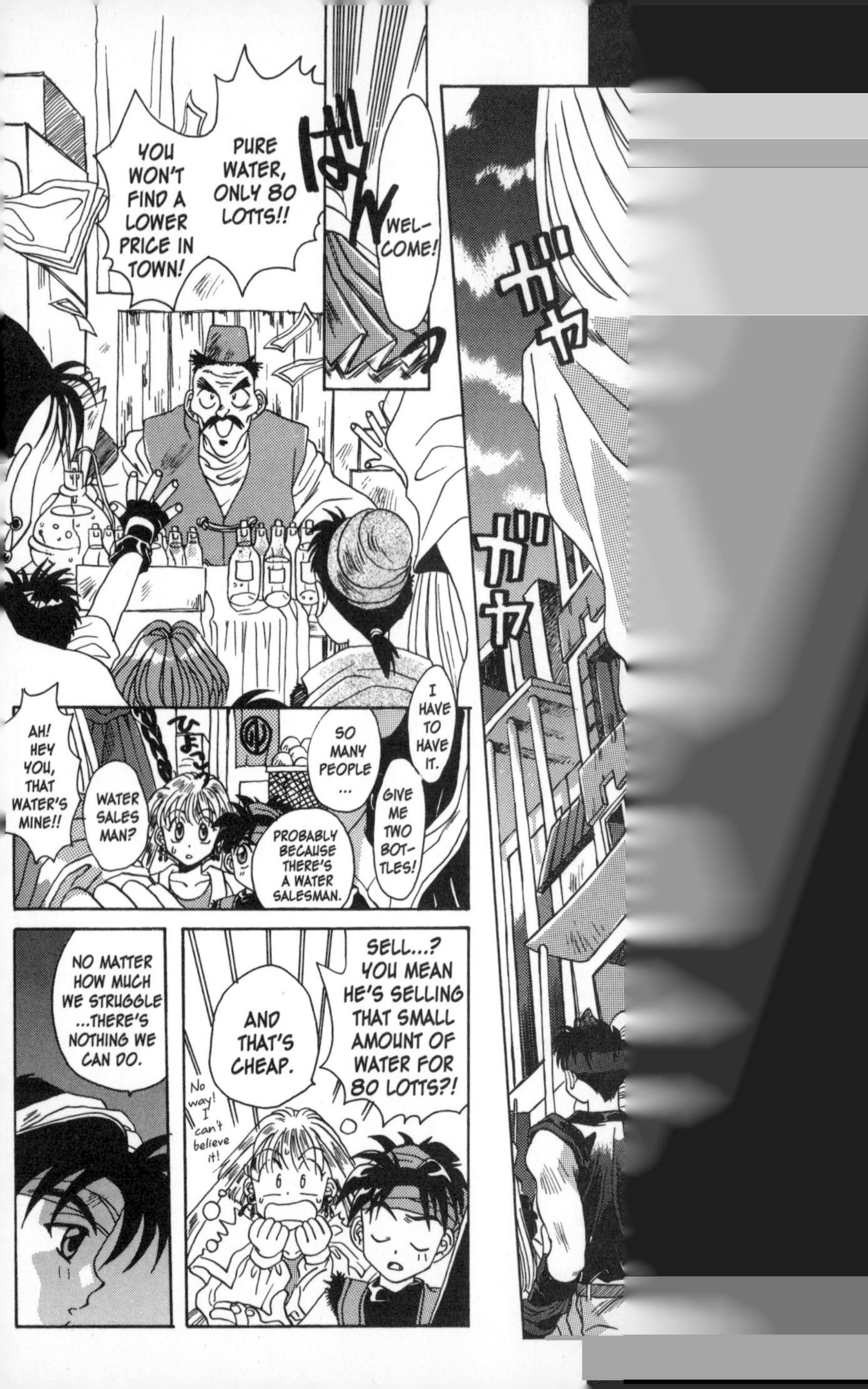
ガヤ
ガヤ
WEL-COME!
ぱん
PURE WATER, ONLY 80 LOTTS!!
YOU WON'T FIND A LOWER PRICE IN TOWN!
I HAVE TO HAVE IT.
GIVE ME TWO BOT-TLES!
SO MANY PEOPLE ...
PROBABLY BECAUSE THERE'S A WATER SALESMAN.
WATER SALES MAN?
AH! HEY YOU, THAT WATER'S MINE!!
SELL...? YOU MEAN HE'S SELLING THAT SMALL AMOUNT OF WATER FOR 80 LOTTS?!
AND THAT'S CHEAP.
No way! I can't believe it!
NO MATTER HOW MUCH WE STRUGGLE ...THERE'S NOTHING WE CAN DO.

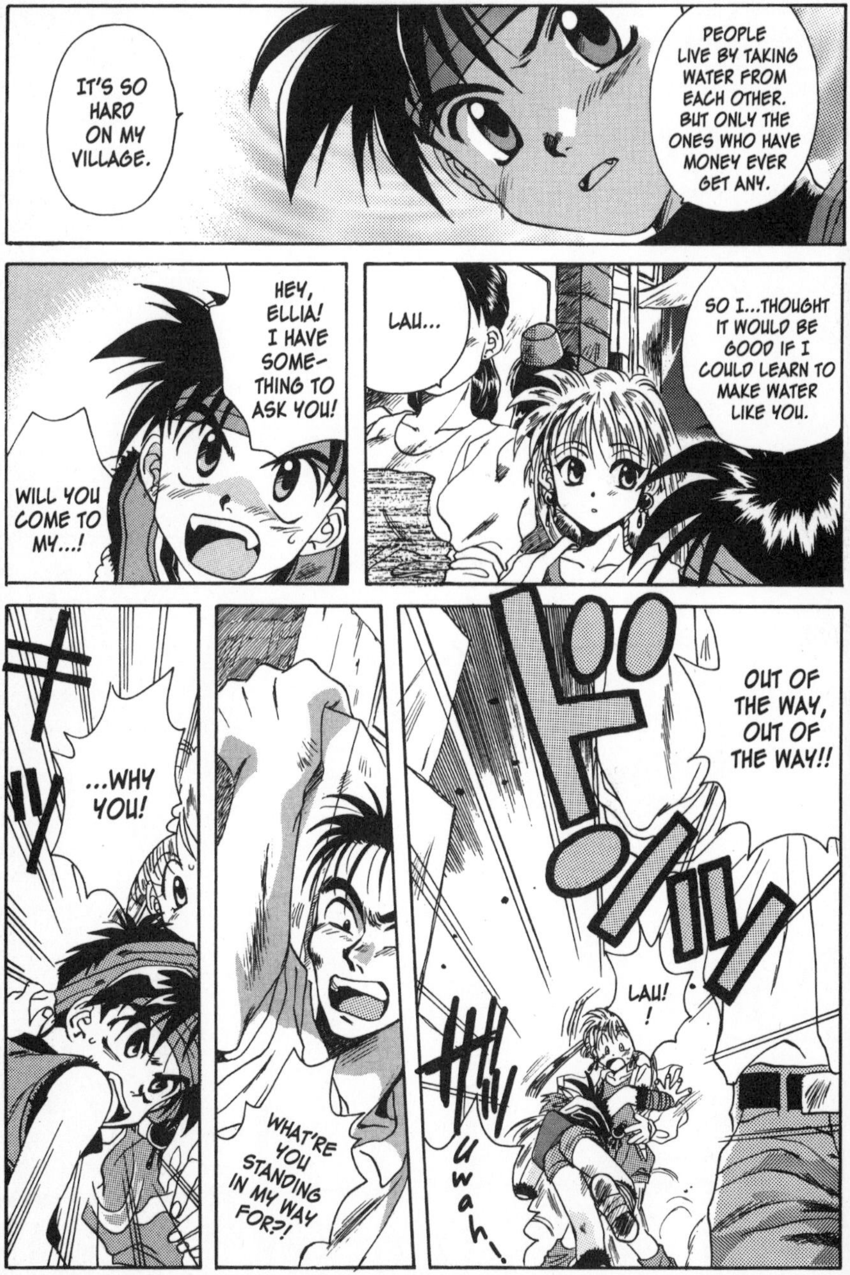
PEOPLE LIVE BY TAKING WATER FROM EACH OTHER. BUT ONLY THE ONES WHO HAVE MONEY EVER GET ANY.
IT'S SO HARD ON MY VILLAGE.
SO I...THOUGHT IT WOULD BE GOOD IF I COULD LEARN TO MAKE WATER LIKE YOU.
LAU...
HEY, ELLIA! I HAVE SOME-THING TO ASK YOU!
WILL YOU COME TO MY...!
OUT OF THE WAY, OUT OF THE WAY!!
LAU!!
Uwah!
WHAT'RE YOU STANDING IN MY WAY FOR?!
...WHY YOU!

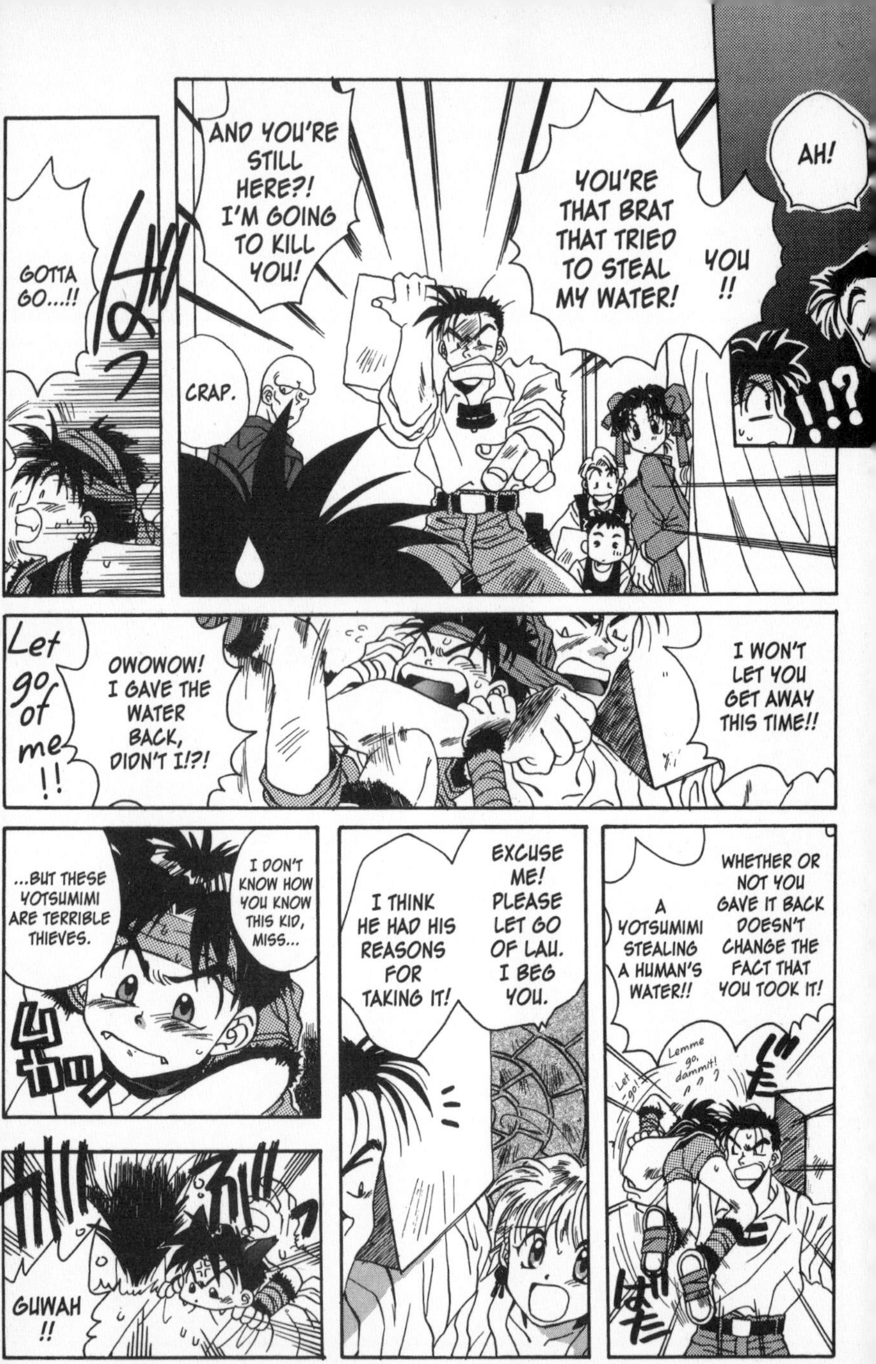
AH!
YOU !!
!!?
YOU'RE THAT BRAT THAT TRIED TO STEAL MY WATER!
AND YOU'RE STILL HERE?! I'M GOING TO KILL YOU!
CRAP.
GOTTA GO...!!
I WON'T LET YOU GET AWAY THIS TIME!!
OWOWOW! I GAVE THE WATER BACK, DIDN'T I!?!
Let go of me !!
WHETHER OR NOT YOU GAVE IT BACK DOESN'T CHANGE THE FACT THAT YOU TOOK IT!
A YOTSUMIMI STEALING A HUMAN'S WATER!!
Lemme go, dammit!
Let-go!
EXCUSE ME! PLEASE LET GO OF LAU. I BEG YOU.
I THINK HE HAD HIS REASONS FOR TAKING IT!
I DON'T KNOW HOW YOU KNOW THIS KID, MISS...
...BUT THESE YOTSUMIMI ARE TERRIBLE THIEVES.
GUWAH !!

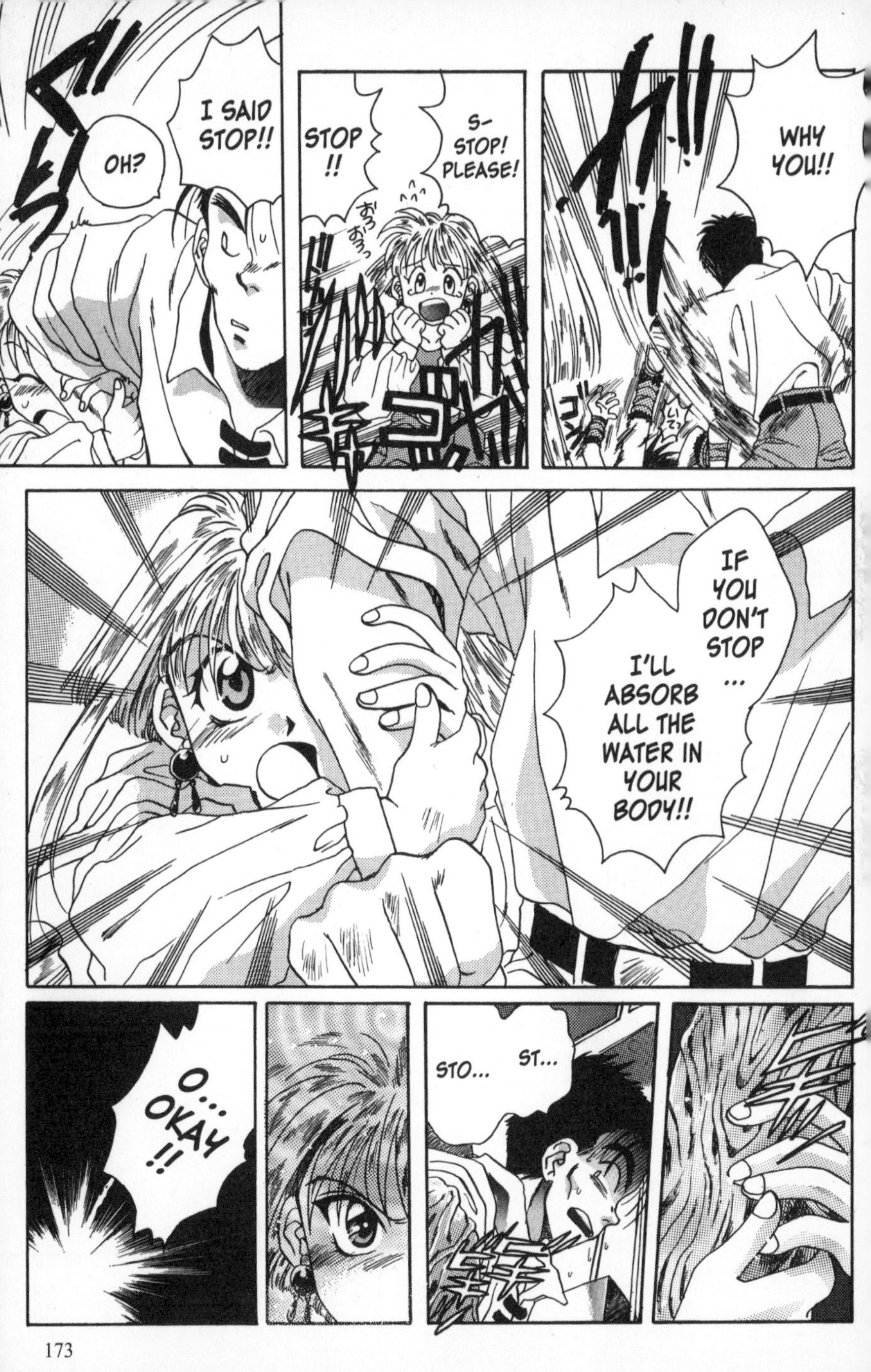
WHY YOU!!
S-STOP! PLEASE!
STOP!!
I SAID STOP!!
OH?
IF YOU DON'T STOP ...
I'LL ABSORB ALL THE WATER IN YOUR BODY!!
ST...
STO...
O... OKAY!!

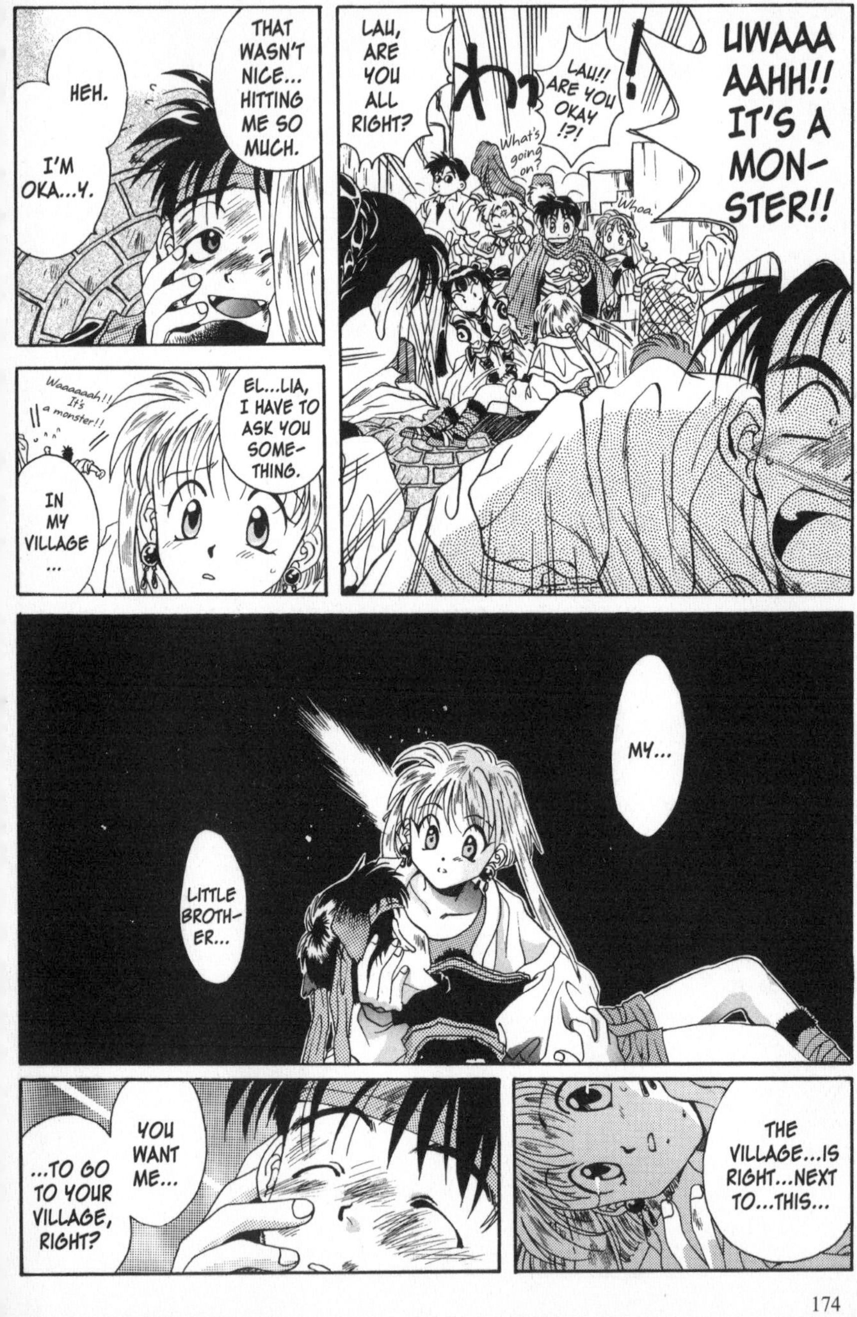
UWAAA AAHH!! IT'S A MON-STER!!
LAU!! ARE YOU OKAY !?!
わっ
What's going on?
Whoa.
LAU, ARE YOU ALL RIGHT?
THAT WASN'T NICE... HITTING ME SO MUCH.
HEH.
I'M OKA...Y.
EL...LIA, I HAVE TO ASK YOU SOME-THING.
Waaaaaah!! It's a monster!!
IN MY VILLAGE ...
MY...
LITTLE BROTH-ER...
THE VILLAGE...IS RIGHT...NEXT TO...THIS...
YOU WANT ME...
...TO GO TO YOUR VILLAGE, RIGHT?

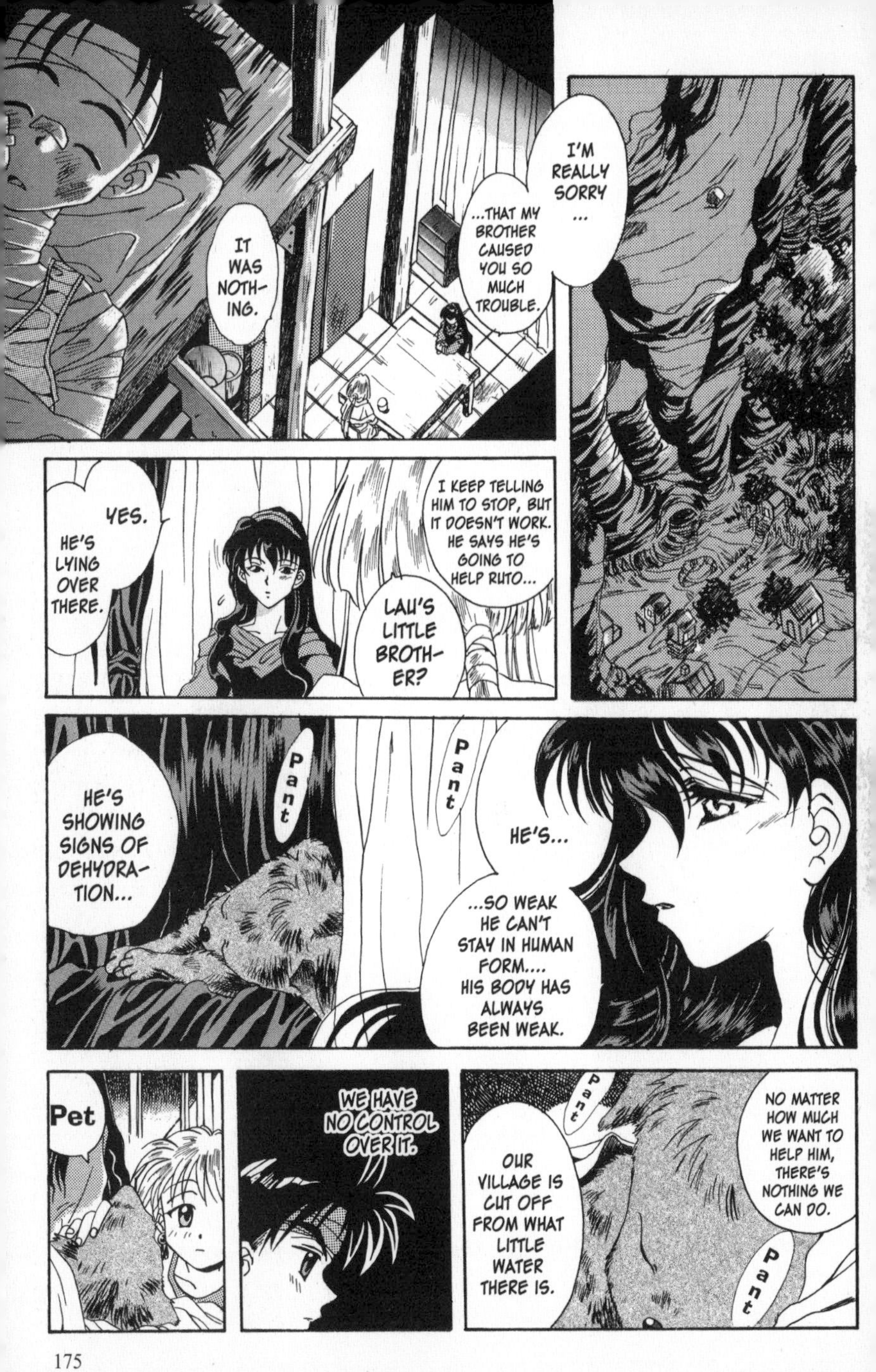
I'M REALLY SORRY ...
...THAT MY BROTHER CAUSED YOU SO MUCH TROUBLE.
IT WAS NOTHING.
I KEEP TELLING HIM TO STOP, BUT IT DOESN'T WORK. HE SAYS HE'S GOING TO HELP RUTO...
LAU'S LITTLE BROTHER?
YES.
HE'S LYING OVER THERE.
Pant
HE'S...
...SO WEAK HE CAN'T STAY IN HUMAN FORM.... HIS BODY HAS ALWAYS BEEN WEAK.
Pant
HE'S SHOWING SIGNS OF DEHYDRATION...
NO MATTER HOW MUCH WE WANT TO HELP HIM, THERE'S NOTHING WE CAN DO.
Pant
OUR VILLAGE IS CUT OFF FROM WHAT LITTLE WATER THERE IS.
Pant
WE HAVE NO CONTROL OVER IT.
Pet

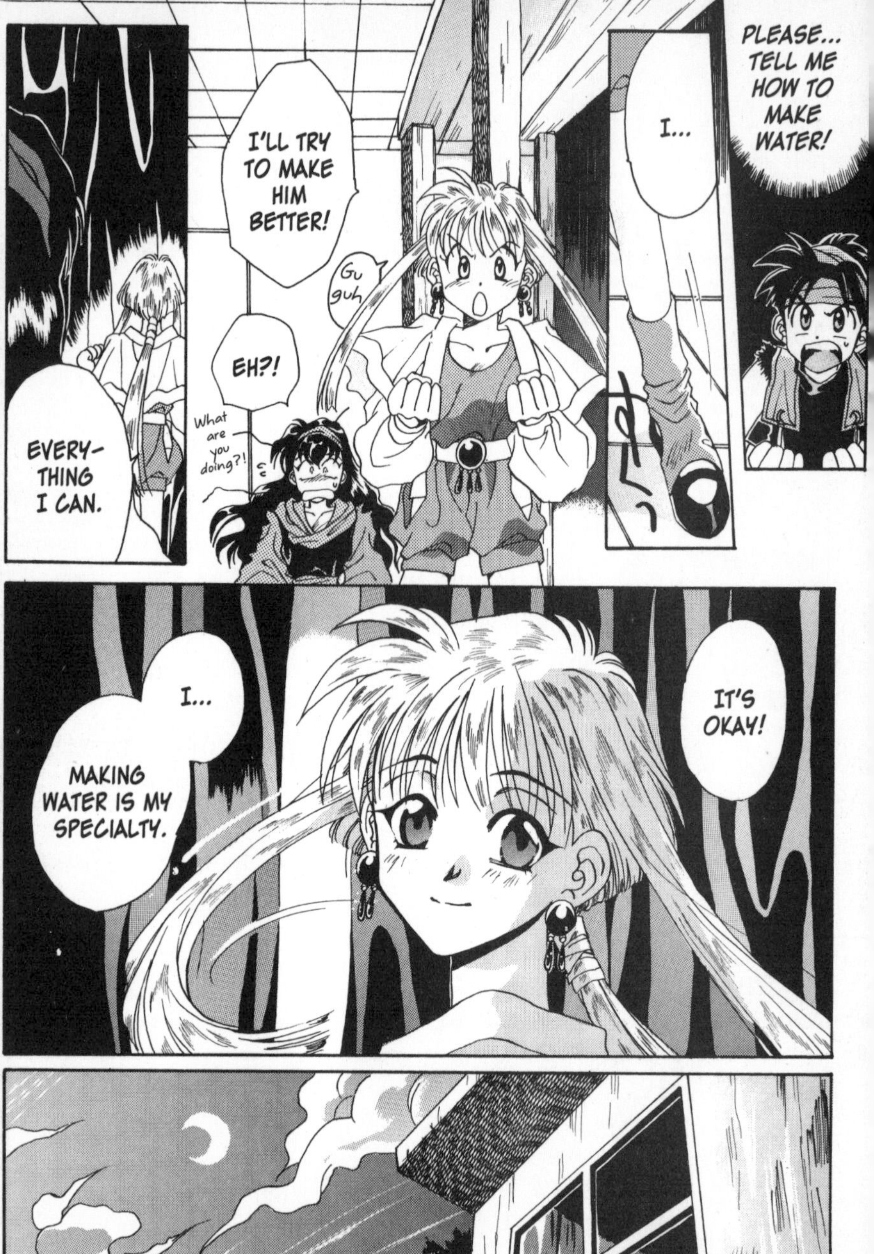
PLEASE... TELL ME HOW TO MAKE WATER!
I...
I'LL TRY TO MAKE HIM BETTER!
Gu guh
EH?!
What are you doing?!
EVERY-THING I CAN.
IT'S OKAY!
I...
MAKING WATER IS MY SPECIALTY.

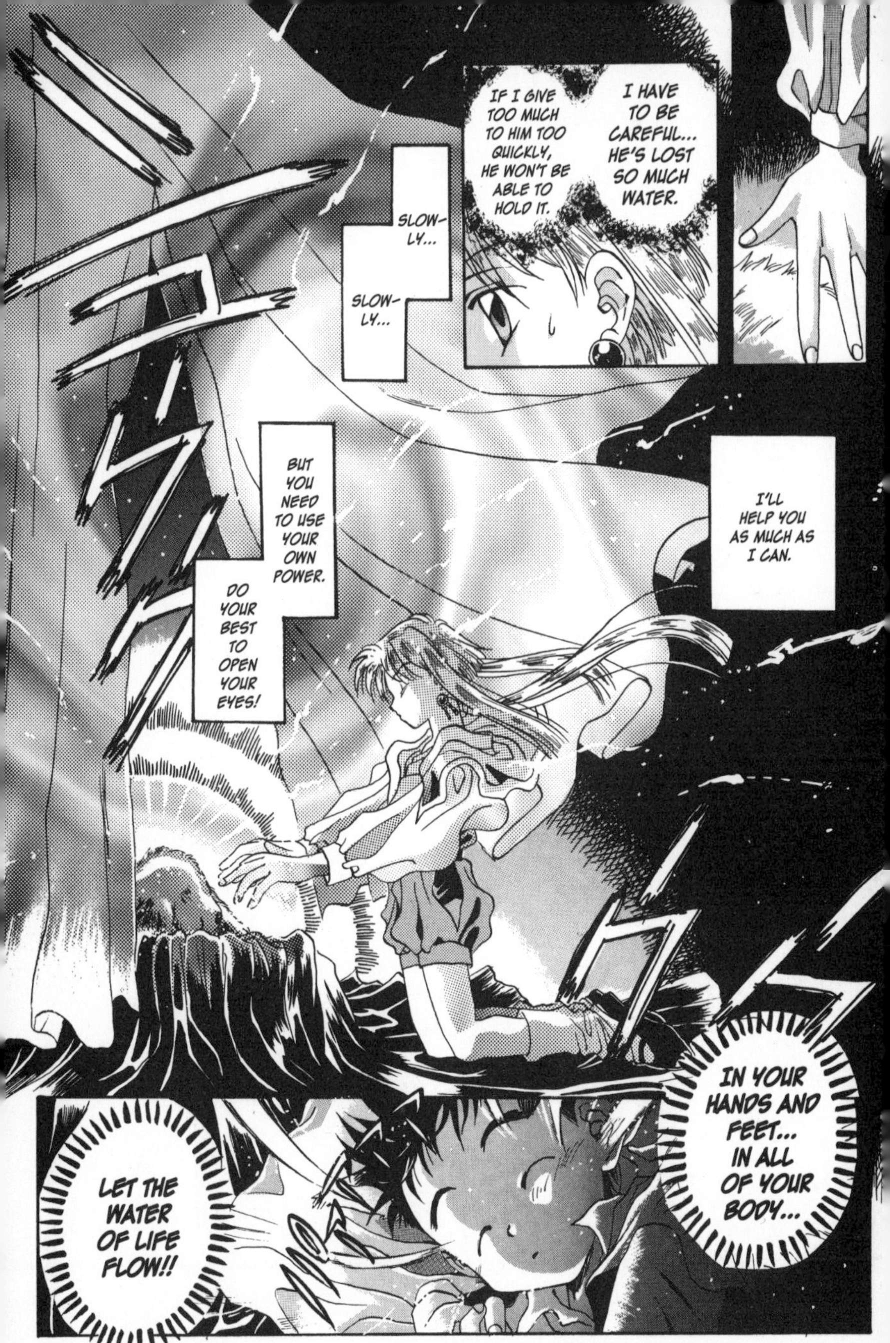
I HAVE TO BE CAREFUL... HE'S LOST SO MUCH WATER.
IF I GIVE TOO MUCH TO HIM TOO QUICKLY, HE WON'T BE ABLE TO HOLD IT.
SLOW-LY...
SLOW-LY...
I'LL HELP YOU AS MUCH AS I CAN.
BUT YOU NEED TO USE YOUR OWN POWER.
DO YOUR BEST TO OPEN YOUR EYES!
IN YOUR HANDS AND FEET... IN ALL OF YOUR BODY...
LET THE WATER OF LIFE FLOW!!

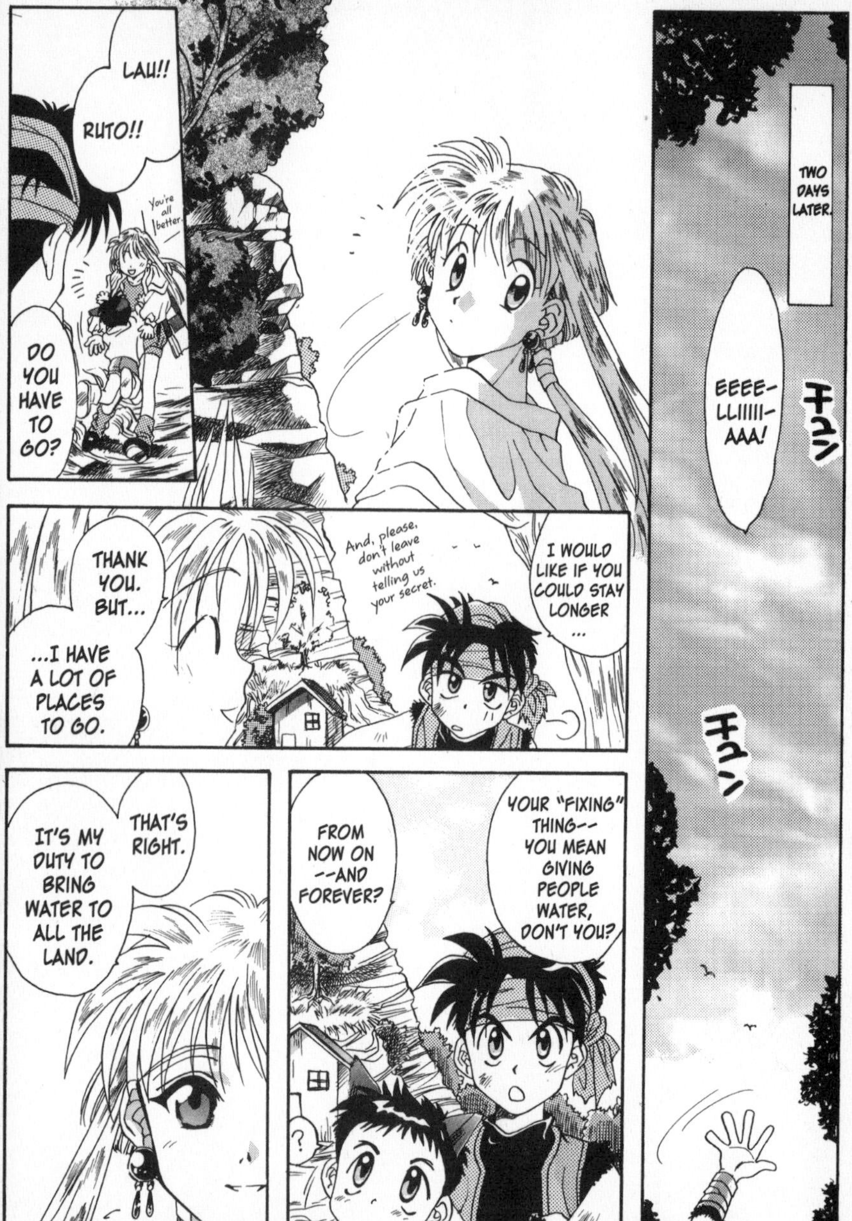

TWO DAYS LATER.
EEEE-LLIIIII-AAA!
チュン
チュン
LAU!!
RUTO!!
You're all better.
DO YOU HAVE TO GO?
I WOULD LIKE IF YOU COULD STAY LONGER ...
And, please, don't leave without telling us your secret.
THANK YOU. BUT...
...I HAVE A LOT OF PLACES TO GO.
YOUR "FIXING" THING-- YOU MEAN GIVING PEOPLE WATER, DON'T YOU?
FROM NOW ON --AND FOREVER?
?
THAT'S RIGHT.
IT'S MY DUTY TO BRING WATER TO ALL THE LAND.

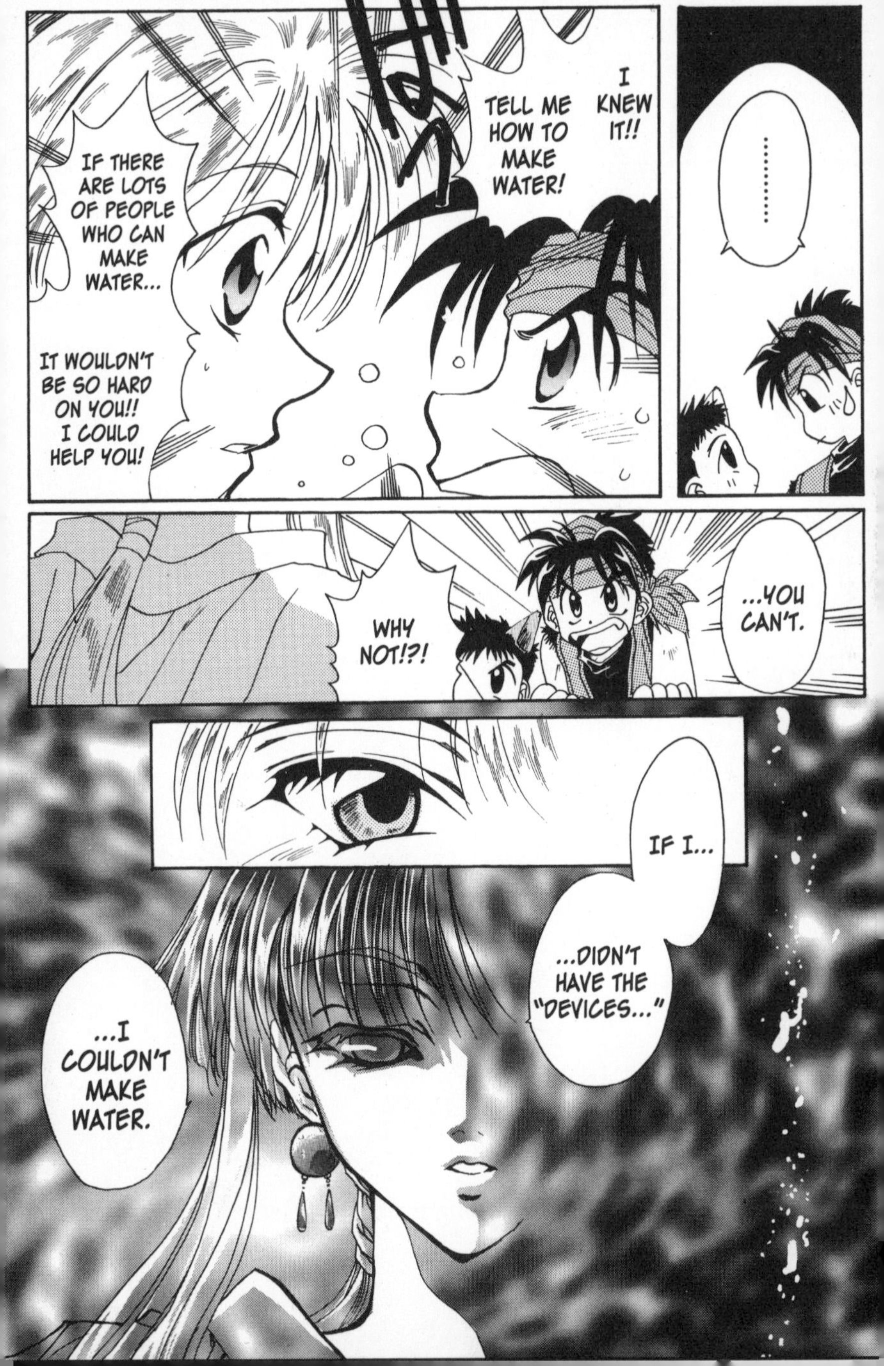
......
I KNEW IT!!
TELL ME HOW TO MAKE WATER!
はっ
IF THERE ARE LOTS OF PEOPLE WHO CAN MAKE WATER...
IT WOULDN'T BE SO HARD ON YOU!! I COULD HELP YOU!
...YOU CAN'T.
WHY NOT!?!
IF I...
...DIDN'T HAVE THE "DEVICES..."
...I COULDN'T MAKE WATER.

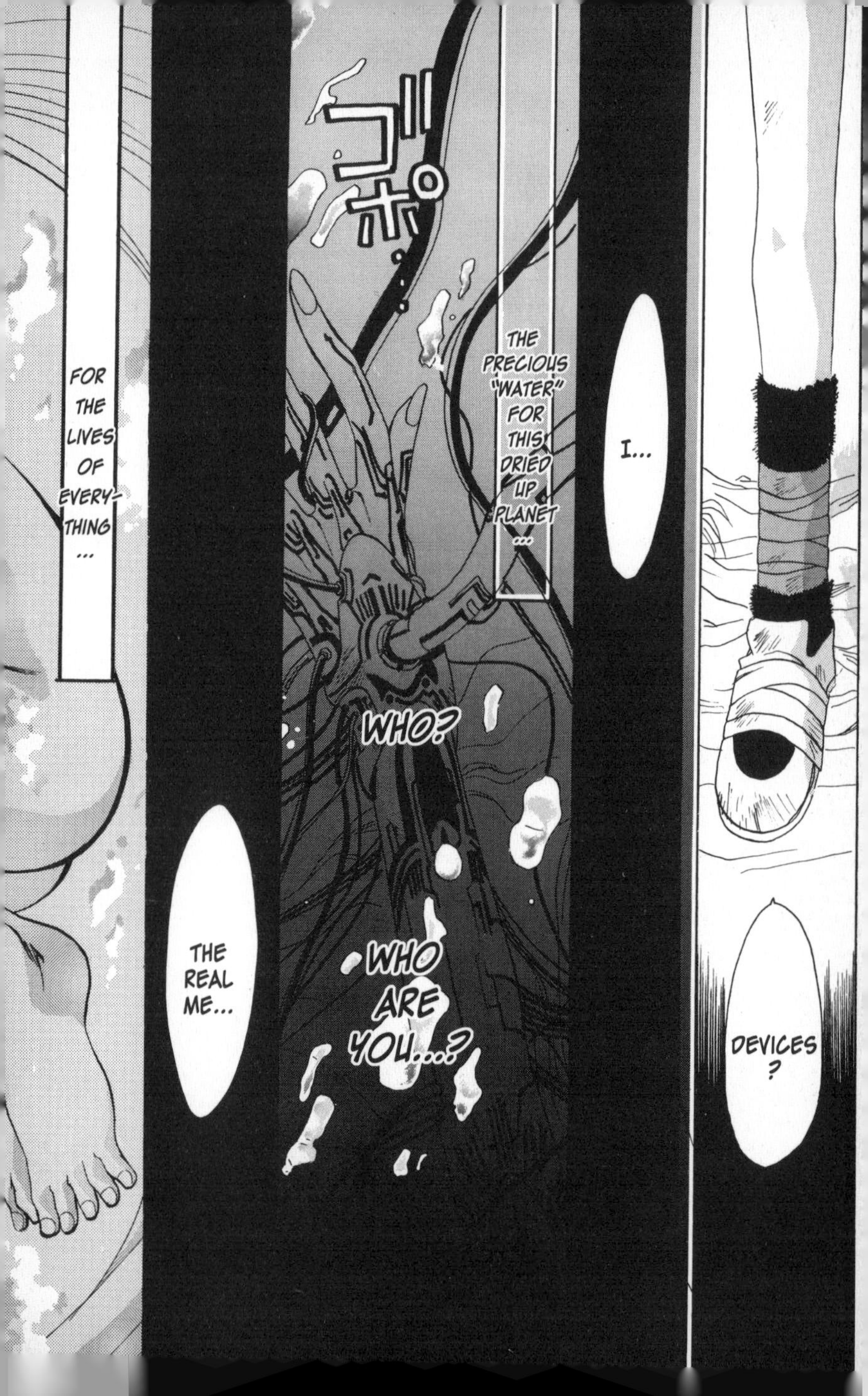

DEVICES ?
I...
ゴポ
THE PRECIOUS "WATER" FOR THIS DRIED UP PLANET ...
WHO?
WHO ARE YOU...?
THE REAL ME...
FOR THE LIVES OF EVERYTHING ...

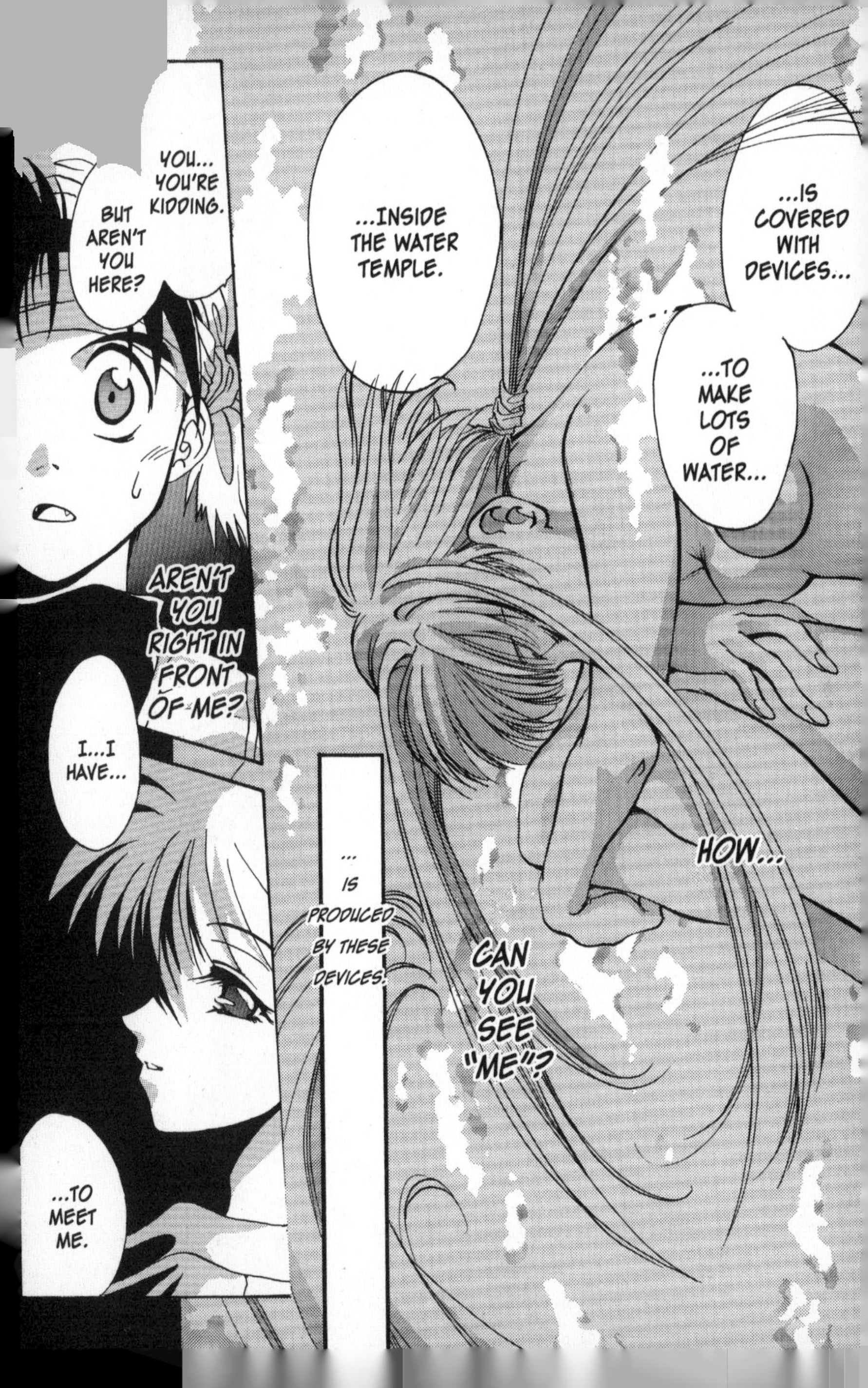
...IS COVERED WITH DEVICES...
...TO MAKE LOTS OF WATER...
...INSIDE THE WATER TEMPLE.
... IS PRODUCED BY THESE DEVICES!
HOW...
CAN YOU SEE "ME"?
YOU... YOU'RE KIDDING.
BUT AREN'T YOU HERE?
AREN'T YOU RIGHT IN FRONT OF ME?
I...I HAVE...
...TO MEET ME.

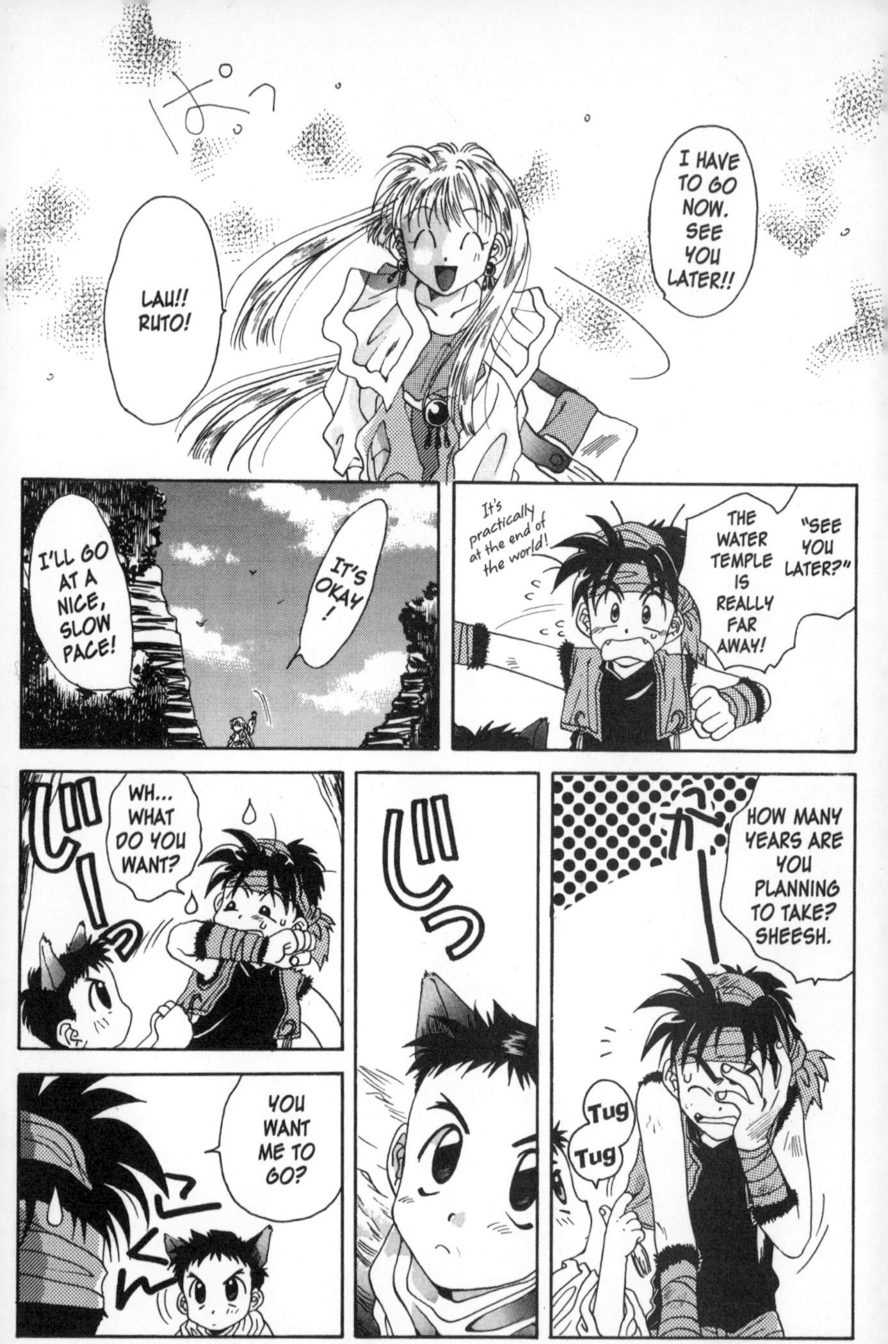
ぱっ
I HAVE TO GO NOW. SEE YOU LATER!!
LAU!! RUTO!
"SEE YOU LATER?"
THE WATER TEMPLE IS REALLY FAR AWAY!
It's practically at the end of the world!
IT'S OKAY!
I'LL GO AT A NICE, SLOW PACE!
HOW MANY YEARS ARE YOU PLANNING TO TAKE? SHEESH.
Tug
Tug
じっ
WH... WHAT DO YOU WANT?
じー
YOU WANT ME TO GO?

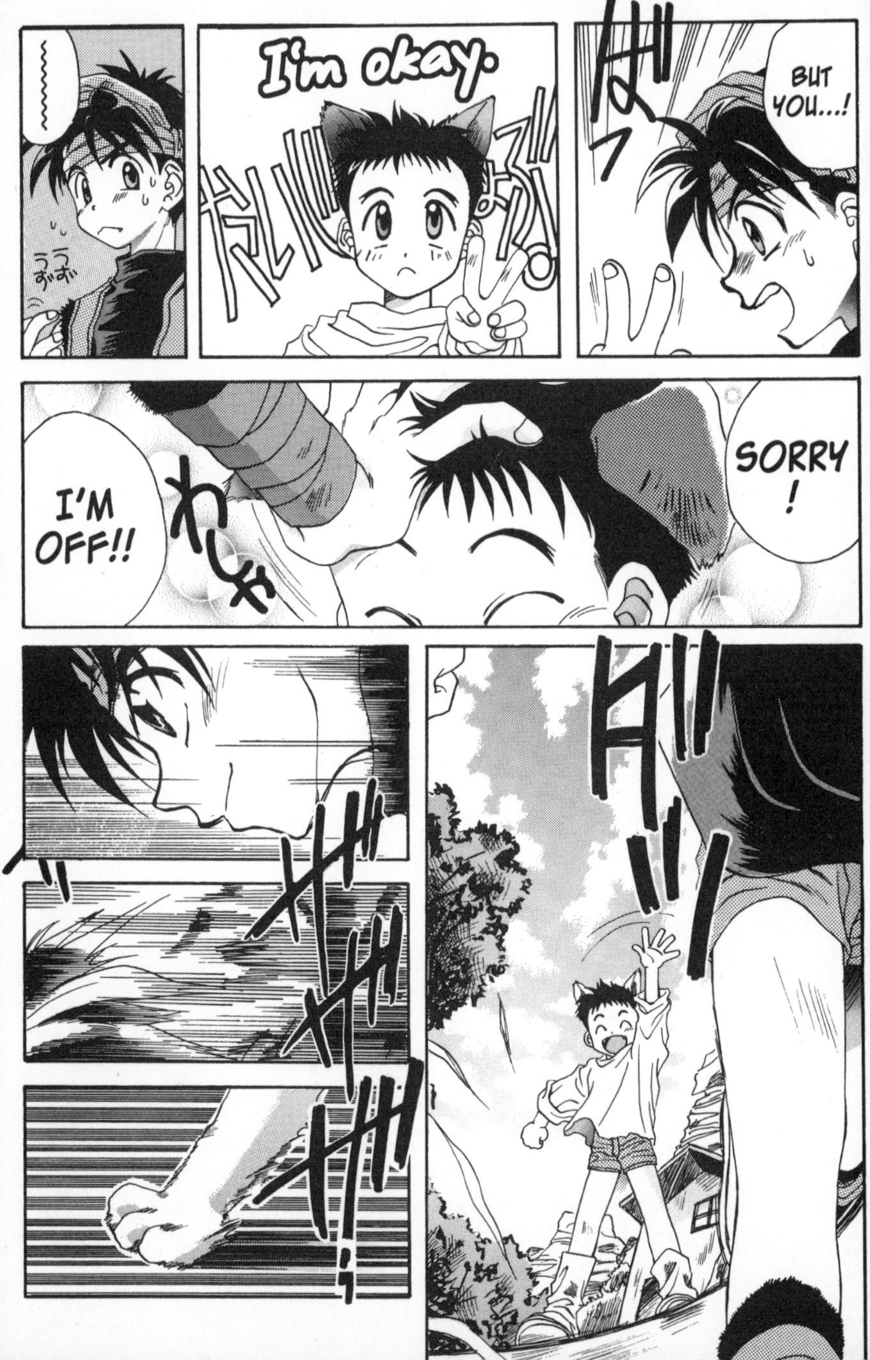

BUT YOU...!
I'm okay.
SORRY!
I'M OFF!!

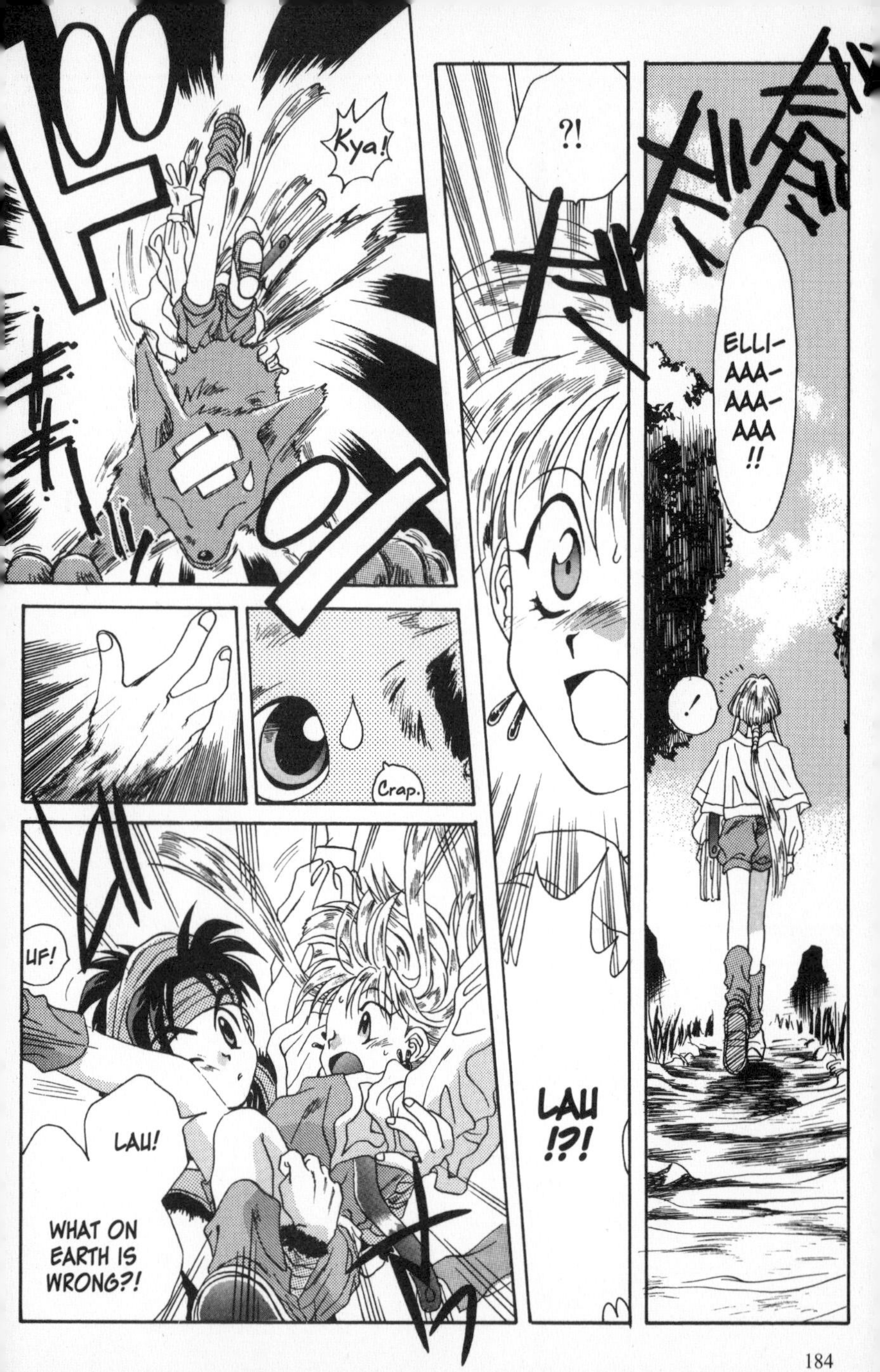
ELLI-AAA-AAA-AAA !!
!
?!
LAU !?!
Kya!
Crap.
UF!
LAU!
WHAT ON EARTH IS WRONG?!

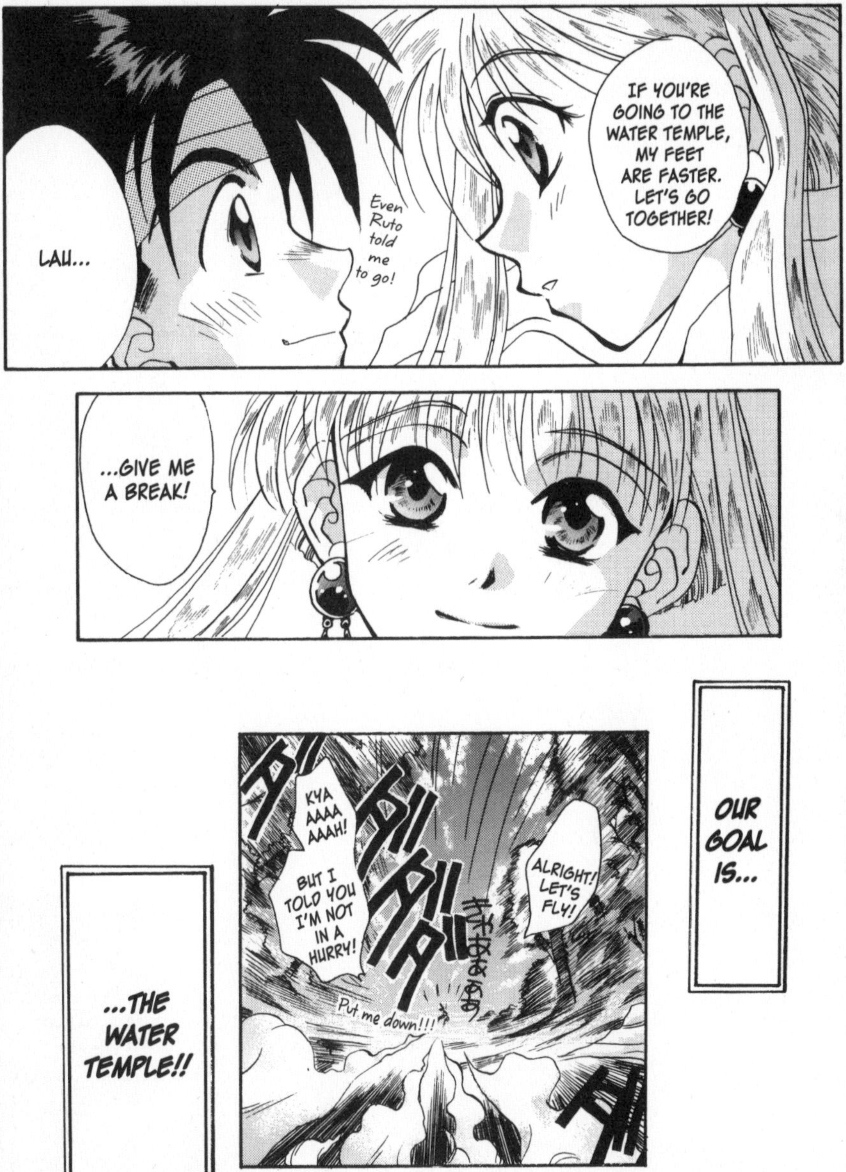
IF YOU'RE GOING TO THE WATER TEMPLE, MY FEET ARE FASTER. LET'S GO TOGETHER!
Even Ruto told me to go!
LAU...
...GIVE ME A BREAK!
OUR GOAL IS...
ALRIGHT! LET'S FLY!
KYA AAAA AAAH!
BUT I TOLD YOU I'M NOT IN A HURRY!
Put me down!!!
...THE WATER TEMPLE!!

MYTH:OX Fin

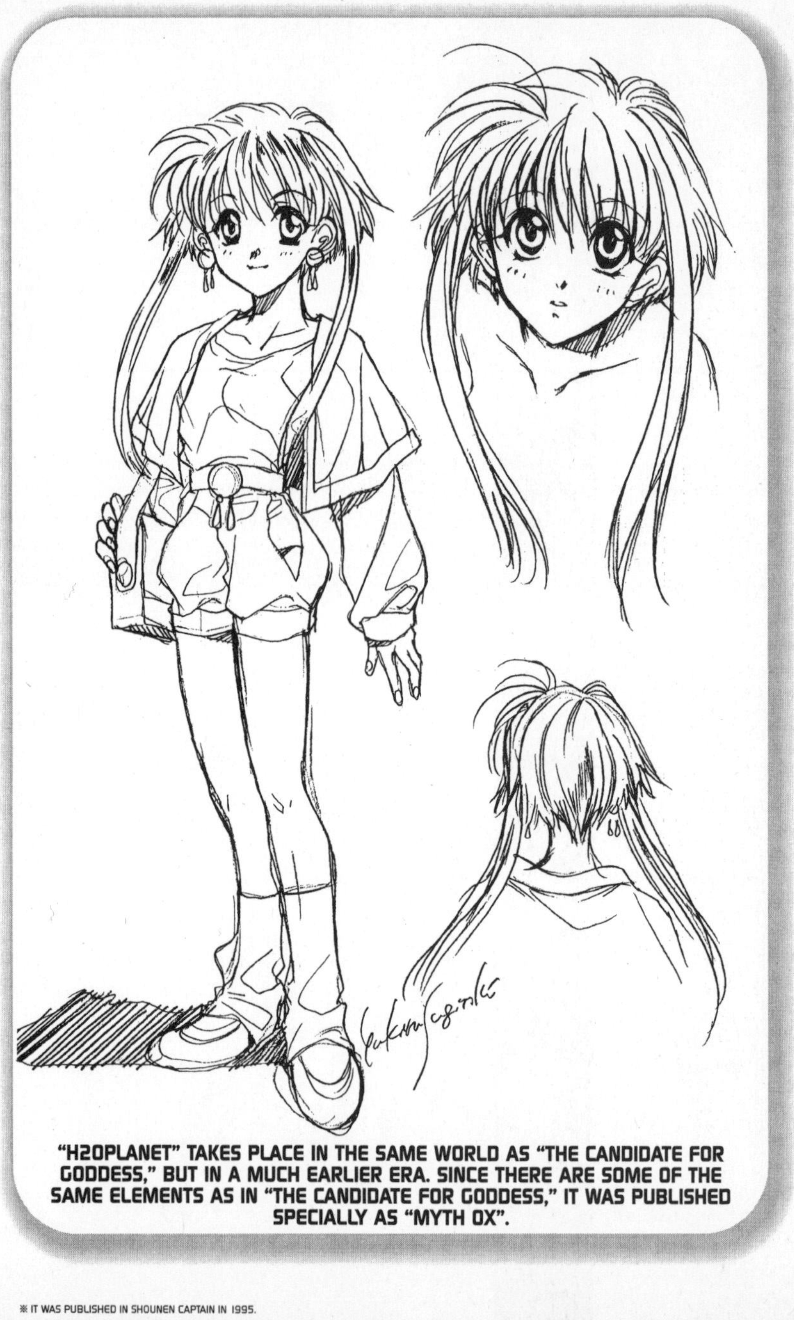

"H2OPLANET" TAKES PLACE IN THE SAME WORLD AS "THE CANDIDATE FOR GODDESS," BUT IN A MUCH EARLIER ERA. SINCE THERE ARE SOME OF THE SAME ELEMENTS AS IN "THE CANDIDATE FOR GODDESS," IT WAS PUBLISHED SPECIALLY AS "MYTH OX".

※ IT WAS PUBLISHED IN SHOUNEN CAPTAIN IN 1995.

Next Page Preview of next volume

Next Page Preview of next volume

Next Page Preview of next volume

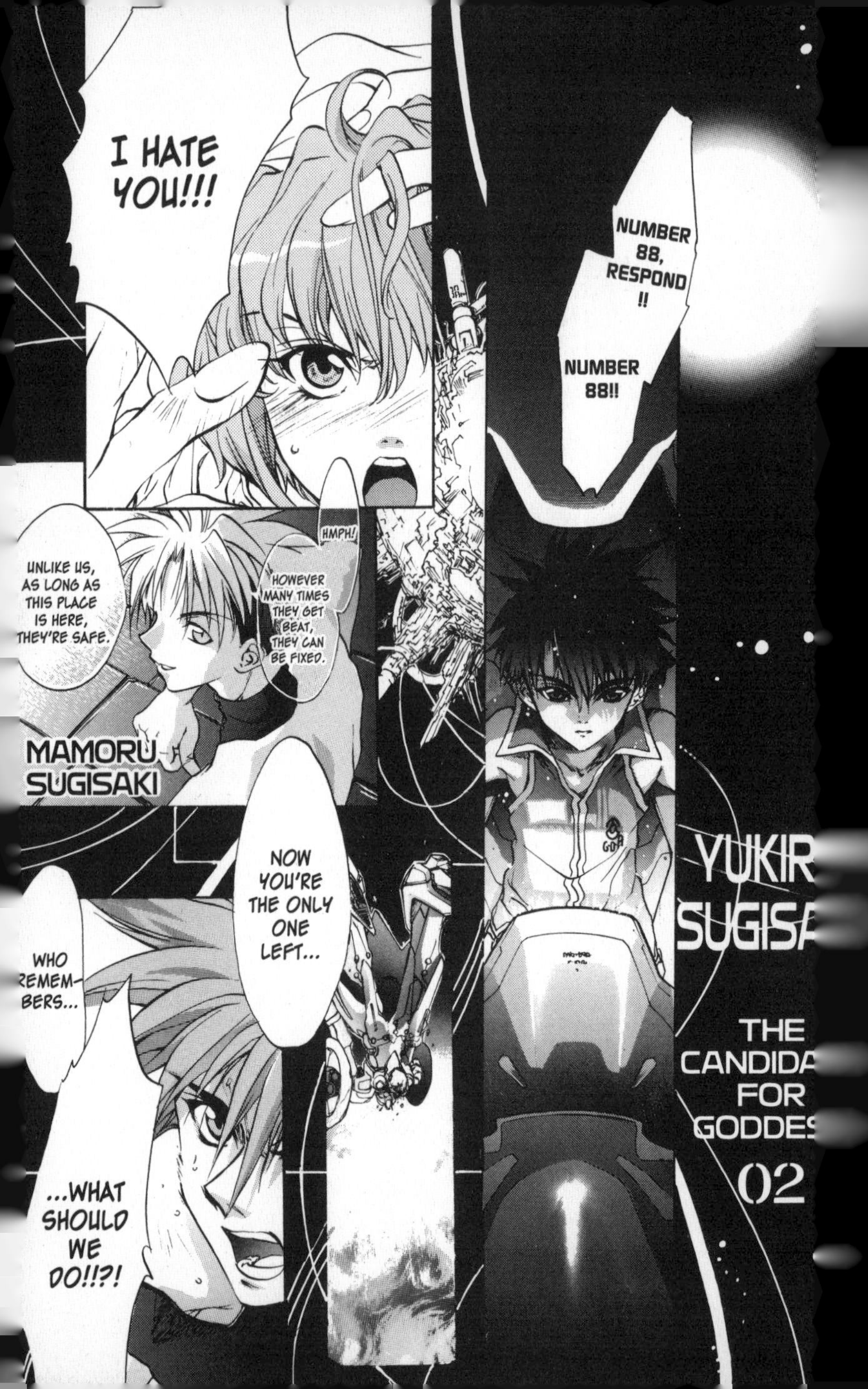
NUMBER 88, RESPOND !!
NUMBER 88!!
YUKIR SUGISA
THE CANDIDA FOR GODDES
02
I HATE YOU!!!
HMPH!
HOWEVER MANY TIMES THEY GET BEAT, THEY CAN BE FIXED.
UNLIKE US, AS LONG AS THIS PLACE IS HERE, THEY'RE SAFE.
MAMORU SUGISAKI
NOW YOU'RE THE ONLY ONE LEFT...
WHO REMEMBERS...
...WHAT SHOULD WE DO!!?!

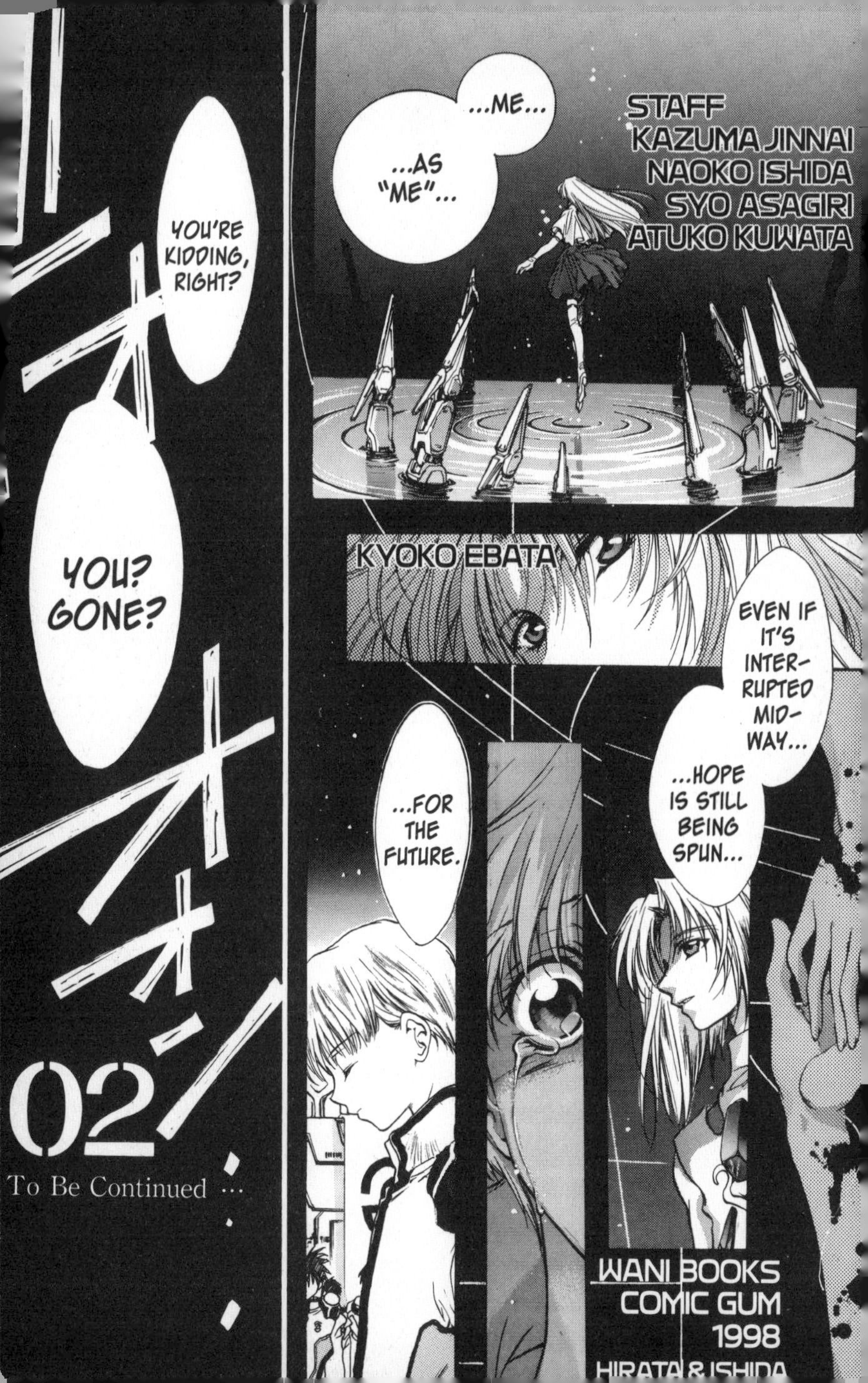
STAFF
KAZUMA JINNAI
NAOKO ISHIDA
SYO ASAGIRI
ATUKO KUWATA
...ME...
...AS "ME"...
KYOKO EBATA
EVEN IF IT'S INTER-RUPTED MID-WAY...
...HOPE IS STILL BEING SPUN...
...FOR THE FUTURE.
WANI BOOKS
COMIC GUM
1998
HIRATA & ISHIDA
YOU'RE KIDDING, RIGHT?
YOU? GONE?
02
To Be Continued ...

WELCOME, EVERYONE.

THIS IS G.O.A. (GODDESS OPERATOR ACADEMY), THE FACILITY FOR TRAINING PILOTS WHO WILL OPERATE THE GIANT HUMANOID WEAPONS, 'INGRIDS', KNOWN AS GODDESSES. G.O.A. WITH YOUR RARE HIDDEN ABILITIES, WE WOULD LIKE YOU TO ACKNOWLEDGE THAT YOU WILL BE ACTING IN A POSITION THAT WILL AFFECT THE FUTURE OF ALL MANKIND. LET US ACKNOWLEDGE THAT ALL OF YOU, WHO HAVE CLEARED THE FOLLOWING STRICT CONDITIONS, HAVE BEEN ADMITTED INTO G.O.A. AS PILOT CANDIDATES:

1
TO BE A HEALTHY MALE OF 14-16 YEARS OF AGE.
2
TO BE OF THE BLOOD-TYPE UNADULTERATED EO.
3
TO HAVE A SPECIAL ABILITY (EX) OR TO HAVE THE POTENTIAL TO HAVE IT.

Eye's Only

YOU WILL BE ENROLLED FOR THREE YEARS.
THE TRAINING IS EXTREMELY HARSH, AND MANY OF YOU WILL PROBABLY DROP OUT.
FURTHERMORE, EVEN IF YOU PASS THE TRAINING, THERE MAY BE NO VACANCY AMONG THE CURRENT PILOTS (DUE TO DEATH OR RETIREMENT BECAUSE OF DEGENERATION OF EX). WHILE YOU ARE ENROLLED, THE CHANCES OF BEING CHOSEN AS A PILOT ARE EXTREMELY LOW.
HOWEVER,
ON THE OTHER HAND, IF YOU DISPLAY ABILITIES SUPERIOR TO THOSE OF THE CURRENT PILOTS WHILE YOU ARE ENROLLED, THE ROAD TO BECOMING A PILOT WILL OPEN FOR YOU.
WE WANT YOU TO BELIEVE IN YOURSELVES, BE DILIGENT IN YOUR TRAINING, AND WIN THE POSITION OF PILOT.
IF YOU HAVE DIRECTION AND AMBITION, WE HAVE NO PROBLEMS HELPING YOU.
WE WILL GIVE YOU THE KNOWLEDGE AND TECHNIQUES NECESSARY TO BE A PILOT.
WE HAVE BUT ONE ENEMY: A GROUP OF UNIDENTIFIED LIFE FORMS WE CALL GISEISHA.
IN THIS BATTLE TO PROTECT THE PLANET ZION, WE, THE LAST OF MANKIND, WILL TAKE NO OTHER PATH THAN VICTORY.
FAILURE IS UNACCEPTABLE.
IN THE BATTLEFIELD, THERE EXISTS ONLY ONE SIMPLE RESULT.
NAMELY, YOU WIN, OR YOU LOSE.
I SHOULDN'T HAVE TO TELL YOU WHICH ONE TO CHOOSE.
THE FUTURE OF THIS BATTLE RESTS ON THOSE WHO HAVE JUST BECOME PILOT CANDIDATES--YES, YOU.

YOUR NUMBER IS...

(EXCERPT FROM THE HANDBOOK FOR NEW STUDENTS)

G.O.A. OFFICIAL HANDBOOK 01, IMPORTANT DOCUMENTS·RESTRICTED.

G·O·A

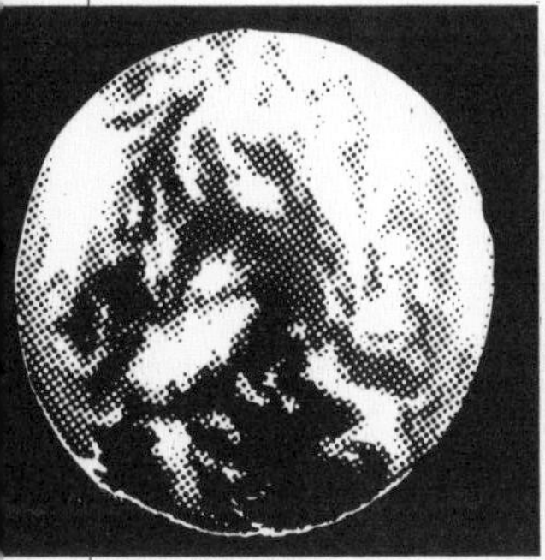

ZION

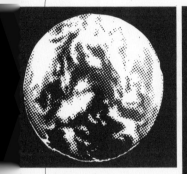

Zion is the last planet, our last remaining hope. All Mankind wishes to someday set foot on that planet. Furthermore, as all information is thoroughly controlled by the government, very little is known about Zion. But there is no doubt that Zion is to us the one and only "Promised Land".

THE DETAILS OF THE FOUNDING OF G.O.A.

Starlog 4088, due to the "Crisis of Systems (Lost Property)", which involved four star systems, we, Mankind, having lost the planets on which we lived, escaped to space. Henceforth, to this day, we have been forced to live in space colonies.

Our last hope, the planet Zion, remains, but the unidentified beings, "Giseisha," cast a dark shadow over that hope.

Mankind concentrated all its efforts into building the giant humanoid weapons, "Ingrids (Goddesses)," which we use to fight the Giseisha. But only those who have met the unusually strict requirements can become pilots of the Goddesses. So, to find and train those few people out of the many applicants to become a pilots, G.O.A. (Goddess Operator Academy) was established.

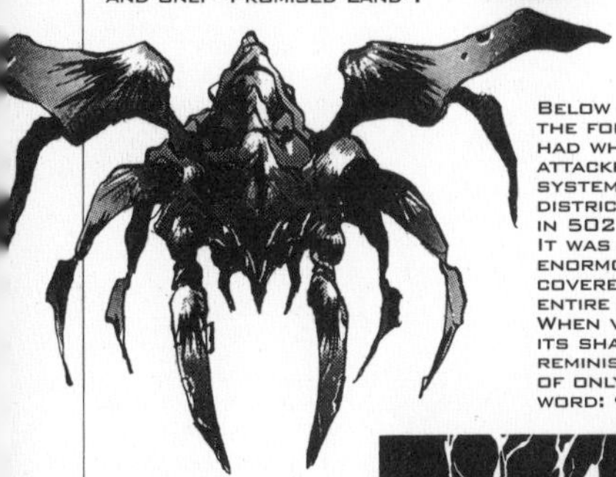

Above, is the form that attacked G.O.A. as it was cruising the surrounding space near Zion in 5030. It is smaller in comparison, but as a result of its terrible fighting power, the Goddess Agui Keameia's manipulator was destroyed.

Below is the form it had when it attacked star system 21NN, district 128 in 5025. It was so enormous it covered an entire colony. When viewed, its shape is reminiscent of only one word: "Devil".

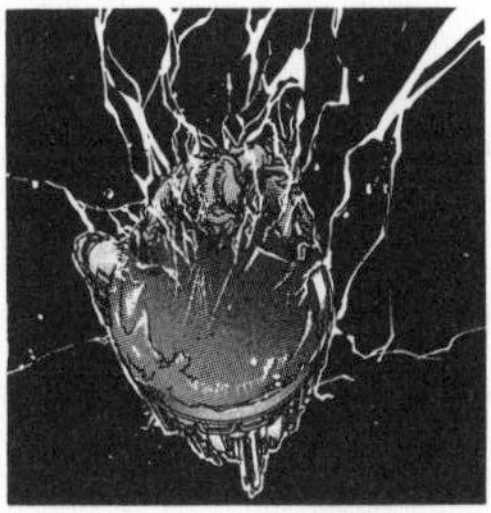

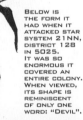

THE ENEMY: GISEISHA

Giseisha is the general term used for the mysterious life forms that have attacked us. As their constitution, shape, and abilities vary, their true nature is completely unknown. As they make repeated invasions on Zion and attack our colonies that are on their way to the last planet, there is no doubt they are Mankind's greatest enemy. Why their goal is Zion, why they are attacking our people, even the reasons for their actions are unknown. But, since the first confirmed sighting happened after the Crisis of Systems, it is said that they may be a consequence of that event.

G•O•A SYSTEM OUTLINE

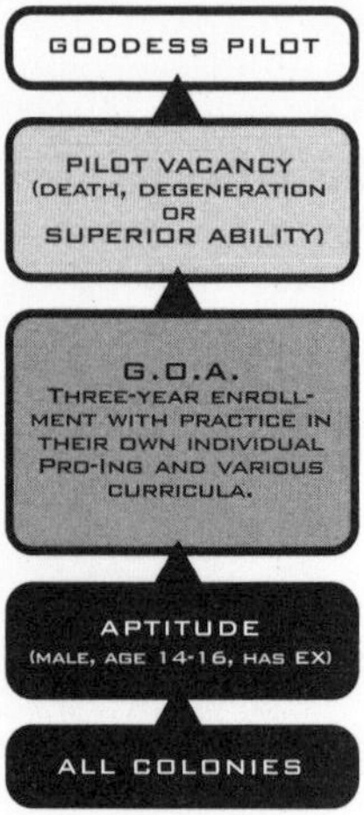

GODDESS PILOT
PILOT VACANCY (DEATH, DEGENERATION OR SUPERIOR ABILITY)
G.O.A.
THREE-YEAR ENROLLMENT WITH PRACTICE IN THEIR OWN INDIVIDUAL PRO-INGS AND VARIOUS CURRICULA.
APTITUDE
(MALE, AGE 14-16, HAS EX)
ALL COLONIES

THIS DIAGRAM IS A SIMPLIFIED VERSION OF THE ACTUAL SYSTEM.

G.O.A.'S SYSTEM:

THE TERM OF ENROLLMENT AT G.O.A. IS THREE YEARS. DURING THAT TIME, THE CANDIDATES LIVE INSIDE THE SPACESHIP. ALL THE FACILITIES NEEDED TO TRAIN A PILOT ARE CONTAINED WITHIN THE G.O.A. SPACECRAFT.

THE TRAINING IS EXTREMELY FIERCE, AND DROPOUTS ARE NOT UNCOMMON. BUT EVEN IF THE STUDENTS MAKE IT THROUGH ALL THREE YEARS, THERE'S NO GUARANTEE THEY WILL BECOME PILOTS. ONE OF THE CURRENT PILOTS MUST STOP BEING ABLE TO PILOT (DUE TO DEATH OR DEGENERATION OF EX), OR THE CANDIDATE MUST SHOW ABILITIES SUPERIOR TO THOSE OF A CURRENT PILOT. FOR A CANDIDATE TO BECOME A PILOT, THOSE ARE THE ONLY TWO PATHS.

FOR THE THREE-YEAR ENROLLMENT, G.O.A. HAS PUT TOGETHER VARIOUS CURRICULA.

IN LECTURE, EVERYTHING ABOUT G.O.A., THE INGRIDS, ETC. IS THOROUGHLY DRILLED INTO THE STUDENTS, STARTING WITH THE BASICS. WHEN NEW CANDIDATES ARE ENROLLED, THE LIMITS OF THEIR PHYSICAL ABILITIES ARE CHECKED, AND THEIR TRAINING PROGRAMS FOR THEIR PRO-INGS ARE ADJUSTED ACCORDINGLY.

FURTHERMORE, WHILE INSIDE G.O.A., ALL THE CANDIDATES' EX ARE NEUTRALIZED TO A DEGREE SO THEY CAN LIVE NORMAL LIVES.

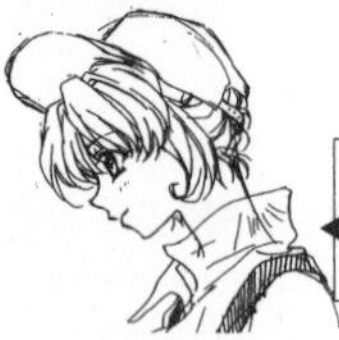

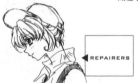

◀ REPAIRERS

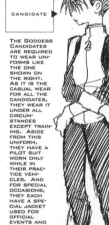

ALL THE NECESSARY PERSONNEL IN CHARGE OF REPAIRING THE PRO-INGS ARE WOMEN. UNLIKE THE GODDESS CANDIDATES, THEY ARE SENT TO G.O.A. TO TRAIN TO BE REPAIRERS; THEY ARE REPAIRER CANDIDATES. THEY STUDY EVERYTHING RELATED TO REPAIRING THE PRO-INGS AND ARE THOROUGHLY TRAINED TO THINK OF PROTECTING THE LIVES OF THE PILOTS AND THE MACHINES. LIKE THE CANDIDATES, THE REPAIRERS ARE REQUIRED TO WEAR UNIFORMS SUCH AS THE ONE SHOWN. THE HAT AND GLOVES ARE ALSO PART OF THE UNIFORM. WHAT THE MODEL'S DONE TO THE UNIFORM IN THIS PICTURE ORIGINALLY SHOULD NOT HAVE BEEN ALLOWED.

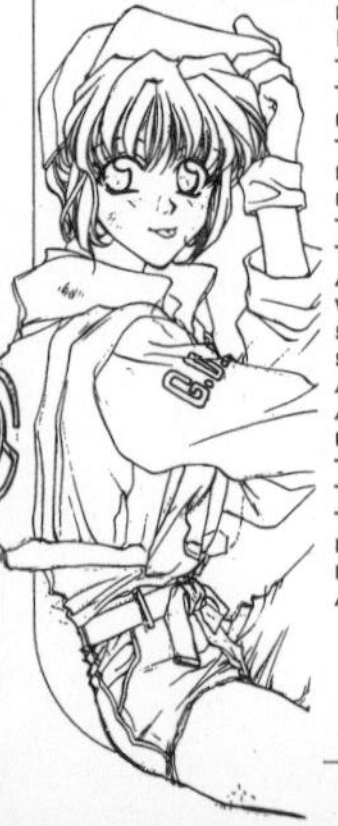

CANDIDATE ▶

THE GODDESS CANDIDATES ARE REQUIRED TO WEAR UNIFORMS LIKE THE ONE SHOWN ON THE RIGHT. AS IT IS THE CASUAL WEAR FOR ALL THE CANDIDATES, THEY WEAR IT UNDER ALL CIRCUMSTANCES EXCEPT TRAINING. ASIDE FROM THIS UNIFORM, THEY HAVE A PILOT SUIT WORN ONLY WHILE IN THEIR PRACTICE VEHICLES. AND FOR SPECIAL OCCASIONS, THEY EACH HAVE A SPECIAL JACKET USED FOR OFFICIAL EVENTS AND SUCH.

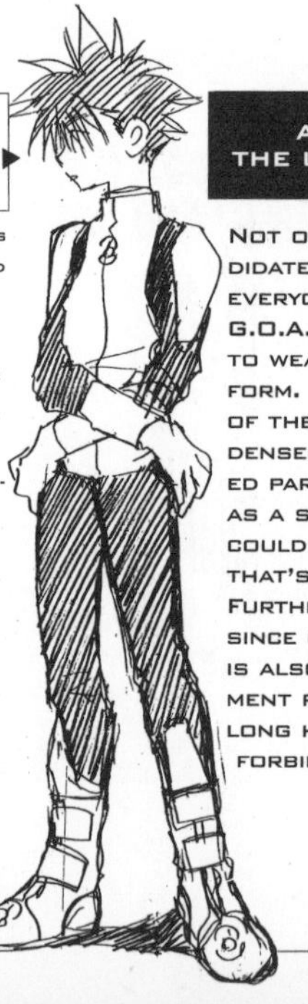

ABOUT THE UNIFORMS:

NOT ONLY THE CANDIDATES, BUT EVERYONE IN G.O.A. IS REQUIRED TO WEAR A UNIFORM. IF YOU THINK OF THE MOST DENSELY POPULATED PART OF G.O.A. AS A SCHOOL, YOU COULD SAY THAT THAT'S OBVIOUS. FURTHERMORE, SINCE CLEANLINESS IS ALSO A REQUIREMENT FOR PILOTS, LONG HAIR IS FORBIDDEN.

1
5
4
3
2

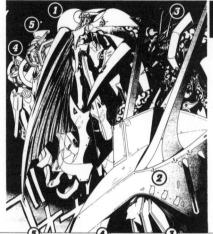

WHAT ARE THE GODDESSES?

THE INGRIDS ARE GIANT HUMANOID WEAPONS CREATED TO PROTECT ZION FROM THE GISEISHA. ULTIMATE WAR MACHINES, ONLY FIVE OF THEM EXIST. AS THEY ARE ALL BUILT IN THE FORM OF WOMEN, THEY ALL HAVE FEMININE NAMES. NICKNAMED "THE FIVE GODDESSES," THEY ARE ELEGANT AND MAGNIFICENT IN BATTLE. THEY CONTINUE TO FIGHT THE GISEISHA THROUGH GENERATIONS OF PILOTS.

BASIC INFORMATION ABOUT THE FIVE GODDESSES:

(1) ERNN LATIES: THE INGRID PILOTED BY TEELA ZAIN ELMES. PUTTING THEM IN ORDER, SHE IS THE TOP OF ALL THE GODDESSES.

(2) EEVA LEENA: AN INGRID IN CHARGE OF ATTACK PILOTED BY GAREAS ELIDD. SHE HAS SEVERAL GUNS FOR ITS INDIVIDUAL USE.

(3) TELLIA KALLISTO: AN INGRID IN CHARGE OF ATTACK PILOTED BY YU HIKURA. POWER IS VERY IMPORTANT TO HER, AS SHE SPECIALIZES IN ATTACKING DIRECTLY.

(4) AGUI KEAMEIA: THE INGRID IN CHARGE OF DEFENSE PILOTED BY RIOROUTE VILGYNA. SHE CAN SPREAD A STRONG DEFENSIVE SHIELD.

(5) LUHMA KLEIN: THE INGRID IN CHARGE OF DETECTION AND ANALYSIS PILOTED BY ERNEST CUORE. SHE CAN EASILY FIND THE ENEMY AND TRANSMIT TACTICAL DATA TO HER TEAM.

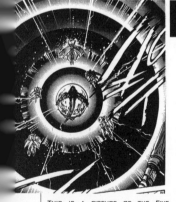

THIS IS A PICTURE OF THE FIVE GODDESSES IN 5025 AS THEY REMOVED THE GISEISHA ATTACHED TO COLONY K-01 IN THE 21NN SYSTEM, DISTRICT 128. AT THIS TIME, BECAUSE THE GISEISHA DID NOT ENGAGE THE GODDESSES DIRECTLY, THE BATTLE WENT MORE SMOOTHLY THAN A SIMULTANEOUS ATTACK IN WHICH ALL THE GODDESSES MUST COOPERATE.

BASIC INFORMATION ABOUT THE FIVE GODDESSES:

THE FIVE GODDESSES ALWAYS FIGHT TOGETHER AS A TEAM. THIS WAY, EACH GODDESS HAS A SPECIFIC ROLE, AND BY COMBINING THESE ROLES, THEY CAN WORK TO THEIR FULL POTENTIAL. CURRENTLY, THE ESTABLISHED PATTERN IS: LUHMA KLEIN FINDS AND ANALYZES THE ENEMY AND SIGNALS THE OTHERS; AGUI KEAMEIA SETS UP THE SHIELD; AND THEN ERNN LATIES, EEVA LEENA AND TELLIA KALLISTO ATTACK AND DESTROY THE ENEMY.

THE SYSTEM IS BASICALLY ONE PILOT (MUST BE MALE), ONE REPAIRER (MUST BE FEMALE), AND ONE INGRID THAT HAS BEEN ADJUSTED SPECIFICALLY FOR THE PILOT, ALL PUT TOGETHER AND USED AS ONE SET.

THE POSSIBILITY OF BECOMING A PILOT IS LIMITED TO THOSE WHO, OF THE FOUR BLOOD TYPES (AA, AB, OX, AND EO), HAVE TYPE EO (AN EXTREMELY RARE TYPE), AND WHOSE EX IS AWAKENED BETWEEN THE AGES OF FOURTEEN AND SIXTEEN.

G·O·A

THE EQUIPMENT OF THE PILOT

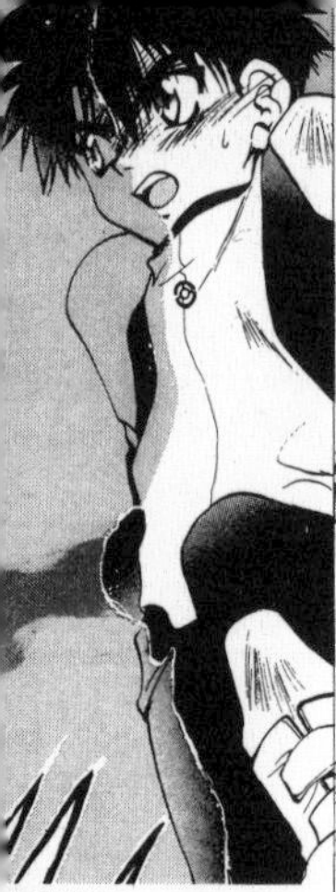

STANDARD EQUIPMENT OF THE FIVE GODDESS PILOTS:

UNLIKE NORMAL SPACECRAFT, THE INGRIDS EMPLOY A CONTROL SYSTEM THAT DIRECTLY READS THE THOUGHTS AND MOVEMENTS OF THE PILOTS. IT'S THE SAME SYSTEM USED IN THE PRO-INGS, BUT THE PRECISION, FEEDBACK, AND OTHER SUCH ATTRIBUTES OF THE INGRIDS ARE SO MUCH BETTER THAT THE SYSTEMS CAN'T BE COMPARED. BUT IN ORDER TO BRING OUT THAT HIGH POWER, SPECIAL EQUIPMENT IS NEEDED FOR EACH INGRID. HERE, WE WILL INTRODUCE EACH PIECE OF INGRID EQUIPMENT.

Z'SKIN:
THE SPECIAL MEMBRANE COVERING THE COCKPIT. NORMALLY BLUE IN COLOR. IF A FOREIGN OBJECT ENTERS THE COCKPIT OR THE MOVEMENTS ARE ABNORMAL, THERE'S A LOT OF NOISE; WHEN THE PILOT IS INJURED, IT TURNS RED; WHEN THE PILOT IS ON THE VERGE OF DEATH, IT BECOMES DEEP CRIMSON. WHEN THE ARMOR IS ABOUT TO FAIL AND THE FRONT COCKPIT PANEL CAN'T SERVE ITS PURPOSE, IT HAS THE EFFECT OF SHOCK-ABSORPTION. TOUCHING IT FEELS LIKE DIPPING YOUR HAND IN LUKEWARM WATER.

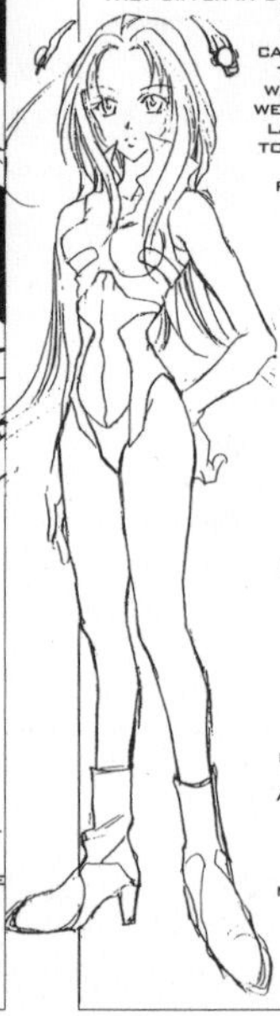

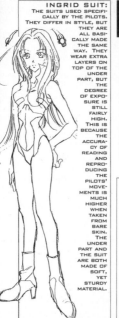

INGRID SUIT:
THE SUITS USED SPECIFICALLY BY THE PILOTS. THEY DIFFER IN STYLE, BUT THEY ARE ALL BASICALLY MADE THE SAME WAY. THEY WEAR EXTRA LAYERS ON TOP OF THE UNDER PART, BUT THE DEGREE OF EXPOSURE IS STILL FAIRLY HIGH. THIS IS BECAUSE THE ACCURACY OF READING AND REPRODUCING THE PILOTS' MOVEMENTS IS MUCH HIGHER WHEN TAKEN FROM BARE SKIN. THE UNDER PART AND THE SUIT ARE BOTH MADE OF SOFT, YET STURDY MATERIAL.

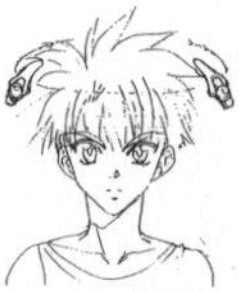

SCANNER:
THE MECHANISM THAT READS THE PILOT'S BRAINWAVES AND CONNECTS THEM DIRECTLY TO THE INGRID. IT COULD BE COMPARED TO A SECOND BRAIN, AND, TO AN EXTENT, IT CAN SAVE THE PILOT'S PHYSICAL CONDITION AND EMOTIONS. FLOATING TWO CENTIMETERS ABOVE THE EARS AND JUST ABOVE THE TEMPLES, IT CAN FUNCTION EVEN IF THERE IS SOMETHING BETWEEN IT AND THE HEAD. IT ALSO ROTATES AROUND THE HEAD.

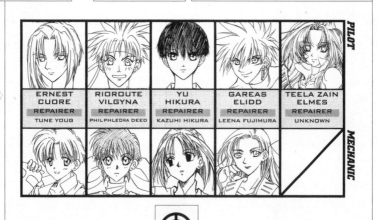

PILOT

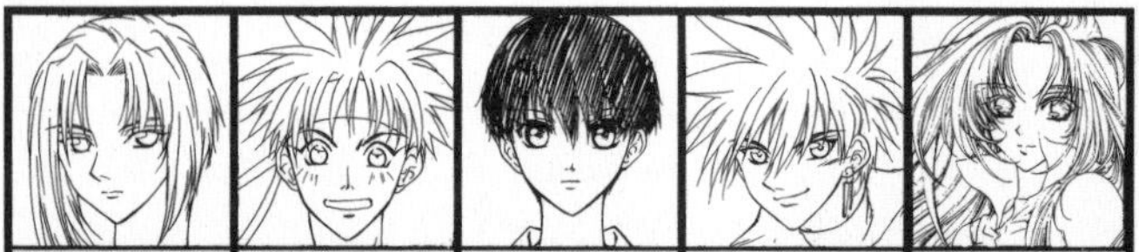

ERNEST CUORE	RIOROUTE VILGYNA	YU HIKURA	GAREAS ELIDD	TEELA ZAIN ELMES
REPAIRER	REPAIRER	REPAIRER	REPAIRER	REPAIRER
TUNE YOUG	PHILPHLEORA DEED	KAZUHI HIKURA	LEENA FUJIMURA	UNKNOWN

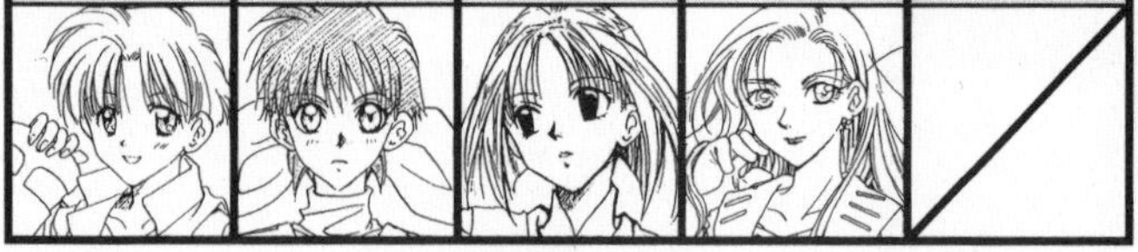

MECHANIC

G·O·A

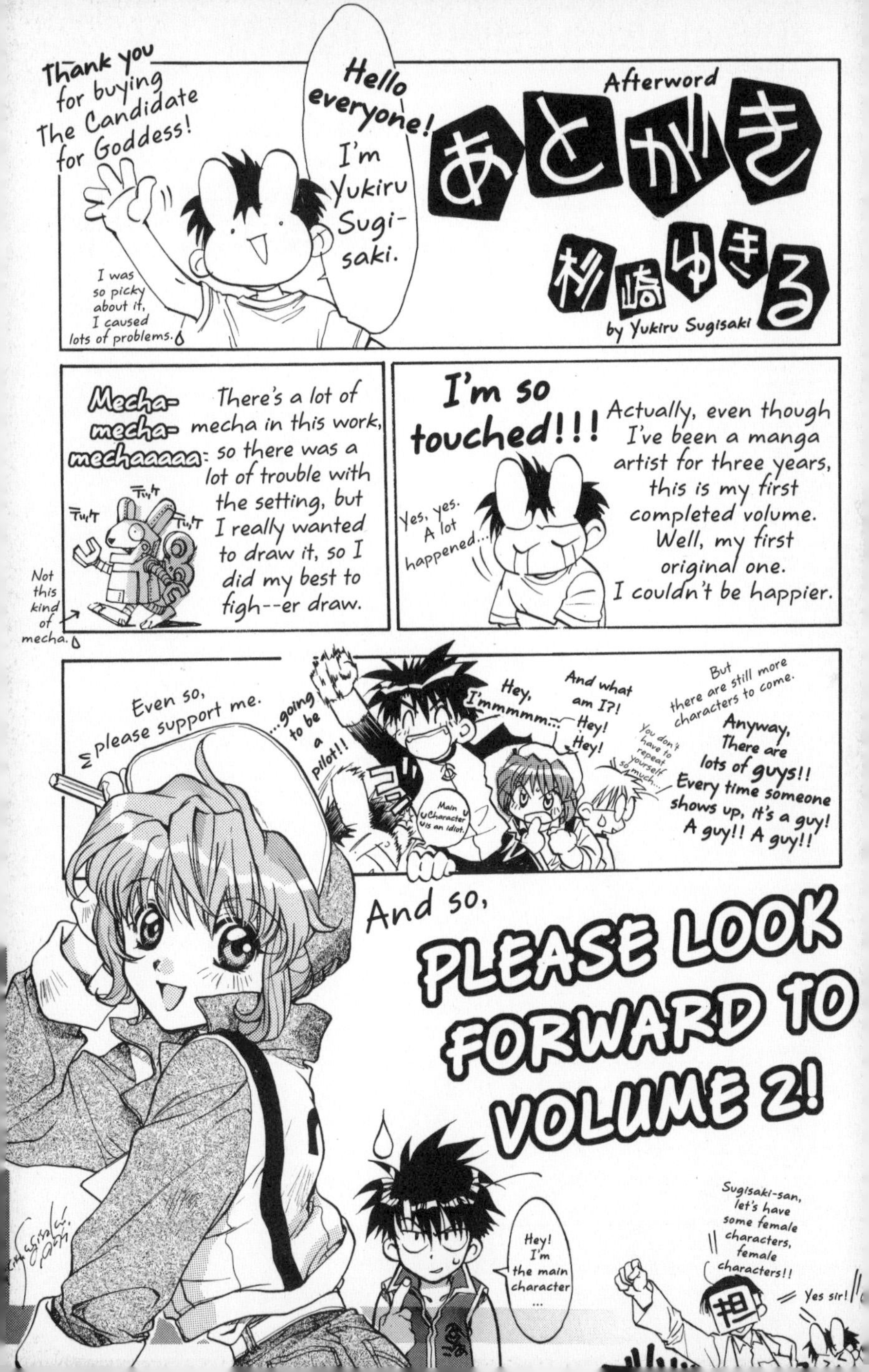
Afterword
あとがき
杉崎ゆきる
by Yukiru Sugisaki
Hello everyone! I'm Yukiru Sugisaki.
Thank you for buying The Candidate for Goddess!
I was so picky about it, I caused lots of problems.
I'm so touched!!!
Actually, even though I've been a manga artist for three years, this is my first completed volume. Well, my first original one. I couldn't be happier.
Yes, yes. A lot happened...
Mecha-mecha-mechaaaaa:
There's a lot of mecha in this work, so there was a lot of trouble with the setting, but I really wanted to draw it, so I did my best to figh--er draw.
Not this kind of mecha.
But there are still more characters to come.
Anyway, There are lots of guys!! Every time someone shows up, it's a guy! A guy!! A guy!!
You don't have to repeat yourself so much...!
And what am I?! Hey! Hey!
Hey, I'mmmmm...
...going to be a pilot!!
Main Character is an idiot.
Even so, please support me.
And so,
PLEASE LOOK FORWARD TO VOLUME 2!
Sugisaki-san, let's have some female characters, female characters!!
Yes sir!
Hey! I'm the main character ...

ALSO AVAILABLE FROM TOKYOPOP®

ALSO AVAILABLE FROM 🐢 TOKYOPOP®

MANGA

.HACK//LEGEND OF THE TWILIGHT
@LARGE
ABENOBASHI: MAGICAL SHOPPING ARCADE
A.I. LOVE YOU
AI YORI AOSHI
ANGELIC LAYER
ARM OF KANNON
BABY BIRTH
BATTLE ROYALE
BATTLE VIXENS
BRAIN POWERED
BRIGADOON
B'TX
CANDIDATE FOR GODDESS, THE
CARDCAPTOR SAKURA
CARDCAPTOR SAKURA - MASTER OF THE CLOW
CHOBITS
CHRONICLES OF THE CURSED SWORD
CLAMP SCHOOL DETECTIVES
CLOVER
COMIC PARTY
CONFIDENTIAL CONFESSIONS
CORRECTOR YUI
COWBOY BEBOP
COWBOY BEBOP: SHOOTING STAR
CRAZY LOVE STORY
CRESCENT MOON
CULDCEPT
CYBORG 009
D•N•ANGEL
DEMON DIARY
DEMON ORORON, THE
DEUS VITAE
DIGIMON
DIGIMON TAMERS
DIGIMON ZERO TWO
DOLL
DRAGON HUNTER
DRAGON KNIGHTS
DRAGON VOICE
DREAM SAGA
DUKLYON: CLAMP SCHOOL DEFENDERS
EERIE QUEERIE!
ERICA SAKURAZAWA: COLLECTED WORKS
ET CETERA
ETERNITY
EVIL'S RETURN
FAERIES' LANDING
FAKE
FLCL
FORBIDDEN DANCE
FRUITS BASKET
G GUNDAM
GATEKEEPERS
GETBACKERS

GIRL GOT GAME
GRAVITATION
GTO
GUNDAM BLUE DESTINY
GUNDAM SEED ASTRAY
GUNDAM WING
GUNDAM WING: BATTLEFIELD OF PACIFISTS
GUNDAM WING: ENDLESS WALTZ
GUNDAM WING: THE LAST OUTPOST (G-UNIT)
HANDS OFF!
HAPPY MANIA
HARLEM BEAT
I.N.V.U.
IMMORTAL RAIN
INITIAL D
INSTANT TEEN: JUST ADD NUTS
ISLAND
JING: KING OF BANDITS
JING: KING OF BANDITS - TWILIGHT TALES
JULINE
KARE KANO
KILL ME, KISS ME
KINDAICHI CASE FILES, THE
KING OF HELL
KODOCHA: SANA'S STAGE
LAMENT OF THE LAMB
LEGAL DRUG
LEGEND OF CHUN HYANG, THE
LES BIJOUX
LOVE HINA
LUPIN III
LUPIN III: WORLD'S MOST WANTED
MAGIC KNIGHT RAYEARTH I
MAGIC KNIGHT RAYEARTH II
MAHOROMATIC: AUTOMATIC MAIDEN
MAN OF MANY FACES
MARMALADE BOY
MARS
MARS: HORSE WITH NO NAME
METROID
MINK
MIRACLE GIRLS
MIYUKI-CHAN IN WONDERLAND
MODEL
ONE
ONE I LOVE, THE
PARADISE KISS
PARASYTE
PASSION FRUIT
PEACH GIRL
PEACH GIRL: CHANGE OF HEART
PET SHOP OF HORRORS
PITA-TEN
PLANET LADDER
PLANETES
PRIEST

02.03.04T

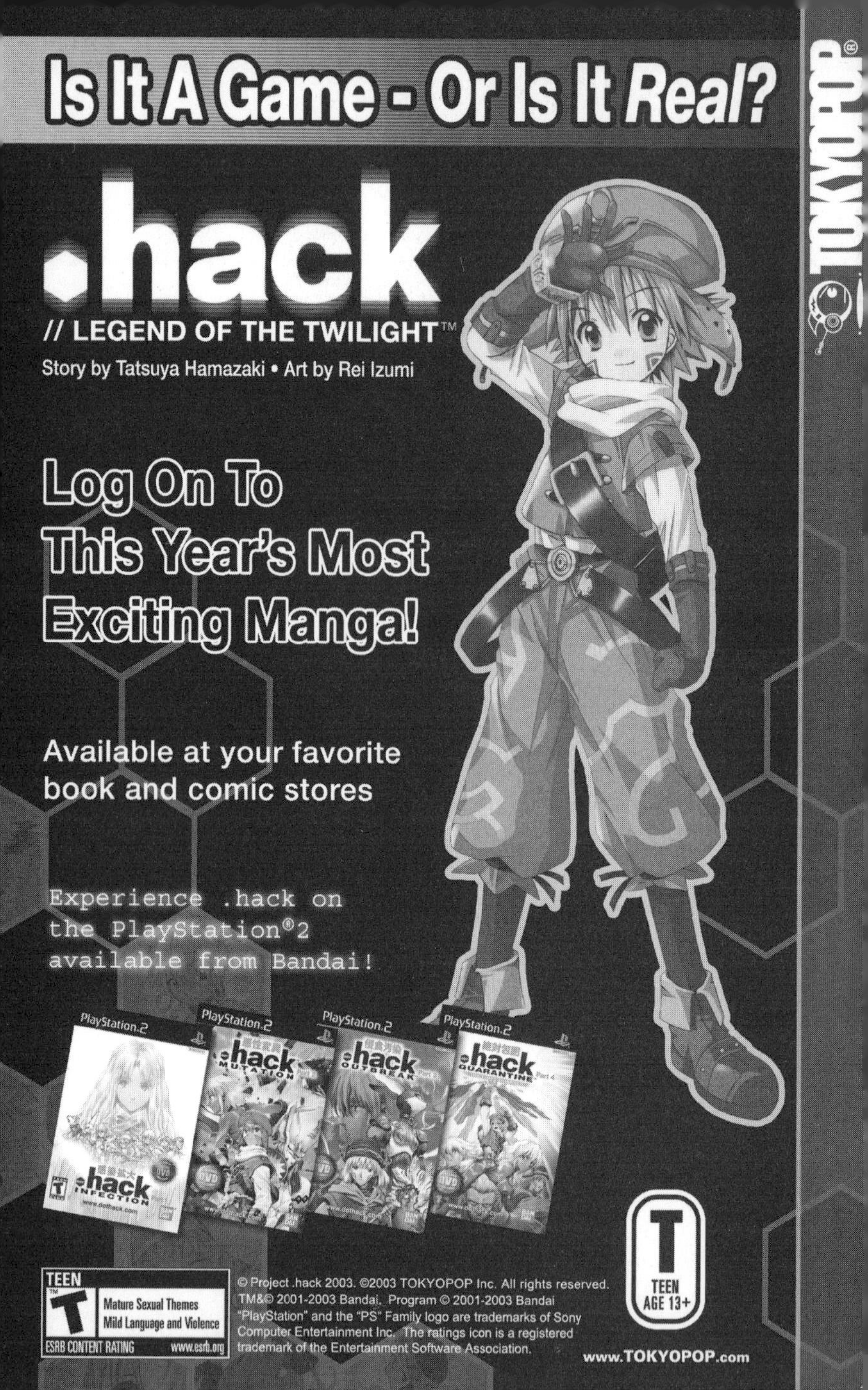

Is It A Game - Or Is It Real?
TOKYOPOP
.hack
// LEGEND OF THE TWILIGHT™
Story by Tatsuya Hamazaki • Art by Rei Izumi
Log On To
This Year's Most
Exciting Manga!
Available at your favorite
book and comic stores
Experience .hack on
the PlayStation®2
available from Bandai!
PlayStation 2
.hack INFECTION
PlayStation 2
.hack MUTATION
PlayStation 2
.hack OUTBREAK
PlayStation 2
.hack QUARANTINE Part 4
T
TEEN
AGE 13+
TEEN
T
Mature Sexual Themes
Mild Language and Violence
ESRB CONTENT RATING www.esrb.org
© Project .hack 2003. ©2003 TOKYOPOP Inc. All rights reserved.
TM&© 2001-2003 Bandai. Program © 2001-2003 Bandai
"PlayStation" and the "PS" Family logo are trademarks of Sony
Computer Entertainment Inc. The ratings icon is a registered
trademark of the Entertainment Software Association.
www.TOKYOPOP.com

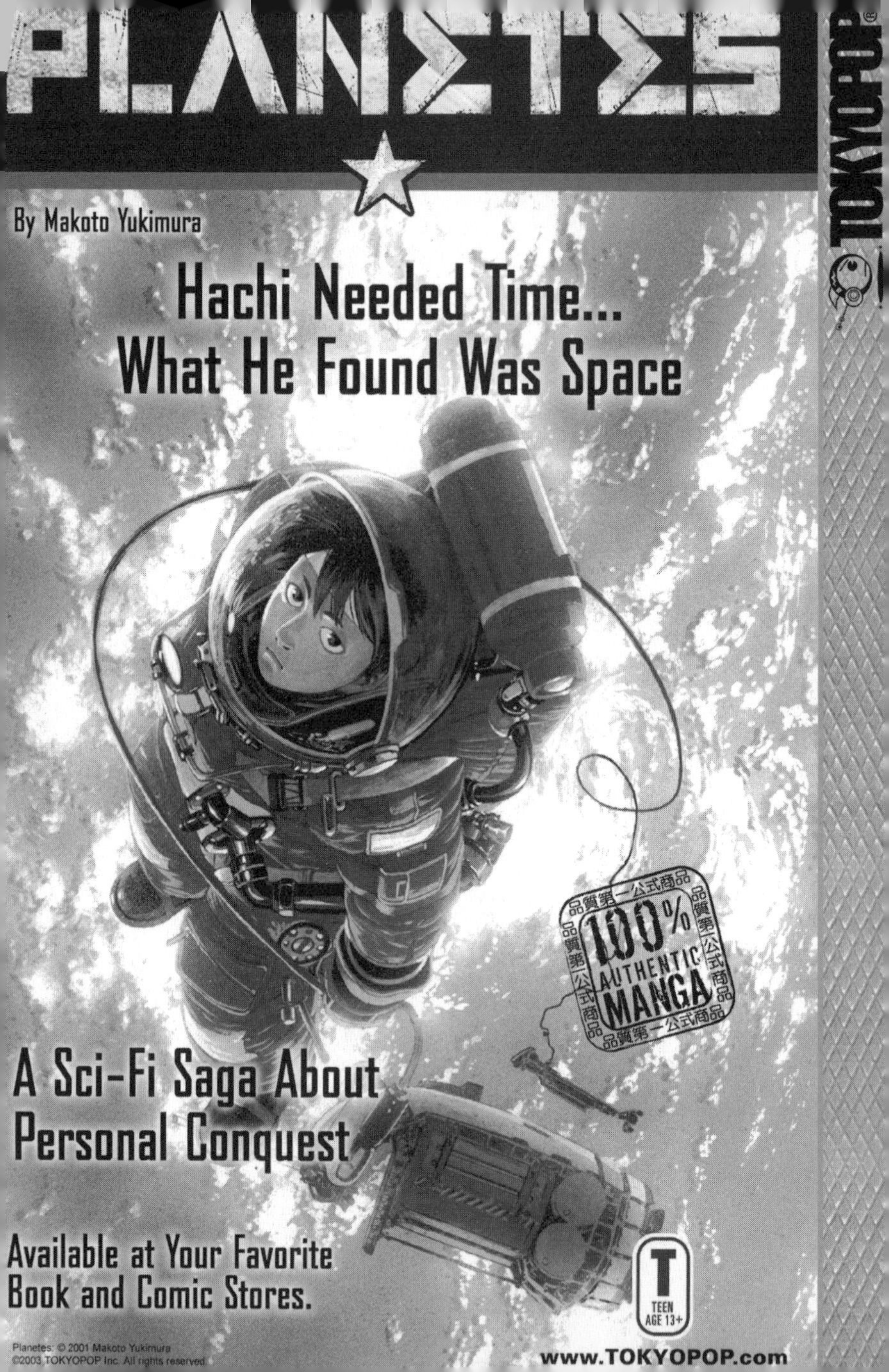
PLANETES
TOKYOPOP®
By Makoto Yukimura
Hachi Needed Time...
What He Found Was Space
100% AUTHENTIC MANGA
品質第一公式商品
A Sci-Fi Saga About
Personal Conquest
Available at Your Favorite
Book and Comic Stores.
T TEEN AGE 13+
Planetes: © 2001 Makoto Yukimura
©2003 TOKYOPOP Inc. All rights reserved.
www.TOKYOPOP.com

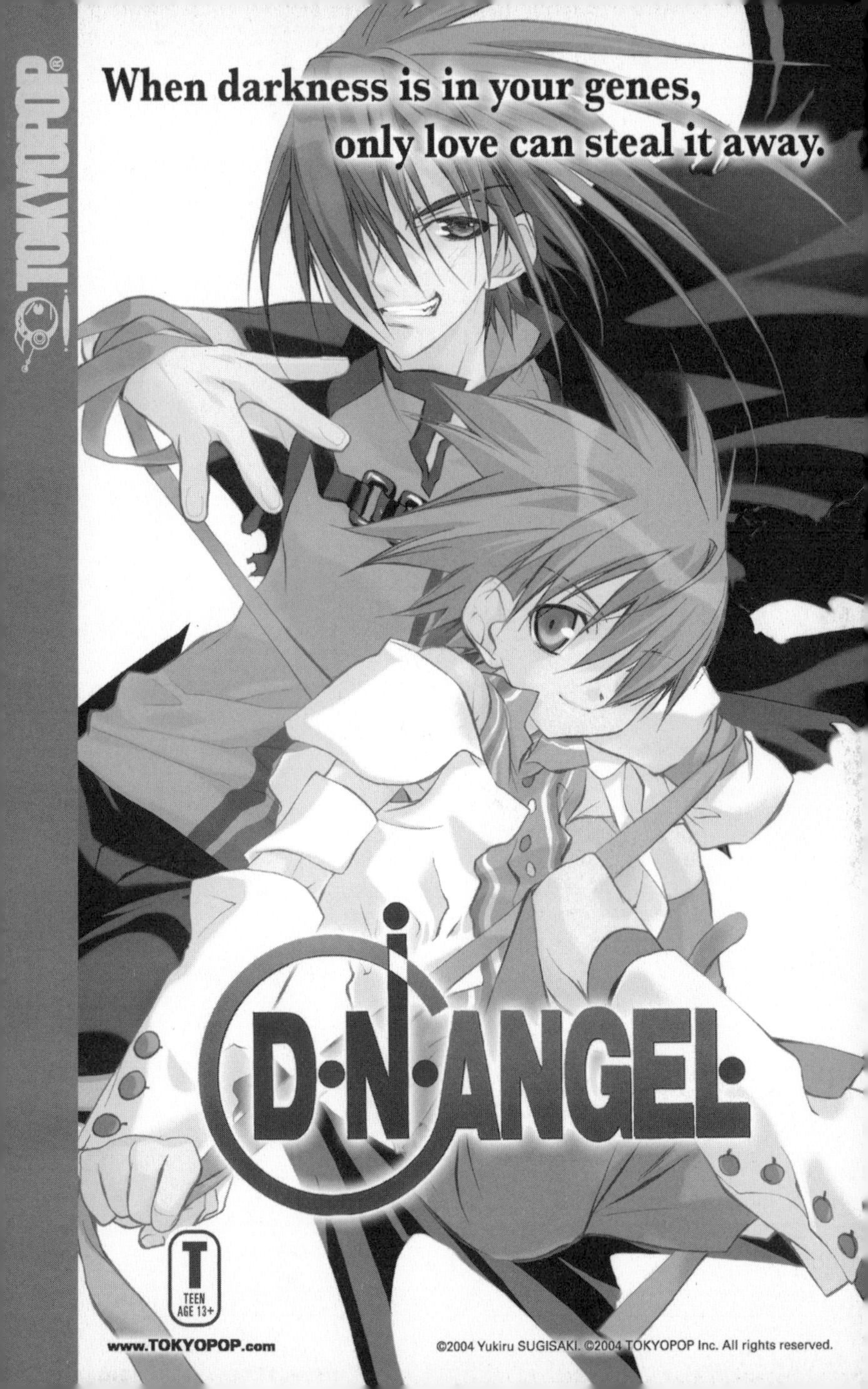

TOKYOPOP
When darkness is in your genes,
only love can steal it away.
D•N•ANGEL
T
TEEN
AGE 13+
www.TOKYOPOP.com
©2004 Yukiru SUGISAKI. ©2004 TOKYOPOP Inc. All rights reserved.

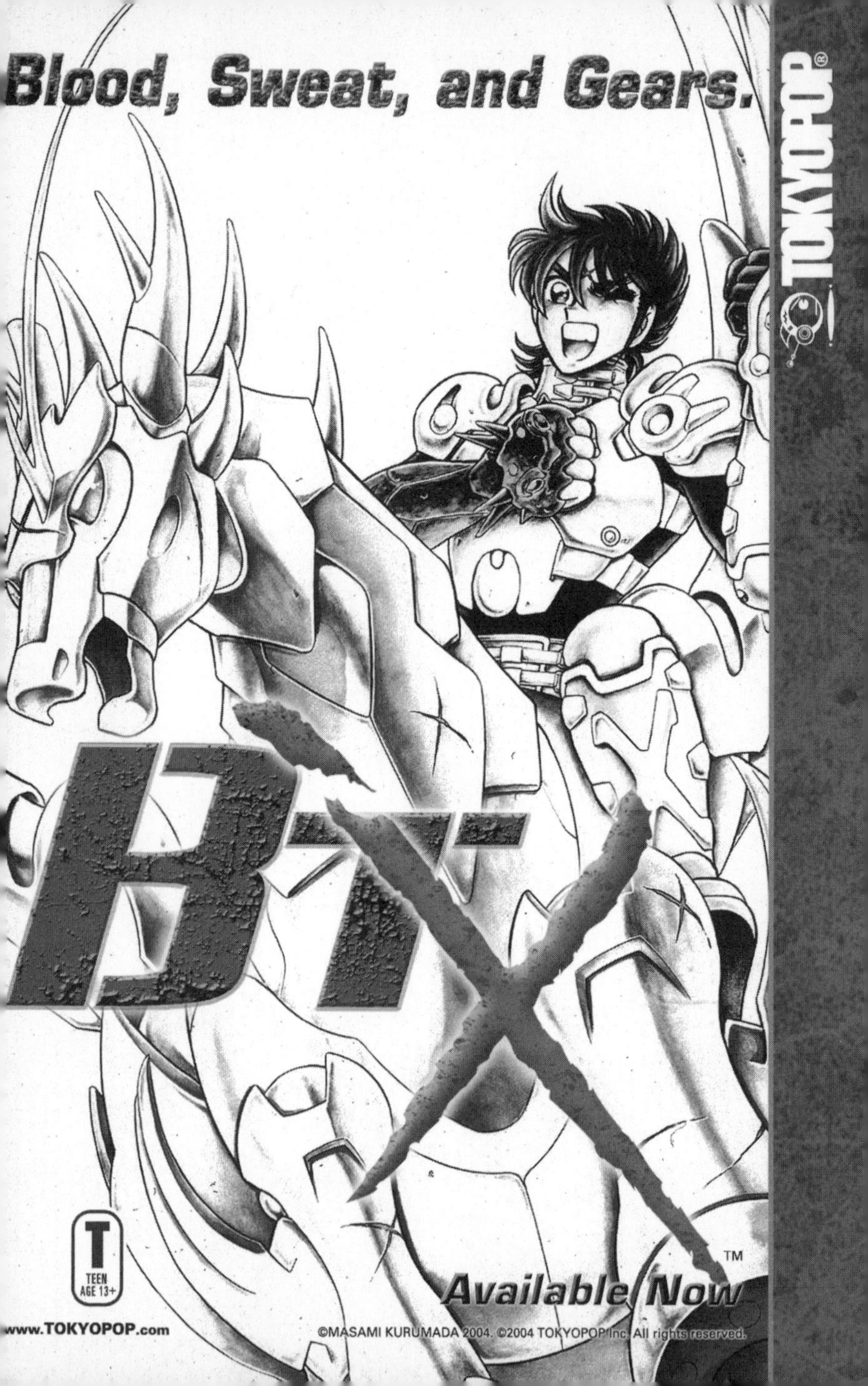
Blood, Sweat, and Gears.
TOKYOPOP
B'T X™
Available Now
T TEEN AGE 13+
www.TOKYOPOP.com
©MASAMI KURUMADA 2004. ©2004 TOKYOPOP Inc. All rights reserved.

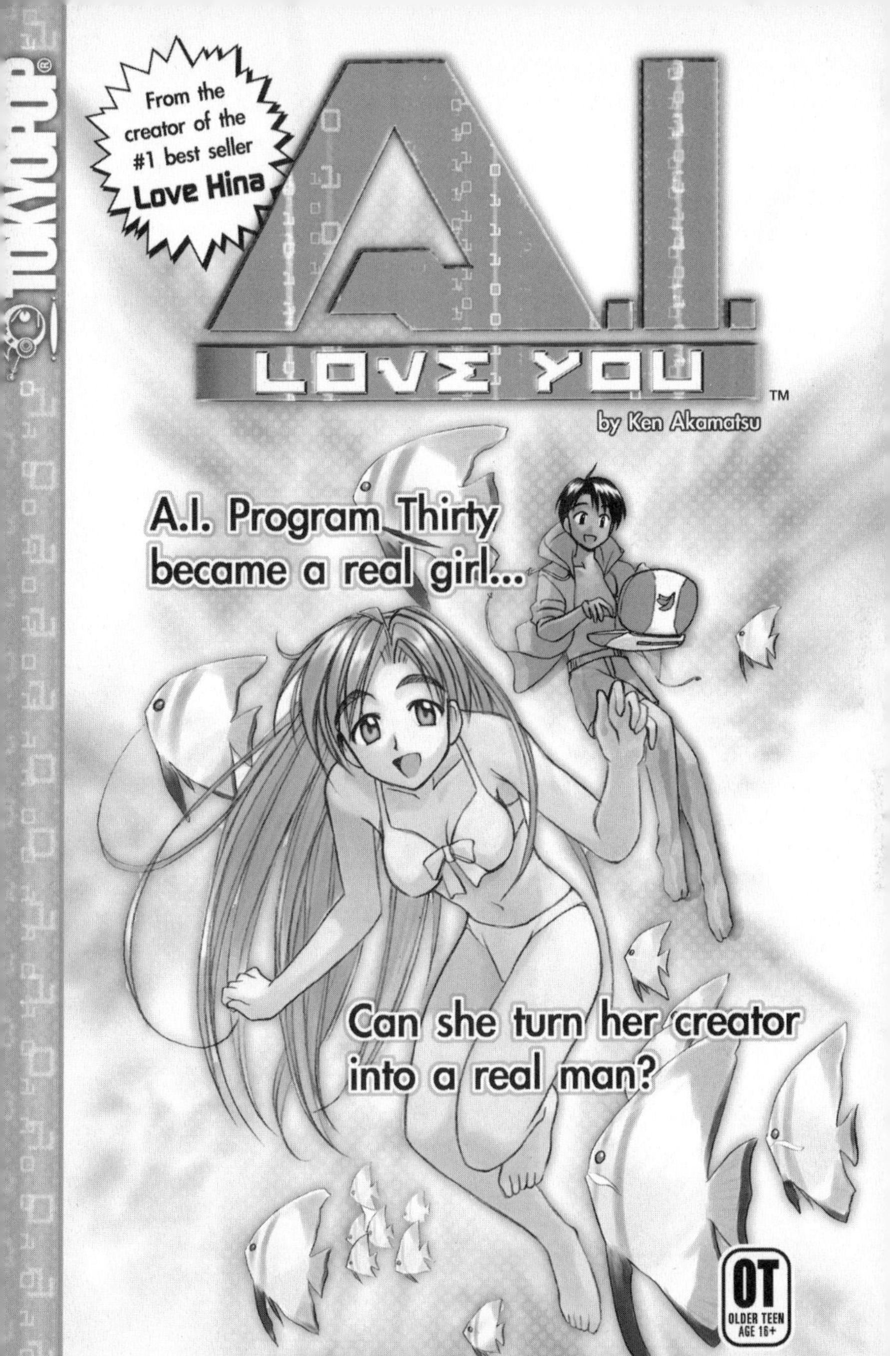
TOKYOPOP
From the creator of the #1 best seller Love Hina
A.I. LOVE YOU™
by Ken Akamatsu
A.I. Program Thirty became a real girl...
Can she turn her creator into a real man?
OT
OLDER TEEN AGE 16+

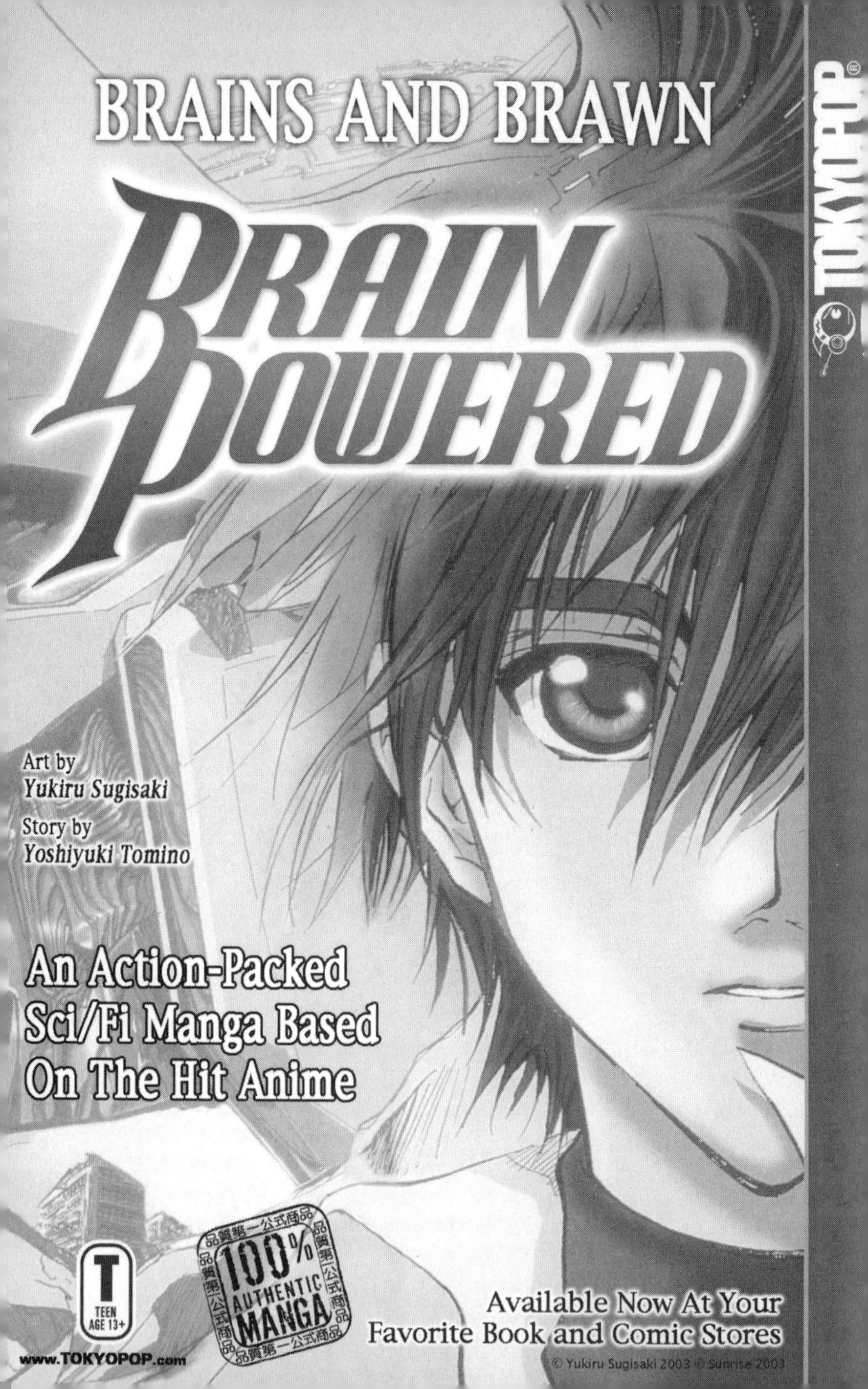
BRAINS AND BRAWN
BRAIN POWERED
Art by
Yukiru Sugisaki
Story by
Yoshiyuki Tomino
An Action-Packed
Sci/Fi Manga Based
On The Hit Anime
T
TEEN
AGE 13+
100% AUTHENTIC MANGA
Available Now At Your
Favorite Book and Comic Stores
www.TOKYOPOP.com
© Yukiru Sugisaki 2003 © Sunrise 2003
TOKYOPOP

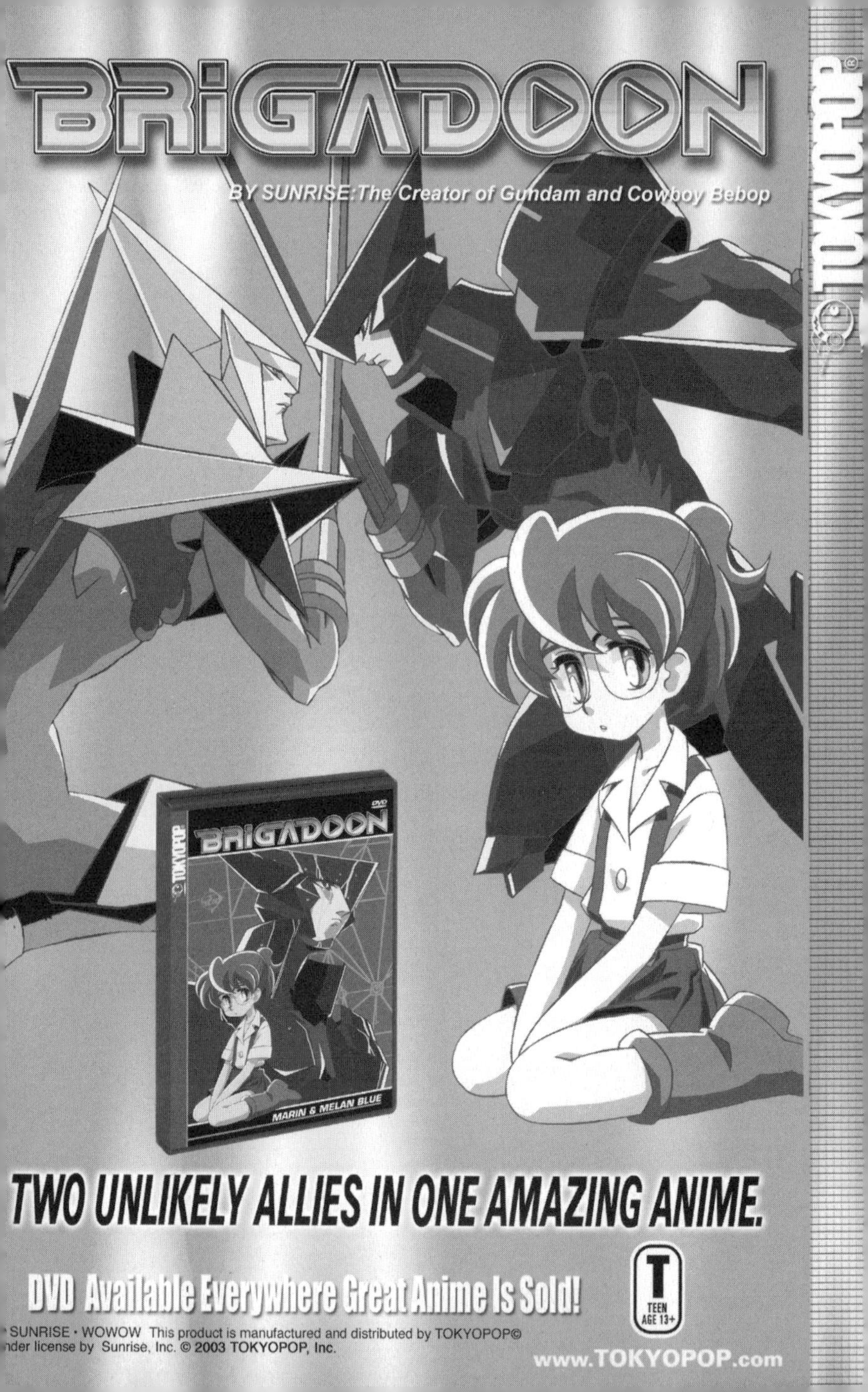
BRIGADOON
BY SUNRISE: The Creator of Gundam and Cowboy Bebop
TOKYOPOP
BRIGADOON
DVD
MARIN & MELAN BLUE
TWO UNLIKELY ALLIES IN ONE AMAZING ANIME.
DVD Available Everywhere Great Anime Is Sold!
T
TEEN AGE 13+
SUNRISE • WOWOW This product is manufactured and distributed by TOKYOPOP©
nder license by Sunrise, Inc. © 2003 TOKYOPOP, Inc.
www.TOKYOPOP.com

MOBILE SUIT

GUNDAM

THE LAST OUTPOST

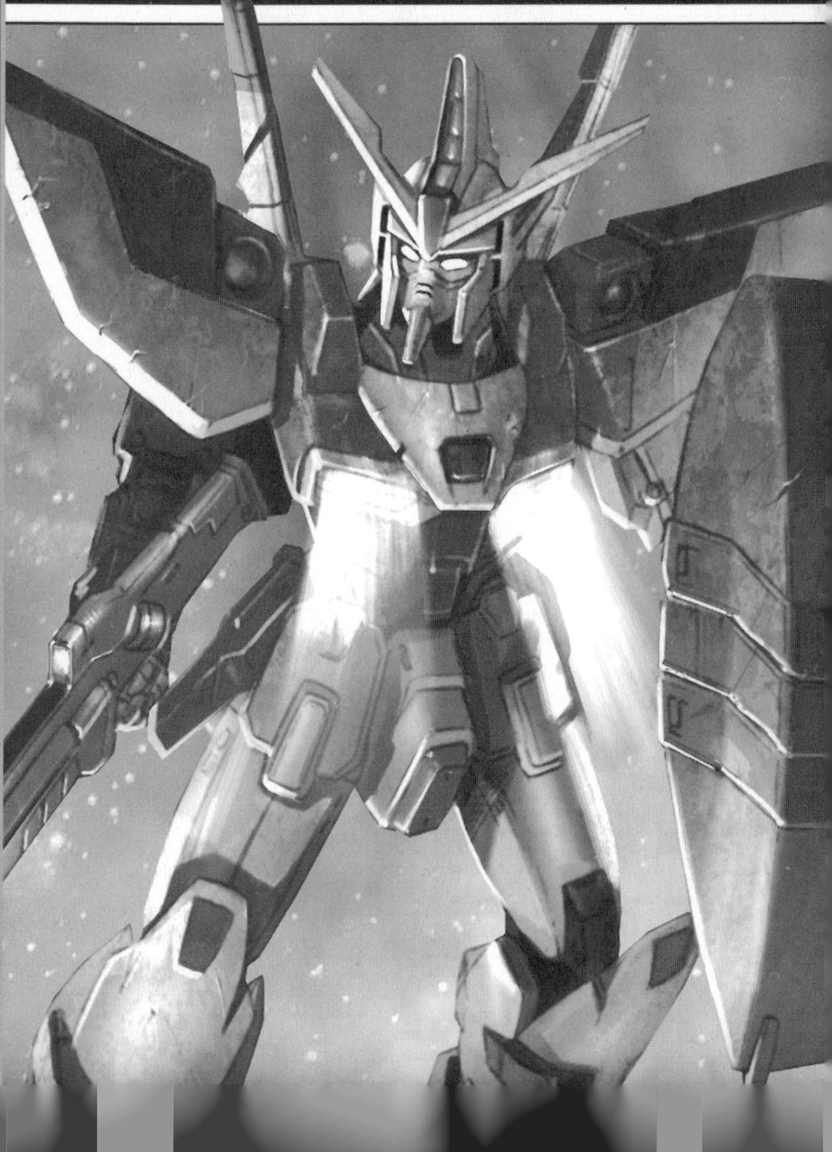

STOP!

This is the back of the book.
You wouldn't want to spoil a great ending!

This book is printed "manga-style," in the authentic Japanese right-to-left format. Since none of the artwork has been flipped or altered, readers get to experience the story just as the creator intended. You've been asking for it, so TOKYOPOP® delivered: authentic, hot-off-the-press, and far more fun!

DIRECTIONS

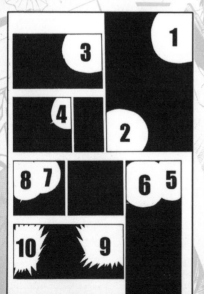

If this is your first time reading manga-style, here's a quick guide to help you understand how it works.

It's easy... just start in the top right panel and follow the numbers. Have fun, and look for more 100% authentic manga from TOKYOPOP®!